Bifurcated Politics
Evolution and Reform
in the National Party Convention
Byron E. Shafer
A Russell Sage Foundation Study

Even today, when it is often viewed as an institution in decline, the national party convention retains a certain raw, emotional, populist fascination. *Bifurcated Politics* is a portrait of the postwar convention as a changing institution—a changing institution that still confirms the single most important decision in American politics.

With the 1988 elections clearly in mind, Byron Shafer examines the status of the national party convention, which is created and dispersed within a handful of days but nevertheless becomes a self-contained world for participants, reporters, and observers alike. He analyzes such dramatic developments as the disappearance of the contest over the presidential nomination and its replacement by struggles over the publicizing of various campaigns, the decline of party officials and the rise of the organized interests, and the large and growing disjunction between what is happening at the convention hall and what the public sees—between the convention on site and the convention on screen. He argues that, despite its declining status, the postwar convention has attracted—and mirrored—most of the major developments in postwar politics: the nationalization of that politics and the spread of procedural reform, a changing connection between the general public and political

Bifurcated Politics

*Evolution and Reform in
the National Party Convention*

Bifurcated Politics

Evolution and Reform in
the National Party Convention

Byron E. Shafer

A Russell Sage Foundation Study

Harvard University Press
Cambridge, Massachusetts
London, England
1988

This book is printed on acid-free paper, and its binding materials
have been chosen for strength and durability.

Library of Congress Cataloging-in-Publication Data

Shafer, Byron E.
  Bifurcated politics.

  (A Russell Sage Foundation study)
  Bibliography: p.
  Includes index.
  1. Political conventions—United States.
2. Republican National Convention.   3. Demo-
cratic National Convention.
I. Title.   II. Series.
JK2255.S49   1988   324.5'6'0973   87-33493
ISBN 0-674-07256-1 (alk. paper)

The Russell Sage Foundation

The Russell Sage Foundation, one of the oldest of
America's general purpose foundations, was established in
1907 for "the improvement of social and living conditions in
the United States." The Foundation now seeks to fulfill this
mandate by supporting research that enhances our
understanding of political, social, and economic problems in
American life.

For Wanda

Contents

Introduction

National Party Conventions in American Politics: The Attractions of the Convention

Even in an era when it is widely viewed as an institution in decline, the national party convention retains a certain immediate, raw and visceral fascination. An institution which is created and dispersed within a handful of days, which nevertheless becomes a small world all its own for participants and reporters alike, which sits astride perhaps the single most important decision in American governmental affairs, and which is observed in passing by a remarkable share of the American citizenry, the convention manages to retain—and somehow to communicate—those same emotional forces which conventions have presented throughout much of American history: the vitality and the tedium, the unpredictability and the inertia, the drama and the vulgarity of combat and maneuvering—of politics—in this most concentrated form.

Yet beneath this quadrennial surface fascination lies a set of intellectual questions and analytic advantages of a more lasting sort. Among continuing institutions of national politics which still take actions of practical consequence, the convention is unique in the degree to which it is spatially and temporally bounded, and hence intellectually manageable. The context for its actions, then, can be examined in an unusually comprehensive fashion. In turn, the product of that examination can hope to contribute to an understanding of the world of practical contemporary American politics, and that must be its most reliable contribution. But the fact that the convention can do this now, even in an era of alleged decline, only underlines the way it has done so historically—and thus the way it can serve simultaneously as a window on the changing politics around it.

Created in response to a set of immediate strategic problems, the convention has endured for over a hundred and fifty years, in part because it has demonstrated a persistent ability to adapt to the changing character of American national politics, in part because that very adaptability has kept it abreast of each succeeding round of counterpart, practical, political problems. In just the years since World War II, the convention has changed in nearly every facet of its operation: in central activities, crucial participants, internal conflicts, and external impacts. Some of this has been evolutionary change, a response to shifts in the society outside—often well outside "politics" as we normally understand it. Some has been change by deliberate reform—though the product seems no less capable of surprising reformers as their opponents. Much of this extensive postwar change, however, has been the result of an interaction between the two, between evolutionary social forces and self-conscious organizational reform.

There is challenge enough in examining the major elements of stability and change in what is more accurately viewed as a seamless web of institutional operation. Nevertheless, a comprehensive look at the major aspects of that operation—at activities, participants, conflicts, and impacts—seems essential to any further understanding, lest important parts of the institutional web be missed, while the nature of their interaction is simultaneously obscured. Real political actions still sit at the center of conventions, tangible ones which serve as immediate rewards for direct participants along with less tangible but often more consequential ones which can move the political world outside. A look at the structure of these actions should thus have inherent virtues. If that look serves as an implicit argument for the further virtues of institutional analysis, then that is a serendipitous side benefit for the scholar.

Regardless, for those who must (or might) *participate* in a convention, and in fact for all those who want to interpret the events of conventions as they unfold, the story of this cumulative postwar change is by far the most important aspect of any analysis, the most concrete and most directly relevant to political life. Even if the convention is potentially a means of addressing larger questions, such as the changing shape of the American political universe, it can only be a tool in these endeavors—a true means, not the ultimate product. Whereas an effective description of convention operations, an aspiringly comprehensive account of the national party convention, can hope for a reasonable closure of its own and can thus leave the reader with some guaranteed benefit, whether larger issues can be resolved or not. Chapters 1 through 8 are devoted to this story, in an effort to describe a changing institution in as full and accurate a way as possible and to address plausible explanations for stability and change.

Each chapter begins with an overview of content and argument, followed by presentation of the evidence for both, in the hope that readers can thereby adjust the text to their own individual purposes and curiosities. Nevertheless, the sequence of these chapters possesses a further formal organization. Pairs of chapters address, by turn, the place of the convention in national politics, the cast of participants within the convention, the patterns of internal conflict which result, and the impact of all that on the outside world. The truth, however, is that any accurate analysis must intercut continually among these concerns in order even to approximate reality. Accordingly, the informal structure to this additional intercutting moves from environmental influences on the convention, to the actions by which its inhabitants both respond to those forces and attempt to shape the external environment, to the contributions of the convention to the larger politics around it. Along the way, a survey of individual nominating campaigns and national conventions of the postwar period, including the major incidents characterizing these conventions, is blended into this (complex and interlocking) story.

Yet scholars who do this kind of analysis often share an additional premise about its essential virtues. They believe, of course, in the subject for its own sake. But they believe implicitly that any institution, movement, group, or even individual, if procedurally central to major aspects of American politics—and that, in this view, is really all that is required—will also provide perspective on the major political developments of its time. Procedural centrality is still a minimum requirement: one would no longer make this claim for the Electoral College, for example. But when this centrality does exist, the phenomenon in question can continue to serve as a window on the external politics around it. At this second level of analysis, then, the elements of the story of the postwar convention become consequential not just for their institutional implications but as a potentially rich source of insights on the political world outside.

Large but evidently abstract developments were in fact filtered through the postwar convention. The nationalization of politics and the sweep of procedural reform, the decline of political parties and their partial substitution by organized interests, a shift in the internal organization and focus of political institutions, an associated shift in the essence of politicking itself—all these surfaced within the convention in limited, concrete, and very observable ways. Indeed, when they had been registered collectively, these developments raised the possibility of a whole new era in American political life, with new principal actors, new intermediary organizations, and new institutional structures—the era of a full-blown "bifurcated politics." That politics still centered on political institutions, though less to build coalitions directly and then bargain over specific outcomes and more to publicize issues and build amorphous but larger external coalitions. It was these coalitions which could subsequently rebound on the organs of government, always with unpredictable timing, often with remarkable force. In any case, this process of building coalitions on two levels was the essence of a politics hovering more in the ether around institutions than in the detailed and deliberate machinations within them.

The coming of this era did not go unrecognized, in its pieces, by political scholars. Yet it remained unassembled—and unnamed—perhaps because diffuseness was itself a defining trait. Worse, its arrival could be viewed either as a fundamental change in the nature of American politics or as an extrapolation of central characteristics which have described that politics for most of its history. Fortunately, this bifurcated politics has an analogy—vague and tantalizing though it too must be—in a growing split within the national party convention. Indeed, the notion of an abstract and general, bifurcated politics derives most immediately from the arrival of a much more concrete and specifiable division in the convention—between the convention on site, as experienced by its participants, and the convention at home, as experienced by its viewers. Chapters 1 through 8 again provide the intrinsic background, the implicit factual basis, for this perception. The concluding chapter then taps the details of that increasing institutional split to search explicitly for the character of the larger politics around it.

Despite all this the basic story of the convention must remain the essence even of these additional implications, since that story can be offered (and defended) in evident detail. Indeed, even this underlying chronicle is in some sense only a prologue to changes still to come. The extent of institutional evolution in the postwar period alone, or the number of times the convention has been the focus of self-conscious reform, is support for the prediction that the convention will continue to evolve, as it is reinforcement for the possibility that more reform is yet in store. Accordingly, any look at the national party convention must close with an attempt to look forward, at the future of the convention as an institution, by applying the interactions of evolution and reform to produce some possible incarnations of the convention as it continues to change. An afterword takes up this task, concluding the text while pointing onward—like politics itself?—to an inexorable new beginning.

1 | The Nomination and the Convention: An Informal Disappearance

National party conventions were created for one specific and eminently practical purpose: to make an effective nomination for president of the United States. All the other formal activities of the convention—from assessing credentials through adopting rules of procedure to drafting a platform—came later, and grew out of arrangements for the nomination. All the other unofficial but potentially consequential activities which sprang up in and around the convention—such as furthering the careers of other participants, furthering political causes grand or picayune, and publicizing the party as an organization—grew up gradually, and later, as well. Before there were any of these associated activities, there was the search for an effective way to make a presidential nomination, and it was this search which produced the institution known as the national party convention.

The first conventions were informal in the extreme. Party leaders or supporters of a particular presidential aspirant, facing strategic problems not easily solved with existing organizations and procedures, turned to a national convention for an interim solution. The device, however, proved sufficiently practical to solve both these and other problems, again and again, so that the convention became the regular and authoritative means for conferring major-party nominations on candidates for president. Over the succeeding hundred and twenty-five years, roughly from 1832 to 1956, conventions played a central—really the central—role in presidential selection. Sometimes this consisted only of ratifying a nominating majority which had already been constructed, effectively though not formally, in the maneuvers leading up to a national convention. Sometimes it meant converting—or just as often failing to convert—this politicking into a nominating majority after the convention assembled. Often it meant creating that majority from activities concentrated at the convention site.

In any case, two institutional constants appeared in the otherwise kaleidoscopic contest for presidential nominations: the convention was at the center of presidential politicking; the nomination was at the center of the national party convention. Along the way, an institution with this degree of consequence anointing one of the two plausible alternatives for chief executive of the nation, acquired regular procedures to deal with recurring (and surely inevitable) conflicts surrounding that decision. The right of putative delegates to participate in the ballot for a nominee had to be certified. The strictures under which proceedings would be conducted had to be confirmed. The general program which the party would offer to the public had to be adopted as well. Given the regularity of these formal activities and the consequences of the main decision from which they evolved, it was not surprising that other, less formal political activities also gravitated to the convention. Important political actors, doing important political things, were reliably present at the convention site. All those with a stake in the behavior of these actors, or with things they wanted to accomplish for themselves, were well advised to be in attendance too.

With such a record of organizational continuity and with a regular set of ancillary processes and politics, it was also not surprising that both participants and observers had difficulty recognizing the situation when, in the mid-1950s, the nomination abruptly departed from the convention. The years to follow would confirm this departure to the satisfaction of almost everyone, but the process by which it occurred did not make this perception (and eventual consensus) any easier to achieve. For the institution of the national party convention, as well as the preceding mechanics of delegate selection, changed only marginally in the period during which the nomination disappeared. Individual conventions might change a rule here or a rule there, but they did not alter their basic institutional outlines. Individual states might change their arrangements for delegate selection in response to peculiarly local forces, but the composite of such arrangements remained as it had been for several decades. Finally, the actors who had to ratify a nomination officially, and whose calculations were the medium through which all those forces which were reshaping the convention had to register their impact, themselves maintained an impressive continuity, at least with regard to their political backgrounds and attachments.

Clearly, then, the environment around the convention, the environment to which these key actors responded, had to be changing in certain substantial ways. The calculations of these key intermediaries had to change from the local to the national in order for the nomination to be drawn out of the convention—and they did, in what might be called the "nationalization of presidential politics." This nationalization had to produce a set of earlier and earlier commitments, along with a resulting earlier and earlier consensus—and it was this very consensus which ultimately removed the nomination from the national party convention and placed it in the process of delegate selection. That nationalization, finally, had to possess a set of major operational components: the growth of national government, the rise of national media of information, the decline of local political parties, the changing shape of the social base upon which all this activity occurred.

Thus the growth of government, and especially national government, gave everyone in society—not just party leaders but interest group representatives and rank-and-file citizens too—an augmented stake in the outcome of presidential politics. The growing reach of national media of information, connecting local developments in the politics of presidential selection and alerting everyone to those developments nationwide, both propelled and facilitated a change in focus. The decline of political parties—as the main localizing agents in presidential politics and as the main resistance to this nationalizing trend—conduced, despite the desire of many political leaders, in the same direction. The changing shape of American society, with a larger proportion of individuals who were determined to participate in presidential politics on an independent basis, who were thus resistant to an intermediary role for political parties, and who were particularly likely to turn to the mass media as an alternative, further magnified the underlying change.

When all these factors, separately and together, had registered their impact, the nomination had left the convention—apparently for good. The Democratic and Republican conventions of 1952 each realized the construction of a nominating majority inside the convention hall. The next fully independent nominations within both parties, the Democratic contest of 1960 and the Republican contest of 1964, showed a very different pattern. No convention thereafter was to approximate the situation in 1952. That is, no convention was to construct a nominating majority within its confines; no nominating majority was to require so much as a second ballot to confirm its existence. That alone was a major evolutionary step for an institution which retained such impressive organizational continuity. Yet it was destined to be a prelude to further, sweeping, deliberate alterations in the mechanics of delegate selection leading up to the convention.

Even this was not the end of the chain of developments initiated, critically, by the departure of the nomination. In the longer run, influences from the nationalization of presidential politics and from the coming of extended procedural reform, when added to the departure of a historically central activity, set the stage for additional changes in every aspect of convention politics. They set the stage for a shift in the cast of participants, who would henceforth constitute the environment for internal politicking. They set the stage for a shift in the major activities of the convention, placing a newly critical conflict at the heart of this revised internal politics. They set the stage, finally, for a new and different relationship between the convention and the general public, after changed participants, contesting changed activities, contributed to a change in the reporting of convention proceedings, one with powerful implications for the resulting public response. All these changes together promised more of the same as the convention moved off into the political future, while they contributed toward defining the direction—or at least the alternatives—for this further change. Yet the movement of the nomination was in some sense behind them all.

The Birth of the Convention

The first national party convention in direct line with the modern version was called by the Antimasonic party in 1831.[1] The Antimasons were based in upstate New York and western Massachusetts but aspired to be truly national. The quickest route to national stature was a presidential campaign, but the new party could hardly launch such a campaign with the dominant nominating device to that date, a caucus of party members in the U.S. Congress, because it possessed none. Accordingly, party leaders hit upon the idea of a national gathering of self-professed supporters, in Baltimore, Maryland, on September 26, 1831. There, 116 delegates nominated William Wirt, an ambivalent candidate who claimed to see nothing wrong with Masonry.

Wirt carried only Vermont in the general election. His party itself collapsed shortly thereafter. Neither nominee nor party could thus be responsible for institutionalizing the device they had helped create.

That same year produced a second national party convention. The National Republicans possessed a greater number of genuine public officials than the Antimasons, but they were otherwise even less of a political party, being primarily a catchall vehicle, little more than a label, for politicians opposed to President Jackson. They were similar to the Antimasons, though, in that they could not use a congressional caucus to nominate a president but aspired to suggest widespread potential in the general electorate and to mobilize widespread support among politically active individuals. They too turned to the national party convention, and 168 delegates had managed to reach Baltimore, in the teeth of severe winter weather, when their convention assembled on December 12. Its delegates nominated Henry Clay, who was decisively defeated by Andrew Jackson. The National Republicans, like the Antimasons, never surfaced again.

The third convention of this election, the national convention of what was still called the Democratic-Republican party, assembled on May 21 and 22, 1832. It was similar to the others in that this gathering was convened to handle an explicit political problem, and to handle that in such a fashion as to mobilize widespread support while conferring national legitimacy. It differed from the others in that the Democratic-Republicans were turning to a device pioneered by two other (proto) parties. It differed from these others as well in that the party calling the convention, soon to be simply the Democratic party, would continue organizationally down to the present. As a result, and most consequentially, it differed from the others in that *this* party would confirm and institutionalize the national party convention.

The problem for the Jacksonian Democrats was not the renomination of President Jackson, a surety under any method. The problem was instead the vice presidential nomination. Jackson and other party leaders desired to dump the sitting vice president, John C. Calhoun, and to replace him with Martin Van Buren, the secretary of state. Calhoun, however, had far more congressional support than Van Buren, so that if party officeholders in Congress were allowed to retain the nomination, a congressional caucus would predictably renominate Calhoun. In response, party politicians in the states decided to call a national convention, justified as reflecting the opinion of all party units and as transferring control over the nomination to the general public. The convention assembled successfully. To the surprise of no one, it slated Van Buren rather than Calhoun. And neither the party of the Jacksonians nor the institution of the national party convention was to pass another election without making a presidential nomination.

The central function—indeed almost the only activity—of each of these original party conventions was evidently and consensually clear. It was the nomination of a candidate for president and/or vice president of the United States. The reasons for turning to the device of the convention were equally straightforward. Either the party did not have enough elected officials to submit the decision to them, while guaranteeing wide geographic support and a semblance of popular legitimacy, or the decisions of such officials were likely to be repugnant to the organizations and individuals who had to do the actual electioneering in the states and localities. The justification for this mode of nomination was immediately apparent as well, even if it was to be realized only unevenly in the hundred and fifty years to follow. The convention would represent a full national sample of self-conscious party adherents; their representatives could deliberate on an outcome of optimal acceptability to all.

It could not have been clear to the participants at these conventions—these Antimasons, these National Republicans, and these Democrats—that they were inaugurating a historic political institution. All knew that the congressional caucus as a nominating device had broken down. But most must have assumed that the convention too was just one more interim means for dealing with the problem of nominations, a means which would itself be circumvented and replaced as subsequent strategic dilemmas decreed. In this assumption at least they were destined to be mistaken.[2] In fact, presidential nominations had been handled directly by the Electoral College, in the manner intended by the Founding Fathers, for only two elections, those of President Washington in 1789 and 1792. Nominations had then been handled by legislative caucus—usually a caucus of party members from the U.S. Congress, occasionally a caucus of party members in a particular state legislature—from 1800 through 1828. But from 1832 through at least 1984, presidential nominations for major-party contenders would be handled instead through national party conventions with only a few, partial, early exceptions. Indeed, every *president* from 1832 on, including Andrew Jackson in his renomination for a second term, was to be nominated by a national party convention.

The Growth of Convention Powers, Structures, and Activities

The permanence of this jerry-built device was neither analytically nor practically evident in its early days. The Whigs, the principal opposition party in the years immediately after the creation of the convention, did not hold a national party gathering in 1836. The Democrats, the dominant party during this same period, did not select a *vice* president at their national convention of 1840. Yet an observer blessed with precocious hindsight could have seen concrete and dramatic indications of the growing strength of the national party convention as a nominating device. For its powers, its structures, and its activities all gave evidence of something more than a transitory existence. Moreover, the speed with which these additional elements both appeared and became regularized created an increased presumption that the institution itself would endure.

The convention, for example, quickly acquired authority over party endorsement. A Whig convention actually deposed a sitting president, John Tyler, in 1844 and then another, Millard Fillmore, in 1852. A Democratic convention then confirmed this ability for both major parties by dumping President Franklin Pierce in 1856. Not only did the convention successfully assert the authority to dispossess an incumbent, it rapidly acquired the capacity to create its own nominee on the spot. Thus the Democratic convention of 1844 nominated the first "dark horse" in American politics, James K. Polk, who was not even a candidate on the opening ballot. The Democratic convention of 1852 then duplicated that feat by slating Franklin Pierce, who entered on the *thirty-fifth* ballot—and whom it was to depose unceremoniously, despite his wish for renomination, a short four years later.[3]

Moreover, so quick and thorough was the rise of the convention as a nominating body that its internal rules rapidly acquired the ability to influence a nomination. The "unit rule," whereby each state was entitled to cast its total vote as a bloc, was to become a mainstay of Democratic convention politics over the next hundred years. Yet it was the adoption of this rule by the Whig convention of 1840 which confirmed the almost instant importance of internal convention regulations, by destroying the chances of Henry Clay despite his position as plurality leader on the first ballot and despite the possible presence of a Clay majority within the hall. Similarly, affirmation of the "two-thirds rule," requiring two-thirds rather than a simple majority for ultimate nomination, was to derail Martin Van Buren in his comeback attempt at the Democratic convention of 1848 despite the evident presence of continued majorities for ex-President Van Buren during all of his first *seven* ballots.

By 1852, the convention had become a certifiably independent entity, without connection to any official organ of government or to the relevant party members therein. The Democratic convention of 1848 was still formally summoned by the Democratic congressional caucus, which had retained this ancillary role in presidential nominations. But that convention appointed a continuing "national committee," with one continuing member from each state, and it was this committee which summoned the Democratic convention of 1852. When the Republican convention of 1856 followed suit and created its own Republican National Committee to handle national party business in the interim between conventions, the independent authority of the convention was confirmed. In passing, the identity of the two major parties which would characterize American national politics from that time forward was confirmed as well.

At the heart of the national convention, then, was the nomination of presidential and vice presidential candidates. Early participants would have regarded the idea of underlining that fact as an exercise in foolishly redundant analysis: what other reason could there be for a national party gathering? Indeed, early conventions were close to having these nominations as their sole collective activity, a fact transparently clear for the conventions of 1831–32, which were truly assembled for no other purpose. But the centrality of a nomination, and of nominating politics, was just a trifle less obvious for the immediate successors to these first conventions, which still argued only intermittently about the credentialing of delegates, the defining of majorities, or the issuing of party programs.

Yet as the nomination gave the convention a reason for continued existence, and as the convention became confirmed as the institutional arena for making a nomination, more and more activities were necessarily added to convention proceedings. Some of these brought with them specific, recurring appendages, such as convention committees, and thus served to elaborate the formal structure of national party conventions. Others were informally but just as effectively added, when those who were attracted by the importance of the nomination, or of one of these new formal activities, or just by the presence of many other powerful actors, came to the convention to try to influence these developments or to engage in distantly related politicking of their own.

A convention which could make an authoritative nomination, for example, needed some regular means for determining who was entitled to contribute to that decision. A credentialing process—and a recurring Credentials Committee—was accordingly born. A convention which was the ultimate if intermittent governing body of the national party had to have some regular means to bring a succeeding national convention into being and to establish its initial operation. A rule-making process—and a recurring Rules Committee—was just as inevitably created. A convention which was the supreme (indeed almost the only) embodiment of the national party had a practical stake in rallying its active supporters back in the states for the coming presidential campaign and in speaking to the general public about the virtues of its ticket. Recurring programmatic statements—and a recurring Platform Committee—were the logical result. Finally, the members of a convention with all these powers had a clear stake in reserving such powers to themselves—and a Committee on Permanent Organization followed logically from that need.

Beyond all this, however, a convention which could make an authoritative presidential nomination was a place where all those with a stake in the identity of the president ought quite logically to attempt to be. Those individuals obviously included party officials of all sorts, but they included the leaders of organized interest groups as well, along with the members of the press, who would report on the doings of all these others. A convention which could attract such influential actors, in turn, was a place where individuals—both delegates and mere visitors and guests—might reasonably pursue their own political careers, quite apart from the careers of those aspiring to be president. By the same token, those hoping to advance a pet political project, from the grandeur of redistributing income to the minutia of repaving local roads, could do far worse than concentrate on the national party convention as the locale in which to pursue their interest.

The Flow of Nominating Activity

For the next hundred years, the convention remained the central institution in the process of presidential nomination, as the nomination remained the central decision in the national party convention. This did not mean that most nominating politics followed even a roughly similar trajectory. It did not mean that most nominating decisions, even within the convention, followed roughly similar patterns. It did mean, however, that the institution which the nomination had created continued throughout this period as the place where that nomination was both formally and effectively resolved. It also meant that those additional structures which the nomination had generated, such as the committees on credentials, rules, platform, and permanent organization, as well as those informal activities which nominating politics had attracted, such as the development of issues and the building of careers, remained of secondary importance to the resolution of the nominating contest.

Throughout this extended period, roughly from 1832 through 1952, the place of the convention in the overall course of nominating politics still varied enormously.[4] Sometimes the practical construction of a nominating majority actually took place well before the official convention and was only, in effect, confirmed there. This pattern was particularly common for the renomination of a sitting president, as with Abraham Lincoln at the Republican convention of 1864 or Grover Cleveland at the Democratic convention of 1884. Yet holding the office did not guarantee such a resolution, and the Democratic convention of 1852 actually dumped Franklin Pierce, as the Republican convention of 1884 dumped Chester Arthur. On the other hand, a quick and consensual resolution was possible even without an incumbent, as with the overwhelming endorsement of Horace Greeley on the first ballot of the Democratic convention of 1872 or the massive affirmation of William McKinley on the opening ballot of the Republican convention of 1896.

A more mixed situation, involving influential preliminary maneuvers but a practical decision still reached within the confines of the convention, occurred whenever a candidate could put together extended support on the outside, perhaps enough to make him the evident front-runner, but then had to hold that support and acquire the rest once the convention had assembled. In such nominations, there were always other contending candidates before and during the official convention; there were always preliminary tests of strength on credentials, rules, or platform; there were ordinarily multiple ballots before the outcome could be realized and confirmed. Thus Lewis Cass put together his nominating majority from a large initial lead and inexorable additions over the first four ballots at the Democratic convention of 1848. Likewise, Winfield Hancock managed to take a proportionately much smaller lead, though one still sufficient to make him the statistical front-runner, and explode it into the rest of what he needed in only two ballots at the Democratic convention of 1880.

The fate of others, however, who could not convert their initial assets into an ultimate nomination served to emphasize how easily such a convention could shade off into one where the nomination was essentially resolved once the convention had assembled, with only marginal relation to activities which had transpired outside and before. With any potential nomination, an initial lead, built up through activities before the convention, was a crucial advantage in subsequent bargaining in and around the convention hall. Yet it was ordinarily just that—an advantage, however major—and it did have to be parlayed into an ultimate nominating majority. Witness the case of James G. Blaine at the Republican convention of 1876, or of Champ Clark at the Democratic convention of 1912, or of numerous other front-runners across American history who began with leads equal to or more substantial than those of Cass and Hancock, yet failed to convert them into a nomination.

More clearly and solely internal to the convention were those nominations which began with a broad range of contenders or with a smaller array of roughly equivalent strength. In such cases, there was no need to consider the degree to which the nomination was practically realized outside: it was realized inside the convention if it was realized at all. Thus the Republican convention of 1888 began with fourteen candidates, among whom the fourth strongest, Benjamin Harrison, was to triumph on the eighth ballot. Likewise, the Democratic convention of 1896 had fourteen contenders, before William Jennings Bryan surged to his fifth-ballot victory. At the extreme among these cases were the true dark horse nominations, where the victor showed no significant activity in advance of the convention and no significant support when the balloting began. James K. Polk inaugurated the pattern in striking fashion at the Democratic convention of 1844—nomination on the ninth ballot, not a single vote as late as the fifth. But Rutherford B. Hayes, little more than a "favorite son" when the Republican convention of 1876 began, also bested the three "serious" contenders and corralled a majority by the seventh ballot.

None of these patterns was particularly dominant throughout these hundred-plus years of convention activity. Indeed, none of them particularly followed from, or produced, any other in the succeeding convention. The unanimous renomination of Ulysses S. Grant by the Republican convention of 1872 could be followed by the dark horse selection of Rutherford B. Hayes at the convention of 1876 and then by a repudiation of Grant (trying for a third term) at the convention of 1880, where James A. Garfield was nominated instead. Similarly, the dark horse selection of John W. Davis, on the one hundred and third ballot of the Democratic convention of 1924, could be followed by the first-ballot selection of Alfred E. Smith (whom Davis had previously defeated) at the convention of 1928 and then by the fourth-ballot selection in 1932 of Franklin D. Roosevelt, who came into the convention as the clear front-runner and then required four ballots to consolidate his strength—at the expense of Smith, whom he in turn had nominated only four years before.

The Disappearance of the Nomination

This kaleidoscope of scenarios—of names, dates, strategies, and fortunes—was united principally by the central role of the convention in the nominating politics which produced the entire array and by the central role of the nomination within the convention. From 1832 through 1952, the eyes of all participants were focused on the convention, and on the nomination within it. It was not that these individuals—delegates and alternates, candidates and their supporters, interest group representatives and issue specialists, private citizens, and, of course, the press—were uninterested in pronouncements on platform, or even in outcomes on credentials or rules. They merely assumed that these lesser convention elements were useful primarily as clues to the identity of the eventual nominee and in turn that this nominee would be the major factor in determining whether platform pronouncements, credentials decisions, or rules alterations achieved any subsequent impact of their own.

Ordinarily then the convention was the key to determining, or at least to confirming, the identity of the nominee. In cases where such confirmation was truly superfluous, as in the uncontested renomination of sitting presidents, it was quite reasonable to assume that other convention decisions would mean nothing at all without the support of those nominees. As a result, it is not surprising that observers had difficulty recognizing the departure of the nomination in the mid-1950s.[5] During the preceding 125 years, there had been occasions (and sometimes stretches) when the nomination within one or the other major party was effectively realized outside the convention and then merely ratified on the inside. Yet these had been followed just as reliably by contests determined almost entirely by developments within the convention hall. The situation from the mid-1950s on, however, was radically different. By 1956, the nomination had effectively departed from the convention, and those very concrete factors which had caused it to depart would prove sufficient to guarantee that it did not return, except in the most unlikely circumstances.

The most immediate product of these forces was the removal of the presidential nomination from the national party convention—in effect, though not in form—and its lodging in the process of delegate selection. But the extended product was to reach much further, to include changes in the social background of convention participants and in the political character of the major activities which could be pursued at conventions. As a result, the disappearance of the nomination began a chain of developments which would alter the practical operation of the national party convention itself while it raised—more forcefully than ever—the question of the probable evolution of the convention as a political institution.

As always, hindsight makes discernment of the departure of the presidential nomination a far easier task than it could conceivably have been for observers enmeshed in the entire complex development. Both conventions in 1952, the Democratic convention which nominated Adlai E. Stevenson and the Republican convention which nominated Dwight D. Eisenhower, realized those nominations through conflicts and maneuvers which occurred right in the convention hall and not in the politics of delegate selection. No convention after 1952, however, at least through 1984, was to do so again. Although there were to be numerous indications of this transformation in the years following 1952, the most obvious and straightforward was the change in the number of ballots ordinarily required to effect a nomination once the convention had assembled. Through 1952, multiballot nominations were still comparatively common. After 1952, they were, quite simply, gone. (See Table 1.1.)

Moreover, the extent of this change is actually obscured by comparing the number of ballots required to reach a nominating majority for all conventions across American history, because renominations of sitting presidents were ordinarily accomplished without substantial obstacles. Often these renominations were completely uncontested; even when this was not the case, the incumbents usually possessed sufficient resources and connections to stamp out their incipient opposition. As a result, when conventions which featured a sitting president who sought renomination are subtracted from the total picture, the break between 1952 and 1956 appears even more sharply. Through 1952, almost two-thirds of all presidential nominations by the two major parties in the absence of a continuing incumbent had in fact required more than one nominating ballot to achieve a resolution. After 1952, again, none did. (See Table 1.1.)

The Thrust of the Nationalization of Politics

The movement of the nomination into the process of delegate selection, and the conversion of the convention into a body which essentially ratified and legitimized a decision reached within that process, was not the result of any direct and explicit decision about the appropriate role of the convention as an institution. Instead, that movement was a response to other, essentially independent developments in American society—some explicitly political, others not. These developments were in no case motivated by a concern with the role of the national party convention. Yet they had as one of their impacts a restructuring of convention activities. These developments were not unrelated, one to the other. Yet only at the very end, after they had already reshaped the activities of the national party convention, was their impact institutionalized—locked into place—through changes in the rules governing the politics of presidential nomination.

The practical explanation for this change in the locus of major-party nominations began—and eventually ended—with what might be called the nationalization of presidential politics. This was the tendency for all the actors in that politics, including candidates, party and interest group leaders, and ordinary citizens, to shift their focus away from the local level—local issues, local activities, and local political leaders—and toward the national level instead. In 1952, the

Table 1.1.   The disappearance of the nomination

	Nominating contests for all conventions			Nominating contests without a sitting president	
	Multiballot	First-ballot		Multiballot	First-ballot
1956–1984	0	16	1956–1984	0	10
1840–1952	27	30	1840–1952	25	14

Source: Developed from the accounts and recorded votes in *Congressional Quarterly, National Party Conventions, 1831–1980* (Washington, D.C.: Congressional Quarterly, 1983), and Richard C. Bain and Judith H. Parris, *Convention Decisions and Voting Records,* 2nd ed. (Washington, D.C.: Brookings, 1973).

politics of presidential selection still retained a heavily local flavor. By 1968, the last election before the onset of sweeping procedural reform, that politics had become heavily national in focus. In between, obviously, the pursuit of local interests, to be bargained out later in some national resolution, had given way to the direct pursuit of that national outcome, as the only way of realizing any local desires.

What this meant at bottom was that the key actors in the selection process—party officials through 1968, rank-and-file participants thereafter—changed the calculations by which they made their commitments to a presidential contender and especially the calendar by which they made these calculations. Before this change, the "bandwagon" which resulted in the nomination of one particular candidate—a peculiarly American metaphor for the rush to join an (apparently) imminent majority—rolled most frequently *inside* the national party convention. After the change, that bandwagon began reliably to roll well in advance of the convention. But if the nationalization of presidential politics led directly to the departure of the nomination, this nationalization is still only a summary concept, a description rather than an analysis, unless it is possible to specify its components.

Accordingly, it was really changes in the scope of government and the locus of governmental decision making, as augmented by both the rise of national media of information and the decline of political parties as organizations, which produced the nationalization of presidential politics—and which explained how this nationalization could change the practical character of nominating politics without changing the formal mechanics of the nominating process. These factors in turn were critically reinforced by rising affluence and shifting patterns of partisan allegiance in American society at large. They then produced, individually and collectively, the nationalization of the politics of presidential selection. That nationalization, finally, by altering the calculations of key actors and the calendar for these calculations, drew the nomination out of the convention and placed it in the process of delegate selection. (See Figure 1.1.)

The Growth of (National) Government

Disentangling the political and social forces which produced the nationalization of presidential politics was probably impossible while it occurred, and remained difficult even after it was confirmed, because

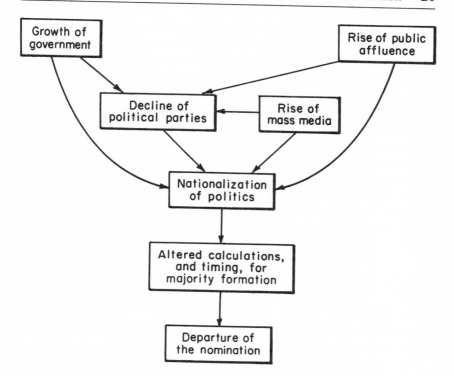

Figure 1.1. Disappearance of the nomination from the national party convention.

all these forces worked roughly in tandem and conduced in the same general direction. But the change which contributed most fundamentally to this gradual nationalization was probably the growth of government—in raw size and in spread of programs—and especially the growth of national government. Like most of the trends behind the gradual nationalization of presidential politics, this one had been going on for some time before its turning point during the New Deal era.[6]

The potential ability of the national government to intervene in various areas of American life had been confirmed as far back as the late nineteenth century, in Republican efforts to manipulate the tariff and foster industrialization. But nearly unbroken control of the presidency by that same Republican party up to the Great Depression prevented the conversion of this power into a shift of policy making from the local to the national level, or into much growth of the national government per se. During their one interlude in power in this period, the Democrats under Woodrow Wilson did increase the financial capabilities of the national government, a key precondition for later activities. But this, too, was of little direct consequence once the short Wilsonian era ended.

The coming of the Great Depression, with widespread demands for relief from its associated misery; the coming of a Democratic government, with a willingness to respond to those demands through what quickly became the New Deal; and the advantageous financial position of the federal government in this response, with an expandable tax base at precisely the point when state and local revenues were exhausted all combined to bring the growth of positive government, of the welfare state, to American society. A series of Supreme Court decisions, centered on the commerce clause, was still required to allow the national government to move into a multitude of new areas: a different set of decisions might have forced the federal government to share its resources with the states and localities and urge them to take the desired actions instead. But the key Court decisions were forthcoming, and both the expansion and the nationalization of governmental policy making did occur.

As a result, the raw size of government began to grow tremendously, so that it became a continually increasing share of national output. (See Table 1.2.) Simultaneously, the impetus for governmental policy making also shifted, to the national level, so that more and more programs were begun in Washington and then extended to, and administered by, the states and localities. Both trends showed subsequent periods when they were ascendant and others when they were essentially static. But the expansion of government during the New Deal years was not halted by the passing of Franklin Roosevelt and the coming of the postwar, post–New Deal era. And the focus of governmental policy making did remain at the federal level despite periods of greater raw growth in the states and localities, because both the programs which these governments were carrying out and the funds which permitted their execution remained heavily dependent on decisions by the national government. (See Table 1.3.)

The Rise of National Media of Information

These changes might have led all the relevant actors, not just interest group leaders and party officeholders but even rank-and-file citizens,

Table 1.2.   The growth of total governmental expenditure

Year	Percentage of gross national product	Percentage change from previous decade	
1980	36.4		
1970	34.1	1970s	+ 7
1960	30.0	1960s	+14
1950	24.7	1950s	+21
1940	20.5	1940s	+20
1930	12.5	1930s	+64
1920	10.3	1920s	+21
1910	9.3	1910s	+11
1900	9.1	1900s	+ 2

Source: Bureau of the Census, *Historical Statistics of the United States: Colonial Times to 1970,* 2 vols. (Washington, D.C.: U.S. Government Printing Office, 1975), p. 224, as supplemented by Bureau of the Census, *Statistical Abstract of the United States 1980* (Washington, D.C.: U.S. Government Printing Office, 1980), p. 418.

Table 1.3.   The rise of federal policy making

Year	Revenue (millions of $)		
	Federal	All state	All local
1980	563,700	212,600	155,900
1970	205,562	88,839	89,092
1960	99,800	32,838	37,324
1950	43,527	13,903	16,101
.....	.....	.....	.....
1932	2,634	2,541	6,192
.....	.....	.....	.....
1902	653	192	914

Source: Bureau of the Census, *Historical Statistics of the United States,* pp. 1123, 1130, and 1132, as supplemented by Bureau of the Census, *Statistical Abstract of the United States 1980,* pp. 279 and 287.

to look increasingly to the national government for a policy response—and to the politics of presidential selection as the most straightforward way to influence national policy. Yet this change in focus was surely facilitated by a major shift in the character of the organizations which connect organized groups and individual actors to the institutions of government. From one side, the mass media of information, especially the news media, which themselves became even more national in focus, became more important as a connector between citizens and their government. From the other side, political parties, at least as fully articulated organizations of party officeholders, became much less crucial as a connector between citizens and government—and parties had long been the major decentralizing (and hence localizing) element in American politics.

Again, the rise of the news media as a crucial intermediary, and its increasing nationalization, had been going on for some time before the disappearance of the presidential nomination from the national party convention, a fact which was partially obscured by the arrival of television and of national network television news.[7] The rise of television did coincide with the disappearance of the nomination, and that rise surely did contribute to the nationalization of political attention: the first national party conventions to be televised nationwide (those of 1952) were actually the last of the old order. But the rise of additional, easily accessible media of information, and their connection into national networks, had been going on well before the arrival of television.

Indeed, these developments can be traced all the way back to the 1840s, to the beginnings of the national wire services with their general (and inevitably "national") press copy for member newspapers across the country. More inescapably, these developments must be traced at least as far back as the 1920s, to the arrival of radio and radio news, and then to the connection of radio news and features into national networks. (See Table 1.4.) In fact, no less a personage than Franklin Roosevelt, in conjunction with the creation and support of his New Deal, became the incarnation of the possibilities for using this new medium to maximum political advantage by communicating directly—and nationally—with the American public. Less often recognized in this regard, but also national in focus and influence, were the newsmagazines—first *Time,* then *Newsweek,* then *U.S. News & World Report*—also beginning to join the ranks of national news media as the 1920s unfolded.

None of these media set out to produce a deliberate nationalization of political focus in the United States. None set out to supplant other organizations, especially political parties, as the major means of connection between the individual citizen and government. Yet each was an additional, easily accessible, more explicitly national source of information about American politics. Each was a means of following that politics not just locally but nationwide. Each was simultaneously a national perspective on that politics and an implicit argument that events elsewhere could eventually have local impact. All were thus inevitable competitors with local organizations, and especially local political parties, for communication about American politics. All were likewise connectors between individual citizens and aggregate politics, connectors bypassing local intermediaries, such as party officeholders.

The Decline of (Local) Political Parties

Throughout this period, parties remained the major institution in American politics which was deliberately and effectively structured in the federal pattern, with the crucial units organized locally, with federations of those units to comprise the party structure at the state level, and with federations of *those* units coming together every four years to nominate a president. But if parties were the obvious countervailing devices to the nationalization of policy making and of political attention by organized interests and individual citizens alike, they were also in a gradual but continual, practical decline. The tan-

Table 1.4.   The growth in the reach of national media of information

| | Percent of household with— | |
Year	Radio	Television
1980	99	98
1970	99	95
1960	96	87
1950	93	9
1940	82	Negligible
1930	46	None
1920	Negligible	—
1910	None	—

Source: Bureau of the Census, *Historical Statistics of the United States,* p. 796, as supplemented by Bureau of the Census, *Statistical Abstract of the United States 1980,* p. 559.

gible resources at their disposal shrank inexorably during this period; their right to make nominations for public office shrank as well.[8]

As with the growth of government and the rise of the news media, the decline of political parties had been going on well before the nomination for president moved outside the convention. In part, this decline had been accelerated by the growth of positive government and by the rise of national media. Thus the very success of the New Deal in transferring the concrete rewards of politics away from local party discretion and into a central government bureaucracy made the most dependent elements in American society far less dependent on the local party, while making that party far less relevant to the distribution of governmental rewards. By the same token, the increased reach and increasingly central focus of the national news media encouraged the less dependent elements in American society to form political opinions and take political action independently, by making the party far less important in providing information about politics and cues to political action.

Yet the decline of political parties as fully articulated organizations for electoral campaigning had begun even before these two developments. Indeed, explicit legislative attempts to weaken political parties had been a feature of American politics since before the turn of the century, through party reforms which were always aimed either at subtracting resources from the explicit disposition of the official party or at removing political decisions from the regular party hierarchy. For example, one of the earliest major reforms, which was argued even in its day to have the potential for weakening political parties as intermediaries between citizens and their government, was the introduction of civil service in personnel decisions. Less visible but perhaps even more influential was the gradual but ineluctable reform of the process of nomination to public office in the states and localities, principally through the imposition of primary elections.

Although such reforms were successful in different places at different times, and although they were differentially successful nationwide, the trend in their overall impact was clear. Civil service, which removed an increasing share of governmental offices from the disposition of political parties, began in the 1880s. At first the offices at issue were principally within the federal government; eventually the trend reached into state and local governments as well. Each extension of the civil service, in any case, was a constriction of the official party. Yet by the postwar period, the trend toward regulated personnel systems was apparently irreversible, and personnel regulations were a serious constraint in more and more jurisdictions. (See Table 1.5.)

Beginning in the late nineteenth century as well was the move to take nominations for public office away from party officials and place them in other hands, usually those of the general public, usually through public primary elections. Again, each victory was an even more automatic loss for the state or local party in question. (See Table 1.6.) Surprisingly, this trend was least successful in the politics of presidential selection, where the reforms which followed the election of 1968 were required to remove the official party from its automatic role in delegate selection and presidential nomination. Yet the nearly complete triumph of primary elections had long since been registered at the state and local levels, and even when that triumph had been in doubt, the role of the primary as a means of weakening the political party was widely recognized and generally acknowledged.

Rising Affluence and Partisan Independence

All these elements were probably sufficient to explain the nationalization of presidential politics. Each was proceeding, even accelerating, throughout the postwar period; all were moving in the same general direction. They did have to acquire their impact through the actions

Table 1.5. The loss of party control over personnel

Year	Number of states with "general coverage" by civil service
1980	47 of 50
1970	39 of 50
1960	28 of 50
1950	20 of 48
1940	15 of 48
1930	9 of 48
1920	8 of 48
1910	5 of 46
1900	2 of 45

Source: Council of State Governments, *The Book of the States 1980–81* (Lexington, Ky.: Council of State Governments, 1980) and its predecessors. The most recent version of the relevant table is "State Personnel Agencies: Coverage, Organization, and Selected Policies as of Late 1979," in the 1980–81 edition, pp. 248–249; similar tables, under varying titles, were presented in most earlier years.

Table 1.6. The loss of party control over nominations

Year	Number of states with mandatory primary for governor
1980	50 of 50
1970	49 of 50
1960	49 of 50
1950	42 of 48
1940	41 of 48
1930	32 of 48
1920	32 of 48
1910	17 of 46
1900	None

Source: Council of State Governments, *The Book of the States 1980–81* and its predecessors. The most recent and relevant single table is "Primary Elections for State Officers," p. 72 in the 1980–81 edition; earlier versions had varying titles as well as varying contents. See also Charles E. Merriam and Louise Overacker, "Direct Primary Legislation, 1899–1927," in Merriam and Overacker, *Primary Elections* (Chicago: University of Chicago Press, 1928), pp. 60–107.

and responses of official party figures, because the bulk of the delegates to national party conventions were still chosen through the official party and because party officeholders were still the most likely to achieve delegate status. Yet it was testimony to the strength of these factors, especially in concert, that they were able to acquire that impact—and thus to remove construction of a nominating majority from the convention. Moreover, they were able to acquire this impact, via the calculations of regular party officials, without much change in the formal rules of delegate selection and presidential nomination.

The composite process which produced this historic shift, however, was further propelled by another continuing change—again beginning well before the 1952 conventions, again moving in conjunction with the other main components of the nationalization of presidential politics, and again reinforcing the impact of all these factors. This final element was economic growth, along with associated changes in American society—in the social base for presidential nominating politics.[9] The attendant elements of economic growth, in rising affluence in general and partisan independence in particular, both magnified the impact of national media and contributed to the decline of political parties, while they added a direct stimulus for party officials to reach an earlier and earlier commitment—and consensus—on a national party nominee. This set of effects was destined to be even more consequential once reform had changed the institutional matrix through which delegates were selected and presidents nominated. But its impact was felt, as an additional influence on the calculations of party leaders, even before the coming of extensive party reform.

Sustained economic growth implied numerous changes in the social base for presidential politics, changes summarized by the notion of rising affluence and including such items as a rising level of individual and family income, a rising level of educational attainment, and a changing occupational structure—ever more middle-class, ever more white-collar. (See Table 1.7.) Americans of higher income, more education, and higher social status had always been more likely to participate in politics, in almost every fashion, than their less advantaged fellow citizens. But wealthier, better-educated, and higher-status Americans were not especially likely to see political parties as the means through which they would attempt to influence governmental policy. Indeed, as rising affluence, education, and occupational standing proceeded apace during the postwar years, an increasing share of Americans began to style themselves as independents rather than as confessed supporters of one or the other political party. (See Table 1.8.)

This development surely contributed something to the weakening of political parties as organizations, since an increasing—and always influential—segment of American society no longer offered even pro forma loyalty, while its members sought other routes to influence over governmental policy. This same development probably contributed to the growing influence of national news media as well, for when the new independents determined to select among candidates for a presidential nomination, without heeding cues from local party leaders,

Table 1.7.   Economic growth and the changing society

Year	Median family income (in constant 1981 dollars)	Median years of schooling	Percentage white-collar
1980	26,136	12.5	52
1970	23,111	12.1	48
1960	17,259	10.6	42
1950	12,548	9.3	37
1940[a]	9,057	8.6	31

Source: Bureau of the Census, *Historical Statistics of the United States,* pp. 297, 381, and 139, as supplemented by Bureau of the Census, *Statistical Abstract of the United States 1980,* pp. 432, 143, and 386.

a. Estimated from aggregate statistics.

Table 1.8.   The rise of independent identifiers

Year	Percentage of all citizens
1986	33
1982	31
1978	34
1974	36
1970	31
1966	28
1962	21
1958	19
1954	22

Source: Drawn from "Table 2.1: Party Identification," in Warren E. Miller, Arthur H. Miller, and Edward J. Schneider, comps., *American National Election Studies Data Sourcebook 1952–1978* (Cambridge, Mass.: Harvard University Press, 1980), p. 81, as supplemented by *American National Election Study, 1982: Post-election Survey File* (Ann Arbor, Mich.: Inter-university Consortium for Political and Social Research, 1983), p. 173, and *American National Election Study, 1986: Post-election Survey File* (Ann Arbor, Mich.: Inter-university Consortium for Political and Social Research, forthcoming).

they almost necessarily turned to these media as a source of alternative, national cues. Yet even more to the point, these individuals were far more likely to become the social base for insurgent movements and independent candidacies, or even for institutionalized opposition to the official party.[10]

The potential for insurgent campaigns, and hence for local alternatives independent of the official party, was thus increasingly enhanced. After reform, these campaigns would express themselves directly, in attempts to wrest away the nomination for a particular champion. But even before reform, they magnified the pressure on party leaders to move early, in response to emerging national developments, so as not to be faced by increasingly plausible challenges to their own authority. Moreover, while the Republican party was the statistical home of the better off, the better educated, and the socially advantaged, this possibility—of indigenous challenges coupled with (or even stimulated by) the campaigns of national contenders—was hardly contained or even concentrated within Republican ranks. The share of party identifiers who were inclined to declare independence from their political party increased sharply for Democrats as well during the quarter-century after 1952. (See Table 1.9.)

Strategic Calculations and the Triumph of Nationalization

All the individual elements of the nationalization of politics played a part in this change in the focus of key participants, and eventually in the location of the presidential nomination itself. The growth of government, and the crucial role of national government within that growth, gave everyone—party leaders, organized interests, and ordinary citizens—a greater stake in nominating politics. The growth and multiplication of national media made everyone better able to follow the progress of that politics. It is true that the key actors remained party officials, and local party officials to boot. But the parties in whose official hierarchies they resided were increasingly enfeebled as organizations, and these leaders found themselves in an environment which increasingly encouraged them to get behind one or another presidential contender, at an earlier and earlier time.

In fact, it was through the calculations—and responses—of these party officials that the evolving nationalization of presidential politics ultimately made itself felt. Party leaders did not necessarily change the calculus by which most of them attempted to analyze presidential politics: they preferred to remain free of any bandwagon until they could judge where it might go but to jump on that bandwagon at a point when their support could still command substantial returns.[11] But the practical framework within which these calculations were

Table 1.9. The rise of partisan independents

| Year | Partisan independents as a percentage of strong partisans | | |
	Democrats	Republicans	Total
1986	58	103	75
1982	55	83	64
1978	93	125	104
1974	72	112	85
1970	50	89	62
1966	50	70	57
1962	30	50	37
1958	26	45	32
1954	41	46	43

Source: Recalculated from "Table 2.1: Party Identification," in Miller, Miller, and Schneider, comps., *American National Election Studies Data Sourcebook 1952–1978,* p. 81, as supplemented by *American National Election Study, 1982,* p. 173, and *American National Election Study, 1986: Post-election Survey File,* pagination forthcoming.

made had changed; changed calculations followed inexorably; and these calculations then cumulated to confirm a new and different political world. In this world, individual party leaders—and hence party leaders collectively—were encouraged to ally themselves with a presidential contender simply because counterpart figures around the country saw the same increased stake in nominating politics, could more easily follow the total process of jockeying for influence over that politics, were less protected from these intrinsic pressures by a strong party organization, and were thus, themselves, moving earlier. But there were important new pressures on these party officials, from below and from above, and these were probably crucial additions in reshaping their political environment.

From below, party leaders were increasingly subject to challenge on their home grounds by other actors who also saw a stake in presidential politics. As political parties became organizationally weaker, party leaders were far more likely to face a challenge from local non-party groups, which were in part the product of economic growth and its associated social changes and which were reliably inclined to act independently in politics. From above, the increasing prospects for local challenges, especially when coupled with declining organizational strength for local political parties, made it easier for national contenders to intervene in state contests over delegate selection. They could rely on media coverage as a partial substitute for regular party support; they could rely even more securely on independents and party dissidents to provide an organizational base for the local version of their national campaigns.

More than ever, then, it was necessary for state and local party leaders to align themselves—early—with a potential winner in order to undercut these potential threats and maintain their own preeminence at home. Again, even this development had probably been arriving, albeit glacially, since about the turn of the century. But in the years immediately following World War II the trend experienced a further extension, to its practical limit.

The End of Nominating Conventions: The Democrats

The nationalization of presidential politics emerges strikingly from comparisons even between the last of the contests to produce a nominating majority at the convention itself and the first of the contests to produce recurring majorities constructed outside, in advance of the official convention. Despite their centrality to this process, party leaders at the time had no reason to see either the implications of this change in their own focus or its permanence. Yet nominations for president were effectively reached at the national party convention for the last time within both major parties in 1952. The very next fully independent nominations within those parties—the 1960 contest for the Democrats, the 1964 contest for the Republicans—were not only resolved outside convention confines but also came to represent and affirm the breaking point, after which nominations were highly unlikely to be resolved inside in anything other than a formalistic sense.

The Democratic convention of 1952 was the last of the classic old-style party gatherings and featured behavior which in its essence would have been familiar to convention participants a hundred years before.[12] The convention required three ballots to secure a nominee, with a majority created at the convention. Moreover, the product of this politicking, the candidate, had entered no primaries and engaged in no direct campaigning prior to his nomination. Instead, party leaders put together his majority after the front-runner coming into the convention proved unable to convert his initial lead into a substantial, successful bandwagon. Yet even that classic but precarious outcome was not guaranteed until the original front-runner had tried a clever and complicated internal gambit, the tactical equivalent of key convention maneuvers stretching back across a century.

Senator Estes Kefauver was the clear public favorite coming into the convention, thanks largely to the televised hearings of his Special Committee on Organized Crime. He had also won by far the greatest number of presidential primaries, although most of these were "beauty contests," having no connection to the allocation of delegates, and although he had lost two of four contested primaries along the way. Despite that, he was actively opposed by no one, at least no one with serious prospects for an eventual nomination. Yet he had failed to create a campaign presence in many states—which is to say in many state parties—and he had actually begun to attack state party leaders as being allegedly in league with organized crime. Kefauver did manage to lead with 340 votes, of 616 needed to nominate, on the first ballot. By then, however, Governor Adlai Stevenson, an undeclared candidate but an obvious resting place for party officeholders from some of the largest states, was already in second place with 273 votes—and that was handwriting on the wall. By then, in truth, the convention had already turned on one brief period, when the Kefauver forces seemed on the verge of executing an internal maneuver which ranked with the most ingenious in all convention history and which might well have altered the balance on the first presidential ballot—and after.

The big fight had come over the credentialing of three southern states—Texas, Louisiana, and South Carolina—whose delegates were probably selected in accordance with applicable regulations but whose leaders gave every indication from the time of their selection of failing to support the national ticket if it continued to present unacceptable positions on civil rights.[13] Accordingly, the key maneuver centered on a loyalty pledge addressing this problem. The Kefauver forces fought for stiff language on party loyalty, in part because they believed that it was ethically appropriate but in part because it might attract the liberal supporters of Averell Harriman, fourth-strongest candidate within the convention, while it alienated the conservative supporters of Richard Russell, the third-strongest candidate, to the point where they would protest and walk out. The roll call on the central provision in this conflict started during dinner and dragged on for over two hours, before it began to appear that the maneuver would succeed. At that point, the Stevenson leadership, finally alerted to the tactical implications, produced a sharp reversal in the Illinois vote (from 15 Yes/45 No, to 52 Yes/8 No), which was followed by a reversal in several other states leaning to Stevenson. Yet another hour after *that* shift had begun, the roll call was resolved with a defeat for Kefauver. The nomination too was effectively resolved, and the next day, after two anticlimactic ballots, Stevenson became the nominee.

The Democratic convention of 1956 might actually have served to comment on the passing of this era, by confirming the shift of the nomination out of the convention and the shifting character of the convention as a result.[14] For the 1956 nomination was openly and fully contested throughout the primaries. Yet a nominating majority was effectively in place by the time those primaries ended, to be confirmed by overwhelming ratification on the first convention ballot. On the other hand, because the nominee (Adlai Stevenson) was still the titular leader of his party in 1956, the Democratic convention of 1960 served as a better instance and guarantor of the degree of change.[15] Even 1960 could not have confirmed this change for its participants—the development was too new to be sure that 1956 *and* 1960 were not mere epicycles—but it was so different from preceding conventions and nominating contests that commentators at the time were moved to pronounce that the character of presidential politics was changing.

The eventual nominee, Senator John F. Kennedy, had sought the nomination fully and openly from the beginning. Kennedy was actually quite similar to Estes Kefauver in that he chose his route principally because he lacked endorsement by the official party and could hope for nomination in no other way. But he then worked at building a full national organization, to squeeze every available delegate out of every approachable state. With this, he entered as many of the states as his organization permitted, courting party officials when possible, threatening them with a local insurgency when not. Ultimately, his preconvention campaign was to feature even fewer contested primaries than that of 1952. Kennedy, however, at least won both of them, against Hubert Humphrey in Wisconsin and West Virginia, providing a testament of electability to official party observers.

There were in fact numerous other contenders in 1960, invisible in the preconvention campaign because they were following a different and much older strategy—one appropriate, as it turned out, only to an earlier era. Senator Lyndon Johnson, Senator Stuart Symington, and Adlai Stevenson again, were all waiting for an inconclusive preconvention campaign to permit them to mount a nominating drive at the convention. In a sense, they had reason to hope—or at least to argue—that the convention would still play the consequential role; two contested primaries hardly constituted a mandate. Yet the front-runner, Kennedy, *had* won them both, along with numerous uncontested others, and he had corralled delegates in most of the major states as well. As a result, these low-profile challengers were to be severely disappointed; there were not even any serious test votes on the way to the opening ballot. The convention was enlivened by a thunderous demonstration for Stevenson from the galleries, one worthy of the great conventions of old and potentially capable of altering momentum—at a different kind of convention in a different era. But when the presidential ballot eventually arrived, the question was never who would achieve a numerical majority but only, in truth, how close the projected (Kennedy) count would be to the actual (Kennedy) outcome.

The End of Nominating Conventions: The Republicans

The Republican contest of 1952 presented interesting twists on the Democratic pattern of that year.[16] It too was a nominating conflict in the old style, with the nomination itself very much unresolved as the convention assembled. It even elaborated the pattern, with a variant of major convention maneuvers which was historically distinctive to the Republican party. The Republican contest paralleled the Democratic in the presence of one candidate who combed the country in search of delegates while his leading potential opponent remained on the sidelines. Yet it offered a twist on that pattern because the active candidate, Senator Robert A. Taft, was also the champion of the regular party, while his most serious threat, General Dwight D. Eisenhower, was the favorite of independents and dissidents. Eisenhower was also to remain in Europe, as commander of Allied forces, for the entire primary campaign.

Despite that, the Eisenhower name ignited the contest with a victory in the opening primary in New Hampshire and with a tremendous write-in response in the Minnesota primary which followed. Despite *that,* Taft managed to win several primaries on his own, including Nebraska and South Dakota, where he directly defeated Eisenhower. By the time the last delegates had been selected, though, Eisenhower had won more primaries, without being entered everywhere, and held the obvious lead in public opinion polls. Yet Taft was just as obviously the favorite of the official party and offered his own primary wins in return. More to the point, he had an apparent delegate edge: the Associated Press made it Taft 530, Eisenhower 427, uncommitted 118, others 131. What followed was not just the classic nominating convention but the classic—and last—Republican version thereof. The peculiarly Republican element was the final incarnation of "the steamroller," a convention maneuver which relied on the fact that the Republican National Committee certified the temporary roll of delegates and that that committee contained a healthy representation of southern members, despite the near absence of a southern Republican party.[17]

The National Committee, true to historic form, decided three key credentials challenges—to the delegations of Texas, Georgia, and Louisiana—in favor of Taft, the champion of the official party. When the convention assembled, the Eisenhower forces retaliated immediately, not with direct challenges to these delegations but with a challenge to the temporary convention rules, which would have allowed challenged delegates to vote on all matters except their own credentials. On this key test the Eisenhower position triumphed, 658 to 548. The subsequent vote on the Georgia challenge, again favorable to the Eisenhower position, was almost anticlimactic. The nominating ballot restored an instant of tension, when Eisenhower fell 9 votes short of the 604 needed to win, leading Taft by 595 to 500 with 101 votes for others. But Minnesota quickly moved to switch 19 votes to Eisenhower, thereby sealing the outcome without the need for a second ballot. Clearly, in the absence of Eisenhower triumphs on procedural rules and then on credentials, the contest would have gone to a second ballot, and perhaps several more. Mathematically, without the credentials decision replacing those three southern states, Taft would have been somewhere between 26 votes ahead and only 10 votes behind when the first ballot was completed.

Because Eisenhower successfully sought uncontested renomination, it was 1960 before events could confirm that changes in the pattern of nominating politics, and a changed role for the national party convention, had arrived in the Republican party as well. That year did go on to provide evidence of change, through a successful effort by Richard Nixon to construct his nominating majority well in advance of the convention and then merely to see it ratified there. But because Vice President Nixon was such a logical successor to President Eisenhower, and because there was no open combat throughout the states as a preliminary to the convention, the Republican contest of 1964 is probably a more convincing affirmation of shifts in Republican politics.

The Republican contest of 1964 actually possessed superficial similarities to the classic traditional contest of 1952, but the nature of the practical conflict, along with the role of the convention in it, marked the two years as sharply different.[18] The 1964 contest again featured a favorite of the regular party, combing the country in search of delegates, who was opposed by one or another contender with support from independents and dissidents. Yet Senator Barry Goldwater, the favorite, also had substantial support from independent activists and conservative insurgents, so that his campaign could be augmented by efforts to take over the official party where it was weak, that is, where party office often went begging, and by efforts to threaten unsympathetic incumbents where party office was occupied, with insurgent challenges if they resisted the national Goldwater campaign.

Despite the impressiveness of that campaign, the primary calendar threatened, for a while, to deflate it fatally. Ambassador Henry Cabot

Lodge won the opening primary in New Hampshire on a write-in, even though both Goldwater and Governor Nelson Rockefeller, his alleged main challenger, were present. Although Goldwater won the beauty contest in several other primaries, he also lost the only other contested primary before the finale, when Rockefeller managed to defeat him in Oregon. But Goldwater bounced back in the final California primary, largest in the nation, capping a drive which saw him go to the convention with overwhelming support. His opponents could manage nothing serious in preliminary test votes, and he was nominated on the first ballot by more than four to one over his nearest competitor. The spotty results of his preconvention campaign, then, served not to suggest that Republican nominating politics worked as it always had, but to prove that in a new era the bandwagon rolling toward a first-ballot nomination did not have to include every primary or state convention contest, nor even every succession of such contests, to build a majority well before the convention assembled.

The Republican contests of 1952 and 1964, along with the Democratic contests of 1952 and 1960, suggested that regular party officials remained formally central to the process of delegate selection (and hence presidential nomination) because the mechanics of that process still buttressed their role. Yet the Republican contest of 1964 and the Democratic contest of 1960 suggested that in order to maintain their practical influence, the influence which could flow from this positional advantage, party officials needed to seek identification with a locally acceptable national contender, to ward off local challenges or to be sure that they did not succeed. This identification, in turn, was necessarily undertaken far earlier than it would otherwise have been, because the candidates were prepared to move earlier, interest groups and independent activists had to move earlier if they were contemplating a challenge to the regular party, and, finally, the party had to move earlier to cut off such challenges and secure its influence on the campaign of an emerging nominee.

All such maneuvers, of course, served to push the contest for a convention majority further and further back into the official process of delegate selection. Not only did the major actors have increased incentives for earlier and earlier commitments, but as those commitments were made and became quickly and nationally known to all the other major actors, candidates gained—or lost—momentum at a point far earlier (and hence with an earlier finality) than would have been true in the past. The result, after 1952, was the departure of the nomination from the national party convention. After 1968, that disappearance was to be institutionalized, through extensive reform of the mechanics of delegate selection and through the additional jockeying which followed from that reform. But by 1968, the disappearance had already, informally, effectively occurred.

2 | Institutionalizing the Disappearance: The Nomination after Reform

Nothing about the politics of presidential selection in the years after 1952 threatened to move the presidential nomination back into the national party convention in any regular and continuing fashion. Occasionally, this politics suggested that a nominating majority might not be assembled by the time the convention gathered. Yet in every case that politics then played out so as to eliminate this possibility, and in every case hindsight suggested that the threat of an actual nominating convention had always been more apparent than real. The nomination, in short, had moved outside the national party convention. It had moved into the process of delegate selection. It had moved in response to a set of powerful forces. Those forces appeared sufficient to keep it outside, barring unforeseen, additional, major change.

Such change in fact arrived, formally and visibly this time, just as most observers were beginning to suspect that the nomination had indeed informally but reliably departed from the convention, and just as most participants were beginning to believe that they understood the dynamics of the new nominating politics. Explosive growth in the number of presidential primaries was the most common measure of this comprehensive change. But it was only the most visible part of what was even then only the most formal aspect of the resulting shift in practical politics. Indeed, formal change this extensive had immediate implications for almost every facet of the practical politics which occurred within reformed institutions. Although that included the nature and timing of the construction of nominating majorities, it was hardly confined—it had hardly even begun—there. The years between 1968 and 1972 brought the greatest break in the formal mechanics of delegate selection since the institutionalization of the national party convention itself. The years after 1972 saw the consolidation of this break, to the point where a radically different politics of presidential selection emerged to accompany sharply changed institutional arrangements.

This new political environment was eventually to produce a reliably different cast of regular participants at national party conventions, of delegates and even of campaign operatives. Just as it was eventually to produce a very different central activity to replace the construction of nominating majorities, an activity with different lines of conflict around it. In turn, the contest among these newly regular participants over this newly central activity was to produce, though with a longer lag, a different pattern of press coverage and even a different relationship between the convention as experienced by its immediate participants and the convention as experienced by the national television audience. Yet long before these effects were confirmed, the new politics of presidential selection was to exaggerate tendencies inherent in the nationalization of presidential politics, to close back over the national party convention, and to lock the nomination itself outside that convention, institutionally.

The initial burst of reform activity, the trigger for all these developments, was a response to a specific consensual crisis, in the disastrous Democratic convention of 1968. But that response was impelled and shaped more generally by many of the same elements which had come together to comprise the nationalization of presidential politics. The product of this initial reform burst then ramified—almost ricocheted—down through the nominating campaigns which followed, as officials in both parties tried to cope with the demands of reform, with the unforeseen consequences of meeting those demands, and with the equally unforeseen composite process which resulted. The outcome, almost immediately, was not just an extensively altered matrix of institutions for delegate selection but in fact a whole new era in the mechanics of presidential nomination. Numerous states added true presidential primaries; numerous others converted older, ineffective primaries into real contests focused on the aspirants for a nomination. The era of dominant primary elections was at hand.

Such a change raised equally immediate questions about the informal migration of the nomination, about whether the components of the nationalization of presidential politics would work the same way in the postreform era and whether the key actors in presidential selection would respond similarly to those forces, however they might work. Answers were not long in coming. The components of the nationalization of politics—the growth of government, of course, but especially the rise of mass media, the decline of political parties, and the changing shape of the social base for all this —not only drove in the same direction in the postreform period but drove ever more intensively. Contested primaries provided a fertile field for mass media to cover. Declining parties not only were unable to resist the general drive toward reform but were far less able to control open presidential primaries than they had been to manage internal party conventions. The new partisan independents, with their ability to underwrite dissident nominating campaigns and their propensity to turn out in open candidate contests, then completed the thrust.

The key actors in this reformed world, on the other hand, those whose strategic calculations would be the most proximate influence on the location of the nomination, also changed sharply, and that shift raised the possibility that one type of change would cancel another. It quickly developed, however, that these newly influential rank-and-file party identifiers, who replaced the previously influential regular party officials, were even more likely to move in the direction in which those party leaders had been going. Party identifiers were inherently less informed about the contenders when the nominating campaign opened, and they were reliably less committed to an extended ideological or issue position as the campaign progressed. On both grounds, rank-and-file party identifiers were *less* likely than party officials to resist existing pressures toward early construction of a nominating majority. When the mass media of information then concentrated on the early states in this reformed nominating contest, the move—almost the stampede—to an early nomination was assured. In short order, the nomination was not only confirmed outside the convention but realized earlier and realized with an institutional inevitability which it had not previously possessed.

The first contest under reformed arrangements for delegate selection, the Democratic nominating contest of 1972, managed to suggest for a short time that these developments were problematic. But the campaigns which followed—as with the contested Republican nominations of 1976 and 1980 along with the contested Democratic nominations of 1976 and 1984—confirmed the apparent inevitability of a decisive preconvention bandwagon. Indeed, these contests confirmed this result in the most convincing way possible, by offering tremendously varied fields, nominating strategies, and incidents along the way, yet the same ultimate outcome—a nominating majority reached clearly and effectively in advance of the national party convention, within the process of delegate selection.

Throughout this transformation, the convention itself maintained a superficial continuity. That is, it not only *looked* much as it had looked in the years before reform; it appeared to play the role it had played before as well. Its central activity—its alleged central activity, as it turned out—not only remained outside convention confines but appeared to be institutionalized there through sweeping party reforms. The convention continued as a nominator of last resort in a set of extreme but not impossible circumstances, when illness, accident, or deliberate injury befell the emerging nominee before the consummation of the nominating ballot. Yet this continuity was in most respects misleading. For once again the convention was destined to change, to evolve, even to decay, in every facet of its operation. A new cast of participants seemed inevitable, for example, especially given the extensive new rules for delegate selection. A new central activity was ineluctable as well, although its practical consequence was very much an open question. As a result, when the reform era sealed the fate and locus of the presidential nomination, it reopened most other questions about convention organization and activity.

The Background to Reform

Changes in the mechanics of delegate selection, and hence in the politics of presidential nomination which occurred within those mechanics—and hence, inevitably, in the place and role of the national party convention within this overall process—followed quickly on one central event. That event was the Democratic convention of 1968. This convention was one of the most contentious in American history. It contributed most directly to the loss by its nominee of the general election. But its largest indirect contribution was an arithmetic progression of institutional change which surfaced continually in the interims between succeeding presidential elections. Yet while this convention was clearly the turning point—the consensual "crisis" for which self-conscious reform of the mechanics of delegate selection could be the response—it was hardly the sole, or even the major, force impelling this change. Nor was it the dominant factor, at least directly, in the chain reaction of reform which followed.

Instead, the major force impelling this change was the nationalization of presidential politics, or at least some principal components of that trend. These were, of course, the same components—the rise of national media, the decline of local parties, and, especially, the spread of middle-class independence—which had led to the departure of the nomination from the convention in the first place. The dominant factor in the subsequent chain reaction of institutional change, in turn, was the numerous unforeseen consequences of the first round of deliberate reform and the reaction of state parties and state legislatures, both Democratic and Republican, as they tried to cope with the (unforeseen) new world of presidential politics which resulted.

Thus the rise of national media of information represented a clear alternative to the local political party as a means of monitoring presidential politics, and probably constituted an implicit argument both for following that politics in this way and even for "participating," vicariously, via the national press. Simultaneously, the decline of political parties meant that they were, in rapid succession, unable to achieve effective legitimacy in their nominating role, then unable to ward off an extended reform movement, and finally unable even to channel that movement to protect their organizational place in the politics of presidential selection. The most consequential background element, however, was probably the changing shape of American society, especially the larger and larger share of white-collar independents which this change contributed to both political parties. These individuals had a different notion of how presidential politics should be conducted, and it did not include working through party organizations. They were an increasingly influential though not numerically dominant group in both parties. As a result, they were to become the "shock troops" of party reform. If both the institutional and the informal products of this reform movement did not ultimately accord with their intentions either, they had still been a major factor in creating those products.

All these forces, however, might have remained mere background had it not been for the Democratic convention of 1968.[1] In most ways that convention was just an orthodox product of the presidential politics of the prereform era. As usual, the calculations of party leaders were central to its nomination. As usual, the nomination was effectively reached, numerous test votes and press analyses notwithstanding, well before the convention assembled. But the desperate contentiousness inside the convention, as augmented by the street demonstrations outside, were probably unrivaled since the Republican convention of 1912—which had produced an even more extreme party fissure and which had also given powerful impetus to a subsequent reform movement.

The withdrawal of President Lyndon Johnson in the face of party division; the rise of insurgent campaigns, first by Senator Eugene McCarthy and then by Senator Robert Kennedy; the assassination of Kennedy on the campaign trail; and the disastrous convention sessions which ultimately nominated Vice President Hubert Humphrey but devalued that nomination in the process: these were among the elements combining to give the convention its surface drama. Despite that drama, they were probably not the equivalent in continuing social force of the rise of national media, the decline of organized parties, and the growth of white-collar independence. But they did unite—implode, really—to shape the convention, and that convention did become the consensual "crisis" to which a self-conscious reform movement could be the response.

Another chain of specific events was again critical in shaping the reform proposals which resulted.[2] An aggressive staff led the key reform commission to its own particular substantive preferences. An initially unsympathetic National Chairman rallied the Democratic National Committee behind this reform package. A wave of new Democratic governors was elected, with a general commitment to reform, at precisely the right point thereafter. Yet the same background forces were again critical as well. The national media, or at least that part which paid any attention, were solidly in favor of structural reform. The regular Democratic party, with temporary institutional disarray added to declining organizational strength, was either insufficiently strong or (more probably) insufficiently mobilized to counter reform proposals which threatened to remove it from the process. And the white-collar independents who loomed ever larger within the party managed, through superior mobilization and superior focus in this peculiarly facilitative environment, to have their way.

Without those grand and continuing forces from the nationalization of presidential politics, then, the impact of the 1968 Democratic convention might have dissipated quickly. Just as without the convention, those forces would have had to work gradually, even glacially, to produce a change in the mechanics of delegate selection. Without the focused drive for reform which resulted, finally, neither these longer-term forces nor the immediate currents arising from the convention could have produced the major initial reform package, its specific component reform proposals, or, by extension, all the subsequent, partially linked adjustments which continued to reshape the selection process. But the background forces were in place when the convention erupted. An explicit reform process was the immediate result. And the politics internal to that process then created a sweeping package of party reform.

The Dynamics of Reform

The inaugural institutional package which emerged from this concentrated reform politics contained sweeping recommendations—broad, deep, and comprehensive—for the handling of party business.[3] Within the realm of presidential selection, these recommendations covered the apportionment of delegates among the states, the slating of delegates within them, the allocation of delegates to presidential contenders, the required demographic characteristics of these delegates, and on and on. Yet the most consequential—and continuing—demand of these proposals was for a changed set of basic institutions for the selection of delegates to the national party convention. As a result, the most consequential aspect of these recommendations, and of the forces they in turn set loose, was a new politics of presidential selection, coalescing quickly around this new matrix of nominating institutions. Although these recommendations for reform were officially internal to the Democratic party, both their products (reformed institutions and a new politics) were to spread quickly to the Republican party.

There were numerous aspects even to the new institutions of delegate selection which the Democratic party demanded for 1972. The largest one, however—and the one which came to characterize the entire package—was a demand for immediate and extended participation by the voters in selecting delegates and nominating a president. In the inaugural irony which went with this requirement, the Democratic reform commission which wrote the key reform report actually believed that it would affect states using a convention system, and thus the character of state party conventions, more than it would affect states using a primary, and hence the character of presidential primary elections. Yet immediately within the Democratic party—and quickly within the Republican party, too, where deliberate, self-conscious, centralized reform was explicitly rejected—the product of these demands and of the general reform movement was an explosive growth in the number of states using presidential primaries to select their delegates to the national party convention. (See Table 2.1.)

The growth of primaries, rather than of reformed state conventions, was thus the first unforeseen element of postreform politics. The extension of this growth into the Republican party—in truth equally—was the second. In part, there was a narrowly political explanation for this impact on the Republicans. In some states, where the Democrats controlled both houses of the state legislature, party leaders simply extended their plan for delegate selection to the Republican party as well, whether leaders on the other side wanted a presidential primary or not. But in addition, many of the forces which were pushing Democratic leaders in this direction fell on Republican leaders, too. They too were sensitive to demands and arguments for "democratization" of the process; they too possessed a large—probably larger—segment of white-collar independents, for whom such reforms were especially attractive.

Beyond that, once started, the process of reform acquired a momentum of its own. Again, this was more self-conscious in the Democratic party, where the very mechanics of reexamining the institutions of delegate selection were institutionalized, with recurring reform commissions after every presidential contest. These commissions invariably produced new reform documents, with both intended and unforeseen institutional consequences for the next round of delegate selection. These consequences then demanded subsequent reform commissions, with new documents, additional ambivalent consequences, and so on.[4] Quite apart from this process, however, the out-

Table 2.1. The growth of presidential primaries

Year	Number of states	
	Democratic	Republican
1984	23	26
1980	34	35
1976	30	30
1972	23	21
1968	17	15

Source: "Presidential Primaries," in Congressional Quarterly, *Presidential Elections since 1789*, 4th ed. (Washington, D.C.: Congressional Quarterly Press, 1987), pp. 7–70.

comes of reformed presidential politics produced a further set of pressures conducing in the same general direction. For example, Democratic leaders in some states which had resisted the urge toward a primary shifted to that format for 1976. The reformed state conventions which they had retained in 1972 had been captured by insurgents and dissidents—usually supporters of Senator George McGovern, the architect of the original reform proposals—and that experience had convinced many local party leaders (whether rightly or wrongly) that they personally would fare better in a primary system. After 1976, in turn, Democratic leaders in states which were still not part of the primary election process had to evaluate the fate—the declining prominence—of their states in presidential politics if they continued to resist the overall trend.

The Republican party had no counterpart continuing commissions on reform. Nevertheless, the unforeseen consequences of Democratic and Republican alterations, as rapidly augmented by a specifically Republican experience, set off much the same dynamic. Thus the same underlying components of the nationalization of politics, enhanced by some mischievous legislators in Democratically controlled states, gave the Republicans the same initial institutional drift. When the first contested nominating campaign under reformed institutions within the Republican party in 1976 produced major gains for insurgent forces, despite the presence of an incumbent president supported by the official party, some state party officials moved additionally to the presidential primary as a hoped-for way to undercut insurgents and to sustain themselves. After 1976, Republican leaders in yet another group of states decided that, in a process dominated by primary elections, they could expect to be slighted not just by the press but even by the candidates if they did not possess a presidential primary too. Once again, reform begat reform—and primaries begat primaries—until the Republican party had actually outpaced the Democrats in some institutional regards. (See Table 2.1.)

A New Era in Delegate Selection

By 1972, the number of presidential primaries had already reached a historic high. By 1980, the number had surged past that. Yet summary figures on states with presidential primaries actually understate their increase, because existing but previously eviscerated primaries took on a new effectiveness in this altered environment. Moreover, summary figures cannot approach conveying the change in the practical politics of presidential selection which arrived, automatically and inevitably, with such extensive reform of the mechanisms of delegate selection. As a result, a different summary of the extent of this change has to begin with a direct comparison to the other major eras in delegate selection and presidential nomination—because the years after 1968 constituted nothing less than a new era in nominating mechanics.

In all the years since the inception of the national party convention in 1831, there had actually been only two great eras of delegate selection. The first was the "pure convention system," from 1832 to 1908, when all states used some variant of the state party convention to select their delegates to a national counterpart. The second was the "mixed system," from 1912 to 1968, which featured a slowly shifting blend of state party conventions and state presidential primaries, to select those same delegates to that same national convention. After 1968, however, there was a third era. This was, effectively, the "dominant primary system," a term of some confusion in the narrowly statistical sense—a sizable minority of state party conventions did, after all, remain—but one which was practically accurate when judged by the character of the resulting politics of presidential nomination.[5]

From the creation of the national party convention itself through the first decade of the twentieth century, delegate selection in the individual states varied tremendously (and idiosyncratically) in its specific details. Despite this variation, there was one underlying institutional prototype in all the states, which themselves grew in number from twenty-three (in 1832) to forty-six (in 1908) during this period. This basic model was the state convention system. Its most common incarnation featured local meetings of party officials (in precincts, wards, townships, towns, or counties), to select delegates to some intermediary level of party convention (in counties, legislative districts, congressional districts, and so on), which selected delegates to a statewide party convention. That statewide convention then chose the national convention delegates, sometimes at large, sometimes by district, sometimes both. Occasionally, this process was truncated by having the state central committee of the party choose the delegates to the national convention. At the other extreme, the system was occasionally varied by opening its initial, bottom level to direct public participation. Regardless, the dominant outline of the process remained a nested set of party caucuses, culminating in the selection of state delegates to the national party convention. The dominant participants, in fact and often even in law, were party officials from top to bottom.

The first (proto) presidential primaries were added to this institutional matrix by Wisconsin in 1905 and by Pennsylvania a year later, in time for the selection contests of 1908. But the serious rush toward effective presidential primaries began in Oregon in 1910, with a primary featuring the actual names of contenders for a presidential nomination. So rapid was this initial rush that the era of the mixed system had actually arrived by 1912, when thirteen Republican and twelve Democratic state parties used some version of the presidential primary.[6] The mix between primaries and conventions varied incrementally and continually thereafter, with a surge toward the primary through 1920 and a drift away by small steps after that. These primaries were always themselves a mix, differing most consequentially on whether the delegates were elected, on whether the names of presidential contenders were present, and on whether the names of presidential contenders were in any way connected with the selection of delegates. But the institutional form of the primary election was the new element, and if the outcomes of these primaries rarely determined the nomination, they were still a means of direct public participation in a few states, and, more important, they did provide a "reality test" for those party officials who would ultimately have to construct a nominating majority. (See Table 2.2.)

There were actually fewer presidential primaries in 1968 than there had been in 1920, the previous high-water mark. But the explosion after 1968, from seventeen to thirty-four for the Democrats and from fifteen to thirty-five for the Republicans, represented the coming of a whole new era. Previously, the mix of the "mixed system" had been heavily weighted toward state party conventions—numerically, but even more so in practice. After 1968, this mix tipped heavily in the opposite direction. The overwhelming majority of delegates were selected in presidential primaries. Primary outcomes swung the result in most of the remaining convention states. The "dominant primary system" was at hand.

Institutional Arrangements in the Postreform Era

These summary tabulations still understate the bedrock institutional change. Many of the presidential primaries which previously existed, and hence many of the states then counted as having presidential primaries, were actually "presidential" in name only. Either the primary could not be used by its voters to affect the fortunes of presidential aspirants or, if that was theoretically possible, most aspirants had good and continuing reasons to shun the explicit contest. The general shift to presidential primaries within both parties after 1968, then, not only added primaries to which these limitations did not apply but actually converted most preexisting primaries into contests in which the identity of the presidential aspirants was paramount. Moreover, once the shift to presidential primaries was under way—and to reformed primaries, at that—those states which retained a convention system began to move in the same philosophical direction. That is, they too became much more likely to offer a variant of their system which was dependent on party voters rather than party officials. The result was an upheaval, almost a revolution, in the basic institutional forms for delegate selection.

Presidential primaries had been divided since their inception between those which permitted the election of delegates only, without regard to their presidential preference, and those which permitted a choice among presidential contenders, quite apart from the identities of the

Table 2.2. Primary and convention systems in the three grand eras of delegate selection

Era	Democratic party		Republican party	
	Average number of states using—		Average number of states using—	
	Primary states	Convention states	Primary states	Convention states
1832–1908	0	32	0	32
1912–1968	15	23	15	23
1972–1984	25	25	25	25
	Average percentage of delegates from—		Average percentage of delegates from—	
	Primary states	Convention states	Primary states	Convention states
1832–1908	0	100	0	100
1912–1968	40	60	43	57
1972–1984	70	30	68	32

Source: "Presidential Primaries," in Congressional Quarterly, *Presidential Elections since 1789,* 4th ed., pp. 7–70; "Key Convention Ballots," in Congressional Quarterly, *National Party Conventions 1831–1980,* pp. 139–196; and "Congressional Quarterly's 1984 Political Calendar" (Washington, D.C.: Congressional Quarterly Press, 1984).

individual delegates. The purest version of the delegate primary featured the names of the individual aspirants for delegates to the national party convention, perhaps with a home address, perhaps with no information at all. The purest form of the candidate primary featured the names of presidential aspirants only, without any information on the slate of delegates pledged to support a given candidate. But there were numerous intermediate versions, including, most particularly, variants which were superficially of one type but effectively of the other. Thus there were primaries in which the voter could both select the individual delegates and express a presidential preference, on the so-called beauty contest line—but in which the two choices could not be effectively connected. Just as there were primaries in which the voter did not get to note a separate presidential preference but in which the names of every aspirant for delegate status had either a presidential preference or "uncommitted" behind them, so that the voter could let presidential preference guide delegate choice.

In any case, the truth about many of the primaries which existed before reform was that they were (for practical purposes) delegate primaries. By the same token, true candidate primaries were far less common than the mere presence or absence of a presidential primary might suggest. As a result, a second but almost equally consequential effect of the shift from state party conventions to state presidential primaries was that these primaries were immediately, increasingly, and then overwhelmingly candidate rather than delegate primaries. (See Table 2.3.) The shift within the Republican party was again a trifle slower, since only Democratic reforms explicitly required candidate primaries in primary states. But in short order, Republicans had equaled the Democratic share of delegates chosen in candidate

Table 2.3.   The share of delegates selected in true candidate primaries

| Year | Democratic party | | Republican party | |
------	% of delegates	No. of states	% of delegates	No. of states
1984	63	23	54	24
1980	76	30	65	31
1976	66	26	60	27
1972	46	16	37	16
1968	23	10	20	8

Source: "Presidential Primaries," in Congressional Quarterly, *Presidential Elections since 1789*, pp. 7–70.

primaries. As a result, again in short order, both conventions were predominantly controlled by delegates from candidate primary states. When further adjustments brought a small move back from such primaries in 1984, the change was already so widely and effectively established that this permutation was just as effectively inconsequential.

A similar, reinforcing change occurred in those states which determined to retain the state party convention. Historically, there were two basic versions of the convention system, paralleling the two basic versions of the primary election. In the historically dominant option, the true party caucus, party officeholders had to activate the opening, grass-roots stage of the delegate selection process. In the other alternative, the participatory convention, party identifiers of any sort were entitled to activate this first and crucial stage. In the years before reform, when most states had used the convention system, the party caucus variant had been additionally dominant. In the years after reform, the crucial fact was still that the convention system as a category had become less consequential than the presidential primary. There were fewer state conventions in total; the larger states, with the larger share of delegates, were especially likely to turn to primaries.

Yet those states which remained with the convention system were henceforth more likely to offer the participatory convention as opposed to the party caucus. On the Democratic side, this tendency resulted from a national regulation: states which used a convention system were required to make it the participatory convention. As a result, states which had once used the party caucus were more likely to change away and adopt the presidential primary; states which changed back from the primary to a convention system were required to make their new plan a participatory convention. On the Republican side, a lesser version of the same trend was apparent. The Republicans did not have a rule forbidding the party caucus. But they began with a larger share of participatory conventions; they turned even more heavily to presidential primaries in their party-caucus states; and the public favor toward the participatory convention encouraged an increasing share of those states which retained a convention system to make it participatory.[7]

Presidential Nominations in the Postreform Era

The result was a strikingly different institutional environment for the politics of presidential selection. A whole new procedural era, that of the dominant primary system, was clearly in existence. A new politics of presidential selection, both outside the convention and within, was an obvious practical possibility. Moreover, while the move to this new era was neither cause nor effect of the shift in the presidential nomination itself, it did raise again the question of the locus and fate of the nomination.

This was true because the summary tabulations which confirmed the arrival of a new era, impressive enough in their own right, strongly understated even the narrow institutional impact of reform. It was true as well because these composite institutional arrangements, once summary tabulations had been adjusted to reflect practical reality, were central to producing a new politics of presidential selection. The historic and still allegedly central activity of the convention, the construction of a nominating majority, had departed well in advance of this reform activity and without any possible influence from it. Nevertheless, whether that nomination remained in the delegate selection process, moved even further back in that process, or actually began to return to the convention was obviously dependent on the character of presidential politics under these new institutional arrangements. So too was the character of the delegates who resulted, in their social background and political orientation. So was the fate of any and all activities which might replace the nomination at the center of the convention if it should not return.

For a period of weeks during the nominating contest within the Democratic party in 1972, there was—or rather, there appeared to be—a quite real possibility that the nominating convention had been restored inadvertently via party reform. The consensual front-runner, Senator Edmund Muskie, was eliminated early. Three factional leaders with apparently solid support, Senator George McGovern, Senator Hubert Humphrey, and Governor George Wallace, then emerged in the middle stages of the primary campaign. But as McGovern began to gather momentum and pull out of the pack, and when he then captured the crucial, final, giant primary in California—and despite a series of test votes within the convention itself—the type of outcome which had characterized nominating politics since the last actual nominating convention (all the way back in 1952) was manifestly in existence once again.[8]

In 1972 then, as in all the presidential contests since 1956, a nominating majority was constructed within the process of delegate selection. In all the presidential years to follow, at least in the Democratic and Republican contests of 1976, 1980, and 1984, the same grand pattern would surface again. Moreover, the factors behind this reassertion were the same as those which had originally combined to create the pattern: that is, every factor which had led to the nationalization of presidential politics in the era before extended reform worked more strongly, more effectively, and in the same direction in the postreform process of delegate selection. (See Figure 1.1.) The nationalization of politics was still obviously integral to the construction of a nominating majority. That had not changed. But when every component ran even more strongly in the same direction in the postreform era, this nationalization was, just as obviously, massively confirmed.

Even then, the continued absence of the nomination from the national party convention—and indeed, its withdrawal further back into the process of delegate selection—was all the more remarkable because there was a new and sharply different set of key actors who had to respond to these augmented forces, by deciding earlier (and consensually) on a presidential nominee. The incumbent party officials who had dominated unreformed presidential primaries and convention systems were largely gone, replaced by those rank-and-file party identifiers who actually turned out to participate in reformed primaries and conventions. Yet even this switch in the identity of the key actors, making the key calculations in the politics of presidential selection, only extended the impact of forces from the nationalization of presidential politics. Even in the Democratic contest of 1972, the one most promising of an alternative outcome, these individuals did reach a preconvention decision. In every contest thereafter, at least through 1984, a similar consensus—often earlier, always in advance of the convention—managed to assert itself as well.

The Nationalization of Politics after Reform

Comfortably before the imposition of sweeping party reform, the nationalization of presidential politics had removed the construction of nominating majorities from the national party convention. Accordingly, if extensive party reform had actually reversed or even reduced the nationalization, this reform (and its subsequent reactions) might have consigned the years of the informal disappearance of the nomination, from 1956 through 1968, to the category of an aberration in the longer evolution of the national party convention. This was, of course, hardly the intent of reformers—or of their opponents for that matter. Yet the matrix of institutions for delegate selection which resulted from their interaction was also hardly the intent of either group. In fact, however, the individual components of the nationalization of presidential politics not only worked in the same direction in the postreform era. They actually worked more forcefully than they had in the years leading up to reform.

The national media of information, for example, all acquired increased influence under the new arrangements.[9] Inevitably, the amount and precision of the information they could convey about developments across the nation expanded. Before reform, the outcome of delegate selection in many states was obscure even to national campaign staffs, and opaque to outside reporters. After reform, the outcome of a presidential primary, especially when it was a true candidate primary, was instantly knowable, instantly known, and instantly translated into delegates won and lost. The outcome of participatory conventions was not as reliably and automatically clear, but it was invariably clearer than the outcome of party caucuses, since aspirants for delegate status ordinarily revealed a presidential preference at the initial (open and public) gatherings to select delegates to the next level of the process.

Moreover, this truly national information was no longer counterpoised to an official party structure, and thus to the responsibilities and commitments of local party officials to each other or to a particular locale. Political parties were still in principle the major counterweight to the nationalization of presidential politics, because their organizational focus was still profoundly local. But they were already in serious organizational decline, and the new institutional arrangements for delegate selection reduced the positional advantage of their officeholders in that process. Party officials in the states had always fared better in party conventions than in presidential primaries. Yet primaries were replacing conventions in state after state. Party officials had sometimes managed to reintroduce themselves, even in primary elections, by using a delegate primary, where local connections might effectively elect the delegates. Yet it was candidate primaries, where the identity of the national contender was critical, which were even more rapidly driving out delegate primaries. Finally, party officials had fared best of all in party-caucus systems, where they themselves conducted—indeed constituted—the contest. Yet the convention systems which remained were more often participatory conventions, open not only to reliable party identifiers but to anyone who *claimed* to be an identifier.

Perhaps the largest change in impact for a component of the nationalization of presidential politics, however, was in the role and influence of the growing segment of white-collar independents in both political parties. The individuals comprising this group had been of increasing significance well before the coming of reform. They had augmented the decline of party organizations by being particularly resistant to participating through an official party structure. They had expanded the influence of mass media by being more likely to take their cues about politics from these media rather than from local intermediaries, especially political parties. They had then added a direct effect all their own by participating disproportionately in those facets of political activity, such as running campaigns or contributing money, which require comparatively specialized skills. As a result, they had become the reliable base for independent and insurgent challenges, and they had served—sometimes by their actions, other times just by their potential—to force an early consensus on a presidential nominee among party officials.

None of these developments changed after reform. Indeed, the character of the institutions for delegate selection which emerged from reform and from subsequent reactions augmented every link in this increasingly consequential chain. National media, the preferred source of information for these individuals, were able to make more information available. Political parties, the disdained channel of participation for them, were no longer organizationally central to delegate selection. The management of campaigns for collecting delegates or raising money, in an environment where each presidential contender increasingly needed an extensive personal organization for both purposes, became an increasingly fertile field for the labors of these partisan independents. The mounting of dissident nominating campaigns—a category in a distinction which itself was destined to weaken in the postreform period—was more open than ever to investment of their energies.

Even at the simplest level, however, as a statistical share of the newly consequential rank-and-file voters, this socially advantaged segment of society became instantly more important. Wealthier, better-educated, higher-status Americans had always been more likely to turn out in any political forum, and that tendency increased as the forum became more specialized.[10] Only the institutional matrix within which such participation could occur—and not the basic tendency itself—changed with the arrival of procedural reform. That fact meant that this putatively independent segment of both parties was much more important in presidential primaries, for example, than in the general election, and more important in participatory conventions than even in presidential primaries. Nevertheless, in this institutional chain, it was the primary electorate, in an era which could be effectively classified as the "dominant primary system," which was crucial. And on that electorate, the effect of reform was tremendous.

The Democratic party, as the party with sharper internal divisions on social lines—on education, occupation, and income, for example—produced a sharper revaluation and a stronger overrepresentation within its primary electorate for its socially advantaged participants. The most highly educated, for example, were disproportionately likely to appear, just as the least educated were disproportionately *un*likely to do so. (See Table 2.4.) But the nature of this relationship, between social characteristics and political participation was so fundamental to primary or convention turnout that the Republican party, although less divided on these same criteria, showed the same clear and sharp patterns of advantage and disadvantage, of over- and underrepresentation. (See Table 2.5.)

Table 2.4.   Participation in reformed presidential politics: The Democrats, 1976 (Overrepresentation = +, underrepresentation = −)

State	Less than high school education (%)	College degree or beyond (%)
California	− 145	+ 100
Florida	− 131	+ 283
Illinois	− 79	+ 117
Indiana	− 90	+ 64
Massachusetts	− 58	+ 100
Michigan	− 50	+ 111
New Hampshire	− 64	+ 150
New Jersey	− 242	+ 68
New York	− 107	+ 150
Ohio	− 113	− 15
Oregon	+ 5	+ 53
Pennsylvania	− 88	+ 47
Wisconsin	− 39	

Source: Developed from Tables 1 and 2 in Commission on Presidential Nomination and Party Structure, *Openness, Participation, and Party Building: Reforms for a Stronger Democratic Party* (Washington, D.C.: Democratic National Committee, 1978), pp. 11 and 12.

Table 2.5.   Participation in reformed presidential politics: The Republicans, 1980 (Overrepresentation = +, underrepresentation = −)

Level	Percentage
Less than high school education	−22
High school and some college	− 2
College degree and beyond	+30
Family income less than $17,000	−71
Family income more than $17,000	+15

Source: Developed from recalculations based on "Table 2.3: Demographic Characteristics of Primary Voters and Other Groups, 1980," in Scott Keeter and Cliff Zukin, *Uninformed Choice: The Failure of the New Presidential Nominating System* (New York: Praeger, 1983), pp. 46–47.

Moreover, this shift in influence within the primary electorate, consequential enough as an indication of the augmented impact of the nationalization of presidential politics, gained additional consequence in the era of extended national party reform. For the key actors who made the strategic calculations in the construction of nominating majorities in this era, replacing the party officeholders who had performed this activity previously, were not some random sample of rank-and-file party identifiers. Instead, of course, they were those party identifiers who, even if they asserted their partisan independence, actually turned out for primary elections. While the white-collar independents were not automatically the dominant subgroup within this population, they were always disproportionately present.

Strategic Calculations after Reform

The underlying cause of the departure of the nomination from the national party convention, well before the coming of reform, had been the nationalization of presidential politics. Yet the proximate cause of the departure had been a pattern of strategic calculations by key political actors, responding to the components of political nationalization and resulting in earlier and earlier nominating majorities. This too had to occur roughly as it did before the coming of reform if the locus of the nomination was not to change again. Before reform, the key actors were party officials; after reform, they were rank-and-file party identifiers. But the practical requirement remained the same: for the nationalization of politics to maintain the nomination outside the convention—indeed, given its increased strength in the postreform era, to drive that nomination further back into the process of delegate selection—these newly critical actors still had to respond to, or at least fail to resist concertedly, the forces of nationalization.

Before there was any practical experience with the reformed process of delegate selection and presidential nomination, there was reason to believe—or at least there were grounds to argue—that very real differences between party officials and party identifiers would produce exactly the opposite result. In this argument, party identifiers, without the strategic advantages for political calculation of regular party officials, would fragment among numerous presidential aspirants, thereby returning construction of a nominating majority to the one available central and subsequent forum, the institution of the national party convention. A more precise comparison between the two groups, however, might have suggested even before the fact that in this realm too, the impact of reform was to exaggerate rather than to reverse the previous trend.

After the fact in any case, after there was even one round of nominating politics under reformed institutions of delegate selection, the major differences between party officeholders and the general public made the emergence of an early nominating majority seem more rather than less likely in the era of party reform. Voters, far more than party officials before them, clearly aspired to make a national choice at their earliest opportunity. In short order, it became additionally clear that a general public which was less acquainted with the aspiring contenders and more dependent on the national media, as well as more ideologically flexible and less concerned with balancing internal party interests, could be expected to be less worried about resisting the nationalization of presidential politics than those party officials had been.

Initially, at the level of a simple awareness of the aspirants for a presidential nomination, of their political histories and group attachments, individuals who were less informed were going to be more responsive to early developments in the nominating campaign. At a minimum, party officials were likely to have known the contenders longer; many were likely to have a personal if still short-run stake in their campaign performance as well. By contrast, even that segment of the general public which turned out for a primary election was unlikely to have followed the careers of out-of-state politicians who had never possessed any direct relevance to their personal fortunes. Under those conditions, they were likely to become aware only of those who were able to fashion quick victories on the campaign trail. Indeed, there was probably a residual but strong tendency for unaware voters to go quickly with the apparent emerging winner, unless there was some clear and personally obvious reason not to do so. The fates of announced candidates for the Republican nomination of 1980, showing this dramatic rise for everyone who was able to win anything early along with the rapid demise of everyone who was not, were quite typical of candidate fortunes in the postreform era. (See Figure 2.1.)

Ideological sophistication surely reinforced simple awareness. An individual who was formally entitled to make these strategic calculations was effectively predisposed to move less quickly, and especially to resist shifting to a previously unknown and ideologically distant choice, if that individual had a well-developed set of policy preferences.

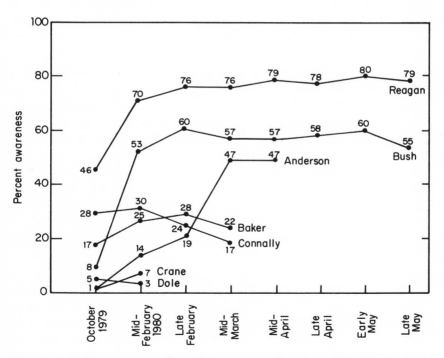

Figure 2.1. Public awareness of candidate names: New Jersey Republicans, late 1979 to 1980. (*Source:* Taken directly from "Figure 4.1, Percentage Able to Volunteer Candidates' Names, New Jersey, 1980," in Keeter and Zukin, *Uninformed Choice,* p. 67.)

One clear difference between party officials and individual citizens, then, was that the officials did hold continuing positions on more major issues, ordinarily holding those positions in a more continuing and consistent relationship as well. This was an obvious, if contingent, anchor in the movement of these officials—party officials were also sufficiently pragmatic to surrender such considerations after a point. They could begin with a preference for a candidate offering a certain set of policy options and group attachments, then transfer to the next most acceptable contender if their candidate did not win, and so on. A general public which was both less aware of these candidates at the start and less ideologically constrained once the campaign began was once again more likely to focus on the handful of contenders who could secure some early victory or even (perhaps especially) on the one emerging candidate who appeared, on the basis of these early results, most likely to be the eventual winner.[11]

The national media of information further accelerated this dynamic. They provided more information nationwide on the results of most state contests than there had ever been before. But this information was also concentrated on the early contests within the list. Temporal placement more than raw size was thus the best predictor of press attention. Moreover, even within early contests this information was concentrated on the candidates who managed to secure early and immediate victories. While this development reflected principally the role of early contests as crucial winnowing agents and as satisfiers of press—and public—curiosity (about the shape of a campaign which had offered no previous tests of reality), it also magnified the effective pressure on the general public to focus on a handful of successful contenders, or even on one emerging candidate.[12] Indeed, when these media were able to anoint an early and consensual front-runner, as they ordinarily were, the impact of early information was additionally magnified. That information, and this press consensus, could not as quickly influence those who possessed prior ideological moorings. But such information and analysis inevitably gained a quick influence on those who lacked the constraint of either knowledge or ideology.

That influence, in turn, was even further magnified by the absence among rank-and-file identifiers of any perceived need to balance constituencies and programs within the field of candidates for a nomination. Party officials, by virtue of their position and the responsibilities it normally entailed for electing a slate of candidates for various offices, had organizational incentives to consider the electoral needs of the extended party at the general election. Some were even sensitive to the coalitional needs of a sitting president in running a government. By comparison, rank-and-file identifiers were always less automatically aware of these needs and much less organizationally constrained to give them weight. Instead, these identifiers were importuned by all the candidates to choose the contender they most preferred. They were under no organized pressure—from other candidates, constituencies, or programs—to resist that importuning. And they could be sure that other primary voters or convention participants faced the same—narrowed—incentives.

The Bandwagon and Nominating Majorities

Perhaps the classic model of the reformed bandwagon, one which rolled inexorably despite the presence of all the elements presumed necessary to derail it, was presented by the Democratic contest of 1976.[13] That contest had a massive field of intendedly national candidates. Eleven had announced their intentions and entered the primaries before the campaign ended. It had three apparently major contenders from the very beginning. Representative Morris Udall, Senator Henry Jackson, and Governor George Wallace each had an apparently strong hold on evidently important factions in the party. The contest had major late entrants as well, additionally serious candidates who were prepared to derail any bandwagon which did roll early. Indeed, Governor Jerry Brown and Senator Frank Church were not only to enter but to win multiple late primaries. The contest even had an apparent—and waiting—compromise choice, should the politics of presidential selection follow older scenarios which this composite field in some ways suggested. Moreover, Hubert Humphrey did any number of things in the course of the campaign to keep this possibility alive.

Yet an obvious long-shot contender, without current public office and with minimal name recognition nationwide, burst out of the pack early and was never headed. Jimmy Carter scored an opening upset in Iowa, in a participatory convention which had been restructured to make the candidate implications of its outcome clear. He parlayed this, plus long-building preparation, into a second upset in New Hampshire, the first of the candidate primaries. And the combination of these initial back-to-back upsets and the intense, early, and national press coverage they generated, was enough to propel Carter through the remainder of the contest—at least by hindsight. There were numerous points in midcampaign when even supporters must have wondered whether this would really come about. Nevertheless, the Carter victory was ultimately so impressive that he was in full control of the Democratic convention when it assembled, had been endorsed by most of the other contenders, faced only token opposition on the ballot, and then saw his nomination rendered unanimous.

The initial boost which Carter received from Iowa and New Hampshire might have been subject to very different interpretations. He had, after all, not won in Iowa but only come in second over a crowded field, while managing to lose to the "uncommitted" preference. He had then won in New Hampshire with only 28 percent of the vote, over another divided field and in the absence of two of the three allegedly serious contenders. Yet these cavils only emphasized the strength of the momentum these early contests created. More emphasis was to come. After Carter had driven the missing candidates in New Hampshire (Jackson and Wallace) from the field, and after he had won nine of eleven candidate primaries by early May, he then *lost* nine of fifteen to late entrants Brown and Church. But even that performance, while it may have indicated something about the depth of attachment to Carter by the same general public which was creating his bandwagon, did not stop its roll.

Carter picked up large numbers of delegates in his wins; he acquired substantial second shares in his losses while his opponents were trading victories. As a result, the combination of an early popular momentum and a late delegate momentum was easily enough to give him a clear majority before the convention assembled. Accordingly, the story of this contest was of the relentless bandwagon for a contender who was not among the top *five* in public opinion polls, in the ratings, or in the opinions of professional analysts when the contest began. That bandwagon was not a simple straight line from the opening contests nor was it generally uniform in its national progress; Carter did best in the South, worst in the West. But it was relentless, and it did roll through the extensively reformed process.

The Republican contest of 1980 offered an equally compelling instance of an even more insistent bandwagon.[14] This contest too featured a large field of aspirants, where seven aspiringly national candidates along with a leading noncandidate who was the potential compromise choice offered every bit as wide a range of ideological positions and group affiliations as the Democratic field of 1976. Yet the Republican contest of 1980 featured one clear front-runner throughout the period leading up to the opening delegate selection, and he in fact managed to convert his assets into an early momentum and then into an overwhelming, even consensual, nomination. If the contest further distinguished itself, it was ironically with both more of an apparent inevitability during most of the nominating campaign than Jimmy Carter had ever possessed and with a point—though perhaps only one—at which an evolving drive threatened to come apart even more profoundly than Carter's more frequently halting campaign ever had.

The front-runner, of course, was Ronald Reagan, who led the active field of contenders in every poll before the opening contest and who was threatened in polls of public preference only by the leading non-contender, former President Gerald Ford. For one brief period, from the Iowa convention through the Illinois primary, it appeared as if actual outcomes might gainsay these polls and produce some real vulnerability. George Bush managed to upset Reagan in the first round of the participatory convention in Iowa. John Anderson came out of the pack in New England, doing far better than expected when he nearly defeated Bush in Massachusetts and Reagan in Vermont. But by Illinois, a scant three weeks after the opening New Hampshire primary—where Reagan had righted himself with the general public and professional analysts—Reagan's bandwagon was again firmly on track.

Bush did win a total of six primaries before he bowed out, citing increased difficulty in raising funds and an apparent inexorability to the Reagan delegate count. Reagan, however, won the twenty-nine others. If there was a moment after Iowa when his campaign looked vulnerable—and Bush did draw even in nationwide polling at that point—it only emphasized the force of the bandwagon which rolled subsequently. So too did a large field with other serious contenders such as Howard Baker, the Senate minority leader, and John Connally, the former governor of Texas; so did the emergence of a pair of other candidates, George Bush and John Anderson, who managed to attract press attention and support; so did the presence of that available compromise, Gerald Ford. All in the end became only further emphasis on the strength—and early victory—of the Reagan candidacy. By convention time the largest problem for the Reagan staff which in any way involved the construction of convention majorities centered on holding their *own* delegates behind the general election strategy of the candidate—and nominee.

Varied Dynamics and Parallel Outcomes

The essentially unilinear trajectories of these two campaigns, of the Carter nominating campaign of 1976 and of the Reagan nominating campaign of 1980, provide forceful instances of the bandwagon rolling toward a clear majority in advance of the convention. Their strength, direction, and resulting early resolution became their most dramatic features, despite an occasional faltering—an occasional blip on the relentless trajectory. Yet in many ways the other campaigns in the postreform period which did not have this simple and one-directional path, again in both the Democratic and Republican parties, provide even stronger testimony to the power of popular momentum under reformed procedural arrangements, precisely because they featured effective construction of a nominating majority before the convention in the *absence* of one long roll from the opening contests.

The Republican contest of 1976, the one transpiring while Jimmy Carter was rolling to the Democratic nomination, was perhaps the classic example of a campaign in which each major contender managed to sustain stretches of victory in the battles for delegates—yet the nomination could still be resolved before the convention assembled.[15] In 1976, the Republican party possessed that most precious of assets, a sitting president. Moreover, Gerald Ford was widely supported by the official party, whose leaders believed, as they would ordinarily have believed throughout American history, that deposing an incumbent would surely lead to defeat in November. Nevertheless, Ford was an unelected incumbent, appointed as vice president when Spiro Agnew resigned and elevated to the presidency when Richard Nixon followed suit. Moreover, Ford faced a reformed environment, in which the support of the official party was no longer a sufficient or even a dominant advantage. Finally, he had one major opponent, Ronald Reagan, who possessed substantial support among dissident party leaders and ideologically conservative independents.

Initially, this Republican nominating campaign gave little indication of deviating from the Democratic pattern. For the first month in fact, Ford won every primary—some narrowly, as with the opener in New Hampshire, others solidly, as with Massachusetts and Illinois. But Reagan managed to keep his campaign alive, though tenuously, with a victory in North Carolina in late March, and while Ford then secured solid wins in New York and Pennsylvania during April, those wins did not immediately translate into momentum because both contests were delegate primaries, whose results could not easily be interpreted by outsiders. Reagan then began a serious reversal with the Texas primary of early May, followed by the Georgia, Alabama, and Indiana primaries. The result, heading into the next contest in Michigan (Ford's home state) was that Reagan was both ahead in delegates and likely to acquire an irreversible momentum if he could manage a win. Ford, however, did take Michigan solidly, along with the uncontested Maryland primary on the same day, and those victories provided the opportunity for the delegates elected earlier in the New York and Pennsylvania primaries to come out publicly and overwhelmingly for the president. In turn, their declarations brought sufficient restoration and momentum for Ford to split the remainder of the contests with Reagan. That split, finally, was enough to secure his renomination, albeit by the narrowest of margins.

The campaign had managed to suggest the possibility of three "different" nominees—first Ford, then Reagan, and then Ford again. It had demonstrated that momentum achieved early would not necessarily continue late, and that no given bandwagon, even when fueled by as many as five or six consecutive primary wins, was enough to roll to a nomination. But if these twists and turns had confounded the experts, they had never produced a situation in which most analysts could not perceive a developing majority—and see how it would lead to nomination before the convention. In that sense, this contest confirmed that even when not just the preconditions but the actual course of nominating politics seemed as facilitative as they might practically be for forcing the construction of a nominating majority at the convention itself, the dynamics of postreform presidential politics could—and would—still prevent that eventuality.

The Democratic contest of 1984 provided a reprise on this theme.[16] As in many of the postreform contests, there was a large field of contenders, with seven or eight entered in most of the early states. But this time there was also one clear front-runner, and he had not only a lead in polls of public preference but a clear lead in campaign resources as well. Walter Mondale in fact won the opening round in Iowa quite comfortably. That contest, however, also offered a major boost to Senator Gary Hart, whose second-place showing was largely unexpected. Hart managed to build that showing into an upset in New Hampshire, the inaugural primary, and then into victories in Massachusetts, Rhode Island, and Florida two weeks later, along with respectable showings in Alabama and Georgia—states where, for all practical purposes, he had not possessed a campaign only two weeks before.

Hart's string of wins and better-than-expected losses put Mondale on the ropes. He righted himself in the Illinois primary and then extended his rally through New York and Pennsylvania, major states which featured large numbers of delegates and augmented their impact with allocation rules that delivered an extra share to Mondale. Mondale never managed to drive Hart (or the other main contestant, Jesse Jackson) from the field. He did not actually win a majority of the primaries along the way. But his April rally after the March debacles was sufficient to return momentum in the delegate column to the Mondale campaign. By the time the last primaries had been conducted, neutral observers knew that the contest was over.

The Mondale-Hart struggle resembled the Reagan-Ford conflict in featuring alternating stretches of wins and losses, with points at which one or the other contender was potentially able to roll to a nomination—or be eliminated. Mondale-Hart also resembled Reagan-Ford in creating a nominating majority, despite this apparent volatility, in the process of delegate selection. The Mondale-Hart contest, however, additionally underlined the role of "expectations" in all such contests, those judgments about how a candidate *ought* to perform which are largely formulated by reporters and commentators but which so powerfully color the strategic calculations of rank-and-file voters. Just as it was particularly pointed in emphasizing the advantages of organization, of active support by organized groups and of organized attention to procedural mechanics in the states and localities.

As the front-runner, Mondale was expected to win. When he won in Iowa, these expectations were not just fulfilled but increased. When he was then upset in New Hampshire, that defeat looked more impressive, so impressive in fact that it had an immediate spillover in the South, where the winner, Hart, was almost entirely lacking a campaign. Indeed, after this stretch of "surprising" Hart performances— four wins and three losses was really the record—the impact on expectations was such that Mondale was widely judged, even by his own campaign workers, to be on the ropes and to need a win in the Illinois primary if he were to stay in the race. The issue of expectations, framed by the press and used to such powerful effect by the general public, was rarely demonstrated with such clarity and force.[17]

Mondale did, in the event, win that Illinois primary, stay in the race, and secure the nomination. Moreover, if the issue of expectations demonstrated some of the inherent risks in being a front-runner, the dynamics of the contest after New Hampshire attested to the problems of a long shot who came out of the pack—and thus to the advantages which an inaugural front-runner still ordinarily retained. For although Hart did win the Florida primary, for example, in that period after New Hampshire when the Mondale campaign appeared to be unraveling, the Hart campaign had not been able—in the absence of momentum before New Hampshire—even to file a full slate of delegates in the Sunshine State. As a result, while Hart won Florida's presidential preference poll, Mondale took a majority of the delegates, a phenomenon which would dog the Hart campaign in states such as New York and Pennsylvania as well, where Hart's delegate totals were even smaller than they could have been, because his campaign had been so organizationally inconsequential when the overall contest began that he could not lay even the procedural groundwork for its improvement.

The Inevitability of a Bandwagon

The Republican contests of 1976 and 1980, along with the Democratic contest of 1976 and 1984—along with each of the missing contests in the postreform period, really—testified to the variety of patterns in nominating politics which could nevertheless produce nominating majorities before the convention assembled. Thus they suggested that the continued absence of the nomination from the national party convention, and its continued lodging in the process of delegate selection, should be accepted—and expected—as the normal course of events, rather than treated as problematic. Indeed, in the absence of even a single contest in which the nomination was constructed at the convention instead, despite the intermittent presence of most of the preconditions which seemed necessary to create that eventuality, there was good reason to believe that an actual nominating convention should be treated as a highly unlikely—a truly deviant—occurrence.

Moreover, the Republican contests of 1976 and 1980, along with the Democratic contests of 1976 and 1984, provided additional insights on why this was so. While the nationalization of presidential politics remained the underlying dynamic and while the strategic calculations of individual voters remained the proximate cause, additional, parallel developments in the nominating campaigns of this period connected and reinforced both sets of pressures. There was, for example, a bandwagon parallel to the accumulation of delegates in the accumulation (or dissipation) of crucial campaign resources, especially support by financial contributors or campaign activists. Financial contributors to nominating campaigns would probably have exhibited a crude bandwagon pattern whenever extended primary conflict occurred. Those able to provide contributions, after all, were not immune to the forces shaping the calculations of other political actors. They too wanted to contribute to an acceptable winner and avoid wasting support on an apparent loser.

Thus it was hardly surprising that when Gary Hart upset Walter Mondale in the New Hampshire primary of 1984 his campaign finances took a sudden turn for the better, just as Mondale's took a sudden turn for the worse. But the coming of extensive finance regulations, with limits on individual contributions and stiff restrictions on spending—a comprehensive reform which arrived hard on the heels of proliferating reform in the mechanics of delegate selection—surely exaggerated this dynamic. Given the narrow limits on individual contributions, a candidate who suffered early reversals could no longer turn to a few large contributors to try to overcome the effect of these poor showings. Indeed, a candidate who began with substantial early funds but inhospitable opening contests, given spending limits governing individual states, could not even concentrate his funding on some subsequent contest to make up for inevitable early reversals.[18]

Campaign activists, those individuals who undertook the organizational labors of a nominating campaign and were thus crucial to its continued existence, followed much the same pattern. They did possess sufficient awareness of the candidates, and sufficient ideological sophistication, to align themselves with a champion who could offer the best return on their personal investment and policy preferences. But they too were unlikely to continue pouring energy into campaigns which were obviously not gaining momentum. If the candidate failed to achieve some early victories, there was not just a rapid decay of support from the voters; there was a counterpart decline among campaign activists too. The most disappointed or narrowly focused simply quit the campaign. The less disappointed or more flexible shifted their energies to the next best alternative. In doing so, of course, they further exaggerated the underlying bandwagon dynamic.[19]

Rank-and-file voters, on the other hand, were still the fundamental building blocks in this dynamic. If they rallied to a candidate, his campaign prospered; if they fell away, it declined. That was their elemental contribution in an era when they, rather than party officials, made the ultimate strategic decisions. Yet although these voters did shift tremendously from one presidential year to another, or even among candidates within the same presidential year, there was one immediate change in their orientations toward nominating politics which still further reinforced the bandwagon dynamic. These voters proved much less likely than the party officials who had preceded them as key actors even to *want* to line up behind favorite sons. Historically, a favorite son was a candidate supported by his home state and perhaps one or two others. He could be a potential compromise choice; he could be nothing more than a device to assemble the state delegation for bargaining at the national convention.

In principle, individual voters might have found this arrangement every bit as attractive as state party leaders had. They could easily have preferred a local champion to a previously unknown national contender; they could even have preferred the explicit strategy of bargaining at the convention. In practice, they did not. Favorite sons were already, almost necessarily, in decline as the nomination moved outside the convention in the prereform years. Party officials, after all, needed to settle on a national contender to maintain their practical influence. But favorite sons were then effectively eliminated as state primary and convention voters reserved their support for truly national contenders, and thus for attempting to influence the true national contest. From 1976 on, not a single political leader was honored at a convention with a majority of the vote from his home state if he was not also an active candidate nationwide. Occasionally, a candidate still tried a modified version of the favorite-son approach, by concentrating his efforts on a home state which happened to have an early primary or caucus, in the hope that this would launch him in the national arena. Reuben Askew of Florida was an example, in the Democratic contest of 1984—as the demise of his campaign was an example of the fate of this approach.[20]

Variety and Inevitability

Yet even these additional elements of reformed contests for presidential nomination after 1968—a finance bandwagon, an activist bandwagon, and a disinclination by the general public to slow either development with the favorite son device—did not imply a reliable straight line from victory in the early contests to effective nomination somewhere along the way. As a result, the ability of the recurring momentum of reformed campaigns to overcome even these more varied and halting routes to a nominating majority became the final testament to the apparent inevitability—or at least the overwhelming likelihood—of an early nomination. Gerald Ford and Ronald Reagan had traded stretches of success during the Republican struggle of 1976, just as Walter Mondale and Gary Hart had during the Democratic contest of 1984. Accordingly, it was still possible for a variety of factors—from particular local preferences through the impact of increased press attention to the consolidation of opposition support—to derail or delay one bandwagon and to cause another to roll. Delegate selection, after all, still occurred in formally independent, sequential state contests. Ordinarily, the nationalization of presidential politics was sufficient to overcome any localized forces—localized issues, localized constituencies, or even locally popular candidates. But a front-runner could still come into a state which was particularly disadvantageous for him, as Mondale did in New Hampshire in 1984 or as Ford did in Texas in 1976, and see expectations of his roll toward victory suddenly and surprisingly violated.

This kind of surprise was more likely when the distribution of social backgrounds and political opinions in a state was different from their distribution in the nation as a whole. It was particularly likely when such a difference was reinforced by favorable trends in press attention, as when Hart zoomed into national focus after his surprisingly strong showing in Iowa in 1984, or by favorable changes in the nature of the opposition, as when that showing in Iowa made Hart the logical—the single logical—alternative to Mondale. In turn, such an outcome acquired its maximum impact when it coincided with, and was augmented by, peculiarities in the rules of the game, as when Reagan entered the Texas primary of 1976 with his campaign on the upswing, with crossover rules permitting the participation of conservative Democrats, with allocation rules which would magnify the impact of any crossovers on his delegate totals, and with the champion of those conservative Democrats, George Wallace, faltering fatally on the Democratic side.

All these contests, however, could not be allowed to obscure one other fact about even such varied patterns of campaign momentum: a candidate who managed to profit from a shift in momentum—and the earlier it came, the more likely he was to profit—might be able to capitalize on it and roll to a nomination, as Reagan did by righting himself in the New Hampshire primary of 1980 and snuffing out the Bush challenge. Or the candidate might not be able to profit sufficiently from that shift, either because particularly hostile states were next on the agenda or because increased press attention then made him less attractive to subsequent voters, as Hart discovered after his early upset showings. In that case, of course, the original front-runner was likely to reassert his momentum and go on to construct a nominating majority, as Mondale in fact did when the Hart boom proved insufficient.

Yet these permutations only reinforced the larger point, that no campaign in the postreform period had managed to produce numerous short stretches for numerous candidates, the pattern best able to undermine the bandwagon dynamic. Indeed, individually and collectively these campaigns appeared to argue that this pattern presented extreme practical difficulties. Moreover, the nationalization of presidential politics and the strategic calculations of individual voters suggested that no campaign *would* be able to demonstrate such a pattern. The parallel pattern of momentum in resources, especially in financial and activist support, along with the apparently permanent change in public orientations toward nominating campaigns, including a strong disinclination toward favorite sons, further reinforced this same suggestion.[21]

As a result, no nominating majority in the postreform period ever threatened to require so much as a second ballot. Indeed, no nominating majority could be said to have been constructed at the convention itself, even if it required only one ballot for confirmation. In the temporarily ambiguous contests, where it appeared that the momentum of one contender might have been stopped without generating decisive momentum for another, hindsight still provides an evident point from which the contest unfolded more or less inexorably and to which a nominating majority could subsequently be traced. (See Table 2.6.) If no contemporary could have confirmed that the grand contest was finished in 1976 when Jimmy Carter defeated Henry Jackson in Pennsylvania, or in 1980 when Ronald Reagan defeated John Anderson and George Bush in Illinois, or in 1984 when Walter Mondale defeated Gary Hart in Illinois, in each case hindsight suggests that this was so.

For doubters, there was even a specific statistic to unearth the point in every one of these campaigns when the nomination was objectively, mathematically determined. Moreover, even for campaigns which were continuously contested, such as the Republican nomination of 1976 or the Democratic nomination of 1984, this point often arrived as early as the beginning of May. (It arrived far earlier, of course, in those which were not seriously contested.) The statistic in question, a *gain-deficit ratio,* had been capable of predicting every nomination under simple majority rule since before the Civil War: it could be extended, with 100 percent accuracy, to every contest from 1972 through 1984.[22] But although its use in most earlier years was in finding the precise point in a sequence of convention ballots when the eventual nominee had effectively emerged, it never found that point in the postreform era at a date later than the last round of presidential primaries. (See Table 2.6.)

Ratification, Legitimation, and Insurance

The high drama of a nomination reached after intricate convention maneuvers, especially a nomination which violated expectations, was thus apparently banished in all but a few extreme though still specifiable cases. Obviously, this development did not eliminate conflict related to the nomination from the national party convention. The Republican nomination of 1976 was in fact confirmed by a very narrow margin. The Democratic nominations of 1972 and 1980 were heatedly contested well into the convention itself, despite the fact that they were not particularly close. The convention was never in any danger of acquiring the ability to make—to unmake and then remake—these nominations. Yet while the construction of a nominating majority had effectively receded from the convention hall, its formal ratification there was still obviously an activity sufficient to generate attention.

This meant that the actual ballot certifying the outcome of the process of delegate selection (and presidential nomination) still occurred at the national party convention—and had to occur if there was to

Table 2.6.   Turning points in postreform nominating contests

Contest	Practical turning point[a]	Statistical turning point[b]	Convention Date
1984 Democratic	March 20	May 8	July 16
Republican	February 27	March 20	August 20
1980 Democratic	March 18	May 6	August 11
Republican	May 3	May 6	July 14
1976 Democratic	April 27	June 8	July 12
Republican	May 18	May 25	August 16
1972 Democratic	June 6	June 6	July 10
Republican	March 7	May 9	August 21

a. That date, judged retrospectively, after which the front-runner was never again in serious practical danger of losing the nomination.

b. The "gain-deficit ratio" as defined in note 22.

be a recognized nominee. In this sense, the convention continued to recognize officially what was a more or less foregone practical conclusion. As a result, the convention continued to confirm for all the relevant actors—for candidates, activists, delegates, and the general public; for winners as well as losers—that a nomination had occurred and was officially settled. If practical determination of that nomination had departed, the legitimation of that nomination remained as a contribution of the national party convention to the larger political system in which the convention was embedded. Once that initial, lone, increasingly ceremonial, nominating ballot was completed, each of the two major parties had a presidential nominee—and the American people had the two individuals from whom they would choose the next president.

Beyond that, the convention continued to exist as a potential nominator of last resort, under a set of unlikely but not impossible circumstances. In each of these consensually unhappy scenarios, the convention could—and presumably would—end up *making* a presidential nomination. These were all scenarios in which the candidate on the way to an apparent first-ballot nomination was derailed before the ballot, by reason of personal health, physical accident or injury, or political disaster. There were in fact no disqualifications due to health in the postreform era through 1984, and the very arduousness of an extended national nominating campaign was an implicit warning to any aspirant with known health problems. But the oldest president in American history, Ronald Reagan, was inaugurated—and reinaugurated—during this period, and one allegedly serious possibility for a nomination, Hubert Humphrey in 1976, did die (of cancer) shortly after the general election of that year. The statistical likelihood that a fatal illness would strike an emerging presidential nominee during that narrow period between practical emergence and a nominating ballot was indeed very low, but it was surely not zero.

The possibility that accident or injury might cause the same result lent itself to similar unlikely but not impossible projections. Lesser illnesses and accidents—flus, infections, twisted muscles, even broken bones—although they might be insufficient to halt an emerging bandwagon, could hardly be absent when a group of individuals mounted nationwide campaigns for a period well over six months. Recent history is less comforting about deliberate injury. Assassination attempts on Robert Kennedy in 1968 and George Wallace in 1972 while campaigning, and on Gerald Ford in 1975 and Ronald Reagan in 1981 while governing, serve as telling reminders that the course of nominating politics can be altered at a stroke by malicious intervention. None of these incidents altered an ultimate nomination. Only the assassination of Kennedy altered actual convention behavior. Yet the possibility was clearly present, and the convention was clearly the forum which would have to make the nomination should that possibility come to pass.

More shadowy and hypothetical, although not beyond the bounds of imagination, was dramatic revelation, emerging in time to halt one bandwagon but too late to set another rolling. One of the charms of a reformed politics of presidential selection, for partisans of reform and for some democratic theorists, was that it permitted lesser-known candidates to compete, build momentum, and ultimately storm to the nomination. One of the risks accompanying that charm, a risk of unknown proportion, was that such a contender would prove to have debilitating secrets—past political associations or lapses of good health—or would commit strategic gaffes on such a major scale that a bandwagon could be stopped before ultimate confirmation. Recent history is again kind in its absence of precise examples. Yet other aspects of recent history, of *vice* presidential choices, for example—Thomas Eagleton in 1972, Spiro Agnew shortly thereafter—demonstrate that this prospect is surely not precluded. Once again, in such an instance, the convention would be called on to play its original role.

Nevertheless, what remained under postreform procedural arrangements was a national party convention effectively stripped of its central decision, the one which had justified its creation and contributed all those other activities and structures which grew up in and around it. The convention retained the authority to ratify—and thus, ordinarily, the ability to legitimize—the outcome of the contest for a presidential nomination. But that contest was effectively settled in the process of delegate selection. Moreover, extensive reform of that process, with the explosive growth of presidential primaries and the newly central role of the general public, strongly suggested—almost institutionally guaranteed—that settlement of the nomination would remain outside the convention. Nearly every other question which had first been opened by the informal departure of the nomination—whether the character of convention participants would change, whether a new central activity would emerge to energize the convention, whether the evolving institution would retain a hold on the general public—was forcibly reopened by extensive structural reform. But the question of the nomination itself was not.

3 | Changing Contours
of Delegate Selection:
The Decline of the Official Party

The major decision once assigned to the convention, the creation of a major-party nominee for president, had thus been moved out—into the individual states, into the preconvention period, and, especially, into the composite process of delegate selection. On its own terms, this move was never a collective or even a conscious decision by those with the formal authority to make it, the official delegates to the national party convention. Their individual calculations were not irrelevant to the shift. But those calculations were originally the product of a set of forces, in the nationalization of politics, having little to do with the identity or preferences of individual delegates. And those calculations became the product of a set of institutional procedures, courtesy of sweeping party reforms, which were never even addressed by the last of the prereform delegates—and which preceded the selection of all postreform counterparts.

The emptying of the convention of its original, formative decision, then, resulted from the interaction of a set of factors almost entirely external to the institution itself. The resulting change in the nature of activity at the convention, however, did not imply that the identity and character of the delegates who attended after the departure of the nomination were unimportant. These delegates remained integral to the operation of the convention as a political institution unto itself; they remained integral to the operation of the convention as a part of the larger political system. Much of what the convention had always done through its continuing internal structure remained consequential, as, for instance, with adopting procedural rules and drafting a party platform—which is to say, shaping an institutional framework, shaping substantive issues, and even shaping candidate fortunes for the future politics of presidential selection. Beyond that, the convention almost automatically acquired new activities, or at least sharply revalued ones, including most particularly the launching of the general election campaign. These activities became the focus of politicking inside the convention. They became the major contribution of the convention to the larger political system. They became the obvious link between developments at the convention and responses by the general voting public.

The practical character of national convention delegates—their social backgrounds, group attachments, ideological proclivities, and political styles—was likely to be a major influence, and often *the* major influence, on the way the convention handled its activities, old and new. That fact, in turn, made the selection of these delegates a matter of continuing consequence. Before reform and well into the period when the nomination had informally departed from the convention, delegate selection, in its institutional procedures and in its practical politics, was easily summarized: The selection of delegates to the national party convention occurred predominantly, indeed overwhelmingly, through the official party. In many states, the official party structure itself served as the practical mechanics for delegate selection. In many others, where formal mechanics did not lead as directly to the official party, party office (and hence connections among party officials) served as the informal explanation of the practical politics of selection. As a result, top party officials, along with the major public officeholders from the official party, were the most likely delegates to the national party convention. Indeed, in many years, however the politics of presidential selection might go, this was all that needed to be said about delegate selection.

The coming of extensive party reform changed all that. The nomination had departed from the convention well before the onset of sweeping structural reform, so that reform was responsible, at most, not for removing the nomination but only for locking it out. Yet it was precisely this reform which set off a chain of impacts on the selection of delegates to the national party convention. At a minimum, reform altered the fundamental, institutional mechanics of delegate selection. In fact, however, the matrix of institutions which resulted from reform (and from its multiple, partially independent reactions) had a consistent thrust which was far more than a simple disruption of previous arrangements and patterns. This matrix, comprised overwhelmingly of candidate primaries and participatory conventions, contributed to a radical reduction in the positional advantage of the official party (and hence party officials) in the politics of presidential selection. That alone was a substantial (and substantially changed) influence on the character of national convention delegates. But it was only the beginning of the changing influences to follow.

Reformed institutions of delegate selection in fact produced a new practical politics of presidential nomination, one requiring independent, national, and personal nominating campaigns for every presidential aspirant. The shift was immediate; general appreciation of that shift lagged by an election or two. Nevertheless, delegates could now be won by any candidate, in almost any state. Accordingly, campaigns to win those delegates had to be built by every candidate, in every state as well. One practical result, perhaps the central indirect impact, was that nominating campaigns could be mounted through the official party for very few, and often none, of these presidential aspirants. An associated result was that any extended national vehicle—party, quasi-party, nonparty, antiparty—would suffice for mounting a nominating campaign.

When the subsequent politics of presidential selection created additional incentives for party officials themselves to hesitate before plunging into nominating politics, like a heightened risk from moving too early and an increased danger to the local party if these party officials moved at all, this constriction of the official party was further augmented from below. When the new politics of presidential selection also created disincentives for national candidates to slate party officials as convention delegates, through the need for a personal rather than a partisan loyalty, the chain of impacts was again augmented, and completed, from above. When it was, the official party had been effectively eclipsed—constricted, encouraged to withdraw, and fragmented when it did not—and party officials had been substantially devalued. Extended state parties in the years after 1968 rarely pulled themselves together to participate in the politics of presidential selection. Participation even by local parties became the exception rather than the rule.

In consequence, party officials, while they did not uniformly pull back from that politics, acted increasingly as individuals rather than as units in some larger organization—and in ways which prevented even those who were successful from restoring much influence to the official party. The decline of the official party and the constriction of party officials were thus the major products of a shift from a politics of presidential selection based in and around the regular party structure to one based overwhelmingly on the independent nominating campaign. There were additional distinctions within this decline, in variations among institutional arrangements for delegate selection in the individual states and among attachments to the official party by individual aspirants for a presidential nomination. Yet the diminution of the official party was the central impact of reforms in delegate selection, as the diminution and fragmentation of party officials as delegates to the national convention was its most immediate product. In short order, both developments began to have a major effect on the convention as a context for internal politicking.

At the center of this effect was a very different set of political attitudes and ideological proclivities among those who attended the postreform convention—in point of fact, those who *constituted* the party in convention. To be more precise, the decline of the official party and the constriction of party officials were key elements in the move by the convention as a collectivity toward the ideological extremes. The received wisdom before extended structural reform was that the Democrats, as the uncontested majority party, were close to the ideological position of the general public, whereas the Republicans were well off from that center—to the right. This wisdom was shaken by the nominating campaigns of 1972, when surveys showed Republican delegates much closer to the general public, while the Democrats were solidly left of the center. But a new wisdom was created in 1976 when Republican delegates, in their first real experience with postreform politics, moved back off to the right—while Democratic delegates stayed well off to the left. That pattern was then confirmed and presumably institutionalized in 1980, when it surfaced in remarkably similar fashion. There were to be still further products from this official party decline, in the organizational base of subsequent nominating campaigns and in the organizational character of the delegates they generated, and these would further alter the convention as an environment for internal politicking. But the ideological reconstitution of that body was a central and immediate product, and the fate of the official party was the prior and more fundamental influence on that reconstitution.

The Move Away from the Official Party

There were numerous noteworthy features of the successive rounds of self-conscious reform in the Democratic party after 1968 and of less systematic change in both parties as Democratic and Republican leaders sought to cope with the changing matrix of institutions for delegate selection. Again, this institutional change resulted in part from the most geographically extensive, procedurally intensive, temporally continuous effort at deliberate reform since at least the early twentieth century, and really since the creation of the national party convention. Again, it was simultaneously the product and then the embodiment of the gradual nationalization of presidential politics, to the point where this institutional change effectively confirmed the informal departure of the nomination from the convention while it institutionalized that nomination, for all practical purposes, in the process of delegate selection.

Aggregate change of this magnitude in the institutions of delegate selection inevitably raised the question of its impact on the character of the individual delegates. They were, after all, the most direct and immediate product of those institutional arrangements. Moreover, a change in their political character was in fact an explicit goal of those who had pushed for extended party reform, as the maintenance of that character was a goal of those who had resisted, reacted, and tried to adjust. Indeed, a change of this magnitude in the institutions of delegate selection raised the question of their impact on the character of the delegates in an additional, more indirect, but potentially more powerful fashion. Because these delegates were also the central reward in the politics of presidential selection—because they were the "votes," a majority of which conferred a nomination—extended change in the mechanics of delegate selection raised the possibility of a larger change in the associated nominating politics. And if that change were realized, it too was likely to have a major impact on the identity of the delegates.

At a minimum, an institutional change of this scope required a shift in the manner by which individuals sought to become delegates. Likewise, it required a shift in the manner by which contenders for a nomination sought to accumulate these delegates. Further, however, an institutional change of this scope held the possibility that the entire operational nature of nominating politics would change. The way national campaigns were organized, the way they were linked to the localities, and even their product—in delegates, nominations, and ultimately presidents—were inherently at issue. But during the period between the Democratic convention of 1968 and the beginning of delegate selection in 1972, the possibility also remained that this extended institutional shift would have neither much effect on the practical politics of presidential selection (and hence no indirect impact on the delegates) nor much effect on individual delegate selection itself (and hence very little direct impact either).

For much of this period, as Richard Nixon was successfully consolidating his hold on the White House and on the Republican party, and as Edmund Muskie was emerging as the apparent consensual challenger on the Democratic side, events seemed to indicate that extensive formal change could coincide comfortably with practical continuity. Nixon had, by definition, been a product of the old arrangements. He seemed assured of being a product of the new arrangements as well. There was no need for him to change his leadership team, or even his convention delegates. Muskie too had been launched under the old regime, thanks to his participation as the vice presidential candidate on the Democratic ticket of 1968. Yet he was the obvious, odds-on favorite for nomination under the new regime as well, piling up an impressive array of endorsements from party officials and public officeholders while amassing equivalent testimonials to his strength from newsmagazines and journals of political opinion.[1] Accordingly, his delegates could be centrally slated to blend the essential elements of the old order with the alleged emerging elements of the new.

The rapid—indeed catastrophic—deflation of the Muskie boom, coupled with a surge to the nomination by George McGovern, demolished these possibilities on the Democratic side. The successful renomination of Nixon over only token challenges delayed a practical test in the Republican party. But four years later, the possibility of new institutions but the same old politics was demolished on the Republican side as well, when long shot Ronald Reagan came within a whisker of unseating President Gerald Ford, who was actively favored by the official party. The precise shape of these first contests under reformed rules of delegate (and presidential) selection was not necessarily the continuing shape of presidential politics. But these inaugural contests did establish certain general outlines for the reformed politics of delegate selection, and they did comment forcefully on the character of the resulting delegates—comments which were to be confirmed again and again during the succeeding nomination campaigns.

At a minimum, these campaigns confirmed that the apparent decline of positional advantage for party officials in the new matrix of institutions for delegate selection, along with the effective demise of party-based institutions in general, did inherently reduce the role of the official party in selecting individual delegates. But beyond that, these campaigns confirmed that this new matrix of institutions for delegate selection did indeed go hand in hand with a new politics of presidential nomination, featuring fully national, essentially independent, personal nominating campaigns—which could not in principle be generally staffed by party officials and in which party officials had certain additional inherent liabilities. Party officeholders faced a new political world, in which they suffered clear institutional disadvantages by comparison with the recent past, clear practical disadvantages should they try to maintain their previous influence by informal means, and evident additional incentives to pull back from the politics of presidential selection. The institutions of delegate selection, the practics of presidential nomination, and the social identities of the central actors—especially of the delegates—thus appeared to hang together in constituting postreform presidential politics.

Institutional Forms and Positional Advantages

The larger societal influences impelling change in this composite politics were, of course, those same factors which had contributed to the nationalization of presidential politics and which had, at one remove, facilitated the departure of the presidential nomination from the national party convention. But the more proximate and specific starting point for the change in all these elements (and especially in the social identity of the individual delegates) was massive reform in the institutional framework for delegate selection. At bottom, each institutional form for selecting delegates—each type of state convention and presidential primary—differed intrinsically in the degree to which it conferred a formal, positional advantage on party officeholders.[2] Moreover, these forms could be ranked along a practical continuum, from those most sympathetic to an official party, through those least sympathetic. The fate of the various institutions in this ranking, finally, was to confirm statistically and forcefully that reform and its reactions had thrown positional advantages for the official party into formal and precipitous decline.

At one end of this continuum of positional advantage was the *committee selection,* whereby the state central committee of the party, or sometimes an even smaller directorate, simply named the delegates to the national convention. High party position was the beginning and end of the ability to select delegates; high party officials and incumbent public officeholders (and aspirants) were the logical choices in such a selection. Party office was everything; delegates were disproportionately likely to be party or public officials. This device was never particularly widespread, but it was a real alternative, always used in a number of states, and it did demonstrate party-based mechanics—and positional advantage for the official party—at their most stereotypical and extreme.

The most widely used of the institutional forms which conferred a powerful advantage on officials of the regular party, however—indeed, the most widely used device for delegate selection in all American history—was the *party caucus.* In a party caucus, party officials at the lowest level (most commonly the precinct committee, often the county committee instead) gathered to select delegates to some higher convention, which either selected the delegates to the national convention or selected delegates to a statewide convention which then chose the national convention delegates. The process, in any case, was in the hands of party officeholders from top to bottom, and party officials, supplemented by the elected public officials and aspirants of the party, were its most likely beneficiaries.

In the middle of the continuum of positional advantage was the *delegate primary,* where individual contenders for delegate status were elected (or not) under their own names only. They might campaign in any fashion they preferred. But their names, plus perhaps an address, were the only identifying labels on the primary ballot. This did mean that anyone who turned out for the primary was entitled to select among these delegate contestants, a clear change from committee or caucus selection. But because the presidential contenders were not involved by name, turnout was often low, as was the level of public information. In return, the possession of party or public office was often sufficient to secure election in what were inevitably confusing contests where local name recognition or political connection were usually the key to ultimate selection.

The *participatory convention* remixed this pattern of assets and liabilities—no formal entitlements but some informal advantages—in a fashion much less salutary for party officeholders. Although the participatory convention was formally structured like the party caucus, with a nested set of meetings culminating in the selection of delegates, the crucial difference was that anyone who wished to take part at the initial stage was entitled, officially and practically, to do so. Party officials held no special status among these initial participants, and there were inevitably more—often far more—nonofficeholders than officeholders in attendance. Party officials might still know more about politicking at such a gathering, but the average nonofficial participant, in turn, might well resent these officeholders as privileged "insiders," so that the significance of their advantage depended crucially on the nature and size of the turnout by others.

The *candidate primary* stood at the far opposite end of the continuum. In a candidate primary, the names of the presidential contenders were paramount. Sometimes the names of the delegate contenders were cited along with their presidential preference; other times only the names of the candidates appeared. "Positional advantage," to the extent that the term had meaning, was formally lodged in the presidential campaign, not in the local party. Candidates might still choose party officials to be the core of their delegate slates, though most campaigns could not even in principle hope to do so. Yet candidates might well—and wisely—prefer delegates who were devoted to their individual candidacy rather than to the local party, with its accompanying slate of state and local candidates and its inevitable concern with the desires of a particular local area.

The Decline of Advantage for Party Officials

The range of positional advantage for party officials was immense: from committee selections where formal entitlements made nothing else necessary, to candidate primaries where the absence of formal entitlements was compounded by the devaluation of informal assets. Moreover, the substance of party reform, the reactions of state parties as they confronted a reformed system, and the drift of institutional change which resulted all played across these institutions in a clear and consistent pattern. In effect, all worked toward the constriction of those institutions which offered the greatest positional advantage to the official party while they worked toward the extension, even the sanctification, of those going furthest to remove that advantage.[3] It was in fact this shift which accelerated the related change in the operational nature of nominating campaigns and especially in the social identity of the delegates which these institutions and campaigns produced.

The speed with which this shift came and the speed with which it ramified through these other areas was truly remarkable. The Democratic party had traditionally made more use of committee selection than had the Republican party, and the share of delegates chosen by committee was actually rising among Democrats as the prereform period drew to a close. At that point, however, national Democratic rules effectively banned the arrangement, and within two elections it had disappeared. (See Table 3.1, col. 1.) The Republican party launched no similar national assault on the device, but the party had never made much use of committee selection, so that its continued employment was truly of minimal consequence.[4] (See Table 3.2, col. 1.)

The reform pronouncements of the national Democratic party were also a direct attack on the party caucus. Remarkably, despite its role as the predominant means of delegate selection across all of American history, this device too was eliminated by the Democrats within two presidential elections. (See Table 3.1, col. 2.) The Republican party manifested no official hostility to the party caucus and in fact main-

Table 3.1.   The changing matrix of institutions for delegate selection: The Democrats

Year	Committee selections (%)	Party caucuses (%)	Delegate primaries (%)	Participatory conventions (%)	Candidate primaries (%)
	(1)	(2)	(3)	(4)	(5)
1984	0	0	0	37	63
1980	0	0	0	24	76
1976	0	0	9	24	66
1972	2	2	14	36	46
1968	13	24	19	21	23
.....	.....	.....	.....	.....	.....
1952	8	27	26	19	19
.....	.....	.....	.....	.....	.....
1936	8	31	31	15	14

Source: See note 4.

tained an explicit policy of leaving the choice of all such arrangements to party members in the states. Nevertheless, the party as a whole was to shift decisively away from the party caucus, in fact within the same two elections. At first, from 1968 through 1976, this was because the demand for public participation in party-caucus states was frequently met with a shift toward the candidate primary *or* the participatory convention. When some of these states abandoned the primary, the drift was maintained because the participatory convention (and not the party caucus) uniformly acquired the switchers. (See Table 3.2, col. 2.)

For much of the twentieth century, state Democratic parties had preferred the delegate primary over the candidate primary. National reformers, however, disliked the device intensely. Once more, within a few elections of the surfacing of a self-conscious reform movement, this venerable institution of delegate selection had disappeared. (See Table 3.1, col. 3.) Through 1968, Republican utilization of the delegate primary had almost precisely paralleled that of the Democrats, since state law generally created two primaries at once. But if there was no counterpart in the Republican party to the national Democratic attack on the device, it was also true that pressure for a direct role in the choice among presidential contenders by the Republican rank and file, coupled with a desire for more attention from these contenders by state party leaders, produced a clear move away from the delegate

Table 3.2.   The changing matrix of institutions for delegate selection: The Republicans

Year	Committee selections (%)	Party caucuses (%)	Delegate primaries (%)	Participatory conventions (%)	Candidate primaries (%)
	(1)	(2)	(3)	(4)	(5)
1984	4	1	8	32	54
1980	2	1	10	22	65
1976	1	4	11	24	60
1972	3	16	20	24	37
1968	5	24	23	28	20
.....	.....	.....	.....	.....	.....
1952	4	26	25	25	19
.....	.....	.....	.....	.....	.....
1936	4	31	32	20	14

Source: See note 4.

primary in the postreform era. This time, however, the absence of a strong national directive did mean that a few states, including New York and Pennsylvania with their major delegations, deliberately refrained from abandoning the device. (See Table 3.2, col. 3.)

The Democratic party had made gradually increasing use of the participatory convention throughout the twentieth century. After 1972, when committee selection, the party caucus, and the delegate primary were banned, its use jumped sharply. There was a subsequent decline, almost to prereform levels, as state after state moved all the way to the candidate primary. But when some of these states backed away from the candidate primary after 1980, the participatory convention was necessarily the complete beneficiary, bringing this arrangement to a new peak of utilization for 1984. (See Table 3.1, col. 4.) Historically, the Republican party had made *more* use of the participatory convention, and its utilization on the Republican side remained roughly stable in the postreform era. It actually dropped a bit when many state Republican parties rushed to the candidate primary. But it recovered when some of these moved back to the participatory convention for 1984. (See Table 3.2, col. 4.)

The single largest beneficiary of all these moves, of course, was the candidate primary. The device had grown gradually in the Democratic party during the twentieth century, though not to the point where it created even a quarter of the national convention delegates by 1968 and not to the point where it was even the plurality leader as the prereform era drew to a close. But it exploded with the coming of reform, to become the predominant device for delegate selection by 1972 and then the overwhelmingly predominant device—with more than a statistical majority of delegates—by 1976. (See Table 3.1, col. 5.) The Republican party experienced its explosion of candidate primaries one election later, for 1976. Yet the direction was the same, and the result was a statistical majority of Republican delegates too, chosen through the candidate primary for 1976 and thereafter. (See Table 3.2, col. 5.)

The Demise of Arrangements Based in the Official Party

The fate of positional advantage for the official party in the politics of presidential selection was thus inevitably tied to the fate of these individual institutions for the selection of delegates to the national party convention. Yet the fate of these individual institutions, dramatic as it was, still understated the composite impact of reform and reaction on positional advantage for the official party, and on the formal influence and guaranteed role of party officials. For the *mix* of these institutions automatically became the framework within which the politics of presidential nomination occurred. Moreover, that mix became increasingly important not just because it represented the sum of these varying impacts but because these institutions themselves divided into two sharply different approaches to a formal framework, with sharply different practical implications—and because one side of that divide was decisively, indeed monumentally triumphant in the postreform era.

On one side were those arrangements integrated into the official party, committee selection and the party caucus, which were formally and mechanically party-based. The delegate primary, though not as formally integral, was practically tied to public office as well and was thus effectively part of this cluster. On the other side were those arrangements independent of the official party, the participatory convention and the candidate primary, which were formally and mechanically candidate-based and which operated, in both intent and effect, outside the official party structure. Obviously, those devices kindest to party officials were in evident, even precipitous, decline, just as those which featured no formal advantage to party officials were dramatically on the rise. Moreover, it was not just the utilization of individual institutions which was changing. It was the utilization of each cluster, as a cluster, which was moving toward the liquidation of the party-based devices and the apotheosis of the candidate-based alternatives.

The situation within the Democratic party was the more striking. In part, this was because the party possessed a centralized national movement for reform, with an evident hostility to party-based arrangements. But it was also because the Democrats had shown a greater reliance on party-based devices in the preceding period. In other words, institutional change went further in the Democratic party both because it was more explicitly pushed and because it had further to go. Even then, the change between 1968 and 1972 alone was actually greater than the change from 1912, the year of the first candidate primaries, all the way up to 1968. After that break, the change was not only grand and dramatic but profound and total. (See Table 3.3.) In 1968, 57 percent of all Democratic delegates were chosen through devices which were essentially party-based; by 1980, none were. For

1984, the national party leadership was to become so distressed by this situation that it would add some party officials to state delegations ex officio, to restore a minimal party presence. But the situation among delegates chosen in the states was still destined not to change at all.

The Republicans, lacking a centralized reform drive from above and having less far to go in the states, moved more gradually at first and more tentatively overall. For them, the largest single break came four years later, between 1972 and 1976. At that point, fallout from the Democratic drive produced a shift toward candidate primaries in *both* parties, via state law. At the same time, a hotly contested struggle for the nomination encouraged Republican convention states to move explicitly to the participatory convention while in other states, it activated dormant participatory arrangements which had functioned like a party caucus in the absence of a nationally organized nominating contest. (See Table 3.4.) Even then, the fact that movement was more gradual in any given year, and not as far-reaching in its totality, could not obscure another central fact about the progress of reform in the Republican party. In 1968, the party still awarded a majority of its delegates through party-based institutions. By 1976, it awarded 85 percent through candidate-based devices.

Almost at a jolt, then, the Democratic party had gone from a process of delegate selection dominated solidly by the official party to one which was overwhelmingly conducted outside the bounds of the regular party structure. The Republican party had made the same change

Table 3.3. The shift from a party-based to a candidate-based process of delegate selection: The Democrats

Year	Party-based (%)	Candidate-based (%)
1984	0[a]	100
1980	0	100
1976	9	91
1972	18	82
1968	57	43
.....	.....	.....
1952	62	38
.....	.....	.....
1936	70	30

Source: Developed from the same figures as those that contributed to Table 3.1. Slight differences in aggregate percentages are due to rounding.

a. Includes only those delegates—the overwhelming majority—chosen as a direct result of state contests. For discussion of the others, see Chapter 4.

more gradually and without the conscious fanfare, but the direction of that change was absolutely the same, and its degree was still so substantial as to make its gradual character (and the presence of some major holdouts) comparatively inconsequential.

This fundamental change promised to have a direct and immediate effect on the identity of delegates to the national convention in both political parties, shifting them from party officials to candidate loyalists. But it strongly suggested the incipient rise of an independent politics of presidential nomination as well. And that rise seemed additionally likely to produce change in the identity of those delegates, in the same—augmented—fashion.

An Independent Politics of Presidential Selection

Such change was not long in coming. Indeed, at the first practical opportunity—immediately for the Democrats in 1972, one round later for the Republicans in 1976—an independent politics of presidential selection sprang up to accompany candidate-based institutions of delegate selection. At its core were campaigns for the presidential nomination which were themselves increasingly based on extended personal organizations. Indeed it was this shift which was to produce a striking change of character in the delegates to the national convention. And it was that change in political character which was to shape the approach of a reformed national convention to those items of political business which continued to come before it.

In fact, what reformed institutions of delegate selection really ac-

Table 3.4. The shift from a party-based to a candidate-based process of delegate selection: The Republicans

Year	Party-based (%)	Candidate-based (%)
1984	13	87
1980	14	86
1976	15	85
1972	39	61
1968	52	48
.....	.....	.....
1952	56	44
.....	.....	.....
1936	66	34

Source: Developed from the same figures as those that contributed to Table 3.2. Slight differences in aggregate percentages are due to rounding.

complished was to change the process of presidential nomination from one based heavily on the official party to one based essentially on the individual candidate campaign. Without this change it might still have been possible to have an old politics in new institutional garb, to have party-based campaigns in candidate-based institutions. Yet this change in the nature of nominating campaigns did follow, and because it did, this new politics of presidential selection was the more consequential influence on the identity of national convention delegates in the post-reform era.

Part of the drift toward independent (candidate-based) rather than integral (party-based) campaigns for presidential nomination was inherent and automatic in what the changed matrix of institutions for delegate selection did to the positional advantage of the official party. Yet party officials did not simultaneously lose the informal assets based on the holding of party office, such as local political expertise and practical campaign experience, so that their eventual—indeed, almost immediate—restriction in or withdrawal from the politics of presidential selection has to be traced to additional factors. More precisely, whenever party officials lost their formal centrality in delegate selection, and whenever they could not substitute informal advantages for this loss, one or more of three basic problems prevented this informal restoration. Either the practical organization of reformed nominating campaigns began to proceed in such a way that party officials could not readily dominate them. Or party officials began to face new (or at least augmented) *dis*incentives for trying to use their very real informal advantages to restore their previous centrality. Or presidential candidates began to see a much different balance of assets and liabilities in these party officials, so that candidates did not turn to them as readily.

As it turned out, each of these conditions characterized the reformed politics of presidential selection generally. The organization of independently constructed campaigns for a presidential nomination did not provide the central place for most party officials which party-based campaigns had. Furthermore, presidential candidates came to look on party officials as much more of a mixed blessing, needing them when they were least available and preferring personal rather than party loyalty when party officials were ultimately prepared to pitch in. Moreover, party officials themselves faced augmented disincentives, in the form of risks to their more local and more important party responsibilities, which discouraged them from trying to overcome these other practical problems. The lessons of immediate postreform history, finally, were available to hammer this situation home, should individual party officials fail to grasp its composite implications.

As a result, at the far end of a chain of impacts from a fundamental change in the matrix of institutions for delegate selection was a change in the identity of national convention delegates, from individuals whose major asset was that they held party or public office to individuals whose major asset was that they had contributed to the preconvention campaign of a specific contender for the presidential nomination. All the other changes in the political character of national convention delegates which were to follow—in social backgrounds, group attachments, ideological proclivities, and political styles—followed eventually and ineluctably from this fundamental shift in the process *and politics* of presidential nomination. The basic element behind them all was the withdrawal of the official party and the devaluation of party officials in nominating politics.

Nominating Campaigns, Integral and Independent

Organizational effects on the nominating campaigns waged under re-formed institutions of delegate selection arose almost immediately. For example, as soon as the process of presidential nomination shifted to candidate-based mechanics for delegate selection, it became necessary for each candidate to develop a fully articulated, independent, and personal campaign in most states—and in all those which possessed candidate-based mechanics. As use of the party-based institutions of delegate selection dropped sharply, and as they were replaced by participatory conventions and candidate primaries, it became possible for any candidate to win delegates through an independent effort in these reformed states. And as it became *possible* for *any* candidate to win delegates there, by mounting an independent and personal campaign, it became *necessary* for *every* candidate to do so or forfeit automatically the chance of obtaining delegates.

Before reform, many aspirants for a presidential nomination did try to have some sort of personal organization in a number of states, as a base for contesting a few candidate primaries and participatory conventions and for cajoling the party officials who would be picking the delegates, through party caucuses, committee selections, and delegate primaries. Other aspirants, however, did not even bother to create such organizations; they relied instead on their contacts among party officials around the country and on lobbying the party-related delegates after they had been selected. The central point, in any case, was that a truly independent preconvention campaign could make a direct contribution to a presidential nomination in only a minority of states and could make little direct contribution at all if the bulk of the official party was actively opposed to the presidential aspirant.

After reform, the situation was immediately different—radically so for the Democrats, gradually but effectively so for the Republicans.[5] From one side, a fully articulated, national campaign was now guaranteed to have a practical chance of producing delegates. From the other side, any presidential candidate who did not mount such a campaign knew that the delegates which that candidate failed to secure would probably be secured by some other contender, rather than remaining available for subsequent personal lobbying. In principle, the official party could still provide a local campaign and a slate of delegates to help any national contender, and in that sense, support from the party was still a valuable commodity. But the more important point in the reformed environment was that any mechanism which could offer a framework for a local campaign and develop a local delegate slate, whether based in the official party or utterly unconnected to it, could be important to the national presidential contender.

Even this analysis understates the extent of change in the organizational environment for nominating campaigns. For as the selection of delegates moved outside the official party structure, and as the level and content of turnout among the party rank and file became the crucial element in allocating delegates, factors outside the control of any local actors—party-based or not—acquired a greater and greater chance of determining both the character of this turnout and the fate of presidential contenders. The outcome in some preceding state, a dramatic development in a national campaign, or the demographic characteristics of the electorate for the current state contest were all capable of overwhelming a given local effort. They did not remove the need to have such an effort: it was necessary to garner the delegates to whom a candidate was otherwise entitled; it might still be the crucial factor in any particular contest. Yet these other factors did additionally reduce the value of having a campaign based on the official party, as opposed to some (any) other vehicle.

Fully articulated, independent, national campaigns, then, became the norm, and no candidate after reform even threatened to secure a nomination without one.[6] In 1968, Hubert Humphrey still mounted the archetypal prereform campaign by announcing his candidacy after the entry date for most primaries and by assembling his nominating majority through long-standing ties to party leaders around the country. On the Republican side, Richard Nixon followed suit and managed to extend the pattern into 1972, thanks to his status as a sitting president who sought renomination without serious challenge. Neither Humphrey nor Nixon could have known that theirs were, quite literally, the last of the limited, party-based campaigns.

The Character of Reformed Nominating Politics

Sweeping reform in the institutions of delegate selection had removed party officials from their prior positional advantage in the politics of presidential nomination. The rise of independent nominating campaigns had guaranteed that their retention of other advantages based on the holding of party office could not substitute informally for the positional advantages which had disappeared. Yet party officials still retained some informal assets, such as local knowledge and experience, which almost automatically accrued to those with tenure inside the official party structure. Similarly, presidential aspirants retained good reason, at least in principle, for wanting to benefit from those assets. Nevertheless, what appeared to be a recipe for moderating the impact of all this change was undermined at once by the nature of the interactions between party officials and presidential candidates in this new political world.

In the opening instance of a new and recurring tension, national candidates needed local support at precisely the point when local party officials needed most to preserve their options. In fact, not only did reformed presidential campaigns need to be fully articulated, independent, and national but they also needed, or at least found it highly desirable, to attain this status early. By definition, the construction of a comprehensive national campaign benefited from as much lead time as possible. Beyond that, the fact that the earliest contests were likely to be pivotal—at least in winnowing the field, perhaps in shaping the ultimate outcome—meant that the earliest organizational efforts might well pay the most dividends. Finally, success in these early organizational efforts could be critical in shaping the subsequent behavior of other key actors, including other political activists and incipient financial contributors.

Presidential candidates, then, did want party officials, but they most wanted them early, well before the first contest. Party officials, from their side, were still willing to play some role, but they had clear organizational incentives to avoid an early endorsement and to watch the mists clear before investing their limited resources in a national nominating campaign.[7] Precisely because they were no longer guaranteed a formal place in the process, they needed to be sure that their preferred candidate was both a serious local and a national possibility; otherwise they would forfeit any chance at practical influence. Moreover, because others would also be soliciting their support, they needed to be sure that they could secure a guaranteed return if they were willing to give automatic offense to these others by committing themselves to one preferred alternative. As a result, many party officials retreated to the role of honest broker rather than candidate partisan in the early days of an evolving nomination campaign.

This dilemma—and the response to it—were exacerbated in many states by state party rules or actual state law. Slates of delegates, especially for a candidate primary, often had to be assembled well in advance of the primary itself. It was extremely difficult for a local party, and perhaps impossible for an extended state party, to pull itself together under these conditions and work for one candidate. In other words, slating had to be done at the point in the process when party officials most needed to preserve their candidate options.[8] Some officials were still willing to take their chances, but they were extremely unlikely to get the official party as an extended organization to ignore the evident problems and to move, as a body, with them. The obvious effect of a successful effort to move the extended party this early was to gamble on one contender and to leave the official party with little role in the campaigns of others. Yet if party officials moved only as individuals at this early date, they were unlikely to be the main force in any of the national nominating campaigns.

The Problem of Party Officials in Independent Campaigns

All these considerations assumed, even then, that each side of the campaign organization would focus primarily on the assets of the other when seeking to solidify campaign roles. But in fact, those on each side of the campaign divide had additional reasons for treating their relationship as problematic in the aftermath of reform, reasons which made party officials even more cautious in seeking a place in the campaign and which made presidential candidates less eager to slate these officials as delegates even when they did come forward.

The problem for party officials was simply but pointedly stated: the focus of party politics was primarily local, secondarily state; presidential politics had always been a sideshow, however fascinating. It was the local party unit which provided the operational base of American political parties; it was local public offices, along with a few state positions, which provided not just the numerically dominant targets but the slots which would determine practical success or failure. As a result, conflict over a presidential nomination was in many ways more a threat to local harmony than it was a promise of any practical gain. This too had always been true, but it was more pressing once reform had removed the positional advantages previously inherent in local party office. If local concerns were still more central to the practical responsibilities of party officials, and if it had just become more costly to worry about presidential politics, then there was that much less incentive to bother.[9]

What really caused the change in incentives, however, was the accompanying change in the practical politics of nomination. For once party officials were deprived of positional advantage, and once most candidates for a nomination were compelled to form independent campaigns, the costs involved in trying to place the extended party in the field early against a number of other serious, independent, and locally organized efforts increased substantially. Once fully articulated, national, and personal campaigns became essential, it was clear that every candidate would at least try to mount such a campaign. It was clear by extension that several of these candidates would possess campaigns in a given area, so that party officials who decided to join one or another of these efforts would acquire a new and automatic, local set of adversaries, who might well—especially if they were intense candidate enthusiasts—remember their previous opponents antagonistically, long after the nominating contest had ended.[10]

Moreover, this decreasing interest on the part of party officials in becoming campaign operatives and convention delegates, or at least in paying the price associated with those roles, was matched by a decreasing interest on the part of presidential candidates in recruiting such officials, especially if recruitment required additional effort. In the reformed world of presidential nominating politics—when the official party could not bring with it a serious positional advantage, when any extended alternative would suffice for creating an independent campaign, when most campaigns could not in principle be built around the official party, when party officials were clearly not going to be available when they were most needed, and when other available organizations would not be prepared to take a backseat to these officials—aspirants for a presidential nomination came to view the official party as a much more mixed, and more costly, asset. Moreover, when presidential contenders needed to build national, independent, *and personal* campaigns, and when they could expect to see these campaigns confronted with other fully articulated national campaigns in the various states and localities, the personal loyalty of party officials was increasingly important.

That personal loyalty, in fact, was not comparatively high. Presidential candidates could expect to suffer some reverses, even in the course of what became successful nominating campaigns. Accordingly, the personal loyalty of the local campaign organization could be crucial to overcoming these reverses should they ultimately prove surmountable. Party officials, in turn, had numerous assets for local campaigning, but an intense and exclusive personal loyalty was not ordinarily among them. Most party officials were unlikely to abandon a presidential contender frivolously; that would reflect badly on them at home as well as with the national campaign. But they did have other responsibilities in local politics, limited resources with which to address the full range of those responsibilities, and a need not to engage in pointless combat, which could only hurt an entire local party.[11] A party official, then, with early reticence, diffuse organizational responsibilities, and a contingent personal loyalty, was no longer the ideal delegate—and not at all the prize which that official might have been before extended party reform.

The Eclipse of the Official Party after Reform

In the face of all this, the official party, as an extended organization, simply withdrew from the politics of presidential selection. No longer would an extended state party adopt one presidential contender, put itself in the field against any and all opponents, defeat those opponents by virtue (at the very least) of superior position, and then claim the delegate slots which came with that victory. The risks in pulling an entire state party together early behind one among many presidential contenders were enormous. The possibilities for doing so were almost nonexistent in any case. Even the likelihood that the candidate would be sufficiently delighted to make the official party the centerpiece of his campaign, when he too faced numerous other claimants for some share in that role, was problematic.

The constriction of the official party, though not necessarily of any given party official, was thus effectively completed. Reform in the institutions of delegate selection had begun that constriction. Change in the practical politics of presidential nomination had extended it. Continuing calculations by party officeholders—and by presidential candidates, for that matter—finished the development, and eclipsed the official party. Occasionally, the leadership of a state party might still find itself sitting comprehensively at a national party convention. But that was ordinarily in response to the uncontested renomination of a sitting president, who had bestowed this arrangement on the official party.

The same constraints fell on local party units, although the reduced difficulty in assembling a local party behind one particular candidate did permit these units intermittently to secure the delegates from their particular areas. Even then, however, they usually did so when there was evident local sentiment for a candidate and when a local party leader was also an intense candidate enthusiast. Indeed, the same incentives and disincentives fell on individual party officials. But at this level, finally, these incentives had a more varied effect. On the average, officials in both parties were more likely to withdraw than they had been before institutional reform and its associated independent politics of nomination. But although the official party as an active statewide unit virtually disappeared, and although the official party as an active local unit was more the exception than the rule, party officials did continue to make it to the national convention, individually and on an idiosyncratic basis.

Lest any of these officials be inclined to misread the practical message of postreform politics, however, the contests immediately after extended party reform provided powerful, final reinforcement. Despite the presence of a new matrix of institutions for delegate selection in 1972, Democratic party officials and public officeholders alike had lined up overwhelmingly behind Edmund Muskie. When Muskie was rapidly cast aside, and when George McGovern—an apparent impossibility of nomination under traditional arrangements—moved to the nomination instead, an object lesson was evidently and painfully provided about the risks of concerted action in reformed presidential politics. Four years later, of course, with the rise of a true national unknown, Jimmy Carter, that lesson was underlined. Carter was even less plausible as a prereform nominee; he acquired support from the official party only when his nomination was certain; and he was never to integrate that party into his government.[12]

The Republican contests of the postreform era offered fewer extended dramatic surprises, and the lesson of those contests was thus less extreme in its import and more gradually registered. Yet Ronald Reagan did almost manage to unseat Gerald Ford in 1976, despite active support by the official party for Ford. And the Republican campaign of 1980 offered just enough additional surprises—the initial defeat of Reagan in Iowa, the apparent rise first of George Bush and then of John Anderson—to reemphasize the same fundamental strategic lesson: the official party had little to gain and much to lose from extended participation in presidential nominating politics. Individual party officials could escape that fate, but only if they exercised suitable caution and only if they were prepared to act on their own—and to live with sharply decreased prospects for influence at the convention.

The Eclipse of Party and the Rise of Ideology

There were to be numerous further effects from the reduced status of the official party in the politics of presidential selection. If the party could not be the central vehicle in most serious nominating campaigns, for example, something would have to take its place—campaigns, after all, still had to occur. If party officials could not be the inherently central delegates to the national convention, someone would have to replace them as well. If the official party was not to be the principal vehicle for successful nominating campaigns and if party officials were not to be its dominant product, then the internal lines of conflict which had characterized prereform conventions would themselves surely shift. All this implied that the convention as an environment for internal politicking would be substantially different. That change suggested that the nature of conflicts within the reformed convention would also be different and that the impact of those conflicts upon the general public could reasonably differ too.

All these subsequent changes—caused in part directly by the retreat of the official party, in larger part by an interaction with those same forces which had contributed to the partisan retreat—were most fruitfully observed through specific incidents. Yet there was a more immediately statistical measure of the impact of the eclipse of the party—the ideological positioning of convention delegates, that is, their self-reported location on a scale from very liberal to very conservative. In the years when the procedural world had been supremely stable, no one had bothered to collect such measures on a regular basis; there was no reason to expect variations reflecting anything more than the peculiar politics of a given presidential year. Accordingly, comparison with the prereform period does require some recalculation from related available measures. For all the years after sweeping reform, however, there are precise measures of the ideological movement which accompanied the retreat of the official party, measures sufficient to chart its course. At first, these measures offered only a partial, and therefore misleading, picture. But in short order, they took on a reliable—and radically different—pattern, which characterized and demarcated the postreform convention.

The prereform wisdom about the relationships among national convention delegates, their fellow party identifiers among the partisan rank and file, and the general American public was stable and straightforward, at least when the focus was relationships among these groups on policy issues and in political ideology.[13] First, the general public was moderate and centrist. Second, Democratic party identifiers were very mildly to the left of this general public, while Republican party identifiers were very mildly to its right. Third, Democratic delegates to national party conventions were mildly to the left of their own party identifiers, and Republican delegates were sharply off to the right of theirs—making them the true outliers in American national politics. There were numerous assessments of the attitudes of these groups on issues of public policy, and while these assessments did not include a direct measure of self-reported ideological position, they did lend themselves to a simple graphic representation in a form parallel to later explicit measures. (See Figure 3.1.)[14]

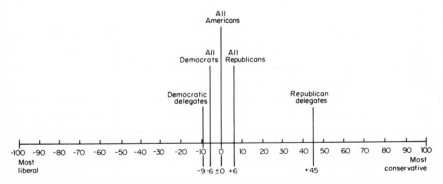

Figure 3.1. Ideological distribution of convention delegates, party identifiers, and the general public. (*Source:* Herbert McClosky, Paul J. Hoffman, and Rosemary O'Hara, "Issue Conflict and Consensus among Party Leaders and Followers," *American Political Science Review* 54 (1960), pp. 406–427, as transformed according to note 14.)

Extensive reform between 1968 and 1972 then became a reason to reexamine these relationships. Indeed, a new set of careful statistical measures was one more, minor aftereffect of sweeping party reform.[15] Moreover, these measures were to attest to a radically changed world in presidential politics, albeit in a manner which was initially and widely misperceived. For what the first surveys of delegate attitudes in the aftermath of reform appeared to reveal was a world turned upside down, the precise reverse of the accepted wisdom about representation and relations between convention delegates and party identifiers—between elites and masses—in the prereform era.

By these measures, in 1972, the general public was again clustered in the political center. Republican party identifiers were again mildly to the right of this cluster, just as rank-and-file Democrats were mildly to the left. But this time, in an apparent major reversal, the delegates to the Republican national convention were only mildly farther off to the right of their own party identifiers, while the delegates to the Democratic convention were sharply off to the left—of the public and even of their own partisans. (See Figure 3.2.)[16] In fact, the difference—and the reversal—was so extreme that scholars at the time considered the possibility that there were two different *kinds* of political party in the United States. One was an old-fashioned entity based on party office, with a composite convention drawn toward

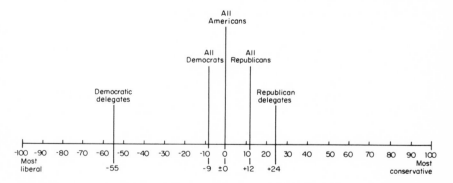

Figure 3.2. Ideological distribution of convention delegates, party identifiers, and the general public, 1972. (*Source: Convention Delegate Study, 1980* (Ann Arbor, Mich.: Inter-University Consortium for Political and Social Research, 1986), variables 8, 21, and 305, and *The CPS 1972 American Election Study* (Ann Arbor, Mich.: Inter-University Consortium for Political and Social Research, 1975), variables 140 and 652.)

the political center. This was, of course, the Republican party. The other was a new-fashioned entity, perennially reconstituted by individual candidates and their campaign activists, with a composite convention leaning toward the political extremes—the Democratic party.[17]

Ideological Divergence and the Composite Convention

Application of the same measures to the national convention delegates of 1976, however, quickly put this initial perception into perspective and led on to what was to become the new received wisdom about ideological positioning. The truly new development for 1976 was on the Republican side. The general public was, as ever, clustered in the center. Republican identifiers were once again mildly to the right of the general public. But this time, and consistently afterward, Republican delegates to the national convention were well off to the right, of the general public and of their own identifiers. (See Figure 3.3.) In 1980, this was confirmed as the recurring pattern of Republican politics, making 1972 rather than 1976 the obviously deviant year.

There was, however, a counterpart surprise on the Democratic side in 1976, one which in effect confirmed the new ideological positioning of national convention delegates by a different route but in an effectively parallel manner. In this surprise, the Democratic convention of 1976 effectively recapitulated its situation of 1972, despite about as different a politics of presidential nomination as it was possible to

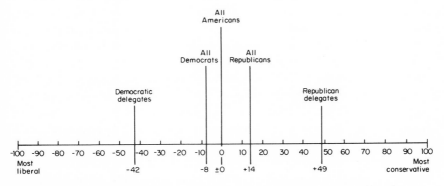

Figure 3.3. Ideological distribution of convention delegates, party identifiers, and the general public, 1976. (*Source: Convention Delegate Study, 1980,* variables 8, 19, and 305, and *The CPS 1976 National Election Study* (Ann Arbor, Mich.: Inter-University Consortium for Political and Social Research, 1977), variables 3174 and 3286.)

imagine. In 1976, Democratic party identifiers were again mildly to the left of the general public, thereby suggesting that little had changed in the society at large. The center, in short, was a true clustering, not an average of two very different sets of rank-and-file partisans. But the Democratic delegates, as in 1972, were well—strikingly—to the left even of their own identifiers. (See Figure 3.3.) Making this finding additionally impressive was the fact that the delegates of 1972 had produced the most liberal Democratic nominee of the postwar period, George McGovern, while the delegates of 1976 had nominated easily the most conservative, Jimmy Carter—yet the two groups of delegates stood roughly in the same position with regard to the general public!

There was still room for debate about the meaning of all this, about the permanence, transience, or deviance of any given year. But when the national convention delegates of 1980 recapitulated almost precisely the pattern of 1976, despite a presidential politics which once again differed sharply, they became not only evidence for the existence of a new basic pattern but confirmation of the associated changes which appeared to explain it, and indeed confirmation of the obvious arguments about connections between the two. In 1976, the Republican party had featured a moderate incumbent president, Gerald Ford, overcoming the challenge of an extremely conservative insurgent, Ronald Reagan. In 1980, the Republicans featured a dominant conservative champion, Reagan, steamrolling an aspiring resistance by a moderate challenger, George Bush. Likewise in 1976, the Democratic party had surfaced a moderately conservative outsider, Jimmy Carter, challenging a diffuse party establishment. In 1980, the Democrats featured Carter as a more moderate incumbent president, facing the dominant liberal spokesman of his era, Edward Kennedy. Furthermore, instead of a tight contest for the length of the nominating campaign, the Republican party in 1980 produced an early bandwagon for Reagan, who drove his last challenger from the field well before the convention. Similarly, instead of a multicandidate field from which an early winner emerged, the Democratic party in 1980 featured two main contenders battling all the way to the convention.

Yet despite all these differences, the larger picture of the relationships among general public, party identifiers, and national convention delegates was essentially unchanged: public in the center; Democratic and Republican identifiers mildly off to the left and right, respectively; Democratic and Republican delegates radically off to left and right, in turn. (See Figure 3.4.) Remarkably, the move from the classic moderate Ford to the archconservative Reagan had almost no effect on the ideological positioning of the Republican delegates as a whole. They had moved far off to the right with the coming of the first contested nominating campaigns after reform, and after the new independent politics of presidential nomination, and they stayed there without regard to the ideology of the candidate who was their putative leader. Similarly but less dramatically, the shift from only minor challenges to candidate Carter by a full panoply of contenders with the full range of ideologies in 1976 to a concentrated challenge to President Carter from a single liberal alternative in 1980 moved the Democratic delegates only a little farther left—and kept them in the *same* relationship to their identifiers.

Partisan Retreat and Ideological Divergence

More to the point, this shift still found these delegates in the same relationship to party identifiers and to the general public which they had demonstrated in 1972. By hindsight then, it became clear that it was not the Democratic delegates of 1972 who had been deviant, capitalizing on a reformed presidential politics to rout the official party and take the composite convention well off to the left. Instead, the *Republican* delegates of 1972 had been deviant, because they represented the shadow, the last hurrah of an old order of party-based presidential nominations. Reformed institutions for delegate selection

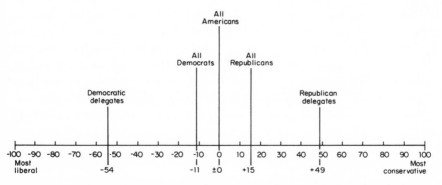

Figure 3.4. Ideological distribution of convention delegates, party identifiers, and the general public, 1980. (*Source: Convention Delegate Study, 1980,* variables 8, 17, and 305, and *American National Election Study, 1980* (Ann Arbor, Mich.: Inter-University Consortium for Political and Social Research, 1982), variables 266 and 267.)

had begun to move through the Republican party as well by 1972, though they would spread a good deal further by 1976. Yet because the Republicans had featured the nearly uncontested renomination of a sitting president, there was none of the competition necessary to bring the impact of new institutional arrangements into practical campaign politics—indeed, President Nixon was free to use the official party as his vehicle for renomination despite the fact that it was operating in a candidate-based, not a party-based, institutional structure.

Reformed institutions of delegate selection, however, had come to both political parties. The independent politics of presidential selection which went with them had come to the Democratic party in 1972, although it was not to reach the Republican party until 1976. Symbolically, the last of the nominees who spanned prereform and postreform politics, Richard Nixon, departed in that interim. As a result a new and similar grand array of major actors and mass publics in presidential politics arrived during that interim too. The results of 1980 made it clear that this was indeed the new shape of postreform politics.

Hindsight, reinforced by the sure knowledge of what actually happened, makes such an outcome appear inevitable. Or at least, there was a ready-made, after-the-fact rationale for such a shift, built on the organizational category of "party official." Part of this rationale stemmed from the alleged social relationship between an official party structure and the geographic area in which it is located.[18] Formally, party officials are responsible for representing at least the modal party identifiers in their jurisdictions, at best a clear majority of voters in the area. Moreover, where a fully developed hierarchy of party offices exists in a relatively stable geographic population, members of that population with comparatively typical attitudes are usually argued to be most likely to rise through the party hierarchy. But the greater part of an explanation built on the category of "party official," and the part with a more immediate political reality, stems not from these alleged social impacts of an extended structure of party offices, but from the direct organizational responsibilities which came with the holding of party offices.[19]

These include, of course, the recruiting of candidates, the mounting of campaigns, and the coordinating of subsequent governmental administrations. Those tasks are in turn united by the responsibility to construct an electoral coalition sufficiently broad to produce—and ideally to guarantee—victory in the general election. For a party official with an array of constituencies and of offices to fill by mobilizing them, this situation implies a comparatively centrist and moderate outlook. Indeed it implies clear additional pressures to move toward the political center, because both the largest number of voters and those most responsive to the appeals of the opposition party are likely to be found there. Nevertheless, these pressures are not sufficient to draw party officials to ideological positions more moderate than those of the party rank and file. Party officials, after all, are more deeply concerned with the issues of politics, and with a broader range of those issues, too. Indeed, many of them have ordinarily been drawn into politics specifically because they care about the sum and substance of such issues, and most of the rest acquire that concern in the course of doing party business.

Accordingly, party officials were predisposed to more extreme ideological positions than those of the general public, and they did indeed manifest those positions. Yet these officials still faced almost unavoidable organizational constraints which held their ideological tendencies in check, and they often faced associated social constraints which had the same effect. When the official party was the central vehicle for nominating campaigns, and when party officials were the central product of those campaigns as delegates, those delegates tended to be farther off toward the extremes in the relevant partisan direction than the general public or even than fellow party identifiers, but not so much farther off that they created major and noteworthy distances from these rank-and-file constituencies. When party officials were no longer the dominant delegates at national conventions, in consequence, the conventions as composites of delegates were free to move off toward the ideological extremes, and they did.

4 | The Rise of the Organized Interests: An Alternative Base for Delegate Selection

The grand story of the change in the political character of convention delegates was the shift from a party-based to a candidate-based process of campaign development and delegate selection. The immediate and central implication of this shift was the withdrawal, the constriction, and at times the erasure of the official party in the politics of presidential nomination, and the associated diminution of party officials as delegates to the national convention. The official party as a formal structure was no longer the effective framework through which delegates were selected; the official party as an extended organization was no longer—and probably could no longer be—the effective means by which nominating campaigns were mounted. Party officials, when they chose to participate under these reformed arrangements, did so as individuals rather than as pieces of some larger organization. As a consequence, they were not ordinarily the backbone of campaigns for a nomination, nor were they the dominant force among the delegations which resulted.

Yet if that was the fundamental half of the story of the impact of structural reform and social evolution on the identity of delegates to the national party convention, it was hardly the whole of that story. For extended national campaigns—more of them than ever, really—still had to be mounted on the way to a nomination. Similarly delegates to the national convention still had to be selected—slated, elected, and sent to the convention. Something had to serve as the organizational base for nominating campaigns, just as something had to characterize the new aggregation of delegates which resulted. Those delegates, in turn, were still inevitably central to decisions at the convention on its traditional and continuing concerns, that is, on platform, rules, and credentials. They were even more critical, as it developed, to the new main focus of the reformed convention, the conflict over launching the general election campaign.

This basic situation led to an equally elementary—but somehow still surprising and ironic—result. For while the supporters of various institutional devices for selecting delegates and nominating presidents argued about the kinds of campaign framework and convention delegate which were likely to follow from adopting their preferences, the environment for presidential politics closed over these arguments and settled them irrefutably. To be more precise, the candidates who needed to mount campaigns and acquire delegates, along with those organized actors who might hope to profit from a campaign role and delegate status, quickly resolved the issue.

In essence, when the official party was constricted within the politics of presidential selection, its place was almost immediately taken by interest groups (that is, organizations constructed around the well-being of the membership) and issue organizations (that is, groups constructed around a particular policy concern). In consequence, when party officials were devalued as delegates to the national party conventions, interest group representatives and independent issue activists quickly took their place. The arguments supporting reform—and these arguments had speculated on the nature of this outcome to a surprising extent—had suggested that "citizen politicians," an aspiringly random sample of the general public, were the likely product of widespread implementation. The environment for reformed politics, insensitive to these or any other arguments, settled the issue differently, by providing only interest groups or issue organizations—the organized interests—as the available framework for independent nominating campaigns, once the official party had lost potential as an organizing framework.

The first nominating campaigns under reformed arrangements, while they did attest to both the extent and the character of this change in the organizational base for delegate selection, were difficult for observers at the time to interpret. Within one or two elections, however, both the trend and its more specific contents were clear. In fact, by 1980, the search for delegates and, through them, for a nominating majority had produced a political arena crowded with interest groups and issue organizations, seeking and being sought, demanding rewards and offering support, while both presidential aspirants and interested partisans tried to secure the maximum benefit from these negotiations. In short, the triumph of the organized interests was the most dramatic product of the demise of the official party. Just as the triumph of the interested partisans, the members of these organized interests, was the accompanying product of the retreat of party officials in the politics of delegate selection.

Organizations did differ in their ability to profit from the reformed nominating environment. Size and geographic dispersion of their membership, demographic characteristics of the members themselves, and formal characteristics of the organizational structure, all contributed to variety in organizational influence, though intense membership attachments might still compensate for any of these. By 1980, in any case, there were remarkable—perhaps even historic—instances of the triumph of individual organized interests, as with the National Education Association on the Democratic side or the Moral Majority and associated religious evangelicals among Republicans. While these particular organizations were not necessarily the statistical norm for the newly advantaged organized interests, they were symptomatic in an additional sense. For although the rise of the organized interests was a crucial further part of the story of the change in national convention delegates, the environment from which such organizations and delegates could be chosen had also changed over time, as indeed had the nature of the organizations which prospered within it.

In both respects, the direction of the shift was the same—toward organizations with intense membership attachments and prospects for substantial membership participation. Among interest groups, this ordinarily meant a white-collar advantage; among issue organizations, it ordinarily favored a narrower focus. For the national party convention, however, it also meant a shift away from the organized interests traditionally associated with the official party—big business for the Republicans and big labor for the Democrats. There were still institutional constraints on this general triumph, since the remaining party-based institutions of delegate selection were least kind to the organized interests, and since even among candidate-based institutions, participatory conventions were kinder than candidate primaries. Moreover, the fate of the candidate to whom a group and its members became attached still critically affected group success or failure. A winning nominee might pull them along to victory as convention delegates, while an early loser might doom the entire organization, at least for that campaign.

Nevertheless, the thrust of the underlying change remained overwhelming, and the rise of the organized interests, along with the triumph of the interested partisans, remained its central manifestation. In fact, the cumulative extent of this trend, within only two or three elections, was so alarming to nominees and to the top leadership of the national parties that these individuals began to look for ways to enhance the prospects of party officials as convention delegates—really to reintroduce them for the Democrats, more to resecure them for the Republicans. The 1984 conventions attested to the success of these maneuvers, involving automatic representation at the convention and revised procedures for slating delegates, respectively. Yet this success also commented on the changing—indeed, the changed—shape of the partisan political universe. For at bottom, a conscious effort to reintroduce the official party to "its" convention only underlined the extent to which party officials themselves had become just one more organized interest.

The triumph of the organized interests, then, was the second half of an explanation for the change in the convention as a context for internal politicking. Without concern for a geographically based electorate but with dedication to a particular group or cause as their principal motive for participation, interested partisans were predisposed to lean away from the political center. This tendency was reinforced by their social environments back home; it was reinforced again by the nature of maneuvering at the convention. In such a world, a partial restoration of party officials would serve more to moderate behavior at the convention than to change the character of nominating politics, especially when more and more of the party officials being restored were themselves primarily motivated by ideological concerns. In any case, the coming of all these new delegates was effectively the reconstitution of the national party convention. Accordingly, these delegates were destined to be critical to a change in the convention's main activity, as they were destined to *comprise* the bases for conflict over changed convention activities.

Theoretical Alternatives to the Official Party

Extended reform in the institutions of delegate selection and extended change in the practical politics occurring through them did not change some of the fundamental requirements of a national nominating campaign. Local campaigns, even if they were not a decisive factor in the local fate of a national candidate, still had to be mounted. Their absence reliably harmed a national effort, by suggesting that this effort was faltering nationwide. Even this ineffectiveness reliably harmed the national effort, because it meant that local successes were not automatically translated into delegates to the national convention. Finally, the strength and ability of the local campaign could occasionally be the deciding factor, the factor which determined whether a particular national candidate won or lost locally, and hence, just possibly, whether that contest became the turning point for a national campaign. Even national candidates without an obvious local following, and even national campaigns which intended to rely on national issues and paid local advertising, thus needed at least a comprehensive, skeletal, local campaign.

By the same token, in the reformed world as in the unreformed, every state (and usually every region within a state) was still entitled to select delegates to the national convention. These delegates were the reward for successful nominating campaigns; they were the accounting system for the contest among aspiring nominees. Accordingly, if delegates could no longer be simply and directly slated, supported, and then selected through the official party, they had to be created and acquired through some other effective means. Moreover, the character of this organizational means, and the identity of the delegates who resulted, was likely to be a matter of some consequence, since those delegates still had to address the business of the convention proper. In the modern era, this meant ratifying rather than nominating the presidential candidate. But it also meant judging the credentials of other delegates, drafting the platform of the national party, and adjusting the rules for the contest four years down the road. It came rapidly to mean affecting the inauguration of the general election campaign, and sometimes of other external campaigns, as well.

In fact, the reformed matrix of institutions for presidential nomination, and each of the institutions within it, had a theory attached to it—or at least a hypothesis of sorts—about the way campaigns would be organized and about the kind of delegations which would be selected. This "theory" was explicit in the arguments of self-conscious party reformers. It was only barely implicit in the counterarguments of deliberate antireformers. It could easily be extracted from less grand arguments over the implementation of any new device (or the retention of any old device) in the individual states, although this state-level debate ordinarily focused as much or more on the way the proposed state system would fit into the national process.[1]

Thus there was a justification even for the prereform system, one rarely offered in public in the course of reform politicking but one often articulated in private by state party leaders. It argued that party-based arrangements were the most appropriate framework for nominating campaigns because the official party was most legitimate, being most broad-based and most generally available, and because party officials were best informed and hence best qualified to make the key judgments about convention delegates and a presidential nominee. In this view, party officials knew the candidates in a way the public never could. They knew the constituencies as well, and so could best estimate their response in November. Moreover, party officials did the ongoing labor of the party, so that they were its appropriate national delegates. They were most concerned with its extended welfare afterward, making them doubly appropriate.[2]

From the other side, the theory—and the intention—of those who supported self-conscious, comprehensive party reform was manifestly, even publicly clear: once the party (often derided as "the party machine" or more commonly "the party bosses") had been moved out of the way, the general public (also known as "the people" or sometimes "the voters") would naturally and inevitably come to control presidential nominations, party politics, and, through them, the presidency itself. This was a right and proper goal for a democratic society; it was a true and scientific analysis of its projected course after reform. One goal of reformed institutions, then, was indeed to displace the official party and replace party officials. Extrapolation from the arguments supporting this goal suggested that the proper public representatives in a reformed political order, mounting campaigns and serving as delegates, were "citizen politicians," in effect a slightly ennobled random sample of "the people."[3]

These arguments were only part of even the opening round of reform politicking and institutional reform. They were certainly not the determining factor in the subsequent course of reform and reaction. Nevertheless, the devices which prospered in the postreform era did possess their own justifications and rationales. These devices, whether candidate primaries or participatory conventions, and whether introduced as a direct response to reform pressures or as a response to the evolving institutional framework, were reliably justified as being more open to public participation—which they clearly were. They were additionally argued to be more likely to represent the general public accurately, a much more equivocal point of reference. They were argued by implication, finally, to be much more likely to produce some sample of that public as campaign operatives and national convention delegates.

These devices were, of course, overwhelmingly triumphant in the postreform era. But whatever the truth about "representation" through them in some abstract sense, the truth about actual campaign operatives and convention delegates was almost immediately clear. Moreover, there was to be a substantial irony in this clear and immediate truth, at least for those attuned to the justification for changed institutions. For the successful removal of the most extensive and best organized contender for organizing campaigns and slating delegates, the official party, did not lead to the assumption of campaign and then delegate status by some random sample of the unconnected general public. Instead—and with a crushing inevitability for reformers, antireformers, and nonreformers alike—it led to the transfer of delegate positions to the next most extensive and next best organized groups and individuals within that public.

The Inevitability of an Organized Alternative

The identity of these groups and individuals, then, became the answer to the question of who was most likely to attend reformed national party conventions—and the beginning of an answer to the questions of what would come before these conventions and how reformed conventions would handle these activities. At bottom, the need to mount fully articulated, independent, national campaigns for a presidential nomination, and an inability to use the official party as the basis for these campaigns, reduced most candidates immediately to three clear options. Candidates could build their state and national campaigns around previously organized interest groups, that is, existing organizations with a focused attention to politics, an attention rooted in the self-interest of group members. Or they could build their campaigns around previously developed issue organizations, that is, existing organizations with a focused attention to some particular public issue, the issue generating and justifying the group. Or, of course, they could combine the two.[4]

Normally, that was the range of choice for any candidate who could not build a campaign around the official party, because these groups were all that existed as a continuing, organizable presence in the states and localities. Candidates were compelled to find some previously organized framework to plug into their national campaigns, since the task of constructing national campaigns person by person from those without organizational ties or political experience would have been impossible. Some candidates, of course, began in such a weak position that they could not attract any number of major organized interests. But such candidates either disappeared quickly, having failed to mount a serious campaign and thus having failed to attract public support, or they scored a few initial successes and began to draw the organized groups and cause-based organizations which would allow them to mount an extended nominating campaign.

From the other side, of course, organized interests discovered a new—and golden—opportunity to extend their influence in presidential politics. Many of these groups and organizations had a long history of attempting to influence presidential selection. Presidents, after all, were likely to be able to make major contributions to their interests or causes. But before reform, these groups and organizations had been forced to operate *through* the political parties, and if that restriction had not always prevented them from achieving their goals, it had ordinarily meant that their direct influence was much diluted. After reform, and after the reformed campaigns which followed hard upon it, these groups and organizations no longer faced that restriction. They could put themselves directly in the service of one or more presidential contenders and demand policy responses to accompany their support.

Organized interest groups were probably a part even of colonial American politics, at least as soon as the social homogeneity and physical hardship which enforced some uniformity on the earliest settlers had begun to meliorate. In any case, such groups had been a widely recognized, and widely debated, feature of the political landscape for most of American history.[5] They were ordinarily distinguished by an official membership and certified leaders, as well as by general policy goals shared by that membership and articulated by that leadership. Moreover, the term *interest group* ordinarily suggested a vision of *self*-interest, in which the goals in question were calculated to advance the social situation of the group or its members, as, for example, with a focus on maintaining higher prices for milk producers or securing job placement for black Americans.

There was no reliable measure of the number and density of interest groups in the period leading up to reform in the institutions of delegate selection. Indeed, scholars of the topic argued over whether, as American society developed and secured the blessings of economic growth and as the technological means evolved to create such groups on a nationwide basis and communicate rapidly among divisions in the states and localities, the number of politically relevant groups had actually increased. Perhaps all that had resulted from these changes was a shift in the nature of available groups, from the community-based to the nation-based. In short order, however, no one bothered to argue that their role in the politics of presidential selections had not absolutely increased.

Issue organizations too had long been part of American politics. They were reliably focused around a particular issue or cause, such as ending a foreign conflict or restoring the moral fiber of the nation, which did not ordinarily have direct pecuniary benefits for their membership. The leaders of these organizations, in turn, were often described as "independent activists," since they ordinarily showed a continuing concern with matters political along with a continuing political participation but without much continuing attachment to a political party. Yet these individuals were more accurately described—and needless to say, more effectively recruited by campaign managers—through their attachments to issue and cause organizations, from which they were surely not "independent."

Again, there was no reliable measure of the population of these organizations during the years leading up to extensive reform. Issue organizations and independent activists had certainly been present—with their insistence on a devotion to particular public issues, political styles, or aspiring candidates, over and above attachment to a specific political party—in all periods of American politics.[6] Indeed, the most dramatic of these political actors long predated reform, as with the abolitionists, the suffragettes, or the prohibitionists. Again, however, regardless of their comparative historical presence, the point is that as the official party withdrew, fragmented, or suffered defeat within presidential nominating politics, these organizations became the obvious replacements—the sole organized alternatives, really—for the mounting of independent nominating campaigns and the slating of national convention delegates. Any given group might succeed or fail in a given presidential year. Such groups as a class were nevertheless the obvious substitute for the official party.

The Rise of Interest Groups and Issue Organizations

In theory, it might have taken even attentive interest groups and active issue organizations an election or two to recognize their new opportunity, develop conscious strategies to maximize it, and thus seize it actively and consciously. In practice, the reformed environment for presidential politics was a quick and effective teacher. The various candidates, once compelled to create nationwide, personal, nominating campaigns and once deprived of the ability to do this through the official party, saw the immediate need to mobilize some existing framework to carry the national effort. It was difficult enough to generate an organized campaign presence in all of the states; it was probably impossible to create such a presence primarily through the use of unattached individuals. From this reality, it was but a short step to seeking out the organized interests. Even then, the generating work of presidential campaigns was to stretch out further and further across the years between actual delegate contests.

Some candidates were quicker than others to make the initial shift. In the first nominating struggles of the postreform era, George McGovern shifted quickly, Edmund Muskie clearly less so. Yet one round of reformed politics was sufficient for most presidential aspirants to learn the lesson and apply the model. By the same token, many of these candidates quickly realized that there were costs as well as benefits in building a campaign on organized interests. Even McGovern was to regret an early dependence on groups such as the National Welfare Rights Organization. The positions which a candidate had to take to attract group support, and the public identification of candidate with organization(s) which frequently resulted, could rebound to reduce prospects in the general election. Yet there would just as clearly be no electoral prospects at all without a successful nominating campaign, and that remained, inevitably, the dominant prior concern.

From the other side, once the organized interests had seen their opportunity, that is, once some had been recruited by a presidential contender and once they had accumulated some experience in nominating politics, their leaders began to press forward and seek advantages from this politics on their own. The Vietnam Moratorium Committee was ready and waiting for the McGovern nomination campaign, as the Moral Majority and associated evangelicals would be waiting for a conservative counterpart in the Republican party an election or two later. The initial move by some groups to identify with and attempt to support presidential candidates who were particularly favorable to group aspirations was as effectively automatic as the initial move by some candidates to find groups to help them carry their campaigns. And the lessons of this experience were just as quickly communicated to other organized groups. The joint result was an environment in which many of the advantages in bargaining over support for nominating campaigns were actually transferred to leaders of the organized interests—and not to candidates for a presidential nomination.

A candidate with apparently greater prospects for nomination was still in a better position to bargain with group leaders than was a candidate with markedly lesser apparent prospects. Again, even McGovern came to rue some of the group attachments which he had accepted in the days when no one gave his campaign much chance. Yet in a world where interest groups and issue organizations could be major elements of any independent nominating effort, the leaders of these groups were reliably in an improved position. They could honestly threaten any candidate who did not give them a major place in his nominating campaign with the prospect that they would shift to one or more of his emerging opponents. As a result, even a front-runner was well advised to acquire the support of as many interest groups and issue organizations as he could, to deprive other candidates of their support and to maximize the chances that his status as front-runner would be converted into an eventual nomination.[7]

Even then, the impact of the new presidential politics was not complete. For the same changes in formal institutions and associated politicking which had eclipsed the official party were an automatic and inherent opportunity for the organized interests to assert themselves, quite apart from any wishes or responses by the candidates. It was not just that the constriction of the official party created a metaphoric vacuum into which other organizations could move. It was also that open institutions, as reliably augmented by candidates competing for campaign support, constituted an automatic opportunity to enhance the place of these other organizations, apart even from the actions of any official party.

The Triumph of the Organized Interests: The Teachers

As with so many other aspects of institutional reform and associated change in the politics of presidential selection, the shift from the official party to organized alternatives as a means of mounting campaigns for a nomination, and from party officials to alternative elites as the delegates produced by those campaigns, arrived earlier and more sharply in the Democratic party. The Democratic campaigns of 1972 served dramatic notice that a new world of presidential politics was in existence, though drama probably outpaced clarity when it came to the precise outlines of this new political world. Edmund Muskie still managed to mount a party-based campaign, with an additional nod toward the dominant groups and organizations of the day. George McGovern was forced to build his campaign on whatever was available outside that framework, including issue organizations such as the Vietnam Moratorium Committee and Americans for Democratic Action, along with interest groups such as the National Women's Political Caucus and the National Welfare Rights Organization.

Yet McGovern did defeat Muskie, and if commentators were more united in noting the specifically deviant characteristics of his delegates than they were in unraveling their generic organizational base, the fundamental shift had nevertheless begun. It was continued four years later in the contest which resulted in the nomination of Jimmy Carter, although again the peculiar details of the Carter campaign, while they certainly advanced the same grand development, continued to obscure its basic character. Because Carter arrived apparently "from out of nowhere," as an unheralded, former, one-term governor of Georgia, it was even more difficult for commentators to characterize his campaign, and especially its associated delegates. Yet those delegates were attached to an array of issue organizations, from environmental groups through "public-interest" lobbies, and if Carter had not been the first choice of the leaders of these organizations, their members had come forward quickly when he began his rise—and needed an organized framework to sustain it.

Moreover, this campaign not only suggested the impending realization of the rise of the organized interests. It also included a particular group linkage which, only four years later, would come to symbolize that rise. For among those who came forward quickly to join the Carter campaign were numerous members of the National Education Association (NEA), the largest interest group for public school teachers in the United States. The strategy of their national leadership in urging its members to get involved with various candidates across the board, and the positioning and willingness of these members to clamber onto the Carter campaign when it surged early, paid off handsomely even in 1976. There were ultimately 172 delegates to the Democratic national convention who were members of the NEA. (There may actually have been some NEA delegates at the 1972 convention too, but they had been unrecognized as an organized bloc and uncounted even by their official leadership.)

In any case, the 1976 campaign, by hindsight, can be recognized as a major learning device for both these individuals and their national leadership. Indeed, it served as a preliminary to one of the great achievements in the history of interest group activity in the politics of presidential selection. For after the Democratic convention of 1976, the national leadership of the NEA decided that support by Jimmy Carter for creation of a federal Department of Education justified the first presidential endorsement in the organization's history—and a chain reaction which would culminate as the Democratic convention of 1980 began.[8] The NEA did indeed endorse Carter. He did secure election, albeit narrowly. He went on to create a Department of Education as one of the major policy initiatives of his term. And the NEA, on the very day he signed that bill—in the fall of 1979, when Carter was otherwise faring badly in the polls versus his possible Republican opponents and even his main Democratic challenger—endorsed the president for reelection. Moreover, in an effort to prove that it had arrived as a force in national politics, the NEA went on to mobilize all its resources behind the Carter campaign—in truth, to *become* that campaign in locality after locality.

The NEA itself was a classic incarnation, almost the embodiment, of an interest group entitled to prosper in reformed politics. It was large; with 1,750,000 members, it was second only to the United Teamsters in total membership. Its members were geographically dispersed, to every congressional district and almost every community, in a fashion no other interest group could emulate. Better yet, these members were all white-collar; they were accustomed to public activity; they carried substantial prestige in many of their communities. That they were also riding a wave of renewed interest in their organization, both locally and at the national level, was a serendipitous but not inconsequential additional asset. Finally, their national leadership was empowered to make a quick endorsement, so that it was ultimately able, from the national level alone, to put fifty staff members and over half a million dollars in salaries and expenses into the field intermittently for a nominating campaign.

The result was more than anyone expected.[9] By the time the convention assembled, there were 302 NEA delegates, a group larger than all but one state delegation. Moreover, the 269 committed Carter delegates within this total were by far the largest Carter bloc, dwarfing any single state and doubling the Carter total in every state but one. Calculated differently, the NEA Carter delegates alone were about 8 percent of the total convention, and almost 16 percent of the total needed to nominate. Individual triumphs within this aggregate were even more impressive. At the Oklahoma state convention, 43 percent of all delegates were members of the NEA, and they had to labor consciously to give away slots as national delegates, so as not to reap continuing local enmity from this sudden local success. In eight states, the NEA had over a fifth of the total delegation, and in all those, the organization had an effective veto over other selections. Its largest bloc in any one delegation, 24 delegates in California, was actually larger than the total delegations of fourteen other states.

Even after these delegates had been selected, however, the national leadership did not rest. It secured 11 of the 155 members of the Platform Committee, 8 of the 34 members of the most relevant subcommittee, and 1 of the 11 members of the drafting committee which created the initial working document—a document promising sharp increases in educational funding during an era of alleged cutbacks and restraints. The national leadership then planned to cover all the expenses of its 465 delegates and alternates until this was ruled contrary to federal campaign finance law; the leadership settled for covering part of the trip to and from the convention site and offering no-cost loans from its credit union for delegates who found the remainder of their expenses a hardship. Beyond even that, the national NEA leadership built a complex whip system to track its delegates on the convention floor, with designated and uniformed floor monitors and an electronic communications network which were widely regarded as the best in the hall—better than either the Kennedy or the Carter operation. Finally, the leaders gained the ultimate satisfaction not only of seeing their candidate nominated, essentially without defection, but of deviating from and defeating him on two platform planks (on women's rights) where they disagreed.

The Triumph of the Organized Interests: The Evangelicals

The factors contributing to change in the politics of presidential selection arrived later, more gradually, and a bit less thoroughly in the Republican party. Yet all those factors did arrive, and if their progress was more gradual and their reach less extensive when compared with the situation of the Democrats, it was still remarkable—quick and far-reaching—when compared with the situation of the Republicans themselves in the period before sweeping party reform. Because the preconditions for change in the Democratic party characterized the Republican party too, then, it is not surprising that a shift to organized interests as the framework for nominating campaigns and to interested partisans as the national delegates produced through that framework occurred in the Republican nomination process as well.

The presence of this similar movement was obscured when the Democrats were going through the tumultuous changes of 1972, because the Republicans were renominating a sitting president. Richard Nixon brushed aside a truly minor challenge from the right, from Congressman John Ashbrook, and from the left, from Congressman "Pete" (Paul N.) McCloskey, with an organization based essentially on the official party. Even informed observers could thus be excused for believing that change had arrived on only one side of the political aisle. Within four years, however, a second sitting Republican president, Gerald Ford, who again built his campaign around the official party, was to face serious difficulty in securing renomination. Challenger Ronald Reagan, the former governor of California, turned to the most conservative party officials and especially to an array of issue organizations, such as Young Americans for Freedom and the Congressional Club, which were devoted to the furtherance of conservative ideological goals. Once again, observers could be excused for missing the extent of the change implied by Reagan's near success, because Ford did manage to defeat Reagan. But once again, in hindsight, the 1976 campaign was testimony to the arrival of the same trends in the Republican party which were being confirmed and propelled by Jimmy Carter on the Democratic side.

The contest of 1980 then brought these trends to fruition—and to public prominence—on the Republican side too. Ronald Reagan was back with a much more explicit and fully developed campaign in the emerging postreform tradition, and this time, of course, he won. He retained the conservative ideological groups; he secured more of the official party from the start; and he added new cause organizations, such as the National Right-to-Life Committee, and new interest groups, such as the National Rifle Association. The result was an overwhelming triumph for the former governor and for the new politics of presidential selection. Moreover, the most dramatic testimony to all this change was the integral rise and success of a new group in Republican party politics, a group calling itself, memorably and combatively, the Moral Majority.

Perhaps the biggest story of the 1980 Republican convention was the rise not just of the Moral Majority but of a larger coalition of evangelical Christians.[10] Yet many of the disparate leaders of these individuals had been educated in delegate politics by activists and materials from the Moral Majority. If they were quick to recognize one another and to act in concert once they had reached the convention, it was even more the Moral Majority which provided events to rally them and initiatives for them to pursue. The evangelicals were never as clearly defined through membership in any given group as the members of the NEA, nor were they as well coordinated and drilled through any whip system. But there were more of them proportionately, and in many ways their achievements, given their inherent handicaps, were more impressive.

The Moral Majority itself was a loose coalition—a mailing list, a television audience, and a small membership, all mixed together—of Protestant fundamentalist ministers and rank-and-file believers from around the country. Its president, cofounder, and moving force was the Reverend Jerry Falwell, headquartered at Liberty Baptist Church in Lynchburg, Virginia, but better known through his nationally televised *Old Time Gospel Hour*. His mailing list of 400,000, with its 72,000 evangelical preachers, was the centerpiece of an effort to convert fundamentalist Protestants from an indifference toward politics to an active role in it. Standard analysis, however, suggested that this effort was inherently limited by the nature of its potential constituency.

While the putative mass base for this operation was potentially as large as those tens of millions of Americans who claimed to be "born again," it was also potentially as small as some fraction of Falwell's central mailing list. This constituency was very unevenly distributed, with a clear concentration in the South and a clear weakness in the Northeast. Moreover, the members were clearly disadvantaged for the politics of presidential selection by their social characteristics, that is, by being less educated, less wealthy, and less white-collar than their fellow Americans. Falwell himself asserted that one of his motivations for forming the Moral Majority was the discovery that many of his own parishioners were not even registered to vote. Finally, although intensity of identification with their local churches was the core of a counterweight to these disadvantages, those churches themselves had historically been organized around the notion that devoted Christians should stand clear of the politics of this world.

For all these reasons, the success of the Moral Majority in the presidential politics of 1980 was at least the equivalent of the success of the NEA, and clearly outshone it in some respects. Like the NEA, the Moral Majority was to acquire full dominance of the delegations in two or three states and an effective veto over the selection of delegates in five or six others. The extent of this success and the element of surprise which came with it were such that none of the news media or academic sources which normally surveyed convention delegates bothered to ask which individuals were members of, or at least recruited by, the Moral Majority itself. But several of these research units were sufficiently alert to ask about a "decision for Christ" or about being "born again."[11] The results were stunning: at the Republican convention of 1980, 513 delegates—over 25 percent of the total and almost 51 percent of the number needed to nominate—had in fact made a decision for Christ at some point in their lives. Moreover, better than half the delegates in Arkansas, Georgia, Kentucky, North Carolina, and North Dakota could make this claim, and more than 40 percent could do so in Alabama, Alaska, Idaho, Kansas, Nebraska, Oklahoma, South Carolina, South Dakota, and Tennessee.

If specific measures of Moral Majority linkage were unavailable within this larger population, specific events staged directly by the national leadership of the Moral Majority, including several prayer breakfasts and a well-covered news conference, were easy to spot. So were pointed contributions to the Republican platform by delegates who were known members of the Moral Majority—on prayer in the schools, of course, but also on abortion, family values, and women's rights (where Moral Majority activists endorsed *defeat* of the Equal Rights Amendment). Indeed, if most delegate surveys did not reflect the presence or absence of Moral Majority delegates, the number of those delegates and the extent of their activities were still sufficient to make the organization itself a major story for most news media and a focus of numerous academic investigations after the convention.[12]

Variations in the Prospects of Organized Alternatives

In remarkably short order, then, the shift from the official party to the organized interests as the main vehicle for independent nominating campaigns, and the shift from party officials to interested partisans as the dominant social types among national convention delegates, was inevitably and effectively completed. Nevertheless, the underlying shift did not imply a uniform benefit—some equal or proportionate gain—for every organized interest (and hence every interested partisan). Instead, the various organized alternatives differed tremendously in their potential for benefiting from this shift, and thus for populating reformed national conventions with delegates who were also organization members. Some organizations prospered massively in a given year; others suffered equally dramatic defeat. Some organizations prospered increasingly year in and year out; others were little advantaged at all.

Several characteristics of individual organizations were especially important in determining their potential standing in the reformed political world. Size and geographic dispersion of the membership were inevitably important in an environment where rank-and-file voters would make the key decisions. The social characteristics of this membership, particularly those characteristics which shaped the likelihood that they would actually turn out in candidate primaries and participatory conventions, were likewise important. The commitment of the membership, the degree to which it identified strongly with the organization, could sometimes be most important of all. Finally, the other resources at the organization's disposal, along with the ability of the leadership to dispense these resources freely, might intermittently compensate for all these other variables.

Size and geographic dispersion of membership were perhaps the most obvious organizational assets or liabilities in the postreform politics of presidential selection. In general, a larger organization was in a better position than a smaller one, because total participants were the main measure of influence in presidential politics. By the same token, a geographically dispersed organization was in a better position than a geographically concentrated counterpart, because the nominating campaign was fated to be truly national in scope. On the one hand then, organizations with both attributes were best able to carry a nominating campaign and claim the delegates who were one of its major rewards. On the other hand, there were enough refinements in these simple rules of thumb to create numerous, and occasionally dramatic, exceptions. Because the earliest state contests were most influential in winnowing the field of contenders, for example, an organization which was small nationwide but large in one or two early states was also in an enhanced position. Moreover, early contests were only a special case of the more general exception: organizations with a large and well-distributed membership in crucial state contests (whether early, middle, or late) were clearly in an enhanced position too.[13]

All of this, however, was still largely dependent on the organization's ability to turn out its membership, and thus to help the candidate or candidates of its choice. Organizational leaders might be able to extract policy concessions and delegate slots even when they could not reliably deliver their members. But if those members could not be brought out in any given year, the candidate favored by the organization was more likely to lose, and if he lost, of course, his policy promises and hypothetical delegates were radically devalued. Moreover, an organization with such a record year after year, no matter how aggressive or administratively able its leadership, was unlikely to continue to receive such concessions. This meant in essence that the membership characteristics most closely associated with turnout, in primary elections and open party meetings, were increasingly valuable. Occupation, income, social status, but especially education were in fact the characteristics most closely related to turnout in candidate primaries, and even more to turnout in participatory conventions.[14] Organizations whose members offered these characteristics were in better shape in the reformed political world than organizations whose members did not.

Even then, there was one intangible factor which added a major twist to these otherwise fundamental relationships: what really mattered was the extent to which the members identified with an organization, cared about its goals and endorsements, and were prepared to come out and support them in person. On the average, a large organization would have a greater raw number of members who cared, even if the average member cared less. On the average, a white-collar organization would have more members who turned out, even if the average member cared no more than the average member of a blue-collar organization. But strong group identifications and intensities of feeling could still overcome these averages—and did in any number of cases. There was room to doubt whether membership intensity could compensate for raw size, wide distribution, or social advantage year after year for any one organization. There was no doubt that intensity could compensate for all these assets in any given contest and thus shake up the politics of presidential selection.

Finally, the structure of the organization, especially the disposable resources available to its leadership and that leadership's ability to act quickly and in concert, might also make a difference. Much of the work on a nominating campaign was done from below, through influences on primary or convention turnout, so that much of the work of capturing delegates was done from below as well. Yet some of the negotiations over campaign endorsement were inevitably done from above, as was some of the bargaining over allocation of delegates within the campaign. In these transactions, a leadership with sizable resources and a free hand in dispensing them, especially if this meant finances or a campaign staff, could make a contribution quite apart from the subsequent activity of its membership.

The Changing Organizational Universe in Convention

Neither the National Education Association nor the Moral Majority could be taken as statistically typical of the organized interests in attendance at conventions in the aftermath of reform. The NEA, after all, was in many senses the most successful of the organized interests which prospered in this reformed environment, as the Moral Majority was the most dramatic product, and the cutting edge, of similar changes on the Republican side. But both groups were diagnostic— perhaps even symptomatic—of larger changes in the character of delegates and indeed of more specific changes within the general shift. For the NEA and the Moral Majority embodied the characteristics which caused certain types of interest groups and issue organizations to flourish disproportionately after reform. Just as they were implicit testimony to a further change, in the universe of organized interests which might populate the convention in a given presidential year.

In each case, the central attribute for success was easy to isolate. Among interest groups, the NEA had all the background characteristics which were additionally valuable after the eclipse of the official party, including large size, geographic dispersion, and a formal structure capable of rapid and decisive action. But what really brought these together was the demographic character of the membership itself, a character summarized by a uniformly white-collar occupational status but captured operationally by the high level of education which reliably came with representing public school teachers and by organizational skills often found in that occupation. In this, the NEA probably did represent the underlying rule: interest groups which prospered in the aftermath of sweeping party reforms were disproportionately likely to feature white-collar memberships; said differently, white-collar membership was the key to interest group influence in deliberately participatory institutions of delegate selection. In fact, this rule went so far as to invade the domain of the largest single category of organizations which were traditionally (and symbolically) blue-collar, that is, organized labor. For in the aftermath of reform, the unions which saw their influence at conventions rise most rapidly were in truth white-collar, the American Federation of Teachers, for example, as well as the American Federation of State, County, and Municipal Employees and the Communications Workers of America.[15]

Among issue organizations, in turn, the Moral Majority (and religious evangelicals in general) made a related point about critical attributes in the postreform era. Moreover, the Moral Majority made that point all the more strongly because it lacked the income, education, and technical skills found in white-collar organized interests. Despite that, the Moral Majority remained diagnostic because of the emotional intensity and substantive narrowness—the two were clearly related—of its issue focus. In the postreform world, an issue organization gained hopes for significant advantage precisely as it did *not* represent all the varied aspects of its members' lives nor all the range of concerns which might characterize a given individual. A narrow focus on matters of little interest to members could still render a group irrelevant, of course. But a narrow focus on matters of central importance to these members—and centrality was surely enhanced by a narrowed focus—could radically improve the prospects of a group, even in the absence of other assets.

The fact that certain key characteristics could provide additional advantage to specific organized interests within the general interested advance had a second implication, one affecting the universe of such groups present at the convention. For if these characteristics were critical to individual group success in the postreform environment, then not only should groups which possessed them be more successful in nominating politics but those groups as a collectivity should become a larger and larger share of the national party convention, and the convention should thus be further reconstituted. The rise of the organized interests was a central fact of delegate selection. The extra advantage accruing to organizations with these key characteristics was a major elaboration on that fact. The product for the resulting collectivity of delegates, the composite convention, should almost inevitably have been an additionally rapid growth of the population of delegates from these organizations.

In truth, the entire constellation of such groups in the larger society may well have been shifting in the same direction.[16] Regardless, the character of those groups which appeared in the convention seemed destined to change in precisely this way—and in fact appeared to do so. Thus one could look out at the Republican and Democratic conventions of 1980, beyond the Moral Majority and the NEA, and see additional representatives of these same developments. Among Republican issue organizations, for example, there were the National Right-to-Life Committee, opposing abortion, and the Congressional Club, propagating conservative ideology. Among interest groups, there were the National Rifle Association, protecting gun owners, and the Sagebrush Coalition, lobbying for a different approach to federal lands. Among Democratic issue organizations, there were the Campaign for Safe Energy, a leading solar lobby, and the Democratic Socialists, endorsing a left-wing social vision. Among interest groups, there were the National Organization for Women, promoting feminism, and the National Gay Rights Organization, fostering homosexual rights.

A different way to see the same phenomenon is to look at the fate of the major interests traditionally associated with the official parties, namely big (corporate) business for the Republicans, big (organized) labor for the Democrats.[17] Corporate leaders had probably never been as consequential at Republican conventions as those with a nostalgia for prereform politics were prone to recall. At least in the postwar period, those businessmen who did surface at Republican conventions had ordinarily been drawn from small-business interests. Corporate leaders, by contrast, had relied largely on party officials for an indirect (but real) influence, because these officials respected their ability to raise money for the general election campaign and saw them as the sort of ideological moderates whom the party would have to hold if it were to win the election. In the aftermath of party reform, however, corporate leaders faced the same sort of calculus as party officials— greater difficulty mobilizing members, more competition for delegate slots, less predictability in the outcome—without even the countervailing advantages of expertise and social connection which came with the holding of party office. As a result, they largely disappeared from the convention.

The fate of organized labor at Democratic conventions was a different and more complex affair. Nevertheless, at bottom, the same pattern applied. Before reform, labor too had relied for its influence on party officials, who respected its ability to help mount the general election campaign and who saw its members as crucial to electoral victory. In such a world, labor did not need a massive convention presence. Attendance by key officials from the national AFL-CIO, their state AFL counterparts, and leaders of the individual unions (national, state, and local) was entirely sufficient to remind party officials of the importance of organized labor. After reform, on the other hand, and unlike corporate business, organized labor did not suffer diminution in the raw total of its delegates. Indeed, allowing for variation from year to year, that total jumped.[18]

Yet only once after 1968, for the Mondale nominating campaign of 1984, were the national AFL-CIO and its political arm, COPE, able to rally behind a presidential contender and help shape the politics of nomination. As a result, those labor delegates who did increasingly reach the convention were split among available candidates and hence among available candidate loyalties; they were uncoordinated in their initial participation; and they often shared concerns and even memberships with the other, newly advantaged, interested partisans. These delegates could still function like the delegates from those other organizations at the convention, that is, they could still mount specific interest group initiatives within the convention hall. But they did not ordinarily manage to function like these organizations in shaping the politics of presidential nomination, much less to buttress the official party in that politics. And their independent initiatives at the convention were more likely to reinforce the behavior of those other newly advantaged delegates and actually to injure the eventual nominee than they were to moderate convention behavior and focus other delegates on the November election.

Institutionalized Constraints on the Advance of the Organized Interests

The onrush of the organized interests in the politics of presidential nomination, and the further rise of certain favored organizations within that general movement, was still not a uniform process. Said differently, even possession of the ideal organizational characteristics, intelligently managed, did not guarantee individual victory in any given area or collective victory in any given year. There were some clear procedural constraints on any uniform advance of the organized interests, in a differentiated pattern of institutional arrangements for delegate selection. Indeed, the Republican party retained some of the older, party-based institutions, and states which used these were reliably less kind to the interested partisans. The Democratic party had dispensed with such institutions, but perhaps surprisingly, distinctions within the candidate-based institutions which replaced them also made a difference to the aggregate fate of the organized interests. Beyond these immediate procedural constraints, there were inherent limitations and contributions to the success of any specific organization from the peculiar course of nominating politics. In the postreform world, the fate of an organized interest was inevitably and intimately tied to the fate of the candidate carrying its banner, and those candidate fates varied enormously—unexpectedly, idiosyncratically, and kaleido-scopically.

While the thrust of reform had been overwhelmingly in the direction of candidate-based institutions, the Republican party had retained some party-based arrangements. By definition—by positional advantage—these institutions were more charitable to the official party, leaving less room for the party to be displaced by other organizations and more room for party officials to shape the success of interested partisans even then. The fate of the religious evangelicals in the contest of 1980 was not the ideal measure of the practical impact of these advantages, since a "decision for Christ" was an imprecise indicator of connection to groups such as the Moral Majority and since the minority of states using party-based institutions was itself not a random sample of the party. Nevertheless, a consistent difference in char-itability toward the organized interests did surface among Republicans in 1980, consistent with the notion that the obvious formal advantages and liabilities inherent in basic plans for delegate selection would be realized in the practical politics of presidential nomination. Accord-ingly, party-based arrangements were indeed less kind to religious evangelicals than were candidate-based counterparts. (See Table 4.1.)

Perhaps more surprisingly, clear differences in institutional contri-

Table 4.1.   Basic institutional forms and the fate of the interested partisans: The Republicans, 1980

Institutional form	Percent of delegates with a "decision for Christ"	
Party-based	22	(N = 216)
Candidate-based	29	(N = 1,557)

Source: Campaign '80 CBS News, *Delegate Handbook: 1980 Republican National Convention, July 14–17* (New York: CBS News, 1980).

bution to the rise of the organized interests were present in the Democratic party too despite the demise of party-based institutions there. Only candidate primaries and participatory conventions, the candidate-based plans for delegate selection, remained in the party by 1980. Yet even these proved to have a differential impact on the rise of the interested partisans. Procedurally, participatory conventions were potentially more responsive to nonparty interests, because they allowed the organized interests to secure their representation directly, by selecting their own members as national convention delegates. Candidate primaries, by comparison, more often forced these interests to work through the presidential candidate and his campaign. This inherently different ability to take advantage of their own mobilization was practically apparent in 1980, when the percentage of NEA delegates chosen in states with participatory conventions was more than twice as high as in states with candidate primaries. (See Table 4.2.)

A different kind of constraint, always present but never institutionalized in the same sense, came from the newly central role of candidate campaigns. In a world of candidate-based institutions for delegate selection, along with independent, national, candidate-based campaigns, the links between individual candidates and specific organized interests were evidently critical to the fate of those interests. Different candidates were differentially attractive to any given interest; different interests were differentially attractive to any given candidate. Moreover, groups and organizations which tried to ignore this fundamental fact and disperse their attention risked ending up with little support in the camp of anyone, including the eventual winner. As a result, interest groups and issue organizations aligned their fortunes with a few candidates—often only one—and the fate of their key can-

Table 4.2.   Reformed institutions and the interested partisans: The Democrats, 1980

Institutional form	Percent of delegates who were members of NEA	
Participatory conventions	15.4	(N = 785)
Candidate primaries	6.5	(N = 2,170)

Source: Published releases by the National Education Association, including especially two addenda to "Memo to Political Editors and Writers" (cited in note 9), "Delegates and Alternates," 24 pp., and "Addendum—Revisions—Delegate Roster," 1 p.

Table 4.3.   Candidate fortunes and the interested partisans:
                The Democrats, 1980

Candidate fortunes	Percent of delegates who were members of NEA	
Carter victories[a]	10.9	(N = 2,099)
Kennedy victories[b]	5.5	(N = 1,203)

Source: Same as Table 4.2.
   a. Includes all states where the first tally after selection of the full delegation showed a Carter majority.
   b. Includes all states where the first tally after selection of the full delegation showed a Kennedy lead (with no Carter majority).

didate or candidates was central to their own success. Active support from significant organized interests did improve the prospects of the candidate, of course. Yet no group was even approximately able to guarantee the nomination of the candidate of its choice, and even collective group support was only one factor among many in the success of individual contenders.

These candidate constraints were present even in the most extreme cases, as in the Democratic contest of 1980, where the NEA was often the organizational core of the Carter campaign and where the evolving Carter renomination in turn did pull the NEA along in many areas. Despite that, the success of the NEA in collecting delegates was noticeably greater in the states Carter carried than in states which went to his rival, Edward Kennedy. (See Table 4.3.) In fact both broad forms of constraint on the interested advance, formal constraints from the institutions of delegate selection and informal constraints from the politics of presidential nomination, were clearly present and clearly cumulative in the presidential politics of 1980. Kennedy failed to carry enough states using participatory conventions to add that category to the comparison, but the other available categories—participatory conventions won by Carter, candidate primaries won by Carter, and candidate primaries won by Kennedy—produced percentages of NEA delegates in precisely that order, as the pattern of inherent constraints suggested they would. (See Table 4.4.)

The abstract potential and concrete presence of various constraints on the rise of the organized interests did not gainsay their general advance or the shift to interested partisans as convention delegates.

More to the point, the presence of both formal and informal channeling devices did not neutralize the simultaneous impact of varying levels of inherent strength on the part of the interest groups in question. For example, when the fifty states were divided into rough quartiles according to per capita membership in the NEA, those quartiles were perfectly aligned with ultimate success in garnering convention delegates, despite varying institutional forms and candidate outcomes. (See Table 4.5.) Indeed, although this further division yielded numerous categories with too few states for comparison, the patterns at the extremes were additionally striking. When those states which used a participatory convention, were carried by Carter, and were very strong for the NEA were compared with their opposite numbers— primary states won by Kennedy with very weak NEA presence—the range in percentage of NEA delegates was a factor of almost sixteen to one. (See Table 4.6.)

The Official Party as an Organized Interest

The larger developments of which the National Education Association and the Moral Majority were only particularly pointed examples were hardly hidden from the participants in the politics of presidential selection. The candidates knew about these developments; they, after all, had to put together reformed nominating campaigns. The leaders of various organized interests knew about them too; their organizations attempted to profit from the changed context. Candidates might lament the political price of reformed nominations. Leaders of the organized interests might enjoy their newly central role or bewail their inability to achieve it. But both sets of actors were fully, if at first not self-consciously, aware of the changing shape of the political world.

It is not surprising, however, that those who knew best, or at least most painfully, about this transformation were party officials. Whether they had been dumped quickly and dramatically, as in the Democratic party, or constricted in a less perceptible and more complex fashion, as in the Republican party, these actors knew at a minimum that the official party was no longer serving as the central element in the mounting of nomination campaigns. Most of them knew as well that party officials were playing a much less central role in the national conventions—some because they had been personally dumped. Beyond that knowledge, many shared the view that the organizations and delegates which had become more consequential were far more concerned

Table 4.4. Institutional forms, candidate fortunes, and the interested
partisans: The Democrats, 1980

Institutions and victors	Percent of delegates who were members of NEA	
Carter conventions	14.9	(N = 708)
Carter primaries	8.8	(N = 1,391)
Kennedy primaries	5.0	(N = 1,126)

Source: Same as Table 4.2.

Table 4.5. Organizational strength and the interested partisans:
The Democrats, 1980

NEA strength in states	Percent of delegates who were members of NEA	
Very strong	13.7	(N = 513)
Strong	11.3	(N = 969)
Weak	7.6	(N = 1,032)
Very weak	5.5	(N = 762)

Source: Same as Table 4.2. Membership quartiles were developed from *N.E.A.
Handbook, 1979–80* (Washington, D.C.: National Education Association, 1979).
Because of tied rankings, these "quartiles" actually contain 10, 14, 16, and 10 states,
respectively, as measured by total membership per state population.

Table 4.6. Extreme cases in constraints on the interested partisans:
The Democrats, 1980

Examples	Percent of delegates who were members of NEA	
Convention states won by Carter with very strong NEA	22.1	(N = 156)
Primary states won by Kennedy with very weak NEA	1.4	(N = 324)

Source: Same as Table 4.2.

with the well-being of their particular interest or issue than with the well being of the party or even of its nominee—and were often willing to use the convention itself to pursue that narrow but intense definition of well-being.

Party officials, on the other hand, were not without assets for an attempt to fight back. Party office, however fully or sparsely filled, did continue in every locality. Many individual officeholders continued as well, as local party leaders if no longer as national convention delegates. While it did take these individuals an election or two to appreciate the severity of their plight, and to develop strategies to address the situation, they had already begun to do precisely that by the interim between the presidential elections of 1976 and 1980. The decline had gone much further on the Democratic side, so that solutions there had to be much more formal and explicit. Yet both parties did address the issue very practically, and both did meet with some practical success. Indeed, in the kind of parallel development which often characterized the parties in the postreform period—a similar structural problem, a similar structural response, adapted for the characteristics peculiar to one party—both in effect turned to formal positional advantage. For the Democrats, this meant guaranteeing a sharply expanded, direct, ex officio representation. For the Republicans, it meant shoring up the place of the party in the slating of delegate contenders, a maneuver at once more conservative and far more extreme than anything on the Democratic side.

Nevertheless, even when these solutions had taken effect, in 1980 and then more extensively in 1984, their principal impact was to rebalance the affiliations of delegates within the convention rather than to reshape the nominating politics which produced most of these delegates. More party officials were ultimately present at both conventions, a clear if limited triumph for institutional engineering. But those officials did not alter the politics of presidential selection leading up to those conventions and thus did little to reverse the advance of the organized interests. In the ultimate irony of counterreform, then, a second effect of this guarded triumph was to confirm the transformation of the official party too, into yet another organized interest. In one year, party officials might operate as an additional restraint on the gains, or at least the behavior, of other interested partisans. In another, they might be dependent on the consent of those other partisans for their warrant to operate at all. What had once been the formal framework and the informal filter for presidential politics, forcing other organized interests to operate through it, had become but one more contender with other major organized interests. If the official party differed in having a potential to brake and channel the concrete gains of other organized interests, it also differed in being dependent on formal guarantees of its own official position in order to have even the potential to exercise that power.

Party Officials as an Interest Group: The Democrats

It was perhaps appropriate that the Democrats, having pioneered the death of positional advantage for party officials and having seen the more thorough eclipse of the official party in nominating campaigns, pioneered the partial restoration of positional advantage too. This effort was never significant enough to restore the official party as the backbone of major campaigns for a nomination—or even to reintroduce it. But it was sufficient to bring some major party and public officials back to the national convention. In the Democratic party, party officials, public officeholders, and their allies struck back through the interim reform commission after 1976, the same arrangement which had contributed so consequentially to their contemporary debasement. In the first halting step, they moved to confer automatic delegate status on a few major positions within their ranks, a move cribbed about at that point by procedural restrictions. When this proved to be formally effective but practically inconsequential, they tried again four years later with a much extended ex officio rule, one which succeeded in adding a larger leaven of party and especially public officeholders to the national convention of 1984.

The Democratic reform commission of 1976–1980 began this move, by noting the rapid and perilous decline of major public officials—governors, senators, and congressional representatives—at the national convention. The argument that these officials were an essential element of the party under any circumstances, because they possessed obvious local constituencies and would be essential to the governmental prowess of any successful president, met a responsive hearing for the first time since 1968. In return, the national commission decided that 10 percent of each state delegation should consist of "add-on" selections; that these should be governors, state party chairs and vice chairs, and senators and representatives; that they should be chosen from an extra allocation, over and above the official delegation totals; and that they should then be pledged to national candidates in precise proportion to the division of presidential preferences in the rest of the delegation.[19]

This move, circumscribed though it was, did stop the erosion of the top state party figures, governors and state chairs, at the national convention. A remarkable 96 percent of all Democratic governors had attended the last prereform convention in 1968, without the benefit of ex officio status.[20] (See Table 4.7.) That figure fell sharply in 1972, and it fell again in 1976. The coming of the add-on provision then stopped this fall, and the governors rebounded as a convention presence in 1980—not to the level of 1968, to be sure, but well above the levels of 1972 and 1976. The chairs of their state parties followed essentially the same trajectory, but the impact effectively stopped with them. The add-on provision did little for lesser state party figures, and, more to the point, it did nothing to stop the disappearance of senators and representatives—who were less favored by the details of the new rule, were often less well tied to continuing statewide politics, did not manage to muscle in to join the very few guaranteed representatives in most states, and were obviously not propelled to the convention through other orthodox political means.

As a result, the succeeding reform commission, more worried than ever about the counterproductive behavior of reformed delegates— in light of the Democratic convention of 1980, at which Kennedy delegates publicly savaged incumbent president Carter—turned back to the problem with a more far-reaching approach. Although the commission actually considered a proposal to make all Democratic senators and representatives automatic delegates, it ultimately settled on the creation of a more heterogeneous class of "superdelegates."[21] These individuals would make up an additional 14 percent of the convention total, over and above the 10 percent add-ons; they would be selected on much more specifically positional grounds; and they

Table 4.7.   Major party and public officials at the convention: The Democrats, 1968–1984

Year	Governors (%)	State chairs (%)	Senators (%)	Representatives (%)
1984	82	94	61	65
1980	72	66	15	13
1976	44	54	18	14
1972	59	58	28	12
1968	96	86	61	32

Source: CBS News briefing books on the coverage of Democratic national conventions for 1968 through 1984. A typical recent volume is CBS News Election and Survey Unit, *CBS News Campaign '84 Democratic National Convention: A Guide to Delegates and Other Participants* (New York: CBS News, 1984).

would, at the time of their selection, not be pledged to any presidential aspirant. Thus at the 1984 convention, the percentage of senators jumped drastically—to the level, in fact, which they had reached in the last prereform convention. Moreover, the percentage of representatives jumped so substantially that it placed them not only on a percentage par with senators (whom they outnumbered in real terms) but well ahead of the level they had reached in the last prereform convention.

On the other hand, the ironies in this apparent and striking statistical success, while less immediately perceptible, were equally impressive. For what this pair of ex officio provisions had effectively done was to recognize the reality of the political status of these top party and public officials and write that reality into party law. In other words, what these provisions had done was to recognize that these officeholders were so enfeebled in the reformed politics of presidential selection, so deprived of formal advantage and so unlikely to restore that advantage informally, that they had to be given special treatment or they would fail to play a consequential role. Yet when they were given that treatment, the result was also to confirm their marginal relevance to the actual politics of presidential selection: some were not chosen until that politics had concluded; the others were still formally and practically outside the crucial contests in the states. All that remained was the hope that these individuals would serve as a force to moderate counterproductive behavior by other delegates at the national convention.

The same raw numbers which trumpeted the return of these officials in fact testified to the sharp change in their effective status in presidential politics and thus to the shift from the official party to the organized interests. For when those public officials who were selected as superdelegates were subtracted from the totals, leaving only those who arrived at the convention through the normal politics of presidential selection, the result was also impressive, but in the opposite direction. Without the superdelegates in these composite figures, the proportion of senators at the national convention had fallen to 5 percent. Without the same advantages but by the same standards, the proportion of representatives had fallen as well, to an inconsequential 4 percent.

These figures, of course, overstate the decline. If the ex officio provision had not existed, some of the senators and representatives who reached the convention as superdelegates would have run through normal political channels, and some would surely have been selected. Yet even when the two populations were treated as a unit in 1984, this huge guaranteed reservoir of public officials had a very limited impact on the actual politics of presidential selection. Many of them did go, early, to Walter Mondale, and that surely enhanced his standing as the front-runner. But both that standing and the contribution of these superdelegates to it surely increased the perception among the general public of Mondale as the creature of special interests and insiders, a perception which was crucial to the rise of Gary Hart as a serious challenger. In one sense, these superdelegates then helped Mondale hold on, by swelling his apparent delegate totals when Hart first upset him in the New Hampshire primary. But in spite of this overwhelming endorsement, Mondale truly was one or two losses from elimination, as even his national staff admitted, and there was no reason to believe that his superdelegates would have done anything other than shift to Hart as a bloc had the challenger been able to secure those additional victories.

It was as a calming influence on the convention itself, then, that these ex officio delegates could even potentially play a more practical and pointed role. Indeed, one of the main arguments for injecting both sets of ex officio delegates, the add-ons and the supers, was that they might restore a concern with the practical, electoral needs of the party. Moreover, by most accounts they did play a version of this (more limited) role, arguing against frivolous dissent and for activities which would support the nominee. Even this effort was not without its detractors, among other delegates who grumbled that the super-delegates were insufficiently concerned with the issues of presidential politics and among reporters who noted that the attendance of these ex officio representatives was well below that of those who had gotten to the convention via normal elective means. Yet quite apart from these alleged virtues and associated vices, the fundamental fact remained: top public and party officeholders were present at the Democratic national convention only because their advocates had succeeded in making a plea for special treatment, as an organized interest.

Party Officials as an Interest Group: The Republicans

The background to delegate selection in the Republican party retained certain major and obvious differences from the Democratic experience. From above, the national party had flirted much less with reform commissions and had never tolerated an independent commission with authority to make changes in advance of the convention itself.[22] From below, the state parties had retained a minority of old-fashioned party-based institutions for delegate selection and presidential nomination. Despite this, the Republican party shared major aspects of the Democratic experience, and these were surely more consequential. The reform currents sweeping the Democratic party had passed through the Republican party too, so that the same overwhelming shift in the fundamental institutions of delegate selection had quickly come to characterize both parties. Inevitably, the same further shift in the character of nominating campaigns, toward independent, national, and personal nominating efforts, had come quickly to characterize the Republican party as well.

Party officials had enjoyed a short period of unconcern about the further effect of all this on their own convention fortunes, because the absence of a serious challenge to the renomination of Richard Nixon had permitted the party to remain a central vehicle for nominating politics in 1972—and party officials to remain comfortably present at the national convention. Many of these officials were shaken from any automatic sense of security in 1976, however, when sitting president Ford, with heavy support from the official party, was almost stopped by challenger Reagan, in a campaign replete with organized interests, producing interest group representatives and independent issue activists as national convention delegates. At that point, on the other hand, the party responded very differently from the Democrats. Rather than look for guarantees of seats at the convention, Republican leaders sought explicitly to shore up their remaining posts in the politics of delegate selection. They settled early on an effort to protect themselves by preserving advantageous rules for the *slating* of delegates, for their nomination to delegate status within reformed institutions. The result was thus less automatic than Democratic provisions for add-ons and superdelegates but was more integral to delegate politicking itself.[23]

Republican party officials and public officeholders had been less damaged by the Reagan insurgency in 1976 than had their Democratic counterparts by the McGovern insurgency of 1972 or the Carter follow-up of 1976, precisely because the Republican contest had been so clear-cut from the beginning. That is, there were two major contenders with clear bases of support, so that those party and public officials who were willing to get involved in the campaign were much better able to judge the apparently obvious local winner and make candidate affiliations accordingly. Although the share of governors did drop in the Republican convention, for example, from 1972 to 1976, this was much less than the earlier Democratic drop-off, from 1968 to 1972. (See Table 4.7.) Moreover and more to the practical point, a second part of the reason why insurgent campaigns were less hard on Republican party officials also became the means by which those officials rallied procedurally to try to limit this change.

In the absence of a sweeping and deliberately systematic, national reform movement, the Republican party had been drawn away from party-based institutions of delegate selection, but it had not seen these reforms extended nearly as far into the process of slating their delegates. In abstract terms, the slating process involves deciding which individuals have the right to stand as delegates for a given presidential candidate, and hence which individuals will go to the national convention if that candidate is locally successful. When the Democratic party banned party-based institutions of delegate selection, it extended this participatory thrust to slating as well: participatory conventions were ordered to abandon the practice of having a single nominating committee to slate delegates at the state convention; candidate primaries were urged to let independent caucuses of candidate supporters do the slating for the subsequent primary.

When the Republican party moved away from party-based institutions of delegate selection, however, it lacked national guidelines for the slating process within reformed institutions. Some states capitalized on this leeway to try to retain a lesser positional advantage for party officials. After 1976, those Republican party leaders who had rallied to President Ford, and indeed many of the party officials (as opposed to the interested partisans) who had rallied to challenger Reagan, affirmed the right of individual state parties to handle the slating process as they saw fit. In doing so, they underlined the possibilities inherent in alternative slating arrangements; indeed, they provided expertise on state practices in that realm. The result was a welter of slating procedures in 1980 and again in 1984—procedures which continued to reserve a far larger role for the official party and party officials than was the Democratic practice.[24]

There was not much room for this variation within participatory conventions, where delegates to the state or district conventions could directly select the national convention delegates. But in candidate primaries, there was a vast array of creative devices for anointing the actual delegates, including devices which consciously attempted to protect party officials. Thus there were states which permitted the Republican state committee or a separate state party caucus to pick the actual delegates, who would then be bound by the result of the primary. There were states where separate participatory conventions *after* the primary could pick the delegates, again binding them to the primary winner but allowing party and public officials to align themselves with that winner and allowing the candidate to organize more effectively his delegate slate. And there were more states whose primaries created delegates who had themselves been put forward by the candidate organizations from centrally developed lists.

It is difficult to measure precisely the cumulative impact of such moves, because formal procedure and actual behavior often differed noticeably. An apparently open participatory convention could effectively be managed by a candidate campaign, just as an apparently centralized slating arrangement could permit substantial public participation—or even be coerced by major organized interests into putting that centralization into *their* hands. What is clearer is that the top offices in the Republican hierarchy, in marked contrast to the situation on the Democratic side, managed to retain their presence at the national convention. (See Table 4.8.) The percent of Republican statewide officials had fallen a bit in 1976, with the first contested effort of the postreform era, but the percent of Republican federal officeholders had not fallen off at all. When the governors and chairs bounced back in 1980, and then back further in 1984, any threat to these major offices appeared to have dissipated.

Unsystematic observers with the experience of multiple Republican

Table 4.8.   Major party and public officials at the convention:
The Republicans, 1968–1984

Year	Governors (%)	State chairs (%)	Senators (%)	Representatives (%)
1984	87	70	53	44
1980	72	66	63	41
1976	69	58	60	36
1972	80	61	50	18
1968	92	74	58	31

Source: CBS News briefing books on the coverage of Republican national conventions for 1968 through 1984. A typical recent volume is CBS News Election and Survey Unit, *CBS News Campaign '84 Republican National Convention: A Guide to Delegates and Other Participants* (New York: CBS News, 1984).

conventions did believe that the percentage of lesser public and especially party officials had fallen off more sharply at Republican conventions in the same period, and there was impressionistic evidence to support them. From one side, almost all observers noted the concomitant rise of the organized interests and their interested partisans, and that rise was so obvious and extensive—at the same time as major public and party officials were being saved—that something had to give. From the other side, when these lesser party officials made a comeback at the 1984 convention—in an uncontested renomination of a sitting president who used the official party as his nominating vehicle and who urged state party officials to use delegate status as a reward for long-standing service—this comeback confirmed their previously diminished state. But in any case, neither this apparent decline nor the evident rise of the interested partisans was sufficient to remove *major* public and party officials, thanks in large part to explicit procedural arrangements. These arrangements were more extreme than their Democratic counterparts in their practical contribution to the power of party officials. They were less extreme in their ultimate formal guarantees. But they were similar in recognizing the official party as yet another organized interest.

The Transformation of the Parties in Convention

A loosening of major constraints which pulled the convention toward the political center had been one of the major impacts of the decline of party officials as convention delegates in both parties. Despite their historical restraining influence, those officials had always been more ideologically extreme than their rank-and-file constituents, since they were more interested in a broader range of political issues and since consistency among these issues mattered more to these individuals. But they had also been pulled back toward the political center by the intrinsic organizational requirements of party office—to build broad-based coalitions and to elect an array of party candidates. The decline of these officials inevitably loosened these constraints. The coming of the interested partisans as a replacement then pulled the convention further off toward the extremes.

Once more, hindsight suggests that this was a logical outcome.[25] Or at least, the interested partisans faced a very different set of organizational incentives than did party officials. For the archetypal party official, issues could matter, often intensely, but an electoral loss was a personal loss too. For the archetypal interested partisan, on the other hand, electoral victory could matter, often intensely as well, but if that victory did not bring advantage to the interest group or issue organization—indeed, if the convention did not bring the first concrete steps toward that advantage—then victory could still be a personal waste. This attitude was reinforced in the politics of presidential nomination, when interested partisans were slated for subsequent election only as they were able to convey an intense attachment to their group or organization. It was further reinforced at the convention itself, when the attainment of programmatic goals, ranging from adoption of a platform plank to selection of a sympathetic vice president, often required logrolling with other interested partisans—so that the more intense ideological interests often came to the support of one another.

In truth, this tendency for interested partisans to pull the convention out from the political center, without much countervailing pressure to hold them within bounds, was probably reinforced even more fundamentally by the social environment from which such delegates sprang. That is, a politics which ordinarily revolved around the promotion of issues rather than the organization of campaigns predisposed most of the interested partisans to care more about (usually more extreme) political positions. Even then, all this might not have pulled the conventions away from the center if the organized interests had been randomly distributed between the parties, seeking advantages of brokerage without regard to other concerns. Such interests, however, traditional partisan interests as well as their newly advantaged counterparts, were much more likely to be attracted to one party than the other on programmatic grounds, so that their composite effect was indeed to capitalize on the weakened role of party officials and to pull the conventions toward the political extremes.

The fact that the Republican convention, with its reliably greater role for party officials, did not hew any closer to the political center was the final aspect of this change in the convention as a composite environment. Said differently, the comparatively stronger position of party officials in the presidential politics of the Republican party gained further interest precisely because it did not contribute the moderating effect which counterreform theorists on the Democratic side had predicted—had predicated there. Some of the explanation for this surprise lay in the political regions from which these officials came, and this part of the explanation had implications for both parties. Throughout the postwar period (and in fact for much longer), each party had operated in large geographic areas where it was reliably in the minority. In those areas, party officials had always needed to be motivated by something other than the building of coalitions and the capture of public offices. Family background and social solidarity had provided some substitute for concrete rewards, but in these permanent minority areas—the South for the Republicans, the plains states and mountains for the Democrats—programmatic concerns and abstract ideology had long had to function as a major incentive too. Party officials from those areas, then, in contrast to their more successful colleagues, had never been drawn toward the political center by organizational considerations.

This fact was probably of major additional consequence in the post-reform Republican party. One of its biggest changes was the growth, gradual and halting though it was, of a seriously organized Republican party in the South.[26] Well into the 1950s—certainly at the last Republican convention actually to make a nomination, in 1952—the southern Republican party was largely a fiction used to channel federal appointments and secure convention delegates. After the 1950s, however, a real party—a real hierarchy of party offices, at least—began to take hold, and ideology, very conservative ideology, was a necessary tool in putting it together. As that newly energized party hierarchy began to acquire national convention delegates, then, those delegates were unlikely to help pull the party toward the political center, even though they represented a partial triumph for party officials over interested partisans.

But at a second level, the experience of southern Republicans, and probably of plains and western Democrats too, suggests a vision of the future for both parties. As the concrete rewards which can be dispensed by party officials continue to decline, and as the formal prerogatives of those officials in nominations to public office disappear almost entirely, the party as an organization will increasingly need considerations of ideology, or at least strong attachments to organized interests, to see that party office is filled and party work accomplished. As parties become more dependent on ideology and related concerns, the distinctions between party officials and the other interested partisans should narrow. They should not disappear, since organizational responsibilities will remain distinct. But they should narrow, as incentives become similar and, indeed, as the same individuals move back and forth. The postreform era, then, has seen a shift in convention participants, from party officials to interested partisans. The attempt at a reaction has been partially successful, albeit by converting the official party into yet another organized interest. But success or failure in protecting formal party advantages in that role, finally, is likely to have less and less consequence for internal convention politics as time passes and as the parties themselves continue to change.

5 | The Convention and the Election: The Structure of Conflict inside the Hall

While the nomination was departing from the convention and disappearing into the process of delegate selection, the convention was also acquiring activities previously located elsewhere. Indeed, these were if anything more crucial than they had previously been to the fate of a candidate who was now being anointed rather than selected at the convention proper. In the most important example of this development, many of the very same forces which had helped to remove the nomination from the convention—the decline of political parties as electoral organizations, the rise of the national media of information, and the spread of partisan independence in the general public—made the convention ever more crucial for the launching of the general election campaign. They made it an obvious place to pull together the diverse elements which would have to work in concert to elect the chosen candidate. They made it *the* obvious place to introduce that candidate, his party, and their program to the general public, under conditions which could not be recreated subsequently. In fact, they combined to guarantee that a potentially influential portrait of nominee, party, and program would be presented to the public whether these supporting activities were successfully managed or not.

Ironically, however, the changing cast of participants, also part and parcel of the reforms which had banished the nomination but made the launching of the general election campaign considerably more important, made successful execution of that launching more difficult. For what the nationalization of presidential politics, in concert with reform in the process of delegate selection, had really done to the convention was to replace a struggle over the construction of a nominating majority with a struggle over the presentation—and publicizing—of the central goals of *all* the major convention participants. The most widely recognized of these goals, of course, was the felicitous launching of the general election campaign. Just as the most influential participants were inevitably the nominee and his entourage, as supplemented by top convention officials. But any number of other convention participants were also free to try to use the convention to launch or extend their major projects, whatever those might be. The identity of these other participants, changing in its quadrennial detail but not in its general character, was thus the key to recurring convention conflict, just as the goals of these other participants, ranging from the launching of a future presidential candidacy to the furthering of specific current policy campaigns, provided the alternative substance for recurring convention struggles.

Thus when it came to the introduction of the nominee, his party, and their program to the general public via the national party convention, the successful candidate and top party officials were often pitted against major factions within the convention rank and file. Sometimes this key internal division crystallized around the split between those who supported the eventual winner and those who supported losing opponents for the nomination. When it surfaced, such a conflict between nominee and one or more challengers was invariably crucial to the place of convention proceedings in the general election campaign. Sometimes, however, the key internal division crystallized around the split between those who were principally concerned with the electoral interests of the official party and those who were principally concerned with the policy desires of issue organizations and interest groups. While it could not by itself achieve the impact of a full-blown candidate struggle, this conflict between a leadership already focusing on the general election and a rank and file still attempting to cap the nominating campaign powerfully conditioned the nominee's ability to use the convention for his own electoral purposes, because it inevitably absorbed time and resources which could otherwise go to these efforts.

Accordingly, this key internal division, whatever its content, became the central means of—and the central obstacle to—using the national convention to pursue the goals of any and all convention actors, be they front-runners, challengers, party leaders, group representatives, issue activists, or all of those. The particular incarnation of this division became the basis for internal conflict at each individual convention. The nature of attempts to manipulate this division gave the convention both its programmatic and its procedural substance. As a result, the specific incarnation of this division presented the central strategic problem of each reformed national party convention for all concerned. Finally, the character of the resolution of this conflict became the pivotal direct factor shaping the contribution of any individual convention to the fate of its presidential nominee in November.

All such conflict was probably exaggerated by the tendency of both parties to increase the raw size of national party conventions, with the goal of spreading the rewards of delegate status but with the effect of further lessening interpersonal controls on conflict. Nevertheless, the first postreform conventions already showed the possibilities inherent in recurring bases of conflict, at what were perhaps their polar opposite extremes. In 1972, a Democratic convention featuring deep divisions between the nominee and his challengers and between the nominee and some of his own delegates was paired with a Republican convention featuring little evident conflict in either area. Yet only four years later, it was the Republican convention which manifested the major candidate conflict, along with exacerbating issue divisions, while the Democratic convention escaped candidate splits entirely and surfaced only minor issue conflicts to fuel its limited struggles. As a result, this second pair of conventions confirmed both the reformed structure of convention politics and the fact that this politics had arrived on both sides of the political aisle.

Beyond confirming the likely structure of conflict at subsequent party gatherings, the first four conventions of the postreform period raised interpretive questions all their own. If the nomination was effectively settled before the convention assembled, why should internal conflict over candidate preferences persist? If that conflict did continue, and if it was frequently augmented by divisions between the convention leadership and the rank and file, why did the nomination, especially in a close convention, not slip back into doubt? Ironically, the answers to both these questions lay in the institutionalization of conflict on the way to a nomination. Seen one way, it was the gradual structuring of this conflict, the gradual deepening of its divisions, which often propelled candidate contests into the convention and then interfered with the efforts of successful candidates to use the convention to launch the general election campaign. But seen another way, the same dynamic which reinforced these candidate divisions effectively prevented post-reform conventions from resuming an independent role in the nomination, thereby choking off any resurgence of their historically central activity.

New Activities for an Old Institution

No one set out to replace the nomination as the central focus of the national party convention. No one had set out to remove the nomination from the convention, and there was probably no need for any single, major activity to replace it when it disappeared. The delegates could still certify a nominee whose majority was actually created in the course of selecting those delegates. They could still pursue the other regularized activities which had grown up over time around the nomination—on credentials, rules, and platform. The convention, in short, could evidently continue without making the nomination. Indeed, it could obviously generate activity sufficient to absorb the time of its delegates, and even conflict sufficient to absorb their energy. If its participants had not lost the nomination through conscious decision, they surely did not need to replace it through any more deliberate effort.

On the other hand, some of the very factors which had helped remove the nomination from the convention did begin to augment another major activity—effectively in its place. That activity was the launching of the general election campaign. In short order, the mere possibility of emphasizing this launching had given rise to an intricate ballet over convention products: party officials discovered that their institution could be used to benefit the general election campaign; other convention participants learned that the convention could be used to benefit their more personal goals and causes; and party officials then looked for strategies which would emphasize the campaign rather than these other goals. In short order as well, this struggle by all the major actors to use the convention began to acquire regular contours, with predictable sorts of divisions inside the convention and predictable patterns of politicking which emanated from those divisions.

In one sense the national party convention had always been integral to the launching of the general election campaign. The nominee of each major party was either confirmed or created there; that act marked the transition from the contest over a nomination to the contest for ultimate general election. In a different and more practical sense, however, the role of the convention in inaugurating the general election campaign grew enormously as the nomination receded. A series of shifts in the contours of national politics meant that the nominee could be propelled toward the presidency via the national party convention, and thus could suffer debilitating initial disadvantage if he failed to secure appropriate propulsion. At the same time a different aspect of that same nationalization of presidential politics implied that the institutional mechanics now existed to launch this candidacy in the requisite manner, if party and campaign leaders could manage convention conflict in a fashion permitting them to utilize those mechanics.

The change from the convention as the capstone of the nominating contest to the convention as a springboard for the general election campaign is a surprisingly recent phenomenon. It was not, for example, until 1932 that a Democratic nominee for president actually appeared before his party convention to accept the nomination personally. The Whig convention of 1844 had invited its nominee, Henry Clay, to do precisely that. But Clay had declined, saying that the practice offended his sense of propriety, and every national convention thereafter had followed this tradition—until Franklin D. Roosevelt shattered it for the Democrats in 1932 and until Thomas E. Dewey broke it for the Republicans in 1944.[1] The appearance of the newly crowned nominee was, of course, only one premature indicator of the grand change to come. More to the point in creating that change were the same factors from the nationalization of politics which were simultaneously thrusting the nomination further back into the process of delegate selection. On the one hand, these factors were emptying the convention of its previously central—indeed, its defining—activity. But on the other, they were creating not just the need but also the means to convert the convention into a launching pad for the general election.

From one side, the decline of strong electioneering organizations among the political parties, along with the concomitant decay of partisan loyalties in the general public, automatically increased the need to use the national party convention, or at least the real advantage in being able to use it, to present both the candidate and his party to the general public. For if the party as an organization was less capable of delivering that public to the nominee, and if the public as individuals was less inherently responsive to its own partisan leanings, the convention remained as one of the only regular, institutionalized means for rallying that public to a partisan choice. Simultaneously, in a nominating process which was increasingly candidate-based, the convention became the first real opportunity to try to bring the candidate and party officials—those who still mattered—together for the election campaign to follow, although this was inevitably a less consequential activity in an era of weaker party organizations and weaker partisan loyalties.

From the other side, the rise of multiple, explicitly national media of information, and especially the coming of gavel-to-gavel televised coverage of conventions, provided a coordinate opportunity to use the convention to advertise the nominee and his party.[2] Again, this general development, the increase in the number of fully national news media offering comprehensive treatment of the national party convention, had been central to moving the nomination out of the convention. But its specific manifestations were also inherently the means—the convention had always been the implicit opportunity—to introduce the nominee to the general public in the most advantageous way possible. These means had actually existed at least since the coming of gavel-to-gavel *radio* coverage in the 1920s. But in the years when the construction of a nominating majority was still the central business of the national party convention, that construction had necessarily been the central focus of everyone, including reporters. Only after the nomination had departed could party and candidate strategists think about using these reporters to begin the campaign to elect the team which they had just formalistically nominated.

Launching the General Election Campaign

So, launching the general election campaign became an increasingly important activity for the national party convention. This would have been true by subtraction alone, that is, it would have been true merely because the convention continued on, while party organizations and partisan loyalties declined. But it became true by addition as well, because an increasingly national news media, especially as embodied in full and national, television coverage, became the means by which public presentations at the convention (and press reports of these and other events) could be turned explicitly to the task of advertising the candidate, his party, and their program. Finally, to this increased need and this increased technical capability was added an essential institutional precondition, the departure of the nomination. A reliably huge national audience—a national *viewing* audience, by this time—could thus be addressed by the convention principals on behalf of their preferred focus, and few were likely to overlook the opportunity.

Party officials had always been concerned about the impact of the convention on the general public, through events occurring at the convention and through coverage of these events by national news media. This concern, however, had necessarily been subordinated to a focus on the construction of a nominating majority when that was still a possible convention occurrence. These officials did not immediately recognize the disappearance of the nomination or the increased opportunity for publicizing the nominee and his program which that disappearance provided. Yet their concern with convention impact did continue unabated. They did, in turn, find themselves in an environment where a concentrated effort at electoral publicity was increasingly possible. Accordingly, they pushed ahead with that effort. Indeed, and not surprisingly, it moved quickly to the center of their convention planning.

Advertising aimed at the candidate, and at his prospects in the general election, was inevitably the heart of any such maneuvering, especially because the process of delegate selection had shifted to feature the candidate rather than the party. Yet the possibility of using the convention and convention coverage to publicize the party too was certainly not absent from the minds of top party officials, or of most nominees, who could see obvious ways to have good publicity for the party rebound to improve their personal prospects. Political parties, unlike executives, legislatures, or courts, are intrinsically difficult to symbolize as active governmental institutions. American parties, often little more than skeletal hierarchies of offices with a party *label*, are probably more difficult than most in this regard. As a result, national party conventions became an additional opportunity—and here perhaps the only opportunity—to display the party as an institution to the American people.

Conventions, accordingly, became more than just a way to introduce a presidential candidate: they became the means to reintroduce an entire, composite political party. This involved an attempt to present and underline a party platform, of course. Of equal or greater importance, it involved an attempt to sketch out a party constituency, that collection of groups and individuals which party leaders judged to be the rightful body of party supporters, the people who "ought" to vote for the candidate of this party if they interpreted appropriately where their best interests lay. Moreover, by the early 1950s, with the coming of nationwide voter surveys, there was actually some objective evidence that conventions were indeed making these introductions and emphasizing these themes, whether candidates and party leaders orchestrated them consciously for that purpose or not.

Again, there is no reason to believe that conventions were not influencing the decisions of some voters well before there was survey evidence to support the possibility. A disastrous convention, such as the Democratic debacle of 1924, which ran to 103 ballots, must have convinced many voters that the party was unlikely to win—and perhaps unable to govern. An electric convention, such as the Republican gathering of 1940, which nominated Wendell Willkie after a whirlwind campaign that did not even begin until the primaries had ended, must have made Willkie a more serious alternative even if he did ultimately fail to unseat President Franklin Roosevelt.[3] Yet the departure of the nomination from the national convention coincided almost exactly with the rise of scientific sampling for the general public. Such samples were never thereafter to lack a significant segment of this general public which claimed that its voting decision was reached during the convention.

In fact, from 1952, the last of the multiballot conventions and the last of those actually to make (rather than merely to ratify) a presidential nomination, through 1984, approximately one American in five claimed to reach a specific voting decision—Republican, Democratic, or neither—during this quadrennial gathering. (See Table 5.1.)[4] These numbers have only a spurious precision; some of those who believed that they had reached a decision during the convention, for example, had surely reached it earlier, merely confirming their impulse while the convention was in progress. Likewise, some of those who believed that they had reached a decision after the convention had surely been predisposed while the convention was unfolding and had merely confirmed that impulse in the convention aftermath. More important were two other, apparently inescapable conclusions. First, some substantial number of Americans did invariably reach a presidential decision during every national party convention. And second, the convention represented one of the few extensively and nationally covered political events directly under the auspices and management of the political parties.

On the average, a fifth or more of the population believed that they had reached a voting decision during this national coverage. If their reports were not to be taken at face value, it was also true that any factors which reduced this figure from one side probably increased it from the other, since the convention sat in the temporal middle of the process of presidential selection. Thus if the flow of politics during a presidential year meant that many of those who believed that they had decided during the convention had really decided in the months and weeks before, only to have their decision confirmed there, that same flow probably meant that many of those who believed that they had decided after the convention had really made their commitment *during* its proceedings, only to have that commitment confirmed thereafter, too. In any case, significantly less than one-fifth of the general public—if that was the accurate, reduced figure—was still sufficient to determine many elections.

Perhaps even more to the point, however, the convention represented one of the few direct opportunities for party leaders to use national press coverage to increase the number of Americans deciding in their favor to its practical maximum. Even if the convention was only capable of locking in some earlier decisions and shaking others, thus making them dependent on the subsequent campaign, that was still a substantial impact—and a major political opportunity. *Whatever* additional Americans could then be fully and finally captured while

Table 5.1. The timing of decisions on the vote

	Percent of decisions		
Year	Before convention	During convention	After convention
1984	51	17	31
1980	40	18	40
1976	33	20	45
1972	43	17	35
1968	33	22	38
1964	40	25	33
1960	30	30	36
1956	57	18	21
1952	34	31	31

Source: Taken directly from "Table 6.56: Time of Presidential Vote Decision," in Miller, Miller, and Schneider, comps., *American National Election Studies Data Sourcebook 1952–1978*, p. 380, as supplemented by *American National Election Study 1980: Pre- and Post-election Surveys* (Ann Arbor, Mich.: Inter-university Consortium for Political and Social Research, 1982), p. 596, and *American National Election Study 1984: Pre- and Post-election Survey File* (Ann Arbor, Mich.: Inter-university Consortium for Political and Social Research, 1986), p. 417.

the convention unfolded were thus a serendipitous dividend and made the potential reward for a successfully orchestrated convention great indeed. In any case, in a competitive context, neither candidates nor party leaders could have been expected to abjure whatever advantages they could squeeze from these ambiguous, indirect, but potentially impressive considerations.

The Struggle to Use the Convention

An attempt to orchestrate the convention, from start to finish and top to bottom, was thus an obvious strategic goal for high party officials and the national staff of the successful candidate. Ordinarily, these two groups worked easily together toward that goal, because party officials—even though they often predated the candidate in national party affairs and even if that candidate had not been the favorite of the official party in the nominating contest—still had a heavy stake in his subsequent success, through numerous other public offices around the country and often through their own positions in party affairs. Despite this easy, incipient cooperation, however, they rarely had a free hand for their intended convention plan. For while their ability to bend the convention toward the general election campaign was growing in principle, and while their awareness of that ability was growing in practice, the ability of others to use the convention toward *their* goals, and indeed their conscious awareness of *that* ability, was similarly on the rise.

As with many other convention developments, the tendency of factions within the convention to try to use that gathering to advance their own central concerns was not strictly a postreform phenomenon. Some candidate operations had always come to the current convention with an eye on some future gathering, just as some organized interests had attended with more of an eye to advancing—or at least publicizing—their particular causes. But when the nomination had been the centerpiece of convention proceedings, these other activities were at least more frequently pursued through efforts to influence the nomination.[5] Moreover, although these activities could still, in principle, have been pursued independently, the focus of other delegates and of the news media on the central struggle for a nomination had inherently limited attention to other concerns. Accordingly, when the nomination was no longer the convention centerpiece but while extended, live, and national coverage of the convention was nevertheless available, the prospects for these other efforts inherently increased.

Such developments made the modern era much kinder to those who intended to use the convention to advance their own "campaigns," whatever the focus of these might be. Yet even if this had not been the case, the postreform era would probably have been characterized much more frequently by these attempts, thanks to the associated shift in the nature of convention delegates. For when the composition of the convention began to move from party officeholders to independent issue activists and interest group representatives, the stage was set for more extended efforts on behalf of candidates or causes not directly related to the current nomination. The newly ascendant delegates, after all, were in large part motivated to participate in presidential politics by these additional, nonnominating factors. When they arrived at the convention, they could hardly be expected to forswear what had motivated them all along. When the reformed convention then proved to be inherently more facilitative of such efforts—by anyone—these efforts in turn could be expected to increase.

As a result, there was a tremendous variety to internal convention conflict in the postreform era, even though the central decision was apparently settled, and known, in advance.[6] Most of this conflict could be traced to two basic sources, the division among the remaining candidates and the division between convention leaders and delegate factions, but that fact did not prevent the individual contributors to the conflict or its particular mix from varying tremendously from convention to convention. Perhaps as surprising as the persistence of this extended internal conflict into the postreform era was the fact that the overall level of conflict tended to move toward one extreme or the other. That is, either internal conflict expanded to reach into most formal activities at the convention, or that conflict was quickly defused, dismissed, and set aside in favor of an ostentatious celebration.

This dichotomy too was probably a direct product of the shift in the central activity of the convention. Or at least, if the emerging nominee was sufficiently dominant as the convention opened, he had good reason to tamp down the contrary desires of the other contestants and to focus the entire convention on the general election, just as supporters of the other remaining candidates, or of causes other than a fruitful launching of the fall campaign, if they remained a large enough minority within the official convention, had good reason to try to guarantee that they gained *something* from the convention itself. The nomination, after all, was apparently settled, and this was their last opportunity to salvage any other goals from the nominating campaign.

Tangible Impacts from Convention Struggles

For the nominee, the very real consequences of this newly important struggle over use of the convention were inescapable. There was that reliably huge audience of occasional viewers, along with a large and more attentive audience of those with a continuing interest in politics—those apt to function as opinion leaders around the country, those most likely to come out and vote. There was also the fact that the convention remained the only major nationally covered event under formal control of the political parties and the largest continuous event focused on presidential politics. But beyond this, and central to the convention's impact on the launching of the general election campaign, was a set of effects stemming directly from the extent and intensity of convention conflict, conflict which evidently and unavoidably shaped the ability of a nominee to orchestrate what would—fairly or not—come to be seen as "his" convention.

At a minimum, by virtue of the varying sources and levels of internal conflict, conventions differed in the time at which the eventual nominee could begin to apply the gathering as a publicized event to the themes and images which he and his party intended to project for November. In conventions which lacked a major candidate split and in which even delegate splits were minor, the nominee could begin orchestrating his convention almost from the start, manipulating most speeches and presentations for coordinated (or at least intended) impact on the coming campaign. In contrast, in conventions which featured a major candidate split, especially if it was further exacerbated by separate factional splits among the delegates, the nominee could not begin this effort in any consistent fashion until the major challenges to his emerging majority and central policy preferences were effectively settled. Sometimes settlement came quickly, after a clear triumph on a major early test. At other times it did not arrive until completion of the balloting for the presidential nominee, or even later. When that was the case, the nominee could not really begin orchestrating the convention until the acceptance speeches of his running mate and himself, usually the final elements of the gathering.

These differences in the level of internal division, however, did not just affect the time at which campaign launching could begin. Instead, they inevitably affected the character of that launching, too, through their impact on the material from which the general public could conceivably develop its impressions of the nominee, his program, and their party. Some of this potential impact was peculiar to those identified with the losing side of convention struggles. Much of it, however, fell among those who had not developed a firm identification with any candidate or position at all. Obviously, the content of significant convention conflicts was a potentially disturbing element not just for those at the convention who lost on these issues but also for those in the outside audience who identified with the losing side. In creating extended convention conflicts, tacticians for the losing sides were prepared to risk this inherent cost of disaffection: their choice, after all, was between such a risk and surrender. But it was the successful candidate who ultimately had to pay this cost.

Yet even those who were not disturbed by the content or outcome of specific internal conflicts might thereafter perceive the candidate as a man not fully in charge of his own nominating convention. Moreover, this was not simply a "perception": the nominee in a sharply divided and then hotly contested convention really was in less complete control of his political environment. He was by comparison less able to stifle conflict. He was by definition less able to restrain such conflict temporally. If his positions lost, *he* was the loser. But even if they won, the obvious evidence of his reduced control could hardly translate into a perception that the nominee was in full charge of his political party. It was only a short step to the perception that this nominee was less of a leader, period. In some abstract world, the general public would have made an allowance for the differential contribution of varying levels of convention conflict to the leadership potential of evolving nominees. But even this allowance would have required an assumption that someone who was not successfully managing his own convention was every bit as able to do so as someone who obviously was.

Even that effect, however, did not exhaust the potential impacts of extended convention conflict. For in an obviously conflict-filled convention, the party too was demonstrated to be publicly divided. Practically, this demonstration meant that the nominee would have to spend more time and other resources *after* the convention, healing, or at least papering over, these divisions. Perceptually, the inescapable appearance of division further lessened the attractiveness of the nominee to any members of the general public who were drawn by the prospect of going with an apparent winner. Finally, if there was significant and continuing conflict—and even more if it sharply compressed the time in which the candidate could strike themes to counteract its effects—then that conflict might remain the dominant public memory of the convention and a major element in the public perception of its nominee.

For anyone inclined to ignore these potential but concrete impacts of convention conflict, the conventions after sweeping party reform operated to magnify the perceived importance of success or failure in using the convention to launch the general election campaign. The impression they gave was not necessarily an accurate reflection of the underlying electoral reality. Yet it did correspond perfectly to the comparative fate of their nominees in November, and that correspondence did serve as one more, barely implicit warning to convention strategists of all sorts. Thus in 1972, the Republicans featured low conflict, the Democrats high conflict, and the Republicans went on to win in November. In 1976, it was the Democrats who featured lower conflict, the Republicans high conflict, and the Democrats who ultimately won. In 1980, the Republicans returned to lower conflict, the Democrats to high conflict, and the low-conflict party, the Republicans, won again. In 1984, finally, although both conventions were pacific when measured against their recent histories, the Republicans were still clearly lower in internal conflict, the Democrats clearly higher, and the lower-conflict convention was still the one that produced the winner in November.

The Sources of Recurring Conflict

There were many reasons not to read the record of postreform conventions in this stark and simple fashion. Some of the conflicts dramatized at national party conventions, for example, only reflected divisions which had surfaced far earlier and had then been sustained through the nominating campaign. Moreover, even in years when the convention was quite reasonably viewed as a "decisive event" in the pursuit of a presidency—that is, an event which shifted the preferences of a share of the general public larger than the eventual margin of victory—there were often other events which could meet the same test. These caveats, however, were in turn largely beside the point. For as the postreform era continued, more and more participants in national party conventions—and probably all those involved with convention planning—became aware of this relationship between convention conflict and election outcome: it might still be spurious; they were not inclined to take that chance.

As a result convention officials and strategists for the emerging nominee needed to think not just about orchestrating the convention for maximum contribution to the general election campaign but about preventing, defusing, or countering the efforts of other convention participants, so as to guarantee that contribution. Obviously, their ability to realize all these goals was itself highly—in practice almost totally—dependent on internal convention politics. The fact that they began with a range of practical advantages meant that any conflict which did develop would normally express itself as a struggle between the effort to focus the convention on the general election campaign and the effort to focus some substantial part of that convention on one or another shifting candidate or group cause: the convention would not be a free-for-all among causes, with the general election campaign only one among many. But the range of advantages for convention officials and candidate strategists, substantial as it was, was not sufficient in itself to determine the outcome of this struggle.

The leadership figures from the full convention and the national campaign of the emerging nominee did begin with certain inherent assets. By definition, they already held the major formal positions in the national party and in the dominant campaign. If they were able to work together, they could control the official agenda, along with the organized responses to any elements of that agenda which slipped from their control. Ordinarily, their positions were indeed coordinated without much difficulty through a sense of appropriate accommodation—the emerging nominee was, after all, the emerging leader of the party—and through mutual self-interest. On the other hand, these individuals faced a few intrinsic obstacles, convention after convention. Prominent among these was the preference of the media of information for conflict as the essence of news coverage. Items of conflict were self-evidently "news."[7] They were also, of course, precisely the points at which a careful orchestration of convention activities might threaten to come unraveled.

But if there were only an institutionalized bias on the part of convention leaders toward consensus and on the part of press operatives toward conflict, the prospects for a successful campaign launching, in the course of some laudatory publicity for the party as a whole, would have been grand indeed. The balance of direct influence over the course of the convention between convention leaders and national reporters weighed heavily in favor of the former. Convention leaders still held the official agenda in their hands. Reporters by themselves could provide little more than the lesser elements of conflict—which might even serve in such a scenario to ensure the convention against becoming merely dull.

What prevented this scenario from being the reality of internal convention politics in the postreform era were two other major, regularized sources of conflict, sources perhaps exaggerated but rarely manufactured by the news media. Conventions might vary tremendously in the identities of their internal protagonists as well as in the mix among them. But two general types of recurring splits among participants still provided a continuing basis for convention struggles. The first was the division between supporters of the successful nominee and supporters of all the alternative candidates, a balance which rose and fell from convention to convention but which always contained a legitimate leadership and a coordinating structure. The second was the division of independent issue activists, interest group representatives, and official party figures among the delegates as a whole, a balance only partially tied to candidate fortunes and thus reliably present even when candidate opposition did not cross any serious threshold.

The Nominee versus the Challengers

The principal basis for organized conflict within a convention—certainly the simplest basis on which to organize any such conflict and normally the most extensive and intense—was the division between the emerging nominee and most other aspirants who had not withdrawn from the contest. The nomination might have moved outside the convention proper; this shift might have been stimulated by the nationalization of politics; that tendency might have been institutionalized through sweeping party reform. Yet all these developments did not guarantee that all the contenders for a presidential nomination would have withdrawn from the field as the convention assembled, nor especially that the delegates who supported these contenders would have disappeared in the interim or even altered their allegiance.

Moreover, there were numerous good reasons, or at least many probable causes, for an aspiring challenger to continue his fight into the convention hall even if the nomination seemed increasingly out of reach. The simplest of these, and the one with the strongest incentives, was a potentially close ballot. No convention since 1952 had failed to produce a first-ballot nomination; none had lacked an obvious front-runner. Yet some contests had been perilously close going into the convention, and this was inevitably an incentive to further conflict: if momentum could be shifted, if a preliminary battle over platform, rules, or credentials could shake some segment of support for the front-runner, or even if some unforeseen external event should accomplish the same result, then a different nominee—or so it perpetually appeared to candidates who had come this far—might yet be crowned *at* the convention.

Prospects for an immediate nomination, however, did not exhaust the reasons for continuing a preconvention contest, even for those who continued to hope to be nominated. The career ambitions of one or more challengers did not stop just because some other contender was most probably about to receive the nomination. Indeed, a challenger who had been willing to come this far might well be willing—indeed determined—to have this nominating campaign contribute at least to some future presidential possibility. The candidate might in effect work to rally supporters for a later nominating contest; he might plan to cement his control over potentially crucial issues for the future. Continued combat into the convention might just be the key to these developments, too.[8]

Moreover, there were other potential reasons, quite apart from the nomination, for continuing this conflict. In an era of candidate-based campaigns, when organized interests had to carry much of the campaign load, the candidate himself could become caught up in the causes of such organizations and groups and might view the convention as one more opportunity to advance them. Indeed, in a kind of chicken-and-egg process, the candidate might have first tested the presidential waters in order to further such a cause, been sustained by its partisans through the nominating campaign, then end up carrying its banner into the convention hall. Alternatively, the candidate could be "caught up" in the causes of such interests in a different sense: having turned his campaign into a crusade for their realization, he might face supporters who wanted to carry the fight to the convention. He could not fail to lead them without appearing to betray everything he had promised along the way, and perhaps compromising his own political future.

There were also countervailing factors, of course. A candidate who effectively damaged the convention of the ultimate nominee could expect to acquire continuing enemies as well as friends. Moreover, a candidate who mounted too much of a convention challenge would eliminate certain immediate career opportunities, such as a vice presidential nomination. Yet these constraints were regularly insufficient to prevent the continuation of some serious remaining challenges, from remaining challengers, who in turn retained all the essential assets for a practical convention struggle. They possessed an existing organization, which could easily be mobilized at the convention. They had a set of concerns—the alleged issues of the campaign—to form the substantive core of such an effort.

The division between the front-runner and all those other aspirants who had not withdrawn from the contest, along with the division between the supporters of that front-runner and the supporters of most other aspirants, active or withdrawn, was thus the leading recurrent basis for conflict within national party conventions. When it surfaced, it was often the most intense basis as well. Moreover, this division was also the most likely to come prepackaged, that is, with organizational machinery in the form of candidate campaigns, which could be turned to rallying potential supporters and thus to converting this barely implicit division into a practical source of political conflict, into a grand political "fault line."

Needless to say, the depth and patterning of this division heavily conditioned the ability of the eventual nominee, even as assisted by top party and convention officials, to use the convention on behalf of his general election campaign. Party and convention officials almost always rallied to the emerging nominee and endeavored to run the convention according to his wishes. Yet a sufficiently large or even a smaller but more dedicated minority in opposition could easily cancel many of their advantages. Such a minority could in fact set much of the agenda for the convention, at least the effective agenda for conflict. Its leaders could—and would—become the obvious touchstones for reporters, seeking the emergent flash points within the convention hall. Its members might even succeed, ineluctably if often inadvertently, in shaping the dominant public view of the nominee and his party long after the convention had recessed.

On the other hand, this candidate-based source of internal conflict did wax and wane from convention to convention. It reached its most intense when the delegate strength of the contenders was close and opposition to the front-runner was concentrated. The Republican convention of 1976, with Ford versus Reagan, or the Democratic convention of 1980, with Carter versus Kennedy, are obvious examples. The potential for conflict via candidates declined as the lead for the front-runner widened and the opposition fragmented. The Democratic convention of 1976, with Carter versus a large but lesser field, or the Democratic convention of 1984, with Mondale facing two lesser opponents, fit this pattern. This potential for candidate-based conflict then declined almost to zero—it was really entirely missing—when the front-runner wrapped up the nomination early and drove other contenders from the field. The Republican conventions of 1972 and 1984, which renominated sitting presidents Nixon and Reagan, were of this type.

The Leadership versus the Rank and File

Nevertheless, the absence of candidate conflict did not guarantee a convention free of division, or even of open combat. For if candidate splits were still the principal source of extended convention conflict, they were not the only regular divisions around which conflict could be organized and contests carried out. In fact, although it rarely reached the level of consequence for the launching of the general election campaign which could be attained when candidate splits were at their most tightly drawn and intense, the second major source of continuing division was far more reliably present. As a result, it was not only the most regular source of internal conflict, the most reliable "fault line" in contemporary convention politics. It was also both the leading source of conflict in conventions where candidate divisions were inconsequential and the leading element of exacerbation in conventions where candidate divisions were present.

This second source of conflict had its roots in the balance among party officeholders, independent issue activists, and interest group representatives within the total delegate population. But it expressed itself as one or another form of factional division between ideological, issue, or interest subgroups. In turn, when it became a significant element of overt conflict, it made its actual appearance as a division between the formal leadership and rank-and-file delegates, including not just those who might still privately oppose the obvious winning candidate but also large segments of the supporters of that emerging nominee. This division too varied considerably from convention to convention. Yet it was always incipiently present because it represented some continuing facets of American politics, as augmented clearly in the aftermath of party reform.

The fact that this source of conflict almost always surfaced as a struggle between leaders and followers, rather than among various leaders or among candidate supporters, was a result of the fact that these leaders and followers reliably possessed very different incentives by the time the convention assembled. Because the nomination was effectively settled, the top convention leadership had one clear goal: to launch the general election campaign in the most effective way possible. That goal, in turn, had one clear prerequisite: to move the candidate away from the dominant ideological thrust of his party and from the specific issue and group identifications of the nominating campaign and toward the ideological center of the political spectrum and a more studied identification with the entire voting public. This requirement held whether the candidate had moved to the left (for Democrats) or to the right (for Republicans) and whether or not he had made pointed issue and group commitments during the nominating campaign. In fact, if he *had* made these moves or commitments—and postreform nominees found it difficult not to do so—this strategic need was all the more pressing.[9]

In contrast, the convention rank and file were reliably unenthusiastic about all such shifts, which they ordinarily viewed as "retreats," coming at the very moment when victory was at hand. In the postreform era, these delegates were reliably more extreme ideologically than the general public; they possessed a greater range of more integrated stands on policy questions; and they held these views more intensely as well. As a result they could not be expected to regard a move toward the center by the standard-bearer for their party with enthusiasm. By the same token, these delegates were more and more likely to be independent issue activists or interest group representatives, with specific causes to push at the convention itself; those causes were, after all, an important part of why an increasing share of them had been drawn into presidential politics. Accordingly, a move to play down these concerns—indeed, to appear detached from "the interests"—could hardly be expected to please them.

Delegates who still had an active candidate at the convention (other than the front-runner) could often hope to have ideological and group concerns expressed through a continuing nomination campaign. Indeed, these concerns could be the basis for preliminary tests of strength by the remaining challenger or challengers. But there were always factions which either preferred or needed to operate outside an explicit candidate framework. Sometimes no candidate would emphasize their cause sufficiently; at other times they could not hope to win their struggle if it became identified with only one contender. Moreover, even those delegates whose champion was in fact the nominee in waiting were subject to these ideological, issue, or interest tensions. In this situation, it was their struggles with their own candidate, or at least the ability of other delegates to pump up those struggles and exacerbate that tension, which created the second, recurring, leader-follower conflicts at conventions.

Both the ideological and the issue-interest aspects of this conflict were probably augmented in the postreform era. It was true that delegates had always been more ideological than the general public, at least as long as surveys of related attitudes had existed, with Democrats leaning left and Republicans leaning right. It was true that the delegates had already produced some historic issue or interest conflicts at national party conventions, as with the hard-money/soft-money split in the Democratic party in the late nineteenth century or the progressive/ standpat division in the Republican party in the early twentieth century.[10] Yet available indications suggested that the convention delegates in both parties were much more reliably polarized ideologically than they had been before reform. Indications were even stronger that the shift from party officeholders to independent issue activists and interest group representatives was at a continuing high-water point.

A major expansion in the number of delegate votes at postreform conventions probably further exaggerated this potential for conflict, between the nominee and his challengers but especially among delegate factions. (See Table 5.2.) In the postreform era, the Democrats did attack the division of delegate votes among numerous individuals— the Republicans had always discouraged this practice—and that attack

Table 5.2.   The growth of the convention in the postreform era

Year	No. of delegates	
	Republican	Democratic
1984	2,235	3,933
1980	1,994	3,331
1976	2,259	3,008
1972	1,333	3,016
1968	1,333	2,522

Source: Extracted from "Figure 1: Size of National Party Conventions, 1932–1980," in James W. Davis, *National Conventions in an Age of Party Reform* (Westport, Conn.: Greenwood Press, 1983), p. 43, as supplemented by the certified totals from *Official Report of Proceedings of the Thirty-third Republican National Convention* (Washington, D.C.: Republican National Committee, 1984) and *1984: Official Proceedings of the Democratic National Convention* (Washington, D.C.: Democratic National Committee, 1984).

prevented creeping convention growth through autonomous state decisions. But convention reformers then discovered more need than ever to adhere to the norm that when the allocation of delegate votes to the states was altered, no state should lose in raw numbers. By that norm, of course, simple reapportionment, explicit recognition of new demographic constituencies, and even a subsequent effort to restore a place for the official party in effect implied that the convention had to grow.

The resulting growth was not a major contribution to convention conflict: the coming of campaign launching as the central convention activity and of the interested partisans as modal convention delegates had much more to do with that conflict. But such growth inevitably reduced the social controls—the interpersonal controls of one delegate on another and the effective restraints of a campaign leadership on its delegates—which might have limited the potential for these recurring sources of conflict to be converted into real struggles. In doing so, finally, this growth attested further to the tendency of both parties to follow the same structural course. The Republican party lacked the regular mechanisms for revising convention arrangements which the Democrats had institutionalized; it possessed an explicit doctrine that the convention should remain a deliberative body and therefore not expand. Nevertheless, the forces which were playing across the Democratic party—the need to reapportion, a desire to reward successful performance, the wish to reach out to new constituencies—played across affected the Republicans as well. In return, the Republican convention followed the Democratic, a little more slowly and not as far, but in the same general direction and with the same overall effect.[11]

Pure Patterns, 1972: The Democrats

It was fitting that the first Democratic national convention after sweeping party reform should manifest most of the signature characteristics of internal conflict at reformed conventions. Reform, the largest single factor behind the shift in the nature of delegates, had been primarily a Democratic initiative. The attempt to achieve that reform in a single, systematic burst was in turn behind most of the specific manifestations of conflict at the 1972 Democratic convention. Indeed, in an additionally fitting symbolic fashion, the central figure in conflicts at that convention was Senator George McGovern of South

Dakota, the chairman of the commission which had produced these recommendations and the eventual nominee of the (first subsequent reformed) convention.

No one at the time could have been expected to see the conflicts at this convention as representative of most convention conflicts to follow. Yet the central rules battle of the convention was an archetypal candidate division, producing a prototypical candidate struggle. The critical credentials challenge was a classic blend of crosscutting candidate and interest group tensions. And the more dramatic of the platform conflicts were almost pure issue divisions, producing almost pure delegate struggles revolving around a temporary split between the emerging nominee and his own delegates. Together with some conflict over the vice presidential nomination, these struggles managed not only to present the full range of convention conflicts but to demonstrate, with a serendipitous high symbolism, the impact of such struggles on the simultaneous attempt to use the convention to launch the general election campaign.[12]

The nominating contest, through the process of delegate selection, had actually gone down to the final day of presidential primaries, down in fact to the crucial winner-take-all primary in California, where George McGovern bested Hubert Humphrey. But despite the apparently decisive lead for McGovern, the margin remained close enough, and divisions among presidential actors deep enough, that his leading opponent, Humphrey, decided to carry the fight to the convention. Humphrey did possess a plausible (or at least a practically possible) strategic gambit, under which McGovern might be stopped. The interim reform commission had recommended but not required that the winner-take-all primary be discontinued. The California primary was thus explicitly legal but officially discouraged. If a majority of convention delegates could be convinced to impose proportional representation, the endorsed plan for allocating delegates, McGovern would lose 151 delegates and fall below a first-ballot majority.

This possibility produced the classic candidate split at a reformed national party convention, an "ABM" ("All But McGovern") coalition to oppose the forces of the South Dakota senator. But that division quickly became enmeshed in a much more confusing and ambiguous split, one in which both factional and candidate supporters played a role and in which the lines were breached in both directions. The ambiguity stemmed from a situation of extreme procedural complexity. The Credentials Committee, minus the California delegation (which could not vote on its own status), had awarded its majority report to the ABM coalition. This report would of course be challenged by the McGovern leadership on the convention floor. But that challenge figured to be sufficiently close that the key test of strength would come on a decision not on the minority report but on the definition of a formal majority.

The convention chairman, Lawrence O'Brien, would rule for the traditional interpretation, a numerical majority of those present and voting. But if this ruling could be overturned, in favor of a numerical majority of the total convention membership, then McGovern might not have enough raw votes to replace the majority report, even if he could otherwise pass the minority report, and would thus lose 151 delegates in California. However, in a final twist, there was a preceding challenge to the credentials of the South Carolina delegation, involving discrimination on the basis of gender and brought by the National Women's Political Caucus. If a ruling on the definition of a formal majority came on that predictably close ballot instead, then convention feminists, who were primarily McGovernites, might indirectly contribute to the defeat of their candidate's position on the proper definition of a majority, affirming the "wrong" definition for the battle over California.[13]

As it developed, the vote on South Carolina, despite some practical mixing of the lines, was unambiguous in its majority and thus produced no ruling from the chair. In part as a result, the California vote was unambiguous too, producing only a pro forma challenge to its definition of a majority. Those with a stake in this outcome were either elated or deflated as their various stakes dictated, but those with the perspective of hindsight would not have been surprised. As had been the case since 1952 and would be in every convention thereafter (at least through 1984), the apparent majority coming into the convention had been confirmed in what all knew to be the crucial test vote. The apparent nomination thus became the official nomination. But, as was also comparatively typical, the candidate division behind that apparent nomination had generated substantial and significant, internal convention conflict.

Moreover, the second generic source of conflict, which had been present but not decisive in the credentials challenge to South Carolina, spilled out in much more dramatic—or at least dramatizable—fashion thereafter. Many of the purest substantive examples came on the report of the Platform Committee, in which several striking minority reports, such as one demanding that the federal government guarantee every family of four a fixed minimum income, were propelled by McGovern delegates but opposed by the candidate himself. However, the dispute which not only exemplified this division but commented most powerfully on the cost of all such divisions to a nominee who could not suppress them quickly came *after* McGovern was nominated. The nominee, having drifted left for the nominating campaign and having made significant issue and interest commitments along the way, was already moving back toward the center and away from narrow and dissident identifications when he began trying to defuse such platform proposals as the guaranteed income. He then continued this move by slating Senator Thomas Eagleton of Missouri, a party regular with strong labor connections, as his running mate.

But at that point, self-conscious feminists, who were, again, overwhelmingly McGovernites but who had been deserted by their champion on the South Carolina challenge, put up a countercandidate, Frances Farenthold of Texas, for vice president. Five other candidates were also nominated, and more than 70 ultimately received a vote—with a majority of all these other votes coming from McGovernites and a majority of the ABM coalition going for Eagleton. One result was that Eagleton was nominated, although with less than 60 percent of the total vote. A second result was that the convention had thus seen the full range of available convention conflict. But a third result was the culmination of a series of blows to McGovern's effort to orchestrate the convention—along with the most striking symbolic blow to this goal in the modern political era. Not only did this full range of conflicts deny the nominee much chance to orchestrate his own convention, not only did it condemn him in effect to open his general election campaign with the closing act of his nominating convention, his acceptance speech, but that speech could not be delivered until 3:00 A.M., Eastern time, when an estimated 80 percent of the earlier viewing audience had already gone to bed.

Pure Patterns, 1972: The Republicans

The Republican convention of 1972 was in some senses the polar opposite pattern to its Democratic counterpart. There was no candidate conflict of any sort. The one small element of internal delegate conflict, which did produce a debate and a roll call, did not interfere with the deliberate orchestration of the convention in any way. That orchestration was in turn the focus, almost the preoccupation, of those responsible for managing the convention, and the absence of major conflicts allowed them to indulge their plans to the full. Yet in other senses, and with the benefit of hindsight, it was clear that the 1972 Republican convention was really a comparatively pure example of a *prereform* convention which lacked significant candidate or delegate divisions rather than the inaugural of the postreform variety on the Republican side.[14]

Procedural reforms were already reaching into the Republican process of delegate selection as the convention of 1972 approached. But without a significant candidate challenge—President Richard Nixon brushed aside two early, token efforts—these reforms did not produce much of the shift from party officials to independent issue activists and interest group representatives which would follow, for the Republicans as well, by 1976. Indeed, the lack of candidate divisions was so total that Governor Nelson Rockefeller of New York, who had opposed Nixon for nomination at the Republican conventions of 1960 and 1968, actually made the main nominating speech. One lone vote against renomination was cast by a delegate for Congressman Paul McCloskey, one of the two early putative challengers to Nixon, but McCloskey himself was never put into official nomination. And that was all there was by way of candidate division at this convention.

Delegate divisions were not much more consequential. There were no splits by issue faction requiring so much as a roll call; there were no such splits by interest group either. The lone debate producing a ballot was over the formula allocating delegates to the states. Because the Republican candidate ordinarily does better in presidential voting among the smaller states, the question of how states shall be rewarded for their performance is a perennial, if lesser, Republican concern. In turn, votes on such disputes are roughly a surrogate for ideological factionalism, because Republicans from small states tend toward the conservative, whereas Republicans from big states tend toward the moderate. The 1972 vote in any case, like most such ballots in the party, found the big-state position in a decided minority. By a vote of 910 to 434, the convention rejected a minority report more favorable to the large states. And that became its only recorded division.[15]

What this meant inevitably was that the convention leadership, as coordinated by the reelection campaign, was free to put the full convention at the disposal of that reelection effort. At the time, the degree to which every aspect of the convention was coordinated with a hoped-for contribution to the November vote was itself a topic of conversation and analysis. With hindsight, it would be clear that this effort was only the culmination of trends gathering strength since the departure of the nomination and was in fact merely a prototype for the successful pursuit of the goal of contributing to the general election campaign via the convention, in both political parties. In focus, then, the convention was thoroughly modern, even if its delegates—and internal divisions—largely reflected the prereform era.

The Reform Era Affirmed: The Republicans, 1976

The Republican convention of 1976, by contrast, was destined to become a landmark of another sort. Again, there was no reason for those who participated in it to look beyond its immediate substance for any different historical significance. Nor was there any way in which participants or observers could have put this convention in its larger eventual perspective. Yet the gathering of 1976 was the first of the true postreform conventions for the Republican party. More than that, it confirmed the arrival of the diagnostic patterns of convention conflict in the party as well, thereby eliminating the suspicion—one possible deduction from the conventions of 1972—that there were two different types of national party convention in American presidential politics, reflecting two types of national political party.

This convention featured intense candidate divisions, producing serious candidate-based conflict and growing (typically) from an extremely close balance between the remaining contenders and from a concentration of the remaining opposition. In addition the convention featured serious delegate splits among ideological factions, producing (again diagnostically) serious tensions between the nominee and his own delegate supporters. None of these conflicts altered the ultimate official outcome nor did they really threaten to do so, the perceptions of many participants notwithstanding. But they did make a powerful contribution to the portrait which the nominee was able to paint by way of the convention. And they did inevitably paint him in a quite different light despite the success of his efforts in the narrow and official sense.[16]

The contest for a nominating majority, through the process of delegate selection, had begun innocently enough. Gerald Ford, a sitting president albeit one who had not been elected to the position, was standing for reelection. He began by defeating his one aspiringly serious challenger, Ronald Reagan, in a succession of opening contests, as incumbent presidents ordinarily did. But a combination of circumstances—a shift into less receptive states, a change in opposition tactics, and a few errors by the Ford campaign—allowed Reagan to salvage his effort fairly early. From then on, Reagan and Ford swayed back and forth across the narrowest of delegate margins. By the end of the campaign, Ford was the apparent—narrow—winner and could expect to be nominated at "his" convention. The obvious closeness of the delegate totals, however, along with the fact that they were divided between only two contenders, raised the automatic lure to the Reagan campaign, that continued conflict, creatively managed, might still upset the apparent outcome.

Accordingly, the Reagan team produced a carefully crafted strategy aimed at splitting off a piece of the Ford forces. This centered on a proposed new Section C of Rule 16, a section dealing with the selection of a vice presidential nominee. Before the convention, in an effort to break some of the Ford delegates loose, Reagan (a dedicated conservative) had announced that Senator Richard Schweiker of Pennsylvania (a moderate liberal) would be his running mate. The ideological mix had made many Reaganites uncomfortable. But faced with a situation which would predictably produce the narrow renomination of Ford, the Reagan leadership had attempted the Schweiker maneuver as a penultimate gambit. They then extended the maneuver with the proposed Rule 16-C, which demanded that every presidential candidate announce his vice presidential running mate before the ballot for president.[17]

The hope of the Reaganites, of course, was that Ford would at the least be unable to use the vice presidency to solidify his support by dangling the possibility before potential contenders, and that he would at best be forced to name someone who would almost surely disappoint some of his convention delegates. The Reagan supporters did not have any hopes for a majority on 16-C in the Rules Committee, but they did hold the necessary 25 percent to bring a minority report to the convention floor, and they did set the stage for doing so. There were additional parts to the Reagan strategy on rules—for example, a challenge to the Ford "justice resolution," which bound delegates to go with the result of their state primary over their individual conscience— but these were always viewed as secondary and subsequent to the fight on 16-C. They would extend the beating if it were possible to defeat Ford on the central issue; they would be of little consequence if it were not.

In fact, those same narrow lines which would produce the nomination itself held, almost to the delegate, in the vote on 16-C. The Ford position triumphed—1,180 to 1,069—demonstrating once again the tantalizing closeness of the balance in the convention. But Ford himself would triumph one day later by a vote of 1,187 to 1,070, demonstrating just as strongly that such tantalizing possibilities were only that, and did not in the postreform era promise the necessary small defections which would restore the nomination to the convention. On the other hand, by the time the crucial ballot came on Rule 16-C, there were already other forces in motion, related but still separate in their background and intent, which would add a different overlay of conflict to the entire struggle. These stemmed from a division among ideological factions, pitting conservatives against moderates and liberals, and that division, although it did follow candidate lines, reached across into the Ford camp—and thus provided one more classic incarnation of the pattern by which the nominee was pitted against a substantial chunk of his own supporters and by which struggles within the same side became the essence of convention conflict.

Early in the convention, some of the pronounced ideological conservatives in attendance, organized around Senator Jesse Helms of North Carolina, had begun a series of platform challenges on foreign policy. Some of these challenges were ultimately driven back by the Ford forces; others were successful in the Platform Committee and were actually written into the draft document. But along the way, the Reagan campaign had reached out to the Helms network and suggested combining a number of their dissident foreign policy planks, criticizing the Ford administration in general and its secretary of state (Henry Kissinger) in particular, in one overall package which they dubbed "Morality in Foreign Policy." This could not win in the Platform Committee either. But it could become a minority report and would thus appear on the full convention floor. The Reagan strategy had called for this issue to follow 16-C, with that rule creating a rift in the original Ford supporters and this foreign policy package then widening the rift sufficiently to deny Ford the nomination.

When the vote on 16-C went wrong, however, prospects for this overall scenario declined radically. In response, the Ford forces, seeing a strong likelihood that they would still lose the foreign policy battle, simply called it off and accepted the Morality in Foreign Policy planks into the composite platform. By doing so, they denied historians a specific roll call to show the extent of the split between formal leadership and putative followership within the Ford camp. But they did not eliminate the obvious evidence that this sort of division too, along with the internal struggle inevitably following from it, had arrived in the Republican party. Simultaneously, the success of the dissident foreign policy planks confirmed the arrival of the full package of diagnostic convention divisions, and associated conflicts, in both parties. Moreover and finally, although this range of disputes did not force Ford to give his acceptance speech at 3:00 in the morning, it surely painted him as a man only marginally in charge of his nominating convention.

The Reform Era Affirmed: The Democrats, 1976

The Democratic convention of 1976 was actually more like the Republican convention of 1972 than it was like the Democratic convention of 1972 or the Republican convention of 1976.[18] There was some remaining candidate opposition, but this was divided among Congressman Morris Udall of Arizona, Governor Edmund "Jerry" Brown of California, Governor George Wallace of Alabama, anti-abortion activist Ellen McCormack of New York, and several other, even less significant names. Besides being divided rather than concentrated, this "opposition" was largely pro forma: the Carter lead in delegates was overwhelming, and there was not even the glimmer of a hope that things might fall together and direct the convention toward someone else. This roster of remaining opposition did prevent the convention from being precisely like the Republican conventions of 1972 or 1984, at which there were *no* remaining contenders. But neither the Carter camp, the advisers of these other candidates, reporters and commentators, nor, presumably, the viewing public took the presence of these others seriously. Shortly before the ballot, Udall removed himself from contention and endorsed Carter. Immediately afterward, Brown did the same.

Even in the realm of delegate divisions, in the intermittent but reliable split between the leadership and some of the delegates, the Democratic convention of 1976 was comparatively tame. This was the area in which divisions, capable of producing some convention conflict, did remain. Committed liberals were still looking for some issue which would at least provide a "test" of the true ideology of their new nominee, but they were never able to coalesce around an especially effective option. There was a roll call on opening the convention floor to an hour of unspecified platform debate, but Carter delegates and some others rallied to the argument that this would merely disrupt the flow of the convention, and the proposal was solidly defeated. Committed liberals tried again with a proposal to return to milder limits, 15 percent rather than 25 percent, on minority reports for the next quadrennial gathering, but this too failed to reach a majority, and a proposal restructuring the next midterm conference actually led but failed to achieve a procedural majority. The result was that these ballots did not reflect on control of the convention by the Carter leadership nor, and this was more important, did they interfere with orchestrating the convention to introduce Carter to the American public in the manner preferred by his campaign team.

There was another incipient division, a major interest group conflict which appeared likely for a time to give the convention at least a slightly different cast. Feminist leaders, organized around the National Women's Political Caucus, wanted percentage guarantees—equal division—for women delegates at the next convention. The Carter leadership was unenthusiastic, viewing this as a "quota" pure and simple and thus as singularly bad policy for their "outsider" candidate, whom they intended to present to the general public as more moderate than the nominee of 1972 and as free of attachments to "the special interests." There were, however, feminist delegates within the Carter camp as well, and it was not clear that the Carter leadership could hold them in line. As a result, the minority report of the Rules Committee, which would have created such quotas explicitly, was amended to urge that state parties look to this standard for the midterm conference and for the next national party convention and to create a separate women's division at the Democratic National Committee, in return for avoidance of explicit quota language.[19]

The division around this proposal, and the fact that it threatened conflict sufficient to require a compromise in the eyes of both sides, did attest to the continuance of some bases for internal convention struggles. The manner of its resolution, however, and the fact that it was resolved without a battle on the full convention floor, attested just as powerfully to the low level of conflict at this convention, while commenting—by subtraction—on the absence of any other bases for conflict. In that sense and by deliberate design, the Democratic convention of 1976 followed the lead of the Republican convention of 1972 in being planned, and then successfully orchestrated, with the November election continually in mind. If it was not as totally lacking in conflict, as Democratic conventions rarely were, it was still far enough from conflict-ridden to make the campaign launching its major, coordinated activity.

The Nomination Revisited

Specific cases thus reinforced what more general observation suggested: First, that aspiring presidential nominees did continue to fight through the convention itself, even though the nomination was effectively settled. Second, that ideological factions, issue organizations, and interest groups did continue to stage revolts, sometimes against their own candidates, even though their main source of potential leverage, an impact on the nomination, was apparently unavailable to them too. Indeed, the Democrats of 1972 and the Republicans of 1976 featured second-rank, *losing* candidates who took their conflict right up to the presidential ballot, just as those conventions featured internal factions which carried their policy desires up to and through the nomination.

Some of this conflict bore only an indirect, though still potentially crucial, relationship to the nomination. Various factions in the delegate population tried to threaten the emerging nominee as a way of using the convention to advance their policy goals. But much of this conflict was directly focused on the nomination itself, despite the continual presentation of examples which suggested that such efforts were ultimately bootless. In fact, examples of both this conflict and of its ultimate futility continued to pile up. The Democrats of 1972 provided one remarkably intricate case. The Republicans of 1976 provided a counterpart, in which a razor-thin delegate margin, in a convention at which the majority of delegates were clearly closer ideologically to the apparent loser, could produce no candidate change at all. Nevertheless, these examples would not prevent repetitions of such efforts in the conventions of 1980 and 1984. There was no reason to believe that they would prevent such repetitions in conventions yet to come.

Two questions followed immediately from this situation. Why did individual delegates continue to labor diligently on behalf of such conflicts when everyone, including the chief strategists for the apparent losing contenders—they were rarely misty-eyed about the nature of their dilemma—agreed that the nomination had been settled in the process of delegate selection? And given that such conflict did reliably continue despite this apparent settlement, why had it *never* (at least through 1984) produced a significant break in the candidate loyalties of individual delegates, and thus a situation in which the convention might actually have resumed its nominating capacity?

The total dynamics of a nominating campaign, especially in the postreform era—the structuring of conflict on the way to a nomination—explained much about the continuation of losing campaigns into the convention itself. Campaign dynamics, of course, inevitably explained why many candidates did *not* continue into the convention. Whenever a nominating campaign could no longer sustain itself, that is, could no longer draw the support of activists, financial contributors, and ultimately voters, it folded up and disappeared from the field— although the delegates which it had secured might still be available for other challenges at the convention. "Campaign dynamics," in this most elementary and global sense, automatically explained the situation of these candidates as the convention approached.

Nevertheless, some losing candidates did survive through the entire process, as with Hubert Humphrey in 1972, Ronald Reagan in 1976, Edward Kennedy in 1980, and Gary Hart in 1984. For them campaign dynamics were even more an essential reason for their existence at the convention and their will to fight while there. This was more than some simple extrapolation from "momentum," although that was ordinarily present too. A campaign which had come this far had been functioning for eight months at a minimum, full-time and intensely. Most had been functioning for at least eighteen months, given the exigencies of building an independent, personal, and national campaign out of largely individualized political actors. Some, such as those of Humphrey, Reagan, or Kennedy, could literally be said to have been operating for years.

Yet inevitably with such a campaign, it was not just an organization but a conflict which had been institutionalized along the way. A set of issues had been raised, and, however grand or picayune, pointed or vague these might seem to outside analysts, they meant something to those who had been laboring under them. A set of constituencies had been mobilized—otherwise the campaign would not have lasted— and these had acquired both an internal legitimacy, as groups which ought rightfully to receive something for their efforts, and the status of a pressure group, to keep the campaign going. Finally, a set of attacks had been made on the emerging nominee, which many in these opposition campaigns took seriously, while a set of attacks on their champion had been endured, making campaign actors additionally sensitive to the comparative virtues of the contenders—and making them again into a pressure group for continuation of the campaign.

All these developments were further augmented by the nature of reformed nominating campaigns, with their reliance on those who were primarily motivated by ideological, issue, or group attachments rather than by party function and partisan duty. They may even have been additionally augmented by an increase—or at least increased prospects—of *contenders* who were themselves motivated by ideology, issues, or group identifications. In any case, it was not difficult to see how, when the lead of the apparent nominee was clearly very narrow, campaigns of this sort would be inclined to fight on. Indeed, it was not difficult to see how such campaigns could reinterpret the margin of the apparent nominee—could narrow any apparent lead—so as to continue. It was even possible, in such an environment, to imagine cases—and the Kennedy campaign of 1980 would shortly provide one, at least in part—in which the candidate himself might have preferred to pull back and reduce conflict but where the rest of the campaign demanded action on behalf of the program, issues, and groups which they had been supporting for so long.

Candidate Loyalty after Reform

On the other hand, many of these same factors from the internal dynamics of a nominating campaign also explained why candidate loyalties did not dissolve and conventions did not break loose, even when conflict over the nomination continued and the margin between contenders was perilously small. In one sense, the stability of these loyalties was more remarkable than the raw numbers indicated, because these delegates were increasingly issue and group products rather than candidate loyalists pure and simple. Yet the raw numbers were also impressive by themselves; they rarely showed more than the tiniest slippage between candidate preferences and votes on what were generally understood to be the key preliminary tests of the entire convention. Thus the tally for the nomination of Ford at the 1976 Republican convention was exactly seven votes more than the ballot for the Ford position on Rule 16-C, the major Reagan procedural challenge—a slippage of .003 of the convention total.

Most fundamentally, of course, the same candidate-oriented nominating campaigns which encouraged major campaign actors to sustain preconvention conflict into the convention itself helped to repress any subsequent shifts, by continuing to draw the lines sharply between candidate supporters. If these campaigns were both successfully mounted and sustained through the entire preconvention period, the very division which sustained them created ever-higher barriers to any movement between candidates. Supporters—delegates—who had aligned themselves with a candidate originally, who had worked hard for that candidate, and who had in turn been attacked by other campaigners, were extremely unlikely to deviate from this basic candidate loyalty. Ordinarily, they had possessed some reason to identify with their chosen candidate from the start. Ordinarily, they had also been screened by the candidate's people to make sure that theirs was a genuine personal loyalty. The extended conflict of the remainder of the campaign had then operated, unintentionally but ineluctably, to strengthen such ties.[20]

These delegates clearly were not immune to attempts to get them to deviate from their candidate's position on a platform plank, a rules plan, or even a minor credentials challenge. They might well shift around, sometimes to the acute embarrassment of the nominee, when the question touched their ideological, issue, or group attachments. But when the question was their candidate attachments, they did not waver. Indeed, although the shift from party officials to independent issue activists and interest group representatives might appear on its surface to increase the strains on candidate loyalty, this shift was itself the product of a change from a party-based to a *candidate-based* process of delegate selection, and candidate loyalties were inevitably central to that.

Moreover, the official convention, albeit frequently the scene of a last attempt at shaking this candidate attachment, also provided numerous reinforcements. Between the time of the last delegate selection and the opening of the official convention, each contender maintained an organized liaison with his delegates, aimed at holding them in line. There was a national staff for this purpose; there was a state operation as well, involving others with whom any given delegate had ordinarily campaigned, fought, and been selected. When the convention itself opened, delegates were automatically housed with their state delegations, the same delegates with whom they had waged the campaign. Thereafter, they caucused reliably, regularly, and throughout the convention not just with their full state delegation but especially with their candidate subgroup.

As if all these encouragements to solidarity were not enough, the very process of lobbying delegates across candidate loyalties—essential to any chance of shifting those delegates—had elements of reinforcement within it too. Such lobbying was always in part an attack on the candidate at its center, the front-runner. This ordinarily bled over into an attack on other delegates who were still loyal to that front-runner, many of whom were necessarily friends and colleagues of the delegates being lobbied. At the same time, this effort involved rallying the already faithful, since they were simultaneously under pressure from the other side. Probably, in an institution as temporally and geographically concentrated and as politically intense as the national party convention it was impossible to separate these facets of the lobbying effort, between rallying one's own side while dividing the other. Probably as well, it was impossible to differentiate between an individual target and the larger group of which that individual was a part, so that impacts on the group could function opposite to impacts on the individual.

Even if all this had been possible, of course, a lobbying effort would still have had to overcome the impact both of the preceding campaign and of the countervailing efforts to hold the front-runner's delegates in line. Even then, even if an individual delegate could potentially be moved in the face of all that, and even if this delegate was thus potentially prepared to desert his or her candidate and vote for some other on the crucial nominating ballot, that delegate still had to face the very personal—the very interpersonal—consequences of doing so. Such a delegate had to face all those other delegates with whom he or she had campaigned along the way as well as all those other non-delegates who were part of the campaign at home. Further, such a delegate had to believe—and probably could not reasonably expect— that having become a "turncoat" and a major prize for the other side, he or she would still be welcomed by opposition delegates, and the opposition campaign, after the convention had ended.

Again, the extent to which these delegates could go in both embarrassing their own candidate and, perhaps more critically, interfering with his efforts to orchestrate the convention for a maximum contribution to the general election campaign was also impressive. The Democratic delegates who were to turn back the California credentials challenge decisively and then nominate George McGovern for president were, immediately after this crucial victory—after McGovern was finally assured of the nomination and could shift to bringing as many elements of the party as possible into line behind him—to *expel* the entire delegation from Chicago, thereby writing off the strongest extended organization left in the Democratic party. The Republican delegates who were to turn back a critical rules challenge on the naming of vice presidential candidates by the same rock-hard margin under which they would nominate Gerald Ford for president could only hours later shift solidly behind a foreign policy package which repudiated the Ford administration.

Yet nothing about these ballots, dramatic as they were when viewed in isolation, suggested even with the benefit of hindsight that the apparent nominee was in any danger of losing his hold on any consequential number of *nominating* votes. As a result, nothing in them suggested that the recurring bases of convention conflict, critical as they were to the public presentation of the entire convention, were likely to restore the nomination itself to the convention. These bases might produce conflicts which affected the prospects of the nominee in November, a not inconsequential contribution. They might produce further adaptations in the structure of the convention itself. Indeed, recurring patterns of convention conflict were quickly to produce their own reliable strategies and counterstrategies for the traditional convention agenda, along with further reforms in internal structure. But they had not at any time restored the convention as a whole to an earlier nominating era, and they continued to appear unlikely to do so.

6 | Recurring Struggles over Tangible Products: Traditional Activities in the Reformed Convention

The shift from the construction of a nominating majority to the launching of the general election campaign as the central activity of the national party convention, because it implied the potential for *all* convention actors to utilize that convention in the furtherance of their own preferred concerns, served as an incentive to convert the inherent and continuing bases of conflict into actual struggles inside the convention. The survival of several nominating campaigns, even when none of the candidates at their center was any longer likely to be the ultimate nominee, became an automatic—and highly effective—stimulus for continued conflict. The mix of (and distinctions among) independent issue activists, interest group representatives, and party officeholders, even when no alternative candidates survived, was a still more common basis for convention disputes.

Yet these recurring struggles, while their precise origin and precise outline inevitably varied from convention to convention, still reliably centered on the traditional activities which every convention would feature. In part, this was because these activities were tailor-made to advance some goals of major convention participants, such as the extraction of favorable policy pronouncements. But in larger part, this focus upon traditional activities was simply a reflection of the fact that these activities continued, and continued to be both central to the convention and readily accessible to its participants. Each of these realms was thus an inherent arena within which relevant substantive desires could be pursued directly. Each was also, however, an arena in which conflict could be mounted with the conscious intent of extracting concessions—policy goals—somewhere else.

Foremost among these traditional activities, of course, was the presidential nomination. Although its ultimate outcome was ordinarily predictable, the nomination still provided the central procedural dynamic of the convention, around which any number of other machinations remained possible. But there was also the selection of a presidential running mate, a potential vice president, and that choice too provided numerous opportunities for convention maneuver. Moreover, there were recurring committee deliberations, constituting the substantive core of national party conventions and hence the core of their procedural agenda. These traditional internal activities involved the certification of delegate credentials, the acceptance of rules for convention business, and the adoption of a party platform; they inevitably provided multiple theaters—innumerable opportunities—for additional conflict.

The resulting conflict most often pitted factions among the delegates—candidate, ideological, issue, or interest factions—against the emerging nominee. These factions had concrete goals to accomplish at the convention in order to cap the nominating campaign. The nominee preferred to refocus that convention on the themes of his successful candidacy, thus launching the general election contest. The result was a set of recognizable, major, recurring strategies for addressing these traditional arenas, strategies so regular that they too could be said to be effectively institutionalized. From one side, dissident delegates sought comparatively extreme policies, so as to "get something" from the convention while dramatizing their alleged gains to external supporters. From the other side, the nominee and his entourage were ordinarily inclined to placate these delegates, even in what were comparatively extreme proposals, so as to avoid open conflict and retain a freer hand in orchestrating the convention.

Only this peculiar strategic dynamic could explain some of the individual struggles over platform and rules in the postreform era. Once again, the battles at a particular Democratic convention, the Democratic convention of 1980, were ideal for enumerating the different bases for convention divisions, the range of struggles these might produce, and the available twists on what were still fundamentally similar, recurring strategies. Yet the convention battles at the Republican gathering of that year, although confined to a narrower range of theaters, were by their very intensity a particularly clear embodiment of the contours of internal politics at reformed party conventions and thus a particularly rich and refined instance of the recurring strategies which made up that politics. When the Republican *and* Democratic conventions of 1984 each featured a comparatively lower level of conflict, that conflict—over rules and platform among the Democrats, over platform alone among the Republicans—effectively confirmed the structure of postreform convention politics by offering the struggles in that politics at their inescapable minimum.

Yet this patterned arsenal of gambits and responses began to go much further than merely constituting and implicitly commenting on the regular character of convention politics. For in the years after 1972, this recurring strategic interplay actually began to produce organizational changes inside the national party convention. The Democratic convention revised its formal committee arrangements, either to focus or to contain committee conflict, while the Republican convention sought the same practical outcome through informal means. Moreover, factions within both conventions worked to extend the reach of their institution outside its boundaries and into other political institutions, including not just the national committee of the party but the presidency itself. Inevitably, however, both these recurring convention conflicts and the structural or procedural responses to them raised one final question, about the practical import of all such efforts: granted that most of those in attendance clearly continued to care, often actively and passionately, about the outcome in these areas, was there still reason for the outside observer to care as well? After all, the nomination was already settled, the impact of the rules was already moot, and the nominee was effectively unfettered by the content of a party platform.

One answer, of course, stemmed from the ability of these conflicts, quite apart from their substance, to shape the launching of the general election campaign. As long as they continued to do that, no analyst, no observer—indeed no participant—was practically free to ignore them. But another answer was rooted in some highly practical if indirect impacts from the outcome of many such conflicts. Rules reforms, for example, could easily affect the outcome of the presidential contest *next time,* albeit in ways which neither proponents nor opponents were very good at foreseeing. Party platforms had an even more indirect but potentially more powerful impact, if they came to represent the programmatic goals of an entire stratum of intermediary actors in presidential politics, who were likely to become the personnel of any subsequent government. In fact, in an era not just of declining relevance for the official party but of shifting coalitions among the organized interests aspiring to replace it, these redefinitions of the rules of the game, and especially these redefinitions of what it meant to be a Democrat or Republican, could end up as activities of the highest consequence.

The Other Nomination

The mechanics of nominating a president, even when the outcome was consensually apparent, still figured centrally in convention politics. At many conventions, some candidates and their supporters still hoped to wrest the nomination away from the front-runner. At all conventions, the emerging nominee and his entourage needed to be sure that nothing interfered with their apparent progress toward certification. Indeed, the key tests of strength at many conventions, while they came in other areas preliminary to the presidential ballot, were "key" precisely because they were linked to an outcome on that ballot. As a result, nominating procedures drew into their vortex many challenges in these other areas—in credentials, rules, platform, even the selection of a vice president—which were mounted quite independently of the struggle for a nomination and which were not even intended to influence its outcome. As a result of that, and finally, other challenges in these traditional realms were mounted in full awareness that they were likely to become linked to progress toward the nomination, so that they could potentially borrow strategic advantage from the need of an emerging nominee to guarantee that they did not disrupt that progress.

Nevertheless, since the adoption of the Twelfth Amendment to the Constitution before the election of 1804, a presidential "ticket" had needed both an aspiring president and a vice president, so designated. With the rise of the national party convention before the election of 1832, the selection of this "running mate" had passed effectively into the new body, where it remained except in cases of death, incapacitation, or withdrawal.[1] Accordingly, the selection of a vice president became automatically subject to all those other pressures, purposes, and conflicts which influenced convention decisions of any sort. On the one hand, then, this selection became one more embodiment of the recurring splits and struggles characterizing the convention. On the other hand it was sufficiently different from the nomination of a presidential candidate that it embodied these conflicts in different, if still quite regular, ways.

The operative criteria for selecting a running mate had always varied as the events of a given political year dictated. But the generic core of these criteria had nevertheless changed sharply with the two great shifts in the overall operation of the convention, the movement of the nomination itself into the delegate selection process and the change of convention participants from party officials to interested partisans. As the nomination came increasingly to be resolved during delegate selection, and as the emerging presidential candidate came inevitably to play a larger and larger role in this effort, the ability of that candidate to designate his own running mate—along with the norm that this was an obvious and reasonable personal concern—grew accordingly. In fact, the last convention of either party to go to a second ballot for a *vice* presidential nominee, the Democratic convention of 1944, preceded by eight years the last convention to require a second ballot for president.

These developments did not mean, however, that the successful presidential contender was fully free to indulge his personal preferences. The practical needs of the general election campaign could powerfully constrain his individual choice. The more immediate needs of his national nominating convention, in converting his apparent majority into a concrete nominating vote, might constrain that choice as well. But the departure of the effective construction of a nominating majority from the convention did guarantee that the front-runner would henceforth be at least the central actor in negotiations over selection of a running mate, just as that departure spelled the end of the era when an autonomous convention might not only settle upon some dark horse candidate for president but create his candidacy as part of a bargain including the vice presidency.

The same reforms in the process of delegate selection which then institutionalized the construction of nominating majorities outside the convention, however, also changed the context for vice presidential selection. Those reforms represented a massive shift from a party-oriented to a candidate-oriented process. The resulting delegates, in turn, represented a shift from party officials to independent issue activists and interest group representatives, although as time passed, even party officials came more and more to resemble these other groups. In any case, as a consequence, in an unforeseen but surely not surprising fashion, the selection of a vice president became subject to the regular and recurring strains among these new convention participants, including inevitably the struggle over use of the convention either to launch the general election campaign or to cap the nominating drive of one or another convention subgroup.[2]

From one side, of course, the nominee and his entourage, ordinarily aided by the formal leadership of the full convention, reliably attempted to coordinate the proceedings, including selection of a running mate, to launch the general election campaign in the most advantageous way possible. This meant, unless other developments intervened, selecting a running mate to "balance" the ticket geographically and factionally, ideally while moving the entire ticket toward the ideological center and toward identification with the general public, ideally in a fashion which reinforced public impressions of the nominee as a person in charge of his convention. From the other side, however, there was always a substantial number of delegates, and often a number of candidates as well, for whom the convention was rather clearly the end of the line. If they could not achieve some portion of their goals from the nominating campaign—the nomination itself having eluded them—they might well leave the convention with nothing at all. As a result, the need for the full convention to nominate and then confirm a vice presidential candidate became one more guaranteed theater in which to pursue their remaining goals.

The effective ability to nominate an alternative candidate for vice president was in fact widespread within the ordinary convention; the ability to threaten to make such a nomination was yet more widely available. Moreover, an explicit vice presidential nomination was a guaranteed way at least to address the convention on behalf of one goal or another. The absorption of convention time resulting from actual conflict over the vice presidency, even if it did not automatically create an impression of weakness on the part of the successful nominee, was an automatic cost, levied upon him. Accordingly, the threat of such an action was itself a bargaining counter, to be traded with the nominee and his entourage in return for something as pointed as a policy plank or as general as additional time on the convention rostrum.

Approval of Credentials, Rules, and a Platform

The internal structure of the convention—not much of a structure but all there ever was—involved a small set of committees. These appeared gradually, to address a set of recurring operational needs: for a definition of entitlement to official participation (Committee on Credentials), for a decision on occupants of major convention offices (Committee on Permanent Organization), for a protocol on the conduct of regular convention activities (Committee on Rules and Order of Business), and for promulgation of a program for the party in November (Committee on Platform and Resolutions). The Committee on Permanent Organization actually emerged and then atrophied, to the point where the Democrats abolished it and the Republicans assembled it for ceremonial purposes only. But the other three, the "big three" committees of the national party convention, became early fixtures. As such, they reliably issued reports for adoption on the full convention floor. These reports, in turn, intermittently contained major substantive proposals, for the implementation of public policy or the conduct of future presidential selections.[3]

Whether these proposals were conceivably major or not, however, the possibility of using them to advance particular convention goals was inherent in anything so integral to the proceedings. Many of the credentials, rules, or platform challenges which followed from this situation were brought deliberately to advance the prospects of one or another presidential contender. Yet because the construction of a nominating majority was the primary focus of most convention actors, for most of the life of the national party convention, many other such challenges, not brought initially to contribute to that outcome, were drawn into the vortex of nominating struggles and came to contribute to—as well as to stand or fall with—the ultimate nomination. Even so, there were ordinarily still other proposals, other majority or minority reports from the Credentials, Rules, or Platform committees, which were never explicitly connected to a candidacy but which became the subjects of convention conflict and ultimately absorbed significant time and energy.

The details of any given set of challenges were inevitably peculiar to the politics of a specific presidential year. Nevertheless, the general character of such challenges did change in certain clear if limited ways. Over time, most such challenges which revolved from the start around one particular candidacy moved from being attempts to influence the climate for construction of a nominating majority to being tests of strength between an emerging nominee and one or more others who hoped to wrest the nomination away. Over time as well, most of those challenges which did not stem from a particular candidacy moved from involving a local electoral problem to involving the policy desires of a specific organized interest. Thus there were credentials challenges brought specifically to advance the fortunes of a candidate or candidates, just as there were credentials challenges arising autonomously and supported only in passing by a nominee or his opponents. There were rules initiatives brought specifically to ensure or disrupt an emergent nominating majority, along with rules initiatives not only brought independently of current candidates but unlikely to have practical effects until some future campaign. There were platform proposals—a stream of them across time and a seemingly interminable flow in the postreform era—from the campaigns of the nomination contenders, from issue organizations and interest groups as a way to influence the fate of those contenders, and from organizations and groups which cared more about these proposals than about any given nomination.[4]

From one side, dissident delegates brought their alternative proposals, their aspiring alternative minority reports, in order to cap their own participation in the nominating drive and realize their goals from that preceding contest. Often, they brought these proposals because the nomination had eluded them, and this was their last chance to secure some reward from all their preceding efforts. Sometimes, they brought these proposals because, having seen their candidate move to the brink of nomination, they found themselves in a position to seek something more, after a judgment that even the nomination of their preferred candidate was not really reward enough. In either case, there was one final twist on this maneuver.

Dissident delegates who were mounting an aspiring minority report always had to trade off the possibility of limiting their demands, and thus having the emerging nominee acquiesce directly and include these demands in the majority report, against the possibility of making those demands sufficiently extreme that the nominee could not easily acquiesce in them as presented, thereby guaranteeing these delegates the ability to use the convention floor—and attendant convention coverage—to publicize their cause directly. In fact, such delegates reliably preferred the second course, with its more extreme demands and its more overt conflict. From the other side, there appeared in principle to be a counterpart choice. The nominee and his major advisers could accept these proposed minority reports, even if they were comparatively extreme, in order to avoid open conflict and orchestrate the convention to the fullest extent possible. Or they could fight the more extreme proposals, so as not to be drawn away from the political center and become identified with dissident groups and causes which would not prove attractive in the general election campaign. In the event, however, nominees reliably preferred the first option, accepting the proposed alternative if at all possible, thereby implicitly confirming—through what was often little short of surrender—that they considered the potentialities in orchestrating the convention to be far more important than the content of credentials, rules, or a platform.

The New Era Realized: The Democrats, 1980

The two conventions of 1980 offered almost an inventory of the types and theaters of internal conflict in the postreform era. Both featured extended conflict in the preconvention period, yet neither threatened to give the convention itself a serious role in the nomination. Each offered serious remaining disputes, revolving around candidate differences among the Democrats, delegate differences (and hence splits between the nominee and his supporters) among the Republicans. These disputes, in turn, came to center on the major, recurring, traditional activities of the national party convention. Finally, these two conventions together, presented most of the major strategies with which key actors reliably attempted to create, and then address, and then resolve these conflicts.

While the Democratic convention was ultimately the more conflictual, and while it certainly did nothing to enhance the electoral prospects of its nominee, the possibility that this convention would break loose and resolve its difficulties by nominating someone else was never great. During much of 1979, the eventual challenger to President Jimmy Carter, Senator Edward Kennedy of Massachusetts, had managed to lead the president solidly in the polls. A series of events late in that year, however—from one side the Iranian hostage crisis, from the other a fumbling start to the Kennedy campaign—effectively erased that possibility. Carter defeated Kennedy in the critical stepping-stone contests of Iowa and New Hampshire. He annihilated the challenger in the sequence of southern primaries which followed. And although Kennedy did keep his campaign alive, actually winning five of the eight primaries in the concluding round, the delegate totals were by then apparently decisive.[5]

Perhaps only the Kennedy name, along with a generation of political attachments, could have sustained this campaign in the face of these results. But probably, the programmatic attachments of most interested partisans—the National Education Association, militantly for Carter, was a striking exception—were equally consequential in sustaining this effort. In any case, the very staying power of a campaign which had never gone as its partisans had hoped was as good an explanation as any for why the contest continued into the convention. A candidate who had managed to sustain a campaign which was apparently never going to achieve the nomination had obviously managed to attract, and maintain, the support of numerous issue activists and group representatives, over and above his personal supporters. These individuals, even if the odds seemed disadvantageous, wanted some sort of fight to justify their continued support. Their candidate moved to give them that fight at the convention.

Despite this resolve, President Carter had over three hundred more delegates than he needed for nomination by the end of the delegate selection process. Moreover, he possessed a rule which permitted a candidate to replace any delegate selected in his name who threatened to vote for someone else with a loyal alternate. Accordingly, in order to continue his own campaign, Kennedy had to attack that stricture, Rule F(3)c, which he did with a minority report from the Rules Committee. The upsurge of the Kennedy campaign in the final round of primaries could provide the rationale for an argument that shifting public loyalties required an "open convention." In turn, failure at this attempt would automatically and immediately doom any nominating aspirations. Yet although the attack on F(3)c inevitably became the centerpiece of the Kennedy nomination assault, it was joined by five other minority reports on rules, addressing such topics as the percentage requirement for bringing items to the floor by petition and the guarantee of a midterm party conference two years down the road.[6]

Some of these proposals were intended as "bargaining chips" in the orthodox sense, that is, as proposals to be traded with the Carter leadership, which remained firmly in control of the formal arrangements—and agenda—for the convention. Some, however, were just as reasonably seen as bargaining chips between the Kennedy leadership and its own delegates, as items which might give those delegates a sense that the campaign had furthered some goals, even if the nomination was not ultimately among them. There was, however, a major Kennedy initiative in the Platform Committee as well. The centerpiece of this effort was a set of minority planks on economic policy, embodying what the Kennedy camp asserted to be the true programmatic heart of the Democratic party. If the rules fight was successful, and if this programmatic judgment proved correct, these planks might be enough to tempt newly freed delegates to join the Kennedy camp on platform—and perhaps stay with it for the nominating ballot.

Specific planks were tailored even more pointedly toward this goal. Thus there was a guaranteed jobs program, to put cross-pressure on black delegates in the Carter camp. There was a promise that the administration would not fight inflation with any means which might raise unemployment, to put cross-pressure on the labor delegates for Carter. And so on. There were also assorted other minority reports on platform, again serving as bargaining chips, either with the Carter leadership or with the Kennedy rank and file. There was even a specific credentials challenge, to six delegates in Virginia, along with a set of minority reports on credentials policy, to create bargaining counters in the Credentials Committee, too.

The drive for an open convention, in any case, and with it the chance that Kennedy might conceivably be nominated, was to end early, on opening night. The Carter leadership, while asserting that its delegates would have stayed behind the president even if there had never been an F(3)c, was not inclined to put that assertion to the test and did not release them. The Kennedy leadership, while asserting that the fight for an open convention was more important than any individual candidacy, was not inclined to facilitate that fight by having its candidate withdraw. As a result, the vote on Rules Minority Report No. 1 —at 1,391 to 1,936—was only about 45 votes off the division between the all-but-Carter forces and Carter's—estimated at 1,348 to 1,981 as the convention assembled. The implication of that vote was obvious, and within hours Kennedy announced his withdrawal, freeing his delegates to vote their conscience.[7]

Kennedy did not, however, abandon his economic policy package, nor did he remove his whip system from the convention floor. Kennedy lobbyists worked hard—with great success—during the morning and afternoon to follow. By Tuesday night, after a long afternoon of platform wrangles in other areas, the Carter bloc was crumbling. Rather than face losses on plank after plank the Carter leadership sued for an agreement. Kennedy would get to deliver his address as planned, but his economic package would be handled by voice vote from the podium. The permanent chairman of the convention, Thomas P. O'Neill, the speaker of the U.S. House, may actually have misannounced the agreed outcome, but four proposals had been accepted and one rejected in advance, and that was the published result of the eventual voice vote. More to the point in any case, the Kennedy platform had been successfully tacked on to the Carter nomination, Kennedy had delivered what was generally hailed as the premier speech of the convention, and the Carter leadership was still awaiting its opportunity to begin orchestrating that gathering for the general election campaign.

The Democratic convention of 1980 was thus destined to be one at which this orchestration did not really begin until the final elements on the agenda, the acceptance speeches of the vice president and president. The Kennedy forces were to hold together through the presidential balloting, despite the fact that their man was not officially nominated, losing only 75 votes from their estimated strength coming into the convention. Indeed, some would argue that effective orchestration by the Carter leadership never arrived at all. For Kennedy was to deliver a slap even after the acceptance speech, by actively avoiding an attempt from Carter at a symbolic clasping of arms, while the red, white, and blue balloons which were poised to shower the hall in another symbolic grand finale largely failed, again on national television, to come down.

The New Era Realized: The Republicans, 1980

The Republican convention of 1980 was noticeably different from its Democratic counterpart. It was different in its overall level of conflict, and that may have been the crucial, practical distinction, because it permitted a much more consistent and extended orchestration of the convention for the fall campaign. Yet it was also different, almost point by point, in component elements, so that the Republican convention completed a near-perfect, composite whole, filling in most of the missing theaters for conflict, along with most of the available strategies for addressing them. Where the Democratic contest had appeared to be settled by the opening primary but had nevertheless extended through the convention, the Republican contest offered early elements of candidate uncertainty, followed by the demise of candidate conflict. On the other hand, where candidate conflict had infused the struggles over rules, platform, and credentials at the Democratic convention, it was factional division—between the ultimate winner and his own supporters—which propelled that conflict at the Republican convention and which added a vice presidential struggle, too.

The Republican contest began, it is true, with an experienced frontrunner, favored in the polls and possessing campaign resources aplenty. Yet Ronald Reagan also faced an extended field for what was, after all, an "open" nominating contest, one lacking an incumbent president. Moreover, there was a major surprise when the apparent front-runner was upset in the opening caucuses, where the Republicans too allowed a public tallying of presidential preferences, so that reporters could know that there had in fact been an upset. George Bush was the new threat coming out of Iowa, but the combination of inhospitable territory for the opening primary in New Hampshire, a continuing lead in resources and the long-established attachment of many Republican voters to Reagan, and some mistakes by the Bush campaign itself, allowed Reagan to right himself quickly. When the campaign then moved south for a series of Reagan wins, to be consolidated with a victory in industrial Illinois, the nomination was effectively resolved, although Bush did manage to hang on through the successful Michigan primary, after which the mounting delegate edge for Reagan and a desperate shortage of activists and finances finally brought the Bush campaign to an end.

As a result, there was never even an illusory threat that the convention would get to make a presidential nomination.[8] Oddly enough, however, the absence of any remaining candidate base for conflict at the convention only served to emphasize the possibilities for delegate conflict, between Reagan and his putative supporters. In fact, this conflict broke open in the Platform Committee, the week before the full convention assembled. While the presence of such a conflict within an overwhelming triumph for the emerging nominee was inherent testimony to the very different interests of delegates and candidates even in such a contest, the response of the Reagan campaign was simultaneous testimony to the dominant counterstrategy of a nominating campaign confronted with convention conflict in the postreform world.

The Platform Committee, as it turned out, was a haven for militant delegates with strong policy preferences. Most were reliable Reagan supporters, but they had joined his campaign to advance their policy goals too, and with the nomination assured, they were free to turn to these. Some of the more idiosyncratic planks which resulted, such as condemnation of the 55-mile-per-hour speed limit, probably received more attention than they merited. But the strongly conservative social policies underlying the platform, including a repudiation of the Equal Rights Amendment, along with stiffly conservative positions on foreign affairs, including a call for military superiority over the Soviet Union, were central features of the resulting document.

As they became aware of developments on platform, the Reagan staff did mount a countercampaign on some of the most extreme proposals. Thus the failure to say anything about the ERA was actually a subsequent compromise, pulling the committee back from aggressively hostile language; the dropping of a promise to return to recognizing Taiwan rather than Communist China was likewise a response to this effort at "damage control." Yet in most areas, the national Reagan team decided that it would be wiser, given the composition of the Platform Committee, not to battle for policy alternatives. Moderates on the committee did not have the 25 percent necessary to mount minority reports. Conservatives could not push their proposals before the full convention—and its television audience—if they were not challenged. As a result the principal strategy of the Reagan leadership was to leave the evolving platform alone.[9]

With neither candidate conflict nor foreseeable disputes on credentials, rules, or platform—there were no credentials challenges at all, and a smaller but parallel revolt on the Rules Committee was papered over by another damage-control team—the main official activity unresolved as the convention opened was the selection of a vice presidential nominee. At the Democratic convention, the vice presidency had not been an issue. Jimmy Carter already had a vice president; Teddy Kennedy never needed one. But at the Republican convention, not just advance speculation but the major news story of convention week came to center on the vice presidency when it suddenly seemed possible, on Tuesday evening, that former President Gerald Ford might be convinced to return as vice president under Reagan.

Discussions around this possibility may always have had more theoretical attraction than practical plausibility. In any case, by the end of the evening Ford was out of the running, and Reagan himself appeared in the convention hall to note that his rival from the nominating contest, George Bush, would be his running mate. In choosing Bush, Reagan made the ultimate, orthodox, strategic move. He focused on the general election and found a running mate who would not only take the ticket back toward the center and reach out to groups in the party who had not been part of his nominating coalition but would bind up wounds from the preconvention campaign as well. The selection of Bush, however, also set off the major "nonstory" of the Republican convention by stimulating another revolt by dedicated Reagan delegates, one which had to be contained aggressively during the next twenty-four hours.[10]

The naming of Bush late Tuesday night triggered anguished protests in numerous state delegations, along with nightlong consideration of a response by some. This potential revolt was concentrated in the southern, plains, and mountain states. It even acquired an incipient alternative candidate for vice president, Senator Jesse Helms of North Carolina. Recognizing the potential at least for embarrassment, the Reagan leadership spent much of the following day trying to move its own delegates back into line. A statement of endorsement from southern Republican state chairs was again circulated actively. Teams of Republican spokesmen made the rounds of various state delegations with the praises, this time, of the Reagan-*Bush* ticket. Campaign operatives were detailed to make additional calls to bolster loyalists in the states. Helms was pressed to withdraw publicly.

The result was a successful, overwhelming ballot for Bush on the next evening, Wednesday. The fact that the maneuvering to firm up support for Bush, like the maneuvering to keep platform conflict out of the convention, was primarily handled off the floor meant that this convention could be turned almost entirely to the task of launching the general election campaign. The podium was used consistently for this purpose, to the point of inserting the president of the NAACP, Benjamin Hooks, as one more example of the promised Reagan outreach. Indeed, the more explicitly scripted arguments about the election campaign—why disgruntled Democrats should turn to Reagan and why he better represented the values of "traditional Democrats"— were able to be presented so thoroughly that when Bush and then Reagan finally appeared for their acceptance speeches, these could serve as the summation, rather than the introduction, of themes for the fall campaign.

The New Era in Repose: Republicans and Democrats, 1984

The conventions of 1984, both of them, were pale shadows of their 1980 counterparts. Once more, the Democratic contest was to sustain some candidate conflict into the convention proper, whereas the Republican contest was to see even the potential for such conflict snuffed out long before. Once more, the Democratic gathering was to have a higher level of conflict overall, even when specific candidate efforts were subtracted. Once more, platform and the vice presidency were to be the traditional activities which highlighted the struggle between using the convention to target the general election and using it to cap the nominating campaign. Yet this time, every one of those aspects was to unfold in a less conflictual fashion, although the Democrats were still to add several new gambits—one a major element, really—to the array of strategies for coping with the nomination-election dilemma.

The small amount of overt conflict which the Republican convention could offer once again centered on the Platform Committee. Although rumblings of a possible challenge to the incumbent president had surfaced in the party around the midterm election of 1982, those rumblings had dissipated, and no challenge of any sort had ultimately materialized. By 1984 in fact, the country was at peace, the economy was on the upswing, the president was personally popular, and the Republicans assembled without the slightest prospect of candidate-based combat. Nevertheless, the more programmatically militant delegates, always attracted to the Platform Committee, again provided some overt tension for the gathering when they began to drive the platform in aggressive new directions. Again as a result, the Reagan leadership had to dispatch a damage-control team to try to rein these initiatives in.[11]

Some mild compromises were the result. Actively hostile language on the ERA was stymied, and a return to the gold standard was lauded as worth studying rather than as a goal for the second term. But on other matters, such as condemnation of the Federal Reserve Board or a detailed promise not to raise taxes, the committee majority could not be moved, and the Reagan leadership preferred to accept the platform as drafted rather than have platform conflict on the convention floor. Moreover, the Reagan team moved to see that not even a hint of conflict accompanied the other possible point of tension, the vote on the vice president. Dissident delegates retained at least the theoretical possibility—and some had the conscious intention—of giving George Bush a less overwhelming endorsement than they did the president. The Reagan team moved to have the two men voted as a ticket and thereby eliminated that possibility.

The Democratic convention was hardly this pacific, and both the amount of time available for setting out the themes of the fall campaign and the coordination of major convention events toward that goal were necessarily more limited. Yet the degree—and especially the depth—of subtractions from that goal were still far less than in the preceding convention. Some candidate-based conflict remained, but it was less intense than in 1980 and more effectively countered. Some delegate-based conflict actually surfaced, and more was initially in the wings, but here too the response was far more effective than in 1980. Indeed, the Mondale leadership managed to fashion a new set of responses by an emerging nominee to the recurring dilemmas of convention management, strategies which were likely to recur intermittently with successors, perhaps in both parties.

The nominating campaigns in the Democratic party in 1984 had never really suggested that the convention itself would get to make a nomination, though they did at times achieve a roller coaster quality. Walter Mondale had begun as the prohibitive favorite, but an onrushing Gary Hart came in a close second in Iowa, upset Mondale in New Hampshire, and threatened to finish him off early if the Mondale campaign could not right itself. That campaign did survive, thanks to a shift to a more favorable set of states and to the loyalty of a coalition of interest groups, and it then moved back inexorably, if haltingly, toward a first-ballot nomination. The fact that Hart managed to win the majority of votes in the last big round of presidential primaries (as Kennedy had done four years before), however, and the fact that Jesse Jackson managed to sustain his campaign too, provided some incentive for continuing those nominating campaigns into the convention.[12]

The concrete upshot was five minority reports from the Platform Committee, but this was still a reduction from the twenty-three of 1980, and these five were in fact handled very quickly. On three from Jackson, the Mondale campaign decided that a fight was desirable, defeating each in turn. On the other from Jackson, on affirmative action, they sought and achieved a linguistic compromise, so as not to appear to be attacking black voters while resisting their candidate. The fifth minority report, from the Hart campaign, proscribing the use of military force in Central America and the Middle East, had the most peculiar career. In committee, the Mondale leadership had opposed this plank, arguing that it would tie the hands of a president while emboldening enemies. But on the floor of the convention, it became clear that the Hart position had a strong majority, including many Mondale delegates. The Mondale leadership attempted to accept the plank, but the Hart leadership, wanting to win its vote rather than have it conceded, demanded a roll call—which was overwhelming after the Mondale endorsement.

The interesting strategic twists from the Mondale campaign, however, came in two other areas.[13] First, as part of an effort to conciliate both Hart and Jackson, thereby mobilizing their supporters behind the Mondale ticket while not appearing to be intimidated or defeated by them, the Mondale leadership gave each candidate a major convention speech during prime television time in return for good behavior. Traditionally, any candidate who could theoretically be nominated for president did not appear in the hall before the nominating ballot, and even Kennedy in 1980 had met the letter of that tradition. All sides ignored the tradition in 1984 in the interest of their separate candidate goals, and it was probably dispatched for good thereafter.

Even more striking, though not as reliably institutionalized, was an attempt to deal with an incipient delegate revolt, one potentially more damaging than the evolving candidate challenges. A minor threat of this sort, aimed at the nomination itself, was floated by some Hispanic delegates, who urged a boycott of the initial ballot to protest an immigration bill before Congress. They were joined by some black delegates, urging a courtesy vote for Jackson on the initial ballot. In principle, these moves might have denied Mondale a first-ballot nomination, but they were quickly defused by a contrary lobbying effort, especially when the Mondale leadership was able to demonstrate that the Hispanics behind this effort were uniformly Hart supporters, operating with the help of the Hart campaign.

More serious in its eventual prospects was an early threat by organized feminists, coordinated through the National Women's Political Caucus, backed by a sizable war chest for the convention itself, and aimed at the very least at the party platform—but potentially at an independent candidate for the vice presidential nomination. What made this threat so additionally credible, of course, was the new requirement that 50 percent of the convention be female. Many of the resulting delegates were recruited specifically to meet the gender quota; many of those who were not so recruited were nevertheless committed feminists. The Mondale leadership, in any case, cut this threat off early by naming a congresswoman from New York, Geraldine Ferraro, as running mate. At a shot, this move eliminated not only the most serious possibility for tension between the nominee and his own delegates but most of the prospect for conflict in traditional areas such as platform as well.

Vice Presidential Struggles

The fact that internal convention conflict in the postreform era was centered on the traditional activities of the convention—on two nominations and three committee reports—was largely a result of the con-

tinuation of these activities at the organizational center of the convention agenda and their ready accessibility there. Perhaps it is not
surprising that this conflict assumed certain regular and recurring patterns as well. In general terms, the conflict in each of these areas tended
to embody the tensions between the convention as the capstone of
the nominating campaign and the convention as the springboard for
the general election. In more specifically strategic terms, the conflict
in each area frequently featured an effort by particular factions among
the delegates to find policy demands sufficiently extreme to be worth
fighting over, in the face of an effort by the nominee and his entourage
to compromise with those demands rather than endure any extended
conflict. Each of these realms, however, was also different in its potential for attracting convention struggles and in the detailed initiatives
and responses which appeared within it.

Nowhere was this potential for conflict, along with this array of
recurring strategies and their embodiment of the tension between
nomination and election, more pointedly illustrated than in the construction of a majority for the vice presidential nomination. Vice presidential conflicts of some sort characterized every convention of the
postreform era, with the partial exception of the Republican convention of 1972, and serious conflicts over this choice ran the gamut of
motives, strategies, and responses. Such conflicts varied most obviously
in their propensity to absorb convention time and energy, but while
any losses in this area were an annoyance to the nominee and his
entourage, the real consequence of these losses was dependent on the
overall tenor of the convention. A successfully orchestrated convention
could stand a little diversion on the vice presidential nomination; a
convention already going sour would be dangerously reinforced by
that same struggle. Accordingly, a much more critical variation among
conventions in these conflicts came in their differing abilities to cause—
really to force—the nominee to deviate from his prospective strategy
for the general election and to compromise with an existing convention
majority.

At one end of the spectrum were those independent, minor vice
presidential candidacies mounted solely to make a convention address.
There were three of these at the Democratic convention of 1976, two
at the Democratic convention of 1980, and one at the Democratic
convention of 1984, to call for, among other things, homosexual
rights, attention to the third world, and an end to conscription.[14] These
initiatives automatically consumed time which nominees would have
preferred to put to other uses. Moreover, they consumed that time at

just the point when these nominees were otherwise assured of devoting the formal agenda to their particular strategies for the general election. On the other hand, this loss was ordinarily minor, it was consequential only when time was already in short supply, and such incidents probably loomed much larger for the nominee's campaign team than for anyone else in the convention or even in the external audience.

More consequential for the direct impact of the convention on the electoral fate of its presidential nominee were efforts by organized factions among the delegates to use the selection of a vice president to protest openly the larger strategic decisions by the nominee, including especially his decision to begin moving toward the political center. One clear case of this in the postreform period was the incipient protest against the slating of George Bush at the Republican convention of 1980. Ronald Reagan did manage to move toward the political center in spite of this threat by ideological and social conservatives, but only after mounting a daylong, comprehensive effort to allay their displeasure. More serious was the actual revolt against the slating of Thomas Eagleton at the Democratic convention of 1972. George McGovern also kept to his general election strategy, but only by enduring an obvious convention protest involving candidates who were both nominated and supported in the vice presidential balloting, only by seeing that protest contribute to a portrait of McGovern himself which he did not desire, and only by having his attempt to begin orchestrating his convention further delayed.

These efforts were distinguished by the fact that they resulted in open convention conflict and by the way this conflict not only absorbed precious time but disrupted the nominee's effort to orchestrate the convention. They were not, however, distinguished by any ultimate success in changing the identity of the proposed vice president nor by forcing the nominee to compromise on his general election strategy and accede to demands rooted in the nominating campaign. The most serious incidents of vice presidential conflict in the postreform era, however, possessed all these additional practical characteristics. Ironically, such incidents were part and parcel of conventions which offered no open division on the vice presidential ballot. Most commonly, of course, that absence of division was testimony to the success of the nominee in orchestrating his coronation, as with the Republican convention of 1972. But sometimes, it was testimony instead to divisions so deep that the nominee had already felt obliged to cater to dissident factions rather than direct his vice presidential selection toward the general election campaign. In those cases the nominee sacrificed not just the vice presidency but a substantial piece of his general election strategy to avoid threatened conflict at the convention.

Thus Walter Mondale managed to defuse the most significant potential protest at the Democratic convention of 1984, but only by anticipating and obviating that protest through the selection of Geraldine Ferraro. Gerald Ford faced a much tougher vice presidential scenario, perhaps the toughest of them all, when his nomination at the Republican convention of 1976 came to turn on a proposed rule for identifying an intended running mate.[15] Ford had to defeat that rule before securing his own position, but even after surmounting this challenge, his hold on the convention remained sufficiently precarious that he felt obliged to select a more conservative vice president. The strategic dilemma in Ford's decision had been made all the more painful by the outcome of the Democratic convention the previous month, which had nominated the relatively conservative Jimmy Carter for president. Indeed, that dilemma was made even more poignant by the fact that Ford already possessed a relatively liberal vice president in Nelson Rockefeller, who was calibrated precisely to help him move toward the political center—and fight Carter. Yet Ford's need to secure his own convention by moving in the *opposite* direction was immediate and paramount, and it ultimately took precedence over this larger strategic goal.

The Vice Presidency among Republicans and Democrats

These individual examples do not suggest much fundamental difference between the parties. As usual, the Democratic party had surfaced vice presidential conflict a trifle earlier in the postreform period, although this was almost entirely an accident of the open nominating contest in the party in 1972 and of the presence of a sitting president in the Republican party that year. Beyond that accidental precedence, the Democrats did reliably feature ritualistic vice presidential nominations, made only to use the podium to address an external audience, of which the Republican party has so far been free. Nevertheless, and more consequentially, serious maneuvering around the vice presidential nomination has characterized both parties since reform. Indeed, the most forceful attempt to use the vice presidency to affect the *presidential* nomination, as well as the most obviously coerced decision to cater to the convention at the expense of the general election campaign through the selection of a different vice president, was a Republican affair.

In few other realms was the structure of politicking at conventions more similar between the two parties. The outstanding distinction, in fact, was not in the nature of the parties outside the convention, or in the structuring of conflict inside that institution, but in a specific rule for delegate selection which the Democrats possessed and the Republicans did not—and in the responses of Democratic nominees to the products of that rule. The rule demanded equal division among the sexes at Democratic national conventions, and it was integral to the situation to which Walter Mondale responded in slating Geraldine Ferraro as his running mate in 1984.[16] His decision was not distinctive in the perceived need to placate an organized interest group within the convention, as with organized feminists in this case. It was not even different in revealing a willingness to placate that group at the expense of orthodox electoral logic; Gerald Ford had certainly done that at the Republican convention of 1976. Moreover, it was remarkably successful in accomplishing its goals at the convention—to the point where Gary Hart, the main opponent to Mondale, felt compelled to announce that he too, if nominated, would slate Ferraro.

Where the difference—the institutionalized difference—lay was in the reason that the group to be placated was present in such substantial numbers. For 1984 was the first year in which the Democratic quota for women delegates—50 percent, equal division—was in effect. No one bothered to argue that the convention would have attained that balance if delegates had been elected on their own; this inability was, after all, the justification for the reform. The delegates selected by direct connection to this rule, however, were disproportionately likely to be feminists; indeed, they would have had difficulty being slated if they had been unacceptable to organized feminists in their states. Thereafter, the chance that they would break from Mondale, for platform challenges and perhaps even a vice presidential contender of their own, was ever present—and constantly discussed.[17]

Most analysts were agreed on what Mondale needed in a running mate by the traditional electoral calculus. He needed someone who could pull votes specifically in the South, else an electoral majority was almost out of the question. Failing that, he needed someone who would at least reduce Mondale's image as a product of the organized interests and who would move him clearly back toward the political center to boot. Ferraro filled none of these needs. She did, however, fill the need to avoid open conflict and permit thorough orchestration of the convention. In fact, she filled that need so well that feminist leaders lamented the lack of intensity among their delegates—because they had secured a historic gain before the convention opened. What made this selection different from anything in the Republican environment, then, was that the faction being placated was at the convention largely because of explicit, reformed, procedural guarantees, so that the Democratic nominee, in responding to incentives from the convention rather than from the election, was in part responding to his own party rules. What remained unclear was whether the Democratic party, in continuing these procedural arrangements, had institutionalized a new notion of the "balanced ticket" for most conventions to come.

The Framework for Committee Struggles: The Democrats

The first postreform convention to be characterized by extended internal conflict, a gathering which produced instances of conflict in every one of the traditional realms, was the Democratic convention of 1972. It was, accordingly, no surprise that the Democratic party was the first to address the question of additional means for constraining, or at least channeling, subsequent conflict. The idea of an interim reform commission for this purpose was no longer novel, since a commission from the interim between 1968 and 1972 had actually contributed to the process which indirectly produced all this newly augmented conflict. In any case, the 1972 convention authorized a new reform body, for the period 1972–1976. This commission was ultimately to have a rancorous public life, building on hostilities from the presidential politics of 1972 and on the continuing intraparty suspicions which were both cause and effect of these hostilities. Yet this commission was also to feature a peculiar unity on internal convention rules, one which would alter the official framework for subsequent convention conflict.[18]

In fact, it was this perverse unity which produced the single largest change in internal convention arrangements for 1976, one with implications not just for politics in its immediate institutional domain—the Credentials Committee—but for the hierarchy of concern among convention delegates with all reformed convention committees. This change involved creation at national party headquarters of a compliance review panel, which would be responsible for approving each state plan for delegate selection as it was developed, granting certification only when every element of the plan was in total compliance with national reform rules. If a state did not achieve certification, the national party would dictate a substitute procedure to select state delegates to the national convention. But when a state did achieve certification—and all were expected to, given the alternative—the only task remaining for the Credentials Committee would be to investigate whether these certified rules had actually been followed.

Despite the fact that this represented on its face a historically new credentialing arrangement for the national Democratic party, there was an odd consensus on the new arrangement. Credentials disputes had been a major contribution to the negative impact of the disastrous convention of 1968. The sweeping reform package developed after 1968 had been partially justified with the argument that it would reduce such challenges sharply. The result of this complex party code, however, had been a record-shattering number of challenges instead. From one side, then, party officials were prepared to go along with almost any arrangement which would extract them from their credentials tangle, by choking off challenges early and by resolving those which could not be choked. From the other side, self-conscious reformers, having developed extensive and detailed regulations to govern the selection of delegates, remained concerned with "judicializing" the credentials process, so that party officials could not undo their carefully crafted procedures at the convention itself. The result was the proposed compliance review panel.[19]

This result, however, was still not the end of changes in the environment for committee politics, and hence in the structure of the national convention. For those at Democratic national headquarters who drafted the proposed calendar for convention committees in 1976, as supported subsequently by the temporary Rules Committee, took this same set of goals—and this same odd unity—a step farther. As convention time approached, they proposed to move the deliberations of *all* their committees back out of the convention, into the month preceding it. Again, party officials, concerned with the impact of convention conflict, were easily amenable to the suggestion that committee business be moved outside the convention and scheduled well in advance of its official sessions. In this way, conflicts brewed in the three major committees could not spill directly into the convention hall, while as many of those conflicts as possible could be resolved—compromised out—before the convention assembled. From the other side, the independent issue activists and interest group representatives, newly advantaged by the reformed process of delegate selection, were also prepared to endorse a change in the basic calendar of the convention. In part, this was because some of the champions of the reform movement, such as George McGovern, were also appalled at the largely pointless divisiveness of the 1972 convention. But in larger part, it was because these individuals were especially invested in the substance of reports from these committees, in and of itself. Accordingly, they welcomed the additional time to consider particular platform planks or proposed rules changes.

Perhaps surprisingly, this reform worked almost exactly as its sponsors had imagined. Indeed, after 1972 (and at least through 1984), there was never again a major credentials challenge at a Democratic convention. Even in 1980, when the forces of Senator Edward Kennedy made a dedicated effort to "open up" the convention, they challenged only six delegates, all from Virginia, although they did produce a challenge to the underlying process as well, that is, to the prior use of a compliance review panel rather than to the sole subsequent use of the Credentials Committee. Yet this larger challenge was introduced mainly as a bargaining counter—many of the Kennedy strategists had been among those most concerned with judicializing the process—and it was subsequently withdrawn, leaving the new arrangements intact and affirmed.

One result was a hierarchy of concern among reformed convention delegates with the committee reports of postreform conventions. The success of credentials reform meant that the Credentials Committee was by far the least interesting, the least intriguing in substance and least promising in the generation of strategic conflict. Of more concern was the Rules Committee, which not only adopted the rules and order of business for the current convention—upon which the current nomination might occasionally turn—but considered the rules for future delegate selection, and hence presidential nomination, as well. Yet even with these possibilities in Rules, it was the Platform Committee which reliably drew the widest and most concentrated attention from postreform delegates, for both its intrinsic substance and its potential influence within the convention. Independent issue activists, after all, entered the presidential contest at least in part to get the party to endorse their positions on the issues of most concern to them. Interest group representatives entered the contest in equal part to secure endorsement of the policy desires of their group. Even party officials were increasingly drawn to party business by ideological, issue, or interest concerns, and these could be most directly celebrated with a plank or planks in the party platform.

Democratic Struggles after Reform: Rules

There was an equally clear pattern of response by presidential nominees to this pattern of delegate interests. The Credentials Committee, of course, no longer required much attention at all. Small assaults on the delegates of the nominee—and assaults were now reliably small—could be directly answered in committee; larger policy questions, for the current year or the future, were unlikely to arise. Rules and Platform, on the other hand, required a different response, since they retained the potential to generate conflict, focus publicity, and absorb time. For delegates, the substance contested in these realms might be seen as a reward in and of itself. For nominees, that substance was often less compelling than its potential to interfere with their orchestration of the full convention and, indeed, to paint an undesired portrait of the nominee himself. Their response, accordingly, can only be understood in light of these concerns. The regular strategy of emerging nominees with serious challenges in Rules or Platform was simply, if at all possible, to surrender to those challenges.

Such surrenders did take different forms in the two committees. In Rules, they ordinarily consisted of acquiescing in yet another interim reform commission, to which the proposals of dissident delegates and candidates could be assigned, often with specific emphasis, occasionally with explicit endorsement. By the time of the convention, the critical part of the rule-bound contest for the nomination, the selection of delegates, had already occurred. The losing candidates might well feel that existing rules had treated them unfairly, but nominees could not acquiesce in changing those rules retroactively without risking their apparent nominations—as Jimmy Carter confirmed at the Democratic convention of 1980, when he refused to release his delegates from the pull of Rule F(3)c. On the other hand, reform packages as extensive as those created by the Democratic party of 1968 did reliably produce unexpected consequences on the way to a nomination, and nominees were usually prepared to placate those aggrieved by these outcomes with the creation of a subsequent reform commission, especially if doing so would sidestep substantial conflict at the national convention.

Analytically, there was a peculiar imbalance to this resolution: while it gave the central product of the rules for a particular year (the nomination) to one side, it gave the rules of the game themselves (for next time) to the other. Yet if they were aware of this irony—trading away the fundamental rules in return for a little short-run peace in response to a set of anomalies which were unlikely ever to occur again—current nominees dismissed it with the view that if they were not just nominated but elected, they would control any subsequent reform commission. Such a strategy did not, of course, take account of what might happen should they *not* be elected, and that element of these negotiations did occasionally add to their complexity. Indeed, perhaps the best example of this entire strategic minuet, including this possibility of a final twist from continuing actors who were institutionally forced to be concerned with the future, came from the rules negotiations at the Democratic convention of 1984.

There, the Hart campaign brought a comprehensive set of reform proposals, their "Democracy Package," to the Rules Committee.[20] This was designed as an abstract accompaniment to a very concrete challenge to over 600 "tainted delegates," chosen with the support of allegedly illegal contributions from organized labor. In return for dropping this section of the challenge, however, one of potentially extreme divisiveness, Gary Hart got Walter Mondale to agree essentially to accept the Democracy Package. But these negotiations, although apparently conclusive, were not quite complete. Mondale supporters on the Rules Committee, and party officials and labor leaders around the country, were so outraged at this apparent agreement, which threw away all the reforms which *they* had sought during the previous interim, that they threatened their own revolt at the convention or in the general election campaign. Mondale then announced that these were proposals to a subsequent reform commission, perhaps even its initial agenda, but certainly not its guaranteed product.

The result was a familiar one, in focused strategic terms. There would be another interim reform commission, and internal politics would determine the precise meaning of all the officially adopted language. The result was familiar in larger strategic terms as well. An extended challenge had been brought, to rectify alleged inequities of the current system and simultaneously provide supporters of the losing candidate or candidates with concrete victories. The nominee had been prepared to acquiesce in these proposals, however extreme, even (in this case) when they repealed a set of reforms which he had supported and which had clearly benefited him. It was left to party officials to rein these proposals back in, either within the convention or within the commission to follow, if they were able to do so. But in a touch, finally, which made the entire incident quintessential, it became clear by the time this new commission was created and the Democracy Package was assigned to it that the arrangements which had been most harmful to candidate Hart in 1984, and which that package had been designed to mitigate, were precisely those which were most likely to benefit candidate Hart in 1988—because they most benefited the front-runner, a status which Hart himself had acquired by the time this commission was appointed.[21]

Democratic Struggles after Reform: Platform

There was always a greater number of counterpart struggles in the Platform Committee—usually representing a much wider range of dissidents—and if they lacked the recurring irony of struggles within the Rules Committee, they were otherwise very similar in their strategic outlines. In fact, even in a convention such as the Democratic gathering of 1980, where the nomination itself turned potentially on convention rules, there were far more dissident platform proposals than dissident rules reforms. Moreover, these planks were brought by a much wider array of convention factions. The most serious, in terms of their potential impact on a nominating majority, were ordinarily produced and supported by the losing candidate or candidates. But there were always other, often major proposals brought by issue organizations or interest groups with only the tacit support of these other candidates, and these proposals also had the clear potential for interfering with the efforts of the emerging nominee to orchestrate his convention. The most painful platform challenges at the McGovern nomination of 1972, for example, such as the proposals for a guaranteed income and for the independent right to abortion, were brought by groups inside the McGovern coalition.

In any case, the general strategy of those bringing such minority reports and the general response of nominees facing them were analogous to those strategies in the area of party rules. Challenging factions sought a proposal extreme enough to justify a battle, one in which the nominee could not easily acquiesce. Nominees sought to reach an accommodation on such proposals if at all possible, on the theory that it was not their intrinsic substance but their prospects for disrupting the convention which constituted their principal impact. Most aspiring minority reports from the Platform Committee in the postreform period partook of this general character. Perhaps the most striking single example, however, was the struggle over nuclear power, and then over energy in general, at the Democratic convention of 1980.[22]

At its center was a small issue organization from the Boston area, the Campaign for Safe Energy. The group had not attempted to secure specific delegates but had concentrated instead on questioning the candidates about nuclear power at every public opportunity, on making contact with delegates as soon as they were selected, and on urging sympathetic delegates to seek a seat on the Platform Committee. The draft platform coming out of the White House had repeated the policy of President Jimmy Carter, namely that American independence from the tyranny of foreign oil required the expansion of domestic nuclear power. Conversely, the proposal from the Campaign for Safe Energy was that nuclear power be condemned and abandoned. Yet when the Platform Committee assembled, despite its Carter majority, the position of the Campaign for Safe Energy, led by a Carter delegate and supported by the Kennedy operation, had a bloc large enough to write the relevant plank. Despite the dispatching of high White House staff for a last-minute appeal, these individuals could not be moved, and the majority report of the committee called for a moratorium on new licenses for nuclear plants and an orderly phaseout of those which did exist.

While the apparent nominee of the party, the sitting president, had thus been defeated on a policy which was so central to his administration that he was even then championing it with his European allies, the striking victory of the Campaign for Safe Energy had its organizational drawbacks for them too. The plank on nuclear power had been intended as the means by which this group would use the convention to publicize its cause to a national audience; victory in the Platform Committee removed that possibility. On the other hand, an even more extreme plank, calling for the federal energy budget to guarantee a larger expenditure on solar power than on synthetic fuels, had secured enough votes for a minority report. As the convention approached, then, the Campaign for Safe Energy began to contact delegates on behalf of this proposal instead. By the time the convention opened, however, it was clear that a majority of all delegates were now lined up behind this minority report, and the Carter campaign again surrendered, making this too part of the platform.

Once more, what was a loss for the president was also a loss for the issue organization, because it again eliminated the ability to use the convention to address a national viewing audience. As a result, the solar leadership began collecting signatures on a petition to nominate Congressman Edward Markey of Massachusetts for vice president, so that he could make a major speech in support of solar power. Given the fact that some of these signatories were again Carter delegates, and that the Kennedy delegates might well vote for Markey despite his intention to withdraw, the possibility existed that Markey would pull a substantial vote. To guarantee against that outcome, the Carter campaign offered Markey a prime-time slot for a major convention address, more time than he would have had through the vice presidential gambit, if he would agree not to be officially nominated. Markey accepted this offer, and the solar lobby in effect received its plank assailing nuclear power, its plank boosting solar power, *and* its major convention speech.[23]

The Framework for Committee Struggles: The Republicans

There was no counterpart to the Democratic reforms in basic committee structure for the Republican party in the postreform era. Indeed, explicit norms of party procedure and the values by which delegates described their actual behavior reinforced a continuing hostility to self-conscious party reform. Yet the same hierarchy of delegate concerns with internal committees did characterize convention politics on the Republican side. Moreover, the same strategic gambits by dissident delegates and candidates were met by the same strategic responses from the emerging nominee and top convention officials. What resulted was in fact an informal recapitulation of the Democrats' deliberate structural changes, along with recurring evidence that the same drives, institutionalized in the Republican party too, might yet produce the same formal resolution.

The absence of a regular reform process, buttressed by a generalized hostility to centrally directed reform, meant on the one hand that the Republican committee system did not move formally outside the national convention. On the other hand, committee struggles continued to be the major obstacle to orchestration of conventions by emerging nominees, so that nominees were constantly alert to means of moderating such struggles. Likewise, the substance of these struggles continued to be of central interest to the individual delegates, in an era when the nomination had eluded them but when they were increasingly recruited on the basis of their ideological, issue, and interest concerns. It was perhaps inevitable, then, that Republican committee proceedings too began to creep out of the period when the full convention was in session and into the week—even weeks—before.[24]

In a similar fashion, an informal counterpart to formal changes within the Democratic party created the same hierarchy of concern with convention committees among Republicans. There were no new compliance arrangements to reduce the Credentials Committee to near-insignificance. But there was an equally effective interaction of party norms against central decision making on state delegate credentials and of practical party building in the states, especially in the South, which eliminated most credentials business. The Rules and Platform committees thus vied among Republican delegates for priority in the postreform era. The Republican Rules Committee lacked the tendency of its Democratic counterpart to intervene in regulations for delegate selection nationwide, but this absence was compensated by a recurring set of rules issues, especially over the allocation of delegates to the states, which the Democratic Rules Committee lacked. Even then, Platform was ordinarily the scene of the greatest number of individual committee conflicts on the Republican side too, from the widest array of dissident factions.

Strategies and Responses in Republican Committee Conflict

Ever since the informal departure of the nomination, credentials business in Republican conventions had been of only marginal concern to anyone. During the period when the Republican National Committee had intervened actively in the composition of party conventions, in the late nineteenth and early twentieth centuries, credentials had been a central, and occasionally a determining matter. Thus the pivotal conflicts at the Republican convention of 1912, which drove Theodore Roosevelt to mount an independent candidacy for president against the Republican nominee, President William Howard Taft—and eventually produced the election of the Democratic nominee, Woodrow Wilson—were ultimately about credentials. Indeed, as late as the final Republican convention actually to construct a nominating majority, the convention of 1952 where Dwight Eisenhower bested Robert A.

Taft, credentials business had been a matter of life or death for the major contenders.

Nevertheless, official Republican doctrine had always left the basic decisions about delegate selection to the "federated units," that is, the state Republican parties. When serious state parties finally began to appear throughout the South after World War II, there was no longer any need for the national convention (or any chance for the national committee) to face the previous and perennial question of who the local party really was. As a result, serious credentials challenges, along with any consequential role for the Credentials Committee, atrophied quickly. The formal potential for this committee to become a focus of conflict in subsequent conventions did, in principle, remain. Yet even the Republican contest of 1976, with the major contenders separated by a handful of delegates as the convention opened, did not produce important challenges to credentials, suggesting that only in truly extreme circumstances might this potential be realized again.

The Rules Committee, on the other hand, retained its status as at least a highly varied theater for internal conflict. In fact, rules battles at Republican conventions gained a different sort of intensity, when contrasted with Democratic battles, precisely because no reforms in delegate selection or convention procedure could be implemented, however they were proposed, if they were not subsequently passed by the full national convention. Thus even comprehensive reform bodies, with comprehensive reform proposals, had to come before the convention via its Rules Committee. The Delegates and Organization (DO) Committee, the internal Republican counterpart to the independent McGovern Commission on the Democratic side, brought such a package, detailed and extensive, to the Rules Committee in 1972.[25] That body accepted most of the recommendations on delegate selection, except those concerning demographic representation, while rejecting most recommendations on convention procedure—a set of judgments which was ratified without change by the full convention.

More common as material for Rules Committee decisions were recurring arguments over the formula allocating delegates among the states. The largest of these disputes in the postreform era, one fought to a roll call on the convention floor, began in the committee at the 1972 convention and became, in truth, the only element of open conflict at that pacific gathering. There were, however, reprises on the issue in 1980 and again in 1984, although the proposal in both years could not get out of committee.[26] Finally, it was of course the Rules Committee of the 1976 convention which handled the challenge with the greatest potential impact on a presidential nomination in the post-reform period. This was the proposed Rule 16-C, which would have forced President Gerald Ford to name his running mate early. It was only when this proposal had been defeated, first in the committee and then via a minority report on the convention floor, that Ford could be fully assured of renomination.

It was still, however, the Platform Committee which drew the most consistent and continuing attention from delegates and which spawned the greatest amount of internal convention conflict. At a divided Republican convention such as that of 1976, platform battles were larger, longer, and probably louder than those in the Rules Committee, even if they were not quite as central to determining the nomination. At an essentially undivided Republican convention such as that of 1980, platform battles were the only major publicized conflicts in the big three traditional committees. Moreover, as in the Democratic party, such battles were most likely to bring out the full array of strategies and responses by all sides. Indeed, and finally, they were most likely to produce strategies and counterstrategies which precisely paralleled those on the Democratic side, completing the inherent partisan symmetry.

As among the Democrats, there was a clear and substantive procedural ballet associated with those Republican platform conflicts which were intended—or acquired the apparent ability—to influence a nomination. At the Republican convention of 1976, Senator Jesse Helms of North Carolina had originally introduced a series of independent proposals on foreign policy, different in major ways (and in a conservative direction) from the Ford draft; Helms's proposals were then gathered, with the active help of the Reagan leadership, into a composite plank dubbed "Morality in Foreign Policy."[27] Its drafters did leave the names of Ford and his secretary of state, Henry Kissinger, out of the document, but they otherwise lambasted both men for everything from losing public confidence, through making secret agreements, to discouraging the hope of freedom for those in totalitarian states. Nevertheless, even though these proposals were adopted by the Reagan leadership, in part because they were almost impossible for the Ford leadership to accept, and even though the Ford leadership was able to hold them to the status of a minority report in the Platform Committee, the Ford leadership saw the handwriting on the wall as this plank reached the convention floor. In the classic response by a nominee to dissident planks which drew him away from the political center, Ford merely endorsed these proposals and had them written into the platform, instead of spending more time fighting them and perhaps having to absorb a clear defeat.

In contrast, dissident proposals which did not become directly related to alternative nominating campaigns were always aimed much more at gaining their explicit substance. In the process, of course, the conflicts these planks engendered invariably expressed the tension between those who desired to cap the nominating campaign at the convention and those who desired to launch the election campaign instead. Often in turn, this tension was more between the nominee and his followers than between the nominee and his opponents. At the meetings of the Platform Committee in 1980, the Reagan leadership would clearly have preferred to temper both the social conservatism and the international pugnacity of its ideological supporters. Yet given the dedication of those delegates to the candidate *and* to these policies, the Reagan leadership quickly realized that the only way to defeat these amendments to their original draft would be to challenge their own delegates on the convention floor—so that it was wiser merely to include these dissident planks in the final document and remain free to orchestrate the convention without platform fights.

Organizational Products from Committee Struggles

In short order, much more than the specific products of this strategic minuet at individual conventions, that is, much more than the particular outcomes of specific fights over rules or platform, began to follow from these recurring committee struggles. Patterns of conflict this regular—with reliable priorities for concentration among committees, reliable strategies for dissident delegates within them, and reliable counterstrategies by emerging nominees—began to spawn efforts to extend the reach of the policy decisions realized at conventions. This implied extending them into other political institutions: it meant extending their hold on subsequent conventions as well. The most obvious but most problematic of these initiatives were efforts to extend the authority of convention decisions into the presidency itself among Democrats, into the National Committee among Republicans. Less immediately obvious but more secure and perhaps more ultimately consequential were efforts—more and more successful—to set out policy positions which were both internally consistent and increasingly distant from those of the other party, and to align the activists in party politics with those positions.

The most aspiringly concrete result of this pattern of conflict—the result with direct organizational implications—was a drive to extend the influence of the reformed convention by comparison with that of other institutions of national politics. Delegates who had succeeded in attending a convention, who could not do much about the presidential nomination but who could hope to influence the current platform and future rules, naturally wanted to see their success in these realms perpetuated. Once again, their responses took a different but clearly parallel form in each party. For the Democrats, this involved an effort to extend the authority of the party platform, the major surviving document of the full convention. For the Republicans, it involved an effort to extend the recognized authority of the full convention itself, that is, of delegate majorities on the convention floor.

On the Democratic side, concern with the subsequent role of the party platform had been bubbling throughout the 1972 and 1976 gatherings, characterized respectively by extended debates on platform through the convention and then by deliberate and repeated but failed attempts to generate such debates on the convention floor. This concern broke into the open, however, and began to acquire concrete manifestations at the convention of 1980. There the forces of Senator Edward Kennedy, as part of their effort to fasten a "truly Democratic" program on President Jimmy Carter, produced a striking new proposal within the Rules Committee. A key minority plank, ultimately accepted by the Carter forces, called for all remaining contenders for the nomination at some point before the balloting itself to offer a written summary, to be read to the full convention, on where each agreed *and disagreed* with the party platform.[28]

In an embarrassing note which his lieutenants at least managed to have read when the television networks were not covering the podium, Carter did ultimately comply. But in fact, the successful minority report from the Rules Committee had gone much further. It called for an explicit Platform Accountability Commission, to meet before the next convention and consider ways to extend the influence of the party platform into subsequent national politics. That commission did meet during the interim between 1980 and 1984; it did create a list of recommendations, including a separate review body at national party headquarters which would assemble at the midpoint in a presidential administration and evaluate the progress of both the president and Congress in converting the platform into national law. There was little reason to believe that such a body would directly cause any given president (or any member of Congress for that matter) to change position in response to its report. In any case, the failure of the Democratic nominee of 1984 to be elected put off any possible test of the impact of this arrangement. Yet as an indicator of the orientation of national convention delegates, as a source of conflicts—and even organizational evolution—at subsequent conventions, and as another possible means of furthering the indirect impact of convention decisions, this new device had already achieved at least a diagnostic character.[29]

The same underlying dynamic surfaced differently in the Republican party. But its motives and drives were remarkably similar, and the move to extend the influence of the Republican convention even broke into the open at the same time, in 1980. This action too started in the Rules Committee. But because it began with the delegates of the emerging nominee, it was focused on constraining not so much a possible president as the National Committee, the embodiment of the national convention in the period between presidential elections. If there was a theme to the disparate motions rumbling out of the Rules Committee, it was not just that the National Committee should follow convention dictates but that, once again, the goals pursued during the nominating campaign should not be diluted by the demands of the general election.

A plethora of subsections gave meaning to this demand. Thus there was a proposal to take the selection of individual committees in the National Committee away from the chairman and lodge it in the full membership; to place the chairman in an extended committee which would pass on all policy statements, expenditures, and appointments; to elect a new national chairman after the November election; to limit any preprimary contributions from the National Committee to candidates who did not have serious primary opposition; to reject giving ex officio seating to representatives and senators on the convention floor; and so on. Most of these proposals passed both the committee and the full convention, without debate on the convention floor. Yet in terms of their intended goal, they suffered an ironic fate when compared to the Platform Accountability Commission on the Democratic side.[30]

Where the platform accountability device failed in its immediate objectives because the Democratic nominee failed to be elected president, these reforms failed in their immediate objectives precisely because the Republican nominee *was* elected. In other words, they failed because they ran afoul of a more intractable fact about national party politics, that a sitting president can ordinarily dominate his National Committee, selecting both the chairman and the committee policies which he himself prefers. As a result, when Ronald Reagan became president, he was effectively able to name his own chairman, and those two men jointly were not interested in having a full committee hamstring any coordinate policy moves. Nevertheless, the drive to have the convention influence even more of national party politics would not—could not—disappear as a source of convention conflict until the nature of convention delegates changed as well. Accordingly, these nascent reforms remained as tangible evidence of the possibilities for still further growth in the realms of conflict, and hence in the activities, of the postreform convention.

Intellectual Products from Committee Struggles

These organizational developments may have attested to the continuing change—and therefore to the continuing vitality—of the national party convention as a political institution. Yet they remained incipient and partial, only weakly institutionalized and still problematic in their ultimate impact. Much more reliably present, though less easily visualized because they did not result in some continuing structure, were changes in the continuing policy positions—the platforms—of both conventions. The positions in an individual party platform, drafted at a specific national convention, were of course easy to note—and easy to denigrate because they were so obviously drafted in response to the events of one particular year and were so clearly binding on absolutely no one. Yet when these documents began increasingly to recapitulate positions, year after year, despite apparently large differences in nominating politics, they suggested at least a certain stability among the values and desires of those delegates as a collectivity, at most a new, consistent, and continuing set of policy preferences among one major set of party elites. Moreover, when these policy packages began to differ more and more *between* the two major parties as well, they suggested at least increasingly divergent pressures on any subsequent party governments, at most a change in the character— the issue content and issue diversity—of the composite national politics outside.

Party platforms as products of national party conventions, whatever the ultimate fate of their recommendations, were tangible documents and thus tangible clues to the politics surrounding them.[31] They were the intellectual residue of some committee struggles; they cataloged the outcome of those struggles between nominees and dissidents, in postreform as they had in prereform conventions. Perhaps most suggestively in this regard as the postreform era progressed, party platforms diverged as sharply as they have ever done without any evidence of economic or international crisis. The platforms of 1972 had differed, of course, because the Democratic platform moved well off to the left while the Republican platform largely lauded the Nixon administration. The gap had been maintained in 1976, when the Democratic platform moved back toward the center while the Republican platform moved well off to the right. But in 1980, and then in 1984 as well, the platforms stabilized—and came to reflect the same development by which the delegates themselves moved well off from the center in directions both conservative (for the Republicans) and liberal (for the Democrats).

As a result, in both 1980 and 1984, the final platform documents were strikingly and consistently different. They differed on basic economic policies, with the Republicans emphasizing the threat of inflation, the Democrats the threat of unemployment. They differed on basic foreign policy, where the Republicans opposed Marxism in all its manifestations, while the Democrats advocated better relations with most other nations. They divided on most of the lesser issues in these realms as well. Thus they differed on medical care, with the Republicans boosting cost containment and private supplements, the Democrats promising national health insurance. They differed on defense, where the Republicans sought military superiority, while the Democrats sought spending cuts. And they divided, perhaps most of all, on a vast array of social issues. The Republicans did not mention the Equal Rights Amendment or homosexual rights; the Democrats endorsed both explicitly. The Democrats did not mention prayer in the schools; the Republicans demanded its provision on at least a voluntary basis. The Republicans supported a constitutional amendment banning abortion; the Democrats favored using Medicaid funds to facilitate it. And on, and on.[32]

There was a sense in which even this substantial divergence merely recapitulated textually what had obviously occurred in the changing backgrounds of the delegates and the changing nature of their concerns. If issue or interest attachments increasingly outweighed party officeholding as the basis for delegate selection, and if this shift implied more emphasis on partisan ideology than on organizational mechanics at the convention itself, the delegates would quite logically be more concerned with the proper substance of platform planks than with tailoring them for electoral needs. Platforms, accordingly, could quite reasonably move away from each other, capping the campaign for nomination rather than launching the general election campaign. Similarly, if even the traditionally dominant forces among these organized partisan interests, big business among Republicans and big labor among Democrats, had lost ground to the more narrowly focused and morally oriented interests—concerned more with appropriate social values and life-styles—then platforms ought reasonably to have reflected this shift too. They ought logically to have increased their emphasis on what became known as social issues, and of course they did. In this way, these intellectual products of committee struggles also became further evidence—and confirmation—of changes in the national party convention.

Committee Struggles and External Politics

There was still room for debate about the external impact of any given platform plank, or partisan difference, in this mix. Indeed, it was still obviously and formalistically true that neither the individual positions within these platforms nor the differences between them were binding on any political actor, including any subsequent president, after the convention. Moreover, the degree to which nominees were prepared to go in absorbing hostile platform planks gave apparent practical support to this formal reality, as attested by sitting presidents with planks which directly contravened central policies of their administrations, such as Ford and "Morality in Foreign Policy" at the Republican convention of 1976 or Carter and a succession of solar energy proposals at the Democratic convention of 1980. Indeed, even the delegates who sought to influence these platforms thought principally in terms of gaining immediate partisan endorsement of their preferences, just as those who sought to influence rules reform thought principally in terms of the role of the rules in the *last* campaign.

Nevertheless, and just as obviously, these facts did not deter those concerned with public policy from fighting over platforms. The outcomes from this conflict could clearly serve as tangible (or at least concrete) rewards for them in presidential nominating politics. After all, they still had to satisfy their groups and organizations at home, and a platform plank could help them do this. Moreover, both the ultimate product and the character of the politics leading up to it were additionally concrete—actual developments with a real external effect—because of their ability to shape the course of the convention and provide the material by which the general public could respond to it. Indeed, this potential impact on the world outside explained much of the intimate strategic byplay around platform or rules proposals in the convention. It is not too much to say that this maneuvering was at the heart of the central activity in the postreform convention, the effort to use the convention to publicize various external campaigns. Yet even that effort did not exhaust the potential impact—apparently real in the postreform period—of proposals which were introduced and then lodged in national party platforms.

This impact was real because these platforms, at base, were still the closest thing American politics possessed to a summary statement of party policy. The National Committees did not issue such documents. The parties in Congress, while sometimes highly coordinated, expressed a program solely through contemporary votes. The program of the president, the only practical alternative, was really just that—the program of an individual officeholder. The platform of the national party might legitimately be subject to satire on many grounds, then, but it was the closest thing to a comprehensive policy statement that American politics regularly generated.[33] Moreover—and this had become the crucial point—although there was a sense in which the platform had always been "party policy by default," it appeared to be becoming much more consequential in the postreform era. Presidential politics was depending more on political activists. Those activists had to be motivated by policy goals. Those goals found a home in national party platforms.

There was, potentially, even more to it than that. Platform battles at the convention, and platform pronouncements when these battles had been resolved, were an effort to educate (or reeducate) the American people. If they convinced any number of Democrats or Republicans that the appropriate party position on a given issue was the one in the platform, then they certainly gained a further impact. But the lasting effect of these battles and their resolution was on the programmatic positions of party elites—independent issue activists, interest group representatives, and, increasingly, party officeholders themselves. The platform gave an undeniable added legitimacy in these circles to the programs it endorsed. As a result, indirectly, almost invisibly, but inevitably, those active in party politics (in the localities, in the states, and at the national level) came to reflect these programmatic emphases, too.

If it was essential that activists in Democratic party politics support an increased governmental role in underwriting abortion, then over time—in a remarkably short time, in fact—it would be inappropriate to be active in that politics without presenting this view. If it was essential that activists in Republican party politics support the reintroduction of prayer in the public schools, then over time—again, with surprising quickness—it would be inappropriate to be active in that politics without offering this position. The degree of emphasis on such views could still vary, but obvious public opposition was no longer acceptable. Campaign workers then expected and demanded these positions of their candidates; candidates expected to (and did) provide these positions in order to mobilize issue activists, interest groups, and party officials. Platforms, accordingly, while they did not enact anything, could aspire to change the views of an entire stratum of political actors, and success at this could have indirect but real programmatic effects of the highest potential consequence.

7 | The Struggle over the Mediated Convention: Televised Coverage and Public Perception

Because the launching of the general election campaign became the central activity from the politics of presidential selection at national party conventions, and because competition between this launching and the publicizing of various other campaigns became the major recurring conflict at conventions as well, the impact of the convention on the general public was a matter of conscious concern to most major participants. Some were concerned directly with the electoral fate of the nominee, or of all those implicitly associated with him. Others were concerned primarily with an issue, constituency, or individual much further afield, to the exclusion if necessary of the prospects of the current crop of candidates. Most participants, in any case, could be expected to try to use the convention to advance their personal political goals. For most, this meant an attempt to use convention coverage to that end rather than some specific, inevitably secondary, decision of the convention.

Yet this struggle was only the most obvious part of the effort to influence the general public through press coverage of the convention. In fact, the success of this effort was also increasingly dependent on the outcome of a simultaneous contest between convention actors and assorted members of the press, as well as the outcome of certain critical, recurring choices within the news media. Each time, this interplay, between and among convention officials and news personnel, produced at least the raw material from which the general public would develop its impressions of individual conventions. Over time, this interplay actually altered numerous organizational and procedural aspects of the convention as a political institution, through an indirect, diffuse, unsought, but nevertheless profound influence.

More precisely, the shift from the convention as capstone of the nominating contest to the convention as launching pad for the general election campaign had coincided with, been facilitated by, and ultimately and increasingly turned on, the rise of television as the major source of impressions about convention activities on the part of the general public. The convention had been an ideal forum for the television networks to launch their live and direct coverage of contemporary political events. In turn the audience for this coverage was immediately and then reliably huge. Such coverage was thus institutionalized, convention after convention. Along the way, television displaced all other media, but especially radio, as the most immediate, live and direct source of information on events at the convention.

These facts, especially the reliable size and composition of the television audience, could hardly have escaped the notice of major participants in convention activities. When these facts were corroborated by an array of polling outcomes, major convention actors were reinforced in thinking of the convention as a forum for influencing the public, especially through press coverage. Indeed, the importance of the distinction between a convention which functioned as a thoroughly choreographed coronation and one which became a protracted struggle over confirmation of the apparent nominee was increasingly rooted in the scope and immediacy of convention events *as televised coverage offered them to the general public.* As with so many other convention developments, no one had deliberately sought that outcome, yet it followed directly from the introduction of television and from the shift in the central activity of the convention.

In short order, then, a specific, reliable, three-cornered contest over coverage of the convention by television news divisions also sprang up—and became institutionalized. No one planned this recurring contest either, but it surfaced again and again to shape the material available for public impressions of the convention. One corner of this contest was the traditional struggle, waged (as always) by elite participants in the politics of presidential selection over activities at the convention—though played out a bit differently in the era of televised transmission. A second, newer corner was the struggle *between* these convention elites, of whatever stripe, and decision makers in the network news divisions, a struggle over what would be presented when, and how it would be covered. The third and newest corner of the conflict took place entirely within the television networks, where news directors chose among convention events in setting priorities for coverage.

The central product of this three-cornered struggle was a set of individual convention portraits. These possessed the most direct and immediate impact on presidential politics; they were the outcome most frequently and vigorously argued—and reargued—when that politics had run its course. Yet there were other, more implicit products of the interaction of this political institution, the convention, and a new medium of information, television. One lesser example was a set of continuing negotiations between convention officials and news directors over formal arrangements for coverage. A second example, resulting less from exchanges or even negotiations but having much clearer operational consequences for the convention, was a set of anticipatory changes in the organization of the institution itself—from redesign of the hall, through alterations in schedule, to changes in the character of convention speeches—all intended to reap maximum potential benefit from promised television coverage.

Eventually, after more than a generation of such coverage, there would be a further implicit impact on the convention as an institution, one dwarfing all these others, when the national networks cut back their convention presentations and revealed the extent to which these other impacts had occurred within a fourth and larger, implicit press decision. But the more direct products from the three-cornered struggle have to be put back together before the full impact of the interplay between national convention and national medium, between convention principals and network newspeople, can be fully appreciated for this earlier period. Indeed, these elements would always be the direct determinants of individual convention portraits, even after the networks had changed the parameters for their presentation.

The Primacy of Television with the Audience for Conventions

There had been a small experiment with television in the Philadelphia area at the Republican convention of 1940, before World War II intervened and directed technological developments and associated resources in other directions. There had been a larger experiment with a chain of cities between Boston and Richmond at the Republican and Democratic conventions of 1948. The first major effort to televise conventions nationwide, however, did not arrive until 1952. Network officials, and especially network news officials, recognized this effort as one of tremendous potential significance. Yet the success of the effort on its own terms, not to mention the birth of a tradition of coverage and public attention which followed from it, surely surprised even them.[1]

Probably, network news officials would have toasted their coverage of the 1952 conventions quite apart from any audience response. The conventions were widely perceived within the industry as a milestone— really a deliberately created bench mark—in the coming-of-age of television news, and indeed of television generally as a central medium of information and communication in American life. So widespread was this view that completion of the nationwide coaxial cable for television transmissions was expedited specifically to provide coverage of the conventions. When all the inherent technological problems, from completion of this cable down to uninterrupted transmission from the convention hall, then proved to be surmountable, network news divisions (along with major network officials) would in all likelihood have proclaimed a triumph, whatever their potential public had seen fit to do.

What happened, however, was far larger than a technical triumph. For the audience for these broadcasts immediately exceeded all but the most optimistic projections. Indeed, the *ratings* for these initial

Table 7.1. Composite Nielsen ratings for television coverage of national party conventions

	Ratings for conventions			
Year	Democratic	Republican	Both	Larger of the two
1984	23.2	19.1	21.3	23.2
1980	24.8	20.5	22.6	24.8
1976	22.5	25.2	23.9	25.2
1972	18.3	29.6	22.0	29.6
1968	28.8	26.6	27.8	28.8
1964	27.9	20.4	23.4	27.9
1960	29.3	12.3	21.2	28.3
1956	24.3	29.4	26.3	29.4
1952	—	—	26.1[a]	—

Source: Ratings by A. C. Nielsen Company, as provided by the Library and Archives of CBS News. Special thanks to Karen Hayutin, who did the actual work of retrieval.
a. Estimated from incomplete ratings figures.

nationwide broadcasts, that is, the share of homes with television which were tuned to these broadcasts at any given time, jumped immediately to the levels which they would maintain by and large for the next thirty years. (See Table 7.1.)[2] The fledgling television industry, given the haste with which convention broadcasts had necessarily been planned and executed, did not secure the comprehensive ratings measures, session by session and hour by hour, which its leaders would subsequently arrange as part of their internal monitoring process. But the piecemeal measures available for 1952 do suggest ratings almost precisely parallel to those which would be derived more systematically in 1956 and after. Moreover, these ratings suggest an audience which *averaged* between 25 and 30 percent of all American households with television sets and which ballooned to approximately twice those figures when the optimum period for viewership, in the early and middle evening, coincided with the presentation of central convention events, such as nomination or acceptance speeches.

The raw numbers implied by these ratings were in their way even more imposing. Conservative estimates for 1952—and network releases after the second 1952 convention were a good deal less than conservative—projected an average viewership of about 4.0 million households, rising to 8.5 million during peak viewing periods. Moreover, these numbers promised a vast numerical increase in the television audience, by means of nothing more than the spread of television *sets* throughout American society. In 1952, only about a third of American homes possessed a television receiver; by 1956, over two-thirds did. (See Table 7.2.) While the ratings for convention viewing were not to rise appreciably over those of 1952—that is, the share of households with television which watched the conventions did not increase—the raw number of households watching the convention roughly doubled, producing an average audience in 1956 of about 9.1 million households and a peak audience—watching live and direct—of roughly double that.

Even these burgeoning numbers did not exhaust the implications of this explosion in the raw size of the television audience. For they also meant that by 1956—only one convention later—television had replaced radio as the major source of direct impressions of these national party gatherings by the American people. Inevitably then, as saturation of television receivers became nearly complete, this displacement became overwhelming as well. By 1960, with 87 percent of American households in possession of a television set, the average measured audience for televised conventions had jumped to almost 10 million households, and the peak audience ranged comfortably over 25 million. As a result, by 1960, the domination of live and direct reporting of conventions by television news divisions was essentially complete.

Again, the mere fact of success at covering the conventions of 1952 might have been enough to convince network executives of the desirability of institutionalizing convention coverage. They had at least demonstrated the feasibility of live and direct transmission; they had removed any aura of inferiority to radio reporters and commentators; and they had arguably established a form of superiority by adding the visual element to anything radio could offer. In the process, television news divisions had performed what was generally regarded as a major public service, by bringing the American people directly into one of their central decision-making forums.

But when the scope of the resulting audience was added to all these considerations, the decision to institutionalize the experiment appeared almost to make itself. Television coverage had immediately achieved what would become the normal ratings of national party conventions. When these ratings were converted into the raw number of television

Table 7.2.   The changes in audience—potential and actual—for television coverage of national party conventions

Year	Total households	Total reach of television (%)	Average composite ratings	Average viewing households
1984	85,407,000	98	21.3	17,828,000
1980	80,766,000	98	22.6	17,888,000
1976	72,672,000	97	23.9	16,758,000
1972	66,676,000	96	22.0	14,082,000
1968	60,813,000	93	27.8	15,723,000
1964	56,149,000	92	24.2	12,501,000
1960	53,021,000	87	21.2	9,779,000
1956	48,902,000	71	26.3	9,131,000
1952	45,317,000	34	26.1[a]	4,021,000

Source: Ratings taken from Table 7.1. Otherwise developed from Bureau of the Census, *Historical Statistics of the United States,* pp. 41 and 796, as supplemented by Bureau of the Census, *Statistical Abstract of the United States 1980,* p. 42, and Bureau of the Census, *Statistical Abstract of the United States 1987* (Washington, D.C.: U.S. Government Printing Office, 1986), p. 42.

a. Estimated from incomplete ratings figures.

households watching the conventions, and when the potential for growth even in that audience was quickly and painlessly attained, a context for decision making about coverage was automatically created. Convention coverage became a staple—indeed, a centerpiece—of network news performance.

Convention Coverage and Public Impressions

That context would not be sufficient, however, to stifle debate about the scope and nature of future convention coverage, both within and without the television networks. Nor would it prevent some explicit changes in the character of that coverage during the next thirty years. But that context did guarantee that network news divisions would thereafter provide live and direct coverage of national party conventions, nationwide. Throughout the succeeding thirty years, regardless of arguments over the character of that coverage, it would reliably attract the major, live and direct audience for conventions. If television also provided a visceral impact which radio or print could not match— as many, perhaps most, commentators would subsequently argue— then even the raw numbers would understate the effect of televised network reporting.[3]

An average audience of this size, and the average viewing time which came along with it, would almost automatically have attracted the attention of those with a concern for shaping public opinion on matters political. Even if the surface manifestations of this opinion, as tracked through public opinion polls, had not shown an apparent impact from convention coverage, nominees, convention planners, and other major participants would probably have approached their activities with one eye on the television viewer. The convention was, after all, a major focused event; the audience for it was, even apart from opinion measures, large and at least intermittently attentive. Accordingly, convention strategists would probably have attempted to influence the impressions which that audience carried away even without a numerical measure of the potential for that effort.

These strategists, however, did not need to rely on logic and intuition to posit a role for the convention in shaping public opinion, for the obvious and continuing measures of convention impact—that is, the personal popularity ratings of the individual contenders along with the trial heats matching Democratic and Republican contenders against each other—showed reliable movement when taken before and after each convention. Through the first several conventions after the arrival of television coverage, public opinion polls were still insufficiently frequent to sort out this change, without the intervention of too many major events besides the conventions. But by 1964, such measures were sufficiently common to suggest certain reliable responses, along with certain reliable types of variation in these responses, variations with obvious potential for affecting the fate of the general election campaigns being launched at these conventions.

Such measures were not particularly good at registering the full effective impact of individual conventions on the general public. Thus they could not capture either convictions confirmed or convictions shaken by events transmitted from these conventions, nor could they begin to tap the effect of movement in general public opinion on the party officials, independent activists, and financial contributors—the specialized intermediaries—who would have to make the campaign function. Nevertheless, a set of poll movements confirming some immediate convention impact were reliably present, year after year. Almost inevitably, for example, no matter how unified or divisive the convention and no matter how satisfying or annoying its coverage was to its participants, the convention produced a rise in personal popularity for its ultimate nominee. On the other hand, the size of this boost could—and did—vary tremendously. Even more to the point, the size of the *gap* between one major-party nominee and the other after both conventions had finished could move in either a Democratic or a Republican direction—and could vary even more.

In the twenty years since there have been sufficiently frequent polls to separate the periods before and after each of the two conventions, no candidate has suffered a decline in personal popularity in the immediate aftermath of his convention. (See Table 7.3.) One candidate, George McGovern with the Democratic nomination of 1972, did move backward in his comparative standing, with regard to the nominee of the other party. Yet even he did not lose in terms of personal popularity. The only other nominee even close to being an exception was Lyndon Johnson, after the Democratic convention of 1964. Yet the essentially static response of his popular rating reflected not disenchantment but an extremely high personal standing going into the convention, along with an extremely large gap (36 percentage points) between Johnson and the Republican nominee, so that there was almost no room statistically for further gain.

This normally positive impact from a national party convention did not, however, imply that the *level* of impact was even roughly similar from convention to convention. Indeed, the same figures which attest to a normally positive impact also attest to the variability in its range. (See Table 7.3.) Some candidates remained essentially static in their personal popularity after their nominating convention; others rose by as much as 10 points. Some *pairs* of conventions boosted the personal standing of both nominees substantially; other pairs boosted one nominee noticeably more than his opponent. Not surprisingly, the gap between some nominees and their opposite numbers remained essentially stable in the aftermath of their conventions, whereas the gap between other pairs shifted by as much as 17 percentage points. Little else, once the field of candidates had narrowed, could produce such temporally reliable movement. Little else, among recurring political events, could achieve such a range of movement either.

The net impact of the two conventions together provided even stronger testimony to the potential gain—or loss—in the battle to shape public impressions through the convention. (See Table 7.4.) Here, there was a much longer stretch of convention history with the

Table 7.3.   Net change in candidate popularity from before to after the convention

Year	Party	Candidate	Movement in popularity (%)	Change in gap between contenders (%)
1984	Republican	Reagan	+ 3	+ 4
	Democratic	Mondale	+ 2	+ 2
1980	Republican	Reagan	+ 8	+15
	Democratic	Carter	+10	+17
1976	Republican	Ford	+ 4	+ 7
	Democratic	Carter	+ 9	+16
1972	Republican	Nixon	+ 7	+ 8
	Democratic	McGovern	0	− 3
1968	Republican	Nixon	+ 5	+14
	Democratic	Humphrey	+ 2	+ 4
1964	Republican	Goldwater	+ 5	+ 8
	Democratic	Johnson	0	0

Source: Developed most directly from "Presidential Trial Heats: An Historical Review," *Public Opinion*, June–July 1984, pp. 40–41, as supplemented by "See How They Run: Reagan vs. Mondale Trial Heats," *Public Opinion*, August–September 1984, pp. 38–39. All figures are originally from the Gallup Organization.

Table 7.4. Net change in the gap between contenders from before to after
both conventions

Year	Net gain	
1984	1%	Republican
1980	2%	Democratic
1976	2%	Republican
1972	18%	Republican
1968	10%	Republican
1964		None
1960	10%	Republican
1956	13%	Democratic
1952	21%	Democratic
1948	1%	Republican
1944		None

Source: "The Gallup Poll: Presidential Candidate Trial Heats 1936–1980," *Gallup Opinion Index*, 183 (1980), pp. 13–29, as supplemented by "See How They Run," pp. 38–39.

requisite polls, since this comparison required only a trial heat between the two emerging nominees before the first major-party convention and after the second. The result, in any case, was another, even more extended range of possible responses to the two national conventions, considered as a unit. Indeed, the direct numerical impact, with all the inherent difficulties of a single measure at a single point in time, ran from a net shift to the Democratic nominee of 21 percentage points to a net shift to the Republican nominee of 18, with all the stops (including no net shift) in between.

Polling Measures and the Impact of Conventions

This range of candidate standings before and after the *two* conventions still obscures much of the practical meaning in any resulting movement. A large movement, such as the 21-point Democratic gain of 1952, might not be enough to threaten an evolving landslide, while a small movement, such as the 2-point Republican gain of 1976, might be critical in a tight contest. Conversely, identical net shifts, even if both were nearly zero, often meant very different things. In a year such as 1984, when candidate loyalties were solidified early, a net shift of 1 percent could coincide with little net change in the personal popularity of the two candidates or in the gap between them, while in a year such as 1980, when candidate loyalties were loose and volatile, a net shift of only 2 percent could coincide with a large net swing in both the personal standing of each contender and in the gap between them. (Compare Tables 7.3 and 7.4.)

Large net changes in polling measures which meant almost nothing for the general election campaign, or small net changes which could be decisive, along with identical net changes which had powerfully different implications for the public opinion behind them, were also warnings: that the absolute magnitude of all such numbers could not be taken as the real public impact of the convention. Had such numbers not shown any impact, or had that impact not varied, campaign strategists might have been deluding themselves about the potential role of convention coverage in shaping public impressions. Nevertheless, once those numbers had attested to some movement in public opinion, and in roughly comprehensible directions and magnitudes, they had gone about as far as they could practically go.

At the most elementary level, such numbers were not precisely comparable across time because the frequency of polling had changed so drastically. The appropriate base for comparison was inevitably unclear, for example, between a year such as 1984, when there were half a dozen national polls between conventions, and a year such as 1964, where there was exactly one. More to the political point, the lasting impact of any gain or loss, even within the same year, could never be judged from these summary numbers. Some increments (and decrements) were mere responses to focused attention and hoopla, and thus were likely to dissipate quickly. Others were attached to additional attitudes or social characteristics of the holder, and were much more resistant to further change. In any case, other political events between convention and election time would surely move these figures additionally, before the ultimate "trial heat," the November balloting itself.

Still more crucially, if the changes produced by a week of convention exposure were capable of decaying with remarkable speed, it was also true that a convention could have tremendous public impact without creating much immediate change in the summary figures for personal popularity or comparative standing. Such figures never even began to assess the share of the public whose convictions had been either confirmed or shaken by perceptions gained from the conventions, although that effect might be critical in the longer run. If a convention did nothing more than lock in the support of those who had been leaning in a given direction, perhaps by reinforcing their partisanship or suggesting that their evolving candidate perceptions were indeed accurate, that was a practical impact of the greatest potential consequence. By the same token, if a convention managed only to lead a significant minority of voters to reassess their current leanings and remain open to messages from both campaigns after the convention, that too was no small practical achievement.

In fact, this was much the way campaign strategists came to view the convention, especially once the launching of the general election campaign became its major immediate activity. The convention was still in a sense only another point in the continuing politics of presidential selection. It was admittedly a major point, one which represented a distinctive stage in the selection process. It was certainly a point which attracted a huge, potentially impressionable audience. But its ultimate impact could come in only four ways—by confirming existing candidate loyalties, by causing existing loyalties to be reexamined, by creating fresh loyalties, or by managing actually to shift and replace old attachments. Campaign strategists approached the convention as a unique opportunity to *attempt* all four of these impacts.[4] Their success with any one, however, was not necessarily captured by the poll standing of the candidates before and after the convention.

The size of the audience, then, was huge: one quarter of all American households on the average, as many as half at major moments. The composition of that audience was unusual: not just committed partisans but weak identifiers, true independents, and even a substantial minority of supporters of the opposite party. The extended focus was almost unique: four or five days, with major blocks of television time but without any role for the opposition party. The available measures of impact, finally, were all positive: if some of them overstated the effect of impressions formed from the convention on the general public, they automatically missed some of the most consequential impacts as well. Accordingly, there was little reason for the participants to forgo a struggle to use the convention—and convention coverage—to advance their political goals. By the same token, on all these grounds, there was every reason to expect the impressions of this audience to be shaped by developments perceived through the convention, whether those developments resulted from the efforts of the political contenders or from other forces in the struggle over coverage, including, perhaps, the behavior of the press itself.

The Coming of a Struggle over Convention Portraits

Initially, when the convention was informally created to deal with the problem of making a presidential nomination, one which would pull the disparate elements of the national party together and impose a single candidate upon them, there was very little organized coverage of the events of the convention, and very little potential influence on the direct perceptions of the general public. Few newspapers sent reporters to cover these earliest party gatherings; almost none could hope to have reports in the hands of their readers before the convention adjourned. "Mediation," then, to the extent that it occurred, was the province of the delegates themselves, reporting on convention developments to the party faithful after these delegates had returned home.

As soon as conventions started to achieve the predictable ability to make one of the two central decisions in presidential selection, however, newspapers began much more reliably to cover them. This tendency was accelerated by the creation in 1848 of the first newspaper wire service, the Associated Press, allowing even papers without a reporter on the ground to provide daily convention coverage. From that point until the arrival of the television era, more than a hundred years later, there were to be only two major changes in the pattern of this coverage. The first was a shift in the norms of news presentation, from a vigorously partisan to an aspiringly nonpartisan approach, from "yellow journalism" to a more evenhandedly critical posture, around the turn of the century. The second was the addition of an entirely new medium of information, the coming of radio and almost immediately of live and direct radio coverage of conventions, in the 1920s.[5]

Both these developments had the potential for altering general public impressions of individual conventions or even the structure of the convention itself. On the one hand, the shift to nonpartisanship in norms of coverage, for example, reduced the encapsulation of various segments of the American public within one or the other major party while it increased the possibility that individuals would be attracted by something discovered about the other party through its convention. By the same token, the coming of radio coverage allowed—indeed, encouraged—the public to form its own impressions, while it provided more of the raw material on which such impressions could be based. On the other hand, both these developments were to realize very little of their potential—thanks to the dominant character of the convention itself at the time they arrived. During the period when the major activity of the convention was the making of a presidential nomination rather than the launching of a general election campaign, that is, as long as nominating majorities were constructed at the convention after the delegates had assembled, there was little room for direct (or even indirect) influence from changed or expanded media coverage.

In both these media developments, in emerging norms of nonpartisanship and in new media of information, the public did gain additional bases for making judgments about candidates and parties. With the coming of radio especially, convention planners also had immediate cause to consider the organization of the convention, both to meet the technological needs of the new medium and to try to reap maximum advantage from radio coverage. Yet while the convention remained of necessity aimed at gaining a nominee rather than at launching his campaign, major convention actors were primarily concerned with influencing *that* decision rather than worrying about any external public—a decision reinforced by the fact that reporters too focused on the nominating contest. Moreover, the eventual nominee himself was often excluded from this process—he did not even appear at the convention during much of this period—so that there was little point in trying to emphasize the launching of his personal campaign. As a result, the realization of these possibilities for using the convention to influence the general public had to await the shift in the major activity of the convention to launching the general election campaign. And because of that wait, this realization was to be effected by television, not radio.

Televised coverage did not create the eventual shift in major convention activity, although television certainly reinforced that shift once it had occurred. Moreover, it was mere historical accident that the first conventions to be covered by network television were also the last to have their central decision made at the convention site. Television did facilitate the nationalization of American politics, which was the driving force behind this institutional development. Yet the nationalization had been building for decades, and its other principal components—the growth of government, especially national government; the decline of political parties, as organizations; and increasing affluence, with increasing education and an apparently concomitant desire for political independence—all predated televised convention coverage. Nevertheless, by the time the nomination itself had moved outside the convention and the central activity of the convention had become communication with the general public, about either the general election campaign or competing items which other convention participants preferred, it was national network television through which such communication could be most effectively pursued.

The Three-Cornered Struggle over Convention Coverage

The actual course of each convention was surely the major influence on coverage by network news divisions, or by most other news media for that matter. The content of this coverage in turn was surely the major influence—or at least the principal raw material—upon which public impressions of each convention were based. Certain central conflicts, the identity of which varied from convention to convention, were almost uniformly granted to be newsworthy by those assigned to cover the convention. Certain routinized highlights of the convention schedule—such as the keynote speech, the nominating address for the apparent nominee, and his acceptance speech—always crossed that same threshold of newsworthiness.

On the other hand, all news media, and television news in particular, had to make some deliberate decisions about what to convey and what to ignore, abbreviate, or reduce in prominence. The simple fact that numerous events were occurring at any given time guaranteed a range of such decisions. Beyond that fact, the character and limitations of each news medium, along with the reportorial resources and time or space available for convention coverage, added to the inherent elements of discretion. Finally, every news division could be expected both to be subject to constraints from the larger organization in which it operated and to subject the convention to constraints which followed from its internal definition of "news."[6]

There were always numerous specialized media of information which provided some convention coverage for their particular publics. These ranged from the membership journals of interest groups, through magazines of analysis and opinion aimed at the political intelligentsia, to local radio and television stations, and their numbers almost surely increased during the television era. But once television had established itself as the major means of access to convention events for the general public, it was the network news divisions to which most convention actors turned their primary attention—just as it was the response of these divisions which could contribute an additional major twist to the efforts of other major convention actors.

Efforts to shape the character and content of televised coverage were an immediate and continuing result. These efforts were always multifaceted and varied enormously from convention to convention— in part because all such efforts had to be pursued simultaneously, given the variety of convention participants and the short tenure of conventions. But these combined attempts to influence the general public still consisted, year after year, of three recognizable subconflicts. Indeed, once network news had established itself as the major means of access to the convention, and once this three-cornered struggle had emerged as the continuing shape of conflict over network coverage, the boundary between convention decisions and network decisions began to blur—such that movements in this boundary could become an additional influence on the continuing character of the convention itself.

Well before that eventuality was realized, however, a continuing three-cornered struggle had become institutionalized. The first of its recognizable subconflicts was a historical mainstay, the conflict among partisan actors—all those with explicitly political ends to extract from the convention—over the use of that convention to further those ends. The second continuing subconflict featured one or another sample of these partisan actors struggling with network reporters and especially network news executives, over the form and character of televised convention coverage. And the triangle was completed by perhaps the least visible (and surely the least covered) conflict, the one occurring, reliably and persistently, within and among the television networks. Together, these three subconflicts came to constitute the quadrennial struggle to shape television coverage of national party conventions. Out of this ongoing set of conflicts, both singly and collectively, emerged a portrait of the convention for subsequent interpretation by the general viewing public.

The Conflict among Partisan Actors in the Television Era

The first and most fundamental recurring conflict, over deliberate use of the convention as a forum to influence the general public, was neither effectively created nor solely sustained by the arrival of television as the major source of convention news. This conflict ordinarily pitted major convention officials and the entourage of the emerging nominee against either the remaining candidates or some sample of interest groups, issue activists, and party dissidents. The strength of this generic conflict in turn was largely reinforced by the departure of the nomination from the convention hall and its replacement with the effort to launch the general election campaign. But the coming of television did not produce this shift in the cast of convention participants and in the central activities which they contested. The effort to use the convention to publicize the concerns of its participants might well have occurred even if radio, rather than television, had remained the major means of communication via the convention with the general public.

Television may have intensified this conflict, by adding to the impact of events "witnessed" at the convention. Indeed, in a kind of self-fulfilling prophecy, television may have intensified this conflict because convention participants *believed* that televised coverage increased the impact of whatever they were able to present via the convention and because these participants then redoubled their efforts to make use of the convention (and television). In any case, it was television, not radio, which became the major means of communication from the convention to the general public. It was television, not radio, to which convention participants attended when they pondered the way to achieve maximum public impact. It was television, once more, which thus added to the complexity of the calculations surrounding all these effects.

The Democratic convention of 1980 provided a particularly strong example of this continuing attempt by major partisan actors to use the convention, of the way they brought television into their calculations at every point, and of the complexity which this consideration added to the total contest. The key dispute was a procedural one, over Rule F(3)c. This rule bound delegates to support the candidate whom they had endorsed during the delegate selection process and permitted the candidate to remove and replace them if they did not. If this rule could not be changed, President Jimmy Carter was effectively renominated. Accordingly, Senator Edward Kennedy made one final effort to wrest away the nomination by attacking Rule F(3)c.[7]

In any era, there would have been negotiations between the two camps, coupled with threats and topped off with bargaining, over arrangements for addressing and then resolving the application of this rule. In the television era, both sides paid particular attention, additionally, to the way these maneuvers were playing—and might play—on network television. Beyond that, both sides paid attention to questions about scheduling and temporal order, and television coverage extended into every aspect of this concern as well. Thus the Carter camp wanted the debate and the vote on F(3)c to come as early in the convention as possible. They expected to win this fight, and they aspired to put it rapidly behind them. The Kennedy camp preferred to have the debate and vote not earlier than the second night of the convention, so that they would have Sunday (as the delegates arrived), all day Monday (the first full day), and most of Tuesday to search for support. Beyond that, they wanted to be assured that the resolution of this dispute was scheduled and covered to attract the maximum— the "prime time"—television audience.

There was, however, yet another dispute tied into this conflict, one which again showed many of the same characteristics. The Kennedy camp wanted their champion to address the convention on behalf of his minority platform planks on economics and social welfare. This would be part of their one-two punch to shake loose the nomination; it would validate their struggles even if they did not gain the ultimate prize. The Carter camp, not surprisingly, was unenthusiastic, arguing that it would be a violation of party tradition for an announced candidate to appear in the hall before he was either anointed or defeated. They feared that a speech by the senator, whether it attracted any additional votes for him or not, would attract votes for his platform planks, thus hanging some obvious losses on the incumbent president in his own convention while prolonging conflict and divisiveness.

At times, it appeared that coverage issues—television schedules— were more important than the substance of these fights.[8] In any case, the eventual resolution, at the intersection of these desires for substance and publicity, kept the upper hand (albeit barely) for the Carter camp while guaranteeing that this convention would be merely a confirmation, not a coronation, as played out on television. Carter partisans held firm on their insistence that the rules dispute be resolved on the first day, but they did not seriously try to schedule it early that day, for fear that *that* would inflame a conflict which would never die. As a result, the Kennedy camp was to get the chance to present their side as the one calling for openness, fairness, and democracy, in the early evening hours in homes across America.

When the F(3)c fight then came off, as agreed, during prime time on Monday night, and when the outcome of that fight was only a handful of votes different from the professed candidate loyalties of the delegates as a whole—and was thus woefully short of any chance at overturning the rule—the nomination was effectively settled. Later that evening, Kennedy withdrew from the race and formally released his delegates. This withdrawal, however, left him free to be slated by the managers of his minority reports as a speaker on their behalf the next evening, without any violation of party tradition. The Carter camp, while never happy with this fallout from their preceding victory, could hardly put these planks anywhere other than prime time without appearing deliberately to court a split with the Kennedy forces, which they were otherwise hoping to avoid. As a result, and unlike most other minority reports, which were to be addressed Wednesday afternoon—when there would be no large television audience and when the networks might well not cover them at all—both Kennedy and his platform proposals drew the maximum national audience for their presentation.

The aspects of these negotiations which involved coverage by network television news were not the central ones for convention politics. The fight over Rule F(3)c would surely have taken place without *any* press coverage, because it was the only chance to avoid an automatic resolution of the nominating contest. In that sense, it would still have been the central, single ballot of the 1980 Democratic convention. Yet the question of potential television coverage, and the potential viewing audience which that coverage represented, were also present at every step of the negotiations. Nothing was done without an eye to that coverage. Moreover, expectations about coverage were crucial to the accommodation which eventually emerged. Both sides clearly believed that television coverage raised the stakes in these negotiations. If that belief increased the *conflict* over them, then it surely contributed something to public perceptions of President Carter and the Democratic party, whether that coverage had inherently raised the stakes in these perceptions or not.

The Conflict between Partisan Actors and Network News Officials

The first recurring conflict over coverage of conventions in the television era thus featured various partisan actors scuffling with each other, in an atmosphere of self-conscious and continual attention to the way these scuffles might be reported, or indeed to the way they might be *choreographed* to influence that reporting. The second recurring conflict over television coverage of conventions was more likely to feature diverse partisan actors, all on one side of a professional dividing line, with network news officials on the other. The extent to which this became an evident, explicit conflict varied tremendously from convention to convention; the potential for it to become a separate conflict, or at least to reinforce and expand any other conflicts, was never far below the surface.

There was always some preliminary jockeying between convention officials and network news executives over arrangements to facilitate coverage, even if the direct political advantage to be squeezed from such jockeying was never very large. There was frequently some more overt maneuvering as well, as convention participants with widely divergent goals tried to enlist network news officials on their diverse behalf and network officials responded in individual ways to these efforts. Occasionally, there could be an even more direct confrontation between partisan actors and network reporters, when the coverage desires of one side clashed with the news definitions of the other, producing the sharpest conflict in all these possibilities.

Some conflict across these lines followed logically, and hence inevitably, from the maneuvering which normally occurred among convention partisans over use of the convention (and hence of convention coverage) to pursue their own ends. Indeed, if tactical decisions about projected conflicts within the convention were reliably made with one eye on the impact of these conflicts upon the television audience, then it was only a small step to bringing the network news divisions directly into these conflicts, or at least into the negotiations surrounding their presentation. Some of this involvement could be secured indirectly, as with the scheduling of official contests at selected times, when the television audience was likely to be at its peak (or nadir). The struggle over the ground rules for the fight about Rule F(3)c at the Democratic convention of 1980, for example, was replete with such considerations.

Yet these maneuvers could be further facilitated by attempting to guarantee—preferably by explicit understanding—that the networks would indeed present the conflict in question when it was scheduled, rather than offering some other aspect of convention activity to the likely audience for that time period. Obviously, such interactions and explicit negotiations featured different groupings within network ranks as well. From one side, some partisan actors would be pressing the networks to cover one set of events or to cover them in a certain way, while other actors would be pressing them to skip those events or at least to cover them in quite another fashion. From the other side, one network might be more responsive to one set of arguments, another to another. In the 1980 Democratic convention, the differential success of Kennedy partisans, with their national debate over economic platform planks in prime time, versus organized feminists, with what was ultimately a purely local debate over women's issues in the late afternoon—when there was no television coverage at all—made the point as well as any.[9]

Such outcomes, blessing some causes and diminishing others, reliably produced public complaint by the losers, at least after the fact. Yet there were also maneuvers and negotiations about scheduled convention events which broke into open conflict long before this, with demands and responses, pressure and resistance, charges and rebuttals between at least some partisan convention actors and some network personnel. Not every convention surfaced such a division, but it was sufficiently common to make it a recognized pattern of conflict. Most commonly, the pattern surfaced when some major, scheduled, convention event which could be anticipated well in advance became controversial precisely because its abstract news value was evidently open to debate.

Perhaps the best—certainly the longest-running—embodiment of this tension was the case of filmed presentations at conventions. Such films, of course, were shown directly to the delegates, alternates, and guests in the convention hall. Yet they were tailored as much or more for viewers at home, and that fact presented from the first, a perceived dilemma for television news officials. On the one hand, these films were often major, even central, parts of the proceedings, and they transpired, obviously, right within the convention hall. On the other hand, they were just as obviously created to capitalize on, or at least make additional use of, the television cameras, to the point where they verged on being "commercials" rather than inherent parts of the program. Perhaps inevitably, news executives saw themselves as responsible for drawing this distinction, and for televising (or not) in accordance with their conclusions. Reliably, convention planners wanted very much to see coverage proceed, unedited and as planned.

It took only one round of experience for party officials to see the added opportunity which television coverage represented.[10] Its success in 1952 (along of course with the audience it garnered) suggested that the parties might add a visual dimension of their own to their communications arsenal, by making films specifically tailored to support the themes of the convention. The Democratic party was the first to try, with a film entitled *Pursuit of Happiness,* to be shown at its 1956 convention in conjunction with the keynote address. Two of the three networks, ABC and NBC, televised the film in its entirety, but CBS offered only the final minutes, filling the remainder of this time with commentary and interviews.

Recriminations never really stopped. Immediately after the film, the convention chairman took the rostrum to announce, to the assembled delegates and to the television audience on all *three* networks, that one of those networks had not covered the film—and to thank the other two by name for doing so. When he subsequently demanded an airing from CBS News, the president of that network fired back with a defense of press freedom, saying that responsible news people, not publicity-seeking politicians, would make these decisions—a rebuttal in which he was joined by spokesmen for both other networks. Nevertheless, convention officials did learn certain tactical responses from the incident, such as the advantage of turning out the houselights when a film was to be shown, so that the networks would at least be unable to do any other live coverage within the convention hall. Network officials, in turn, were confirmed in their wariness toward all convention films, so that successors faced even more skepticism about the value of direct transmission.

Such controversy was never absent thereafter from conventions featuring filmed presentations; it may have reached its zenith in the Republican convention of 1984.[11] There, party leaders planned to introduce President Ronald Reagan on the night of his acceptance speech with a specially prepared film highlighting some aspects of his first term and presenting the man himself as his supporters preferred to have him perceived. Upon announcement of plans for this device, however, the networks instantly began arguing about "news" versus "propaganda." Convention officials immediately responded that this film was an integral part of the convention and obviously not an interlude, so that a decision not to show it would once again be a deliberate attempt to censor coverage of the convention.

For three days, from Monday through Wednesday of convention week, the relevant officials volleyed back and forth, elaborating their positions. Eventually, on Thursday evening, ABC decided to show the film in its entirety; CBS and NBC elected to pass, substituting comments from their anchor teams in the main television booth. From the viewpoint of convention officials, the networks had made an increasingly common editorial decision, which interfered with public perceptions of the convention as it had unfolded. From the viewpoint of network officials, an effort to manipulate network news had been thwarted, while the real political events of the convention had been covered live and in full. Regardless of viewpoint, this conflict between convention officials and network officials—sharp, explicit, and continuing—had been one of the few public struggles of the entire convention. In this case at least, the networks had won.

The Conflict among Network Actors in the Television Era

A third and final set of decisions about television coverage of the convention was every bit as omnipresent throughout this period but differed from these other corners of the recurring struggle by occurring almost entirely within the television networks. These were the decisions about priorities for coverage at the individual networks—the choices among a myriad of available events for broadcasting—and if these too did not necessarily lead to open conflict, they often featured open argument inside the networks; they occasionally featured sniping between network news divisions; and they frequently produced complaints, though inevitably after the fact, from convention principals.

The exercise of journalistic discretion by television news executives, even if it had not been considered part of their mission and responsibility, was an intrinsic part of covering a convention. Unless "the convention" was conceived solely as the current proceedings on the rostrum, the possibilities for choice—and alternative broadcast—were extensive. There were often several official events, such as meetings of convention committees, even during the time the full convention was in session. There were ordinarily numerous other, open and public, formal meetings of major interest groups or candidate campaigns, called to reach (or implement) decisions which would clearly have some subsequent impact on the course of events in the convention hall. Beyond even that, there were a multitude of other developments, without formal announcement or process, which might shape the course of the convention.

Most aspects of this choice among matters to cover on television, and of the extent and manner of coverage, were not powerfully different from most aspects of the same choice in other media. Television news people, like most others, reliably evinced a preference for "the real story" of the convention rather than its formal proceedings. This preference ordinarily translated, as it would with most other news media, into a preference for items of conflict. Even these generally shared approaches, of course, tended to receive more scrutiny—and complaint—on television than on radio or in the print press, precisely because network television had become the central means of live and direct presentation of the convention to the general public. If television did add an emphasis beyond this, one intrinsic to the medium, it was through a preference for items of conflict with a heavy visual—or at least visualizable—element. Yet it was not any such immanent difference, anything inherent in television news as a medium, which most often fueled this third aspect of the recurring struggle over convention coverage.[12]

Instead, it was a combination of the institutional organization of television news with its standing as the largest and most immediate source of convention information for the general public. For where television differed additionally from all other news media except radio, which it had displaced on quite other grounds as a news source, was in the speed, and then the finality, with which news decisions had to be made. Film (and later videotape) arrived and in effect demanded an immediate decision to broadcast, delay, or ignore. Events deferred— be they proceedings from the podium, an alternative item about to be pulled from the screen, or the incoming film or tape—might well not be back again, since there were always numerous other events which might expect to have the same advantage of temporal priority when *they* arrived. Added pressure for a quick response—and added finality, having made one—derived from the presence of two other networks, simultaneously involved in the same enterprise. Beating these networks to a story was the television counterpart of rushing out an "extra" in the bygone days of newspaper supremacy. It was also the route both to prestige among the networks and to potential audience rewards, as the public switched channels in response to a breaking story.

Since the very beginning of televised convention coverage, network news teams had in fact offered some mix of three general types of visual presentation, aimed at conveying the total and complex reality of the convention to the general public. First, they presented the current proceedings of the full convention, assembled in the hall. Second, they provided reports from news people scattered throughout the hall and throughout the convention city for that matter—sometimes in the form of interviews with convention participants, sometimes in the form of stories about previous or forthcoming convention developments. Third, they offered commentary from their anchors, high above the hall in specially constructed booths, commentary which could assess current proceedings in the hall but which could also refer to events earlier or events unfolding elsewhere.[13]

The *mix* of these three types of presentation inevitably varied from convention to convention, as events made one or another emphasis appropriate. But the mix of formality, informality, and analysis also varied over time in a more regular fashion. At the first televised convention, by far the largest share of coverage was indeed reserved for events at the podium. The desperate haste of preparation, when added to comparatively cumbersome equipment, contributed to this approach. As the networks acquired experience with covering conventions, however, and as cameras, for example, became lighter and more mobile, news teams sought to expand the range of events covered, although at first even this was largely a matter of covering the proceedings of the official committees and of the scheduled events of major official actors. Over time, the share of coverage devoted to reports from various points around the convention city and to commentary by network anchors increased further, at the expense of this formal focus. Even then, however, the largest single block of televised time was devoted to events at the podium, to a much greater degree than recurrent complaints about network discretion would have suggested.

Obviously, all such coverage decisions—in priority, weighting, and approach—had an element of discretion about them. Again, the more noteworthy phenomenon was the extent to which such decisions were most often effectively dictated by the schedule of the convention itself, along with the extent to which the networks appeared to exercise their discretion in effectively similar fashion. Yet whenever network presentations did differ significantly, that difference was grounds for charges and countercharges from convention principals, who were aggrieved (or advantaged) by some element of the difference. Moreover, whenever their exercise of discretion led the networks to desert the formal proceedings at the podium for some other event or report which was not likely to contribute to the positive launching of the general election campaign, whether they did so as a group or not, the likelihood of aggressive complaint by convention leaders was extremely high.

The complexity of the decisions which could—and had to—be made entirely within the network news operations, as a product only of a "best news judgment," was perhaps most effectively illustrated at the

Democratic convention of 1968. That convention was probably the most divisive and dramatic of the modern era. Although much of its drama was produced by real convention principals and certainly not by television news people, major elements of this drama were also occurring simultaneously, so that the need for choices was ever present. The most controversial of these, and probably the one which most thoroughly marked this convention in the public mind, concerned the relative priority of the Humphrey nomination itself and of the street violence occurring shortly before that nomination.[14]

Given the scale of the street demonstrations outside the convention hall, network news people could hardly have avoided reporting on them. Party officials did argue that many of the demonstrators were there because they could rely upon the television cameras. The demonstrators, however, were real enough, as were the events they helped produce, and the cameras were guaranteed to be present under those conditions. What *could* have been different, and what produced the bulk of subsequent argument, was a set of decisions by news executives within these overall parameters. The one most widely argued after the fact, of course, and the one which made the point about differential public perceptions of the convention based on network news judgments, was the decision about the relative priority for film of the violent confrontation between demonstrators and police outside the convention hall. This film was finally ready, and immediately presented, just as Hubert Humphrey was being nominated for president inside.

Perhaps nothing would have altered the impact of this convention on the launching of the general election campaign. It was an unhappy and conflictual gathering almost from start to finish; it did indeed paint a portrait of its nominee as a man not in charge of—and perhaps not up to—the situation. In any case, the networks would probably have made their decisions about news priorities in much the same way they ultimately did, even if they had possessed the benefit of similar experiences. The footage screened in the middle of the Humphrey nomination was arguably the most visually riveting of the convention. It was evidently "news" by any standard. Yet the obvious logical alternative—presenting the central event of the official convention *followed by* the confrontation between police and demonstrators—was certainly available.

It was also given only brief consideration. Those nominating speeches really were the first opportunity for the Humphrey campaign to counteract the damaging events of the convention to that point and begin to launch the election campaign in the most positive way possible. Yet the networks, operating on a consensual standard of newsworthiness and under direct and fierce competition to get their version of the most newsworthy events on the screen first, effectively eliminated—really annihilated—this possibility. Instead, they presented an extended incident which became the embodiment of the tensions of that unhappy gathering. This incident was inherently dramatic, so that its impact on the viewing public was likely to be as large as such an impact can be. There would certainly be no alternative version of history, to test whether the events which followed might have unfolded differently with a different network news approach.

The Impact on Conventions of Television Coverage

Many network news decisions, while they lacked the extraordinary character of those for the 1968 Democratic convention, did partake of their essential nature. That is, a news director had to decide while something happened whether that event was to be put on the screen then, held off to be put on the screen later, or saved for presentation only if nothing else occurred of evidently greater newsworthiness. News directors—sitting, in the modern era, in front of a bank of television screens filled with the ongoing and available network footage—did make such decisions all the time; that was, after all, a central part of the job. On the one hand, their most common decision remained a choice of footage from the podium at the moment. On the other, they were most likely to pull away from the podium and present some other, unofficial development with precisely those events which were most likely to cause subsequent controversy.

In any case, these decisions were always the third and final contribution to a recurring three-cornered struggle over the explicit content of televised coverage of the convention. As such, when placed on top of the actual events transpiring at any individual convention, these coverage decisions completed the presentation of the largest part of the raw material from which a huge portion of the American public would draw its impressions of that particular gathering. The product of the three-cornered struggle was thus an individual convention portrait. The product was also in effect the largest single presentation of the mediated convention itself. This mediated convention, finally, this combination of network coverage decisions and of the convention events being filtered through them, became a major part of the contribution of this individual convention to the general election campaign. These, then, were the explicit contributions of the national television networks to eventual public impressions of individual national conventions.

Yet if the networks always made some contribution to public perceptions of these conventions, and if that contribution was always not just their most widely perceived but also their most widely debated impact, it was not—ever—the only impact of network coverage on the convention. There were also implicit impacts, for example, from the simple process of arranging to have the networks cover the convention. There were far more important impacts from the *operation* of that coverage—working gradually but cumulating strongly over time—on the organization and procedures, the very framework, of the convention. The negotiations over network arrangements for coverage always created some small additional effects, not just on the resulting picture of an individual convention but also on the convention as a continuing institution. Of a similar sort but more substantial were the anticipatory reactions of the convention leadership across time to the continuing character of television coverage, reactions which produced further small but more consequential changes in the convention as a political institution.

Arrangements for Coverage and Convention Portraits

The aspect of this influence which was least visible in principle to the general public involved advance arrangements to facilitate televised coverage. There was always a set of opening negotiations over technical preparations for coverage, often spreading over many months. The networks needed fairly extensive supporting facilities, or at least agreements, from the national parties. The parties hoped to use these arrangements to build goodwill in general and to secure some marginal specific advantages if the opportunity presented itself. These negotiations never shaped the ultimate portrait of an individual convention in a major way. They never altered the operation of the convention in ways of continuing, major consequence. But they did produce regular, concrete outcomes, and these did occasionally turn up as obvious elements in the total convention portrait.[15]

Before the advent of network radio, there was little formalized interaction between convention officers and press representatives. In the earliest days of the convention, newspaper reporters came and went much as anyone else, and little was done—little could be done, and there was little reason to do it—in trying to influence what they might write. As the convention became more institutionalized, there was some minimal effort to accredit journalists in order to provide them with (or deprive them of) specific forms of access, but even this was a relatively haphazard operation, with little reason to believe that it would secure positive commentary or impede negative. Key convention officials might well try to see that unfriendly reporters (or all reporters for that matter) were barred from crucial private negotiations, but that effort was only an extension of their normal approach to political reporting and was not judged noteworthy by those on either side of the journalistic fence.

The advent of radio coverage began to change some of this. Live and direct radio transmission did require prior arrangements for the placement of microphones within the hall and for their support through additional broadcasting equipment, inside or out. Radio anchors also needed prearranged positions from which they could view the convention floor and coordinate convention reporting. Quite apart from these arrangements, the earliest days of radio coverage featured some additional jousting between partisan actors and news officials as radio networks introduced technical innovations which allowed them to pick up aspects of convention conversation which partisan actors believed—and intended—to be private. The associated prior arrangements, however, rarely acquired adversarial overtones.

The advent of television coverage took the scope of these advance arrangements a good deal further, since television came to require huge camera platforms which could dominate the hall and since television anchor booths had to be even more complex than those for radio. In fact, the first convention covered by network television provided an example of the extent—and limits—of such mutual arrangements. For 1952, both parties planned to hold their national conventions in Chicago, and both expected to hold the sessions themselves in Chicago stadium. But the networks argued strongly that the stadium was insufficient to handle even their direct broadcasting equipment, much less the technical support which necessarily came along with it. In response, both parties agreed to move their conventions to the International Amphitheater.[16]

Lest it appear, however, that the networks uniformly had their way with convention arrangements, it should be noted that the 1952 conventions were also the last to be held not just in the same hall but even in the same city until 1972. All three major television networks had a strong preference for this arrangement, since it cut costs and eased logistical burdens; all three expressed that preference repeatedly and forcefully. Yet each national party saw an independent stake in being able to put its convention in the most politically and individually advantageous spot—for electoral reasons, for symbolic reasons, or just to hold down its own costs. Accordingly, for the next four conventions, each party chose to let these considerations override repeated calls from the television networks for conventions located in the same city.

Most of the discussions between national party leaders and network news officials about coverage of the conventions did, however, produce the arrangements the networks requested. Some of these were quite remarkable, visually and symbolically. The main camera platform, right up the middle of the convention hall, was easily the dominant structure on the floor, towering over party leaders and enshadowing entire delegations. The network anchor booths, around the rear of the convention floor and immediately above it, rivaled the podium itself in both sheer physical size and attention-getting physical presentation. More substantively relevant developments reflected the same situation. Thus although convention officials might prefer to limit the number of camera placements apart from the main camera platform, as a means of forcing greater concentration on events at the podium, the networks also got their way reliably on the placement of numerous smaller cameras throughout the hall—which were indeed both intended and suited for sweeping the floor, covering the stands, and in general pulling back from the podium for other internal shots. Whatever marginal gains convention officials might squeeze from advance arrangements, then, had to derive primarily from the goodwill acquired through facilitating them rather than from precise—and predictable—limitations and structures.

The two parties did differ in one noticeable regard with respect to these arrangements. The Republicans were always more resistant to demands for floor passes (and hence floor access) for network reporters and camera crews. This resistance stemmed from an emphasis, much greater among Republican than among Democratic party officials, on the convention as a deliberative—and dignified—body. This implied that the aisles should be clear during official sessions, so that the delegates themselves could concentrate on the podium. It meant that floor passes for anyone, including members of the press, should be limited, so that those aisles could in principle be cleared. In practice, this difference between the parties was only ever one of degree. In 1964, Republican convention officials and Goldwater campaign leaders actually proposed limiting floor passes to delegates and alternates, but the outraged response of the entire press corps caused them to retract the suggestion.

Thereafter, the notion of keeping the convention more effectively deliberative was still more often saluted by Republicans than by Democrats, but the product of this notion did not ordinarily inconvenience either the television networks or major print news outlets. The Republicans did reliably bestow a lower total number of floor passes, but the greater share of the burden from this fell on the smaller news media and on other groups with a concern for floor access. In fact, whatever goodwill the Republicans may have forfeited, in contrast to the Democrats, by continuing to hold to this general attitude was probably more than compensated by the general character of support services for the press offered by both parties. Press representatives continually noted the Republican party's more comprehensive and effective liaison operation. And the Republicans did indeed make the lives of reporters reliably less complicated, by offering a broader range of background materials to aid in coverage, by seeing that these materials were available more generally and on an appropriate schedule, and especially by coordinating the total support operation much more consistently.

The Process of Coverage and Convention Structure

A more visible and much more consequential set of impacts from network television coverage on the structure of the convention also followed the introduction of the television cameras—and television reporters, and ultimately the huge television audience—into the convention hall. Although these effects were physically visible in every case, and although they were not only continuing but actually integrated into the organizational framework for subsequent conventions, they were easily missed by ordinary viewers of individual conventions. Indeed, these continuing responses to the arrival and character of television coverage normally went unremarked, at least as self-conscious reforms in the operation of a major political institution, even by those who were involved in realizing them. Yet the structure of the convention, its organization and procedures, did change noticeably during the television era—and in direct response to television coverage.

Once again it was not unprecedented for the national party convention to show some concrete effects from a major change in the media presenting it to the general public. The appearance of live and direct, gavel-to-gavel, radio coverage in the 1920s had been just such a change, and it had been met by a few shifts in the organization of the convention proper and by a multitude of arguments about the need to do more. Indeed, the first convention to receive nationwide radio coverage, the Democratic convention of 1924, had become a source of sardonic humor, thanks to the combination of its historic duration (seventeen days and one hundred and three ballots) with this live and direct coverage. At the same time, however, the central activity of the convention had remained the *making* of a presidential nomination, so that there were strong and very narrow limits on the shifts which could occur in response to changes in the mere reporting of convention developments, however much convention officials might claim to desire those shifts.

No such limits were functioning throughout most of the television era, and the corresponding responses were thus both more numerous and more serious. Because the central activity of the convention was now the launching of the general election campaign, this activity not only failed to brake the influence of live and direct, gavel-to-gavel, television coverage, it actively facilitated that influence. If modifications in the convention itself, especially in its surface organization, could improve the effectiveness of the convention in its new political role—in either launching the general election campaign or in securing attention for some competing cause or causes—then few convention actors were prepared to oppose those adjustments. They might not perceive the larger genesis of these reforms; they were likely to view them as attractive nevertheless. Accordingly, the convention as a comprehensive pageant was consciously redesigned, to secure maximum visual impact. Scheduling was considered, so that significant events fell at times calculated to attract the maximum television audience. The overall pace of the convention was the object of special focus, to try to sustain the attention of that audience once captured.

Some of the resulting change was narrowly visual, as befitted the response to a medium which had just added that element to all the existing news approaches.[17] For example, after only one round of experience with televised coverage, convention organizers in both parties began to assess the physical appearance of the rostrum and the hall and make changes aimed at enhancing it. Consultants specializing in design and in video presentation were deliberately added to the convention planning staff. They recommended changes in coloring, podium construction, lighting, and so on, recommendations which were quickly implemented. At the same time, convention officials began exhorting the delegates themselves, to a degree unprecedented in the era of radio or newspapers, to remain vigilant about their appearance and the appearance of their total delegations while the convention was proceeding—and while *television cameras* were looking on.

But the changes promoted by the arrival of television and produced by a deliberate response to that arrival went far beyond the decorative and cosmetic. Indeed, once convention planners began to consider the tremendous size of the composite television audience and the visual impact of the convention on it—a consideration which, again, gained force from the belief of these planners in the heightened impact of television as a medium—a much more extended set of adjustments resulted. Most of these followed more or less directly from an explicit concern with the pace of the convention, that is, the flow of events and the potential of that flow to hold an audience. But this concern was always mixed with a largely implicit set of beliefs about audience values, about what would seem attractive or unattractive to contemporary television viewers.[18]

A trivial embodiment of this growing concern was the introduction of national entertainers at the Republican convention of 1956, as a way to fill the inevitable gaps when there was literally nothing occurring at the podium. More consequential embodiments stemmed from the arrival of an explicit *script* for the convention, along with an attempt to follow it precisely. The need for a script grew most pressingly from the desire to have critical events fall at times of maximum viewership, or occasionally at times of minimum viewership instead. But this pressure was reinforced by a desire to see that all these events made their appropriate contribution to (or minimized their likely detraction from) the goals of their proponents. This effort, once again, brought not just the particular demands of televised coverage but the perceived shifts in the values and mores of viewers into the equation.

One of the first casualties of an emphasis on effectively scripting the convention was old-fashioned, stem-winding, convention oratory. If key events were to fall in critical time slots, and if other events were to make their appropriate contribution, then everyone who had the opportunity to appear at the podium had to be committed to precise limits. Neither the lesser speakers at off-hours, who could by their disregard of this criterion push the major speakers into off-hours as well, nor the major speakers themselves could be permitted to decide, once at the podium, how long they were going to speak. That decision would permit them, by immediate extension, to take the central impact of the convention into their own hands. There had to be specific and agreed limits for each speaker, and this requirement even led eventually to a programmed rehearsal of every speech, so that a verbal consent to remain within limits could be confirmed practically.

A second casualty of the scripting era was the old-fashioned partisan demonstration. Supporters of a given candidate had historically celebrated his alleged chances with shouting, chanting, and marching in the aisles at any appropriate (and often inappropriate) opportunity. In the era when the convention actually made the nomination, these demonstrations not only provided rank-and-file delegates with something to do but gave them the chance to help create the impression of wide and deep support, an impression which might then draw others to the cause. But in the era of televised coverage, when nominations were being ratified but not created, such demonstrations threatened at the very least to disrupt the schedule of convention events. At the worst, they contained the possibility of creating a negative impression—of division, dissension, or mere unseemliness—for the general public and even for potential supporters of the candidate at their center. In response, the Democrats through formal rules and the Republicans through clear norms and procedural roadblocks abolished the old-fashioned demonstration and substituted a fixed period of cheering by the delegates from their seats.

All these changes followed from the arrival of live and direct television coverage at national party conventions. All of them altered the appearance and operation of the convention as well. All of them, finally, came in addition to the portraits of individual conventions, which became a central part of convention impact on the general public and were also shaped, powerfully, by network television. Yet all of them also occurred within an even larger implicit framework, provided by the standard of gavel-to-gavel coverage. It was that framework, comprised by those overall parameters, which was about to change in the late 1970s, in a development with the potential for outweighing all these others.

| Coverage Levels and
Institutional Character:
The Coming of the
Bifurcated Convention

The shift to promotion of various external campaigns as the central
activity at the national party convention meant that press *reporting*
of the convention had become immediately and inevitably crucial. The
fact that the audience for this promotion, in turn, was overwhelmingly
the audience of direct local participants meant that the central news
medium for live and direct coverage of the convention was especially
important within this overall equation. That medium, of course, which
appeared within the convention just as the nomination was departing
and which rose to dominance in the period of ascendancy for the
campaign launching function, was network television. It began to work
changes on every aspect of convention operations.

The arrival of television had been met almost immediately with
lesser organizational and procedural changes in the convention, in
everything from the shape and color of the convention podium to the
length, placement, and content of convention speeches. Their potential
for concrete impact, though circumscribed, was quickly realized. The
arrival of television also meant a recurring contribution to the impact
of the convention on the general public, through the presentation of
individual convention portraits. Much of the substance of these portraits was still dependent on central events at the convention, with
some added influence from the preference of television reporters for
visual possibilities. But much of it stemmed as well from the necessity
for numerous decisions about priorities within convention coverage,
present in any era but multiplied, telescoped, and given an added air

of finality in the era of television. Yet these developments still occurred within a larger context which powerfully shaped them all—a context provided by the consensual standard of *gavel-to-gavel coverage* by network television news.

The gavel-to-gavel standard was hardly invisible; news directors or viewers could readily have attested to it if asked. Yet its all-enveloping impact was both unnoticed and perhaps unnoticeable as the television era progressed. In any case, the extent to which all the other explicit struggles over press coverage of the convention had occurred within and been shaped by its implicit parameters was starkly revealed in 1980, and underlined even further in 1984, when the major national networks cut back—almost decimated—their broadcasting of the convention. At a stroke, this reduction intensified all the existing issues about media choice of events for presentation. At a stroke, it changed not just the amount but the substance of the material with which most of the general public would make sense of the convention. As a result, it produced what was in essence the "bifurcated convention," with one version for participants and another for viewers—and a large and growing disjunction between the two.

For most of the television era to date, from 1956 through 1976, the norm of gavel-to-gavel coverage was the one saluted by the national networks. That norm could always be interpreted to permit exclusion of the most routine, nonsubstantive, and nonconflictual sessions, just as it came to encourage inclusion not only of formal events outside the official sessions but, especially, of informal developments which might influence the course of convention politics. The norm emerged "naturally," almost without discussion, in the aftermath of network successes with the conventions of 1952. It governed network news behavior for more than a generation, making it appear that the major impacts of television coverage were through network decisions about priorities for particular events or through convention adaptations to the character of television news.

Yet from the first, these other impacts not only occurred within but were powerfully dependent on the larger context contributed by gavel-to-gavel coverage. And from the first, there was always an argument within the networks over whether the scope of this coverage was justified. The players in this argument, along with many of their premises, were essentially unchanging. From beginning to end, network news divisions opposed programming and marketing divisions over the issue of extended coverage national party conventions. For over twenty years, the resolution was unchanging as well. ABC News did cut back on its broadcast in 1968, so that its version could no longer conceivably be described as gavel to gavel. But through 1976, CBS and NBC, the two networks with the largest audiences for convention reporting, were to retain their original coverage pattern. At any point within the first generation of televised conventions, then, the networks could assert that the norm, gavel-to-gavel presentation, was also their practice, and the ordinary convention viewer would have had to agree.

Despite this surface continuity, there were developments within the networks, and more so within the wider world of politics, which would eventually produce a change of major proportions, a restoration of uniformity among the three networks at a new and much reduced level. The economics for decision making about convention coverage inside the networks came increasingly to strengthen those in favor of a cutback. At the same time, the political context for that decision making, which involved both the place of the convention in the process of presidential selection and the array of other events and institutions in that process, changed even more extensively, to reinforce the same position. Thus burgeoning primaries reduced the importance of the convention from one side; presidential debates subsequently reduced it from the other. The networks inevitably turned their attention to covering both.

They also turned to a decision, in 1980, to pull back consciously from the gavel-to-gavel standard of convention coverage. When the organizational and, especially, the political events of 1980 did nothing to undermine this decision, there was an even more substantial cutback for 1984. The result of these successive and cumulative cuts was a change in the overall parameters of network convention broadcasting, the enveloping context for live and direct coverage of conventions, on such a scale that it threatened to rework public impressions of individual conventions—while it reworked the convention as a continuing political institution, more thoroughly than anything since the beginning of the television era. Inevitably, when the total time available for coverage of the convention declined by *60 percent* within the period of only two elections, the influence of network decisions about news priorities surged. Inevitably as well, when total coverage declined by that magnitude in so short a time, the need for top party officials to adapt the organization and procedures of the convention itself to these new parameters intensified to an unprecedented degree.

What resulted was nothing less then the bifurcated convention. Even in the years leading up to 1980, the interplay between and among convention officials and news personnel had produced a growing disjunction between the convention as a local event, for on-site participants, and the convention as a mediated event, for those watching at home. But the cutbacks of 1980 and then of 1984 vastly increased the distance between the convention as experienced by participants in the locality and the convention as perceived by those who ended up watching, not the total event, but the declining (and shifting) sample of it presented on television—to the point where the disjunction between the direct and the mediated experience, between the *two* Democratic or the *two* Republican conventions of 1984, was perhaps more directly consequential than the actions taken by real participants on the local scene.

The Birth of the Gavel-to-Gavel Standard

Only an observer with a perspective gained from the next thirty years could have seen an incipient split over the appropriate level of convention coverage after the first experiment with television broadcasting in 1952. Moreover, any observer who did come up with such a prediction—featuring two clear sides to the debate, with two defensible arguments and the ultimate triumph of the side which counseled a reduction—would surely have been dismissed, and probably drowned out, by the general euphoria in the television industry at that time. Nevertheless, the seeds—indeed, the full alignment—of such a conflict were present in the aftermath of the first conventions covered nationally by the television networks.

Immediately after those conventions, a small series of articles did suggest that while millions of homes had indeed watched the conventions for the first time ever, millions had also turned them off.[1] Their statistics suggested that the average audience for network presentations during the period when the conventions were being broadcast was only about two-thirds what it would have been if standard network programming—variety shows, situation comedies, contest giveaways, and the like—had been offered instead. One analyst went so far as to summarize convention coverage as "a bomb." But these analyses were brushed aside in the aftermath—the afterglow, really—of network coverage of the 1952 conventions. Television news officials were aggressive in saluting their triumph, recognizing in it the potential for displacing radio news as the central source of information about public affairs for the largest share of the American public.

More critically, top network executives also supported this judgment. Indeed, they viewed convention coverage as a triumph for the entire industry, in demonstrating an ability to bring major political events into the homes of millions of Americans. They were delighted to accept the accolades of most other analysts and commentators, to the effect that they had provided a major public service; they repeated these judgments to each other as well. The practical response of those executives, moreover, was not only to authorize a repetition in 1956 but to encourage an expansion to more peripheral convention events, such as committee meetings, external rallies, and so forth. When an increase in the viewing audience appeared to justify this response once again—the ratings of the convention did not go up at all but the number of viewers doubled, thanks to an increase in the number of households with television sets—the continuation of the venture was assured. The conventions of 1960 were the last in which expansion of the audience could be gained through major expansion in the share of households with televisions, but that possibility did exist. When it was again realized, a tradition—of comprehensive network coverage of conventions—was simultaneously confirmed.

No such simple and direct, audience-based rationale for this coverage was available with the conventions of 1964. But by the time these conventions were on the horizon, network news teams had another, quite different version of the market argument for substantial coverage. In late 1963, all three networks had expanded their evening news programs, from the previous fifteen minutes to half an hour. Network coverage of the conventions was an automatic opportunity to showcase the expanded news teams, in a setting where they were almost guaranteed a more varied audience than their usual array of (evening) viewers and where they were potentially able to go head to head with their evolving competition.[2] The large overall audience which convention coverage seemed to guarantee was an implicit promise that these news teams would be seen by the widest possible range of viewers, occasionally switching channels in the interest of novelty and thus not only encountering alternative teams but perhaps preferring what they saw—and being drawn across to alternative news programming on a regular basis. Under those conditions, even if the conventions lost viewers by comparison with regular entertainment programming, convention coverage could be seen as a kind of "loss leader," providing aid for the network news divisions in their ratings battles with each other over the four years to follow.

As a result gavel-to-gavel coverage retained not just a public service and prestige rationale but a marketing and financial defense too. By the end of the 1964 conventions, then, the networks had developed a clear and dominant pattern of coverage. CBS News was typical: from 1956 through 1964, and ultimately through 1976, CBS offered roughly 3,300 minutes—fifty-five hours—of explicit convention coverage per presidential year, and these numbers did not include additional attention on the early and late evening news programs. (See Table 8.1.) Coverage of the individual conventions within these totals varied a bit more, with longer conventions generating longer coverage. But a second simple statistic suggested how regular and reliable this coverage, under the gavel-to-gavel standard, had become: throughout this period, CBS was never on the air with fewer minutes of explicit convention coverage than the convention itself was in formal session. In every case, the network lived by its version of the gavel-to-gavel standard.

Table 8.1.   Total minutes of coverage by CBS network news compared with length of official convention sessions

Year	Network coverage	Official sessions
1984	1,361	2,884
1980	2,557	3,818
1976	3,365	2,944
1972	3,345	2,999
1968	4,133	3,148
1964	3,364	2,486
1960	3,054	2,755
1956	3,360	2,979

Source: Figures for 1956 through 1968 were derived from "Table 6.2: Number of Sessions and Duration of the Major Party National Conventions, 1952–68," in Judith H. Parris, *The Convention Problem: Issues in Reform of Presidential Nominating Procedures* (Washington, D.C.: Brookings, 1972), p. 150. Figures for 1972 through 1984 were extracted from convention records of the national parties, typical recent examples of which include *Official Report of the Proceedings of the Thirty-third Republican National Convention* (Washington, D.C.: Republican National Committee, 1984) and *1984: Official Report of the Proceedings of the Democratic National Convention* (Washington, D.C.: Democratic National Committee, 1984).

The Rise of a Debate on the Level of Coverage

The basic network decision about the scope of convention coverage, accordingly, remained roughly the same throughout this period. It committed the networks to a defensible version of completeness; it characterized all three television networks. Yet the absence of change was never the absence of internal argument. Very early in the history of televised coverage, a debate began inside the networks over the appropriate amount of resources—and television time—to be devoted to the conventions. The leading actors, their basic positions, and their arguments were to change hardly at all. What did change eventually was the organizational and political environment *around* these actors and arguments. And at that point, the institutional context for the debate, in both the networks and the wider political world, would push for a markedly different resolution.

From the first, whenever an argument about the scope of coverage surfaced, it pitted news divisions against programming (entertainment) and marketing (advertising) divisions. The news divisions argued reliably that coverage of conventions was a major public service, which brought the American people into one of their central forums for decision making. In this, they were buttressed by institutionalized self-interests, in the perception of the conventions as the "World Series" of news coverage, and in the even more concrete fact that such coverage provided major exposure for the largest possible numbers of reporters, helping numerous reportorial careers.

The programming divisions always argued that the conventions were badly overrated as newsworthy events, though they varied the specifics of this indictment over time. They too were buttressed by institutional interests, which spilled out in a second argument, to the effect that convention coverage was not only costly in direct financial terms but evidently disruptive to normal programming schedules. In this argument, they were perhaps inevitably joined by the marketing divisions, which were charged much more explicitly with emphasizing the "bottom line"—that coverage of conventions always represented an increase in direct expenditures while it coincided invariably with a sharp decrease in revenues.[3]

All three networks followed through in applying the gavel-to-gavel standard to their coverage of both 1964 conventions. The actual ratings for network coverage of these conventions, however, were to produce the first defection from the standard and to signal a change of much greater ultimate import—a change in the overall environment for network decision making about convention coverage. At first, this defection was only an experimental shift, by the smallest and economically weakest network. But while the experiment itself would not produce much immediate impact on the total amount of convention available to the viewing public, it would become an important part of an eventual, much larger, chain reaction.

It was ABC News which became the vehicle for this break. After 1964, the ABC network was almost forced, by ratings alone, to re-examine its decisions about convention programming. From one side, ABC news officials were not enthusiastic about a turn to the criterion of ratings. The conventions were still the biggest routinized event they presented, and news people had no difficulty in drawing the practical implications for coverage of conventions from any decisions based on recent audience response. Network executives, from the other side, while they may or may not have judged these numbers to be any more or less catastrophic in the abstract, read them to suggest that more than a simple juggling of personnel was necessary to address the underlying problem.

What they saw was that ABC had not just suffered losses relative to regular (entertainment) programming, a serious enough matter for the economically weakest network. It had also suffered losses—massive losses—in competition with the other networks. (See Table 8.2.)[4] Once again, as it had for every convention since the beginning of national coverage, ABC had placed third in the competition for viewers. Worse,

Table 8.2. Nielsen ratings, by network, for coverage of conventions

Year	Democratic			Republican			Combined average rating		
	CBS	NBC	ABC	CBS	NBC	ABC	CBS	NBC	ABC
1984	8.1	7.2	7.9	6.4	5.8	6.9	7.3	6.5	7.4
1980	8.6	8.3	7.9	7.1	6.9	6.5	7.9	7.6	7.2
1976	7.7	7.2	7.6	9.0	8.8	7.4	8.4	8.0	7.5
1972	6.6	7.2	4.5	10.1	10.6	8.9	8.4	8.9	6.7
1968	9.7	10.6	8.5	7.7	11.2	7.7	8.8	10.9	8.1
1964	9.9	13.8	4.2	6.9	10.7	2.8	8.4	12.3	3.5
1960	10.7	14.4	4.2	5.3	5.8	1.2	8.0	10.1	2.7
1956	12.2	8.8	3.3	13.6	11.7	4.1	12.9	10.3	3.7

Source: Library and Archives, CBS News.

that competition was not even close: ABC had managed to draw only about a third of the average audience for each of its competitors. For the Republican convention of 1960, it had already been reduced to a rating of 1.2—1.2 percent of the total public with a television set. For 1964 this figure had improved inconsequentially to a miserable, uneconomical, 2.8.

A Breach in the Gavel-to-Gavel Standard

The response was perhaps unavoidable. For 1968, network executives at ABC planned sharply condensed coverage of the national party conventions. Live and direct transmissions would be cut, to the point where they eventually stood at just over *25 percent* of what had been offered in 1964—despite the fact that the two conventions of 1968 actually ran longer in formal session. ABC was to supplement this reduction with some additional news, to be used either for summarizing developments at the conventions or for presenting special reports on external events as the situation dictated. But ABC would also present far more of its standard entertainment programming than it (or any other network) had done before.

The change worked strikingly. In 1968, with regular entertainment programming as a lead-in, ratings for this reduced portion of convention coverage on ABC News jumped dramatically, more than doubling the figures from 1964 and making ABC roughly competitive with the other two networks—a status which the network had never before attained. (See Table 8.2.) But if the experiment had to be judged a clear success on its own terms, it still did not create an immediate precedent for the other networks. Indeed, so strong was the gavel-to-gavel tradition (and the arguments associated with it) that ABC itself hesitated, despite the apparent lessons of 1968.

What caused ABC to reconsider was the *political* character, and hence the inherent news value, of the 1968 conventions and the doubts which this raised about other arguments on convention coverage. In fact ABC had been the first network not just to cut its coverage but to surface a major argument about why this cut was justified on the traditional ground of newsworthiness. After 1964, ABC had not been prepared to go all the way to argue that the convention had lost the nomination for good and was thus no longer a decision-making body. But ABC executives did assert—an argument with the evident ring of truth—that conventions differed tremendously in their potential for significant decisions, or even substantial conflict over preordained outcomes.

The conventions of 1952 had made the nominating decision. Those of 1956, 1960, and 1964 had not. Moreover, the conventions of 1964, especially the Democratic one, had underlined just how inconsequential an uncontested renomination could be. On the other hand, the conventions of 1968 had challenged this wisdom. The Democratic convention of 1968, in particular, had been as conflict ridden as any in modern times, so that if conflict was the standard of newsworthiness, this convention had been manifestly more newsworthy than ABC executives were willing to admit—or at least than their level of coverage would argue. For 1972 then, ABC executives authorized an increase in their coverage of the first convention, the Democratic, although they still offered less than the other two networks. But when the ratings response was again disastrous, with 4.5 percent of the total audience, the network cut back its coverage of the Republican convention sharply. (See Table 8.2.) When its ratings then rebounded, to be essentially competitive, a development of far more consequence— and of consequence to far more than ABC officials, or even viewers— had occurred.[5]

At a minimum, the ABC news division itself would never again offer half of the total minutes of convention coverage which it had presented in 1964, its last year of efforts at gavel-to-gavel presentation. (See Table 8.3.) But the experience of ABC in 1972 would actually set the stage for an increasingly public debate over the value of that

Table 8.3.   Convention coverage by ABC network news: Total minutes and Nielsen ratings

Year	Democratic		Republican	
	Total minutes	Neilsen ratings	Total minutes	Neilsen ratings
1984	566	7.9	513	6.9
1980	636	7.9	831	6.5
1976	690	7.6	948	7.4
1972	1,164	4.5	470	8.9
1968	485	8.5	425	7.7
1964	1,380	4.2	1,985	2.8
1960	1,540	4.2	1,320	1.2
1956	2,070	3.3	1,300	4.1

Source: Developed from records in the Library and Archives, CBS News.

sort of coverage in general. With the passage of one more convention, that debate would set the stage for a change in policy on all three networks.

Argument over a potential change in network attention to the conventions surfaced, much more frequently and explicitly than ever before, in the period leading up to the conventions of 1976. The substance was hardly new, but by the time the networks began to prepare for these conventions, the larger *environment* for this argument had changed in numerous—and substantial—ways. It was not until 1980 that real cutbacks in coverage began, and not until 1984 that the full range of impact from these cutbacks could be seen unequivocally. Yet the period leading up to the conventions of 1976 brought out the serious arguments. And the events of presidential politics in that year then converted one side of these arguments into network policy.[6]

The Environment for Decision at the National Networks

At a minimum, of course, ABC had already acted on the dissident side of this argument. By trimming its coverage of the conventions in 1968 and then by testing—and reconfirming—that decision in 1972, ABC had effectively breached the united front on coverage of conventions. But if gavel-to-gavel coverage was still the saluted norm at the other networks—and this tradition had always meant inattention to the most routine convention events, coupled with extra attention to convention developments outside formal sessions—there were now major environmental changes with the potential for reinterpreting that tradition. These lay in both the organizational context for coverage decisions at network headquarters and in the larger political context for such decisions, at the heart of which was the convention itself. It was these contextual changes which were about to fuel a shift in the fundamental, consensual decision on the time allotted to conventions.

The alignment for internal network debates remained essentially as it had been. News divisions were strongly in favor of comprehensive presentation. Programming divisions, although not opposed to coverage itself, were in favor of limits. Marketing divisions supported their programming colleagues, more openly and vehemently than ever before. Part of the argument was the same as well. News executives argued that coverage of conventions was a major public service. Programming executives underlined the opportunity costs of convention coverage, in disruption and displacement of other productions. Marketing executives emphasized these costs in a more concrete fashion, by introducing the deteriorating balance sheets they occasioned. The remainder of the argument, however, was newer, and was powerfully dependent on references to the contemporary environments for organizational decision making within the networks and for political decision making around the conventions.

Both environments had shifted dramatically in the course of a generation. The original internal arguments by news officials in favor of extended coverage were clearly irrelevant by the late 1970s. The television industry was firmly established. It had vanquished radio by every measure, from public support to advertising revenue. A total disregard of the conventions might risk rallying a collection of critics on the outside; a *cut* in coverage would actually strengthen the financial position of the networks. The evening news programs were thoroughly institutionalized too. Indeed these programs were so well established that the original argument about convention coverage as a loss leader—that viewers who strayed to the coverage of one network might stay with that network's news team throughout the year—was probably reversed: those same evening news shows were probably more useful in convincing their permanent viewers to watch the conventions on their usual network.[7]

Proponents of a cutback, however, found both augmented support for their original arguments and a new set of supporting assertions in this changed environment. The programming divisions had never been happy with the disruption to their schedule occasioned by extensive convention coverage, and they were no more happy in the late 1970s than they had been in the 1950s and 1960s. But by the late 1970s, they were actually in a position to turn the loss-leader argument on its head. By then, it was the programming divisions which could argue that viewers who strayed from convention coverage on one network *to entertainment programming on another* might well stay with that network once the conventions were gone. By 1976, of course, the possibility was not a mere hypothetical: ABC had cut its coverage of conventions, in part to take deliberate advantage of this opportunity.

That prospect alarmed more than the programming divisions at the other two networks; it alarmed their marketing divisions as well. Originally, sponsors willing to buy large blocks of television time were themselves a rarity, and the sponsoring of convention coverage was viewed as a "prestige" activity. In that context, the financial losses associated with extended coverage had been comparatively small. But as the networks had become established, everything in this equation had changed. The direct costs of covering conventions had escalated sharply, from personnel, through logistics, to technical support. The costs per minute of advertising time—and hence of any advertising time forgone—had increased even more rapidly. All the while, the notion of advertising at conventions as a prestige activity was losing out to a more scientific approach to television markets, based on measures of how many individuals of what background might be watching at a given time—and these measures were frequently unkind to national party conventions.[8]

The Environment for Decision in Presidential Politics

All these changes in the internal environment for decision making about convention coverage, then, ran in the same direction—toward a reduction—and they might have been sufficient by themselves to precipitate a cut. Network news divisions could still be expected to argue against that decision. Network executives did try to estimate the response of outside critics if such a decision were announced. But what really armed the proponents of a cutback, and further undercut the potential response of opponents, was a set of basic changes in the convention itself, and in its place in the larger political system. The first conventions covered nationally, in 1952, had created their nominating majorities before the television cameras. Since that year, however, no convention had made a nomination, and as time passed this fundamental change did not escape notice.

The possibility remained that a given convention would differ. Indeed any number of conventions in the interim—the 1960 Democratic, the 1964 Republican, the 1968 Democratic, and the 1972 Democratic—had shown some early threat of doing precisely that. But the reality of the situation also remained painfully clear. The convention had lost its alleged central activity and the task which had led to its creation. Only under extreme and deviant conditions could it expect to recapture the nomination even temporarily. Moreover, network news officials had long since not only recognized but acted on this fact. For if the nomination had effectively departed from the convention, it still had to be realized somewhere.

That new locale was the formal process of delegate selection. More specifically, it was a handful of key state conventions and a proliferating chain of state presidential primaries. Not only could these institutions be covered by television news, but a reasonable definition of newsworthiness argued that they should be covered. Network news divisions wasted no time in moving out to report on these new forums, occasionally with special programs before a key primary or caucus, often with a special evening feature as the returns began to come in.[9] This development, however, further devalued the convention as a central newsmaking event for the public and even for news officials. That public could be expected to know the outcome of key contests, and then of the nomination itself, well before the convention assembled. Not only would network news reporters know that outcome but they would already have participated in numerous nominating specials, which further reduced the importance of the convention—as an opportunity to cover stories and to showcase their abilities.

Yet even these considerations did not exhaust the developments contributing to the devaluation of the convention as a center for political decision making—and a focus for network attention. For 1976 was also to bring a resurrection of direct presidential debates, in the aftermath of the conventions. The networks immediately became the prime venue for these encounters. Indeed, they were always described as "televised debates." Audience response, in turn, fully justified such televising. The first debate of 1976, as measured by Neilsen ratings, was the largest single political event of the year. But the debates also served as an additional major forum for introducing the nominees to the general public, over and beyond what those nominees could accomplish at their national conventions.[10]

As a result, the proliferation of primaries and caucuses (and of news reports thereof) subtracted from the importance of the convention in the nominating contest, just as the reappearance of presidential debates—as an obvious and competing forum to frame arguments for the general election—subtracted from their importance as launching pads for the general election campaign. Campaign launching remained the central activity of the convention, and the convention retained the potential for serious impact on the electoral fate of its nominees. But the public might just as reasonably conclude that a better way to get the measure of those nominees was in televised debates. Indeed, a larger share of the American public was destined to watch the inaugural debate of each succeeding series than would watch, for example, the acceptance speech of either nominee at his convention.

The Coming of a New Era in Television Coverage

Accordingly, both internal and external criteria for coverage of conventions pointed, in the abstract, toward a cut. Nevertheless, the combination of these factors did not produce any immediate practical change. It did generate a more open and extended discussion on the issue, but that discussion was destined to be inconclusive for 1976. Perhaps more surprisingly, it was ultimately the external, political criteria (rather than the internal, organizational criteria) which led to reduced coverage in 1980—and then encouraged a much more extensive reduction for 1984. In fact, these cutbacks were to occur step by step and in precise coordination with specific developments in presidential politics. As the year 1976 began, the networks still had only one experience with covering the extensively reformed process of presidential selection created by Democratic party rules after 1968. They had no experience at all in covering that process on the Republican side. As a result they concentrated on applying what they had learned from the first round of postreform politics to nominating contests in both parties.

The summary figures for coverage in 1976, then, suggest continuity. NBC and CBS offered almost exactly the amount of coverage they had provided in 1972, and indeed, almost exactly the average amount they had offered over the preceding five conventions. (See Table 8.4.) Moreover, this actually represented an increase in coverage as a per-

Table 8.4. Total minutes of televised coverage by network news divisions

Year	Democratic convention CBS	NBC	ABC	Republican convention CBS	NBC	ABC	Both CBS	NBC	ABC
1984	728	702	566	633	651	513	1,361	1,353	1,079
1980	1,328	1,373	636	1,229	1,356	831	2,557	2,729	1,467
1976	1,696	1,776	690	1,669	1,762	948	3,365	3,538	1,638
1972	2,201	2,164	1,164	1,144	1,105	470	3,345	3,269	1,634
1968	2,163	2,220	485	1,970	1,875	425	4,113	4,095	910
1964	1,367	1,390	1,380	1,997	2,180	1,985	3,364	3,570	3,365
1960	1,639	1,575	1,540	1,415	1,630	1,320	3,054	3,205	2,860
1956	2,010	2,160	2,070	1,350	1,275	1,300	3,360	3,435	3,370

Source: Derived from records in the Library and Archives, CBS News.

centage of official deliberations, because the combined total of formal convention sessions in 1976 was a bit smaller than in 1972. Despite that, it was not the continuity represented by these summary figures, but the additional events and experiences contributed by the presidential politics of 1976, which would determine the network response for 1980. In short, these summary figures mask the extent to which the *events* of 1976 reinforced and added new arguments to the case for reduced coverage.

At a minimum, the two overall contests of 1976 confirmed the observation that the nomination had moved out of the convention and into the process of delegate selection. Accordingly, they confirmed the simultaneous observation that particular state conflicts within this composite process had become the key to a nominating majority. Beyond that, these contests confirmed, if such confirmation was any longer needed, that the networks could effectively cover key conflicts in individual states as they occurred. The conventions, once again, were intrinsically diminished within this first (nominating) phase of presidential selection. But as if that was not enough, 1976 then reintroduced presidential debates to the second (electing) phase, thereby further diluting the importance of the conventions.

All that was missing in this push toward reduced convention coverage was a solution which could respond to this new environment without fueling the charge that the networks had abandoned an important public service and, especially, without tempting the ever-apparent (though probably chimerical) possibility that the convention would rise up and retake the nomination. In the planning for coverage of the conventions of 1980, that solution, perhaps inevitably, appeared. The networks would still send sufficient reporters and technicians to cover the convention—and any potential return to serious decision making—comprehensively. In the absence of such a return, they would plan to cut coverage deliberately.[11]

Once this resolution had been enunciated, network news divisions were effectively undercut, both within their organizations and in the wider world of politics. Internally, this arrangement would not deny them the *resources* to cover conventions in full, including the deployment of a large number of reporters at the site. Externally, it left the fate of these reporters entirely dependent on the importance, or at least the conflict and drama, of the conventions themselves. If these advance analytic judgments proved wrong, the networks could quickly reexpand their coverage. *Unless* they proved wrong, a reduction in coverage was not only logical but programmed.

A New Network Consensus on Coverage Levels

As a result, CBS and NBC promised for 1980, not gavel-to-gavel transmission but rather presentation of all developments of significance. Under this rule, the two networks were ultimately to reduce their total minutes of coverage noticeably. When the second convention adjourned, they had offered about 75 percent of the average total minutes which they had provided for the five conventions from 1956 through 1972—a reduction of 25 percent overall—with reductions of 30 percent for the Democrats, who had the much longer convention, and 20 percent for the Republicans, who were less troubled by (time-consuming) internal conflict. (See Table 8.5.)

The size of this break gained emphasis from its relationship to the actual, official duration of the conventions. The television era had already, in fact, seen a major change in the formal length of these gatherings. But that change had come between 1952 and 1956—and it had come in direct reflection of the disappearance of the nomination. In 1952, both conventions were in session for over forty hours. After 1952, no convention ever achieved that duration. From 1956 through 1980, however, there was no additional patterned decline in the length of conventions. (See Table 8.6.) Indeed, the two conventions of 1980 together were actually the *longest* since the original transmissions. It was not the convention, then, but the *networks* which had altered the available total of live and direct convention activity. The convention as an event was actually longer than it had been four years before; convention coverage had nevertheless dipped noticeably.

Table 8.5. Total minutes of televised coverage, as percentage of average minutes between 1956 and 1972

Year	Democratic convention			Republican convention			Both		
	CBS	NBC	ABC	CBS	NBC	ABC	CBS	NBC	ABC
1984	39	37	43	40	40	47	39	38	44
1980	71	72	48	78	84	76	74	78	60
1976	90	93	52	106	109	86	98	101	86

Source: Developed by recalculating the figures in Table 8.4.

Table 8.6.   The length of official proceedings of national party conventions

Year	Party	Number of sessions	Duration of sessions
1984	Democratic	4	31 hr, 33 min
	Republican	6	16 hr, 31 min
1980	Democratic	4	39 hr, 48 min
	Republican	5	23 hr, 50 min
1976	Democratic	4	25 hr, 34 min
	Republican	5	23 hr, 30 min
1972	Democratic	4	32 hr, 39 min
	Republican	5	17 hr, 20 min
1968	Democratic	5	28 hr, 48 min
	Republican	5	23 hr, 40 min
1964	Democratic	4	14 hr, 31 min
	Republican	5	26 hr, 55 min
1960	Democratic	5	27 hr, 55 min
	Republican	5	18 hr
1956	Democratic	9	31 hr, 39 min
	Republican	5	18 hr
1952	Democratic	10	47 hr, 10 min
	Republican	10	41 hr, 1 min

Source: Figures for 1952 through 1968 were taken directly from "Table 6.2," in Parris, *The Convention Problem*, p. 150. Figures for 1972 through 1984 were added in the same format and were drawn from convention records of the national party committees.

Nothing about the presidential politics of 1980 served to countermand this cutback. Both nominating contests were extended and conflictual, so that there were numerous battles along the way which the networks could—and did—cover spontaneously. Nominating majorities had evidently been constructed, however, before either convention assembled. After the nominations, in turn, the presidential debates were repeated, suggesting that they were at least on their way to being institutionalized. Moreover, nothing about the audience response to a cutback in coverage of the conventions of 1980 served to countermand this decision either. Ratings did not go up, from any public concentration on those parts of the convention which were still available. But neither did those ratings go down, through any public desertion of conventions when available coverage shrank. (See Table 8.7.) The loss in ratings from normal entertainment programming in 1980 was thus essentially the same as it had been for the preceding twenty years. But that loss was figured on a reduced period, so that it represented a reduced loss, in viewers, advertising, and revenue.

For 1984, then, the same basic decision was extended. The networks again planned to offer all the key state contests on the way to the nominations, however many that might be.[12] They again planned to offer all the presidential debates, however many that might be as well. They again planned to reduce transmission of the conventions—in a fashion calculated to make their cuts of 1980 look tame. By the time the year was out, events themselves would have modified the amount of broadcasting of the politics of presidential selection generated by these criteria. But those events would not reduce the magnitude of this decision as it applied to coverage of conventions.

As 1984 unfolded, there was to be a nominating contest on the Democratic side only, so that network commitments were reduced by political reality here. At the same time, there was to be only one presidential debate between the two major candidates, reducing coverage there as well. But the conventions in between were to do nothing to threaten the trend toward contraction of coverage. As a result, for the two conventions together, CBS and NBC offered less than *40 percent* of what they had provided on the average from 1956 to 1972.

Table 8.7.   The loss in rating points and audience as a result of convention coverage

Year	Average convention rating	Average entertainment rating	Drop-off in rating points for convention	Percent of audience retained
1984	21.3	34.7	−13.4	61
1980	22.6	40.7	−18.1	56
1976	23.9	42.3	−18.4	57
1972	22.0	43.6	−21.6	50
1968	27.8	40.3	−12.5	69
1964	23.4	39.6	−15.8	59
1960	21.2	38.8	−17.6	55

Source: "Average convention rating" is taken directly from Table 7.1. "Average entertainment rating" is the Nielsen rating for the comparable time period during the week preceding the national convention, again courtesy of Library and Archives, CBS News.

(See Table 8.5.) They had discarded about 25 percent of this average presentation in 1980; they dropped another 35 percent in 1984—for a whopping total decline of 60 percent.

The gap between CBS and NBC on the one hand, and ABC on the other, did remain after the 1984 conventions, with ABC still offering measurably less in total minutes of coverage than its competitors. But the other two networks were now far closer to the normal ABC position than they had been since the initial breach of the original consensus—and far closer to the ABC level than to their own historical standards. As a result, a drastically reduced consensus on the proper amount of the conventions to be presented by the networks was effectively in existence. The raw figures guaranteed that this new era of coverage would be different from the old. But even those figures did not convey the qualitative difference which accompanied the new era—and which itself held the potential for further shaping the convention as a political institution.

Reborn Conventions, on Site and at Home

The impact of this reduction in coverage would necessarily be determined over a period of conventions. Network officials would adjust their programming to new constraints on available time; convention planners would surely try to adapt the institution both to these time constraints and to the adjustments of network officials. Yet the most general impact of this reduction was evident immediately. From this point on, the decisions of network news officials—in selecting aspects of the convention to be covered and ignored, along with determining the extent and manner of coverage for those aspects which were selected—would be increasingly critical to the public presentation of the convention. They would thus be critical to the success of all those attempting to use the convention to communicate with the general public. They would likewise be critical to the impact of the convention on that public, quite apart from individual efforts at manipulation.

The simple presence of these decisions, of course, did not constitute a new development. There had always been a need for selecting among options for broadcast and for establishing a set of coverage priorities—even in television, that most direct and apparently "unmediated" of communications media. Yet the sharp cut in available time for coverage of conventions brought the need for these decisions—their number and centrality—to a new and qualitatively different level.

Again, television had always provided a substantial mix of direct transmission from the podium, supplementary reporting from the convention site, and comment from network anchors. Moreover, total network transmissions had always absorbed more total minutes than the formal convention sessions. In other words, for every convention since 1952, those networks with a commitment to gavel-to-gavel coverage had been on the air with convention reporting for longer than the convention itself had been in session. (See Table 8.8.)

These statistics might not have provided any comfort to convention officials who were annoyed with the content of network presentations. And in truth, even when such broadcasts had reached 130 or 140 percent of total time in formal session, news directors had felt compelled to make selections among available items for reporting. But when the total time available for transmission declined to 70 percent of the period in formal session, as it did in 1980, the need for these decisions was obviously intensified. When the total time available declined to *47 percent,* as it did in 1984, this need reached epic proportions. Very little of the convention could be offered directly, even in principle. Less could be offered in practice, unless network news people were willing to give up their own central activities, the defining activities of reporters and anchors.

In fact, this shift was so substantial that it began to produce a qualitative difference in coverage, and thus a qualitative difference in the convention itself. A shift of this magnitude implied that the associated change in the character of coverage would consist not just of a proportionate reduction of everything that had been presented. Rather,

Table 8.8.   Network television coverage, by network, as a percentage of total convention proceedings

Year	CBS	NBC	ABC
1984	47	47	37
1980	67	71	38
1976	114	120	56
1972	110	106	33
1968	131	130	29
1964	135	144	135
1960	111	116	104
1956	113	115	113

Source: Developed from Tables 8.4 and 8.6.

it implied that coverage in the new era of televised limits would consist of a noticeably different composite picture. In turn, this shift in the character of coverage was so substantial that it raised the possibility almost of two conventions, one unfolding in the convention city and one unfolding on the television screen—the convention on site and the convention at home.

Elements of this disjunction—this clear and growing divergence, really—had always been present, at least incipiently. Republican party officials and Goldwater campaign leaders, for example, had been dreadfully unhappy with the character of press coverage of their 1964 convention, arguing that the "real convention" had been quite different from the one the television viewer saw. In particular, they had been distressed with coverage of Goldwater delegates responding to their opponents at the podium with catcalls, fist shaking, and general disruption, while the less conflictual aspects of the convention—which appeared to include many of the speakers setting out the preferred program of the nominee—received significantly less (televised) attention.[13]

There was no doubt that the network definition of news did emphasize conflictual aspects, rather than some statistical sample from the podium, at the Republican convention of 1964 as at most others. Moreover, it was probably true that the focus on these aspects did magnify their impact, through nothing more than the addition of the visual—and visceral—element to their reportage. It was also true, however, that the events which most irked Republican strategists really had occurred—and would have been considered news by almost any journalist. Beyond that, if television journalists had sought to emphasize the visual aspect, that was, after all, the heart—the major advantage—of their medium. As a result, the differences in available perceptions of the convention could be assigned more to the inevitable task of news operatives in mediating an event than to the particular role or limitations of television. More to the point, these effects surely were not sufficient to make those two sets of perceptions qualitatively different and hence to produce a truly bifurcated convention.

But in the aftermath of a cutback in the scope of convention coverage, especially a cutback on the scale begun in 1980, this inherent disjunction was inevitably exaggerated. Even in theory, if this condensation was sufficiently large—and a drop from more than 100 percent to less than 50 percent certainly appeared to meet that standard—and if television news was still to offer some events live and direct rather than merely summarizing them all, then the possibility of two distinct conventions was instantly present. If that possibility was then realized in practice, convention after convention, this would surely become the most obvious product of the new era in television coverage, to the point where the impact of the convention as a whole might be radically changed and the behavior of those attempting to use the convention might reasonably change as well.

The Evolution of the Bifurcated Convention

The power of this possibility, almost for two separate conventions, was captured symbolically by the case of the vice presidential selection at the Republican convention of 1980. The extent of the difference between two composite conventions, the Republican convention on site and the Republican convention at home, could not be appreciated until the full convention had adjourned. Yet the short but intense effort to create a "Ford vice presidency," the centerpiece of one side of convention politicking Tuesday night, was a major event almost totally divergent in its relationship to the formal sessions and to the home (television) screen. As such, by Wednesday morning, it had underlined the possibilities inherent in cutbacks in network coverage—and in the coming of the bifurcated convention. When the statistics for network coverage then put data behind these possibilities, and when the next pair of (bifurcated) conventions, in 1984, put incident after incident into the same general pattern, that coming was not only confirmed but elaborated.

Going into the Republican convention of 1980, Ronald Reagan was already the evident nominee. His last remaining opponent, George Bush, had withdrawn; the convention seemed destined to be a classic coronation. The front-runner for the vice presidential nod, in turn, was Bush. For one long and intense evening, however, the Tuesday evening prior to nominations for president, it appeared—to the television audience though not necessarily to the audience in the hall—that Gerald Ford, the former president, had become the leading contender. Yet by the end of that evening, variously boring or intense, Ford was back out of the running, if he had ever seriously been in, and Bush was the choice of nominee-elect Reagan.[14]

There were numerous elements of political curiosity in these developments. This would, for example, have been the first time that a former president had returned as vice president, or even as vice presidential nominee. The practical details for such an arrangement would have been every bit as precedent breaking and intrinsically interesting as well. But the largest institutional lesson from these developments came not from the details of this potentially curious and unprecedented possibility, but from its overall role as a diagnostic case of the growing disjunction between the convention as a local event and as a mediated phenomenon. Indeed, that disjunction could be plumbed quickly by comparing the events of Tuesday evening from the perspective of two related audiences—of convention observers who were guests in the convention hall and of convention observers who were "guests" via televised reporting.

The hypothetical discussions of a vice presidency for Ford came concretely and vigorously to life early that evening when Ford suggested, in an interview with the CBS anchorman, Walter Cronkite, that such an arrangement was not out of the question. Six-plus hours of intensive negotiations between the Ford and Reagan camps followed over the details of that possibility, at the end of which both sides apparently concluded that it could not be realized in practice. Quite apart from the role of Cronkite in breaking (if not creating) this boomlet, and the role of the other network teams in propelling what they all took to be the lead story of the evening, the place of this story in the lives of its two audiences remained its must suggestive aspect.

It was quite possible for those in the hall to be unaware of this development almost in its entirety—and for it thus to be close to a complete "nonevent." Anyone who came to the hall before the transmission of the Cronkite interview, or who watched the news on a channel other than CBS, would have arrived with no notion of the Ford possibility. Such a person could quite plausibly have sat through a long evening which centered on the reading of the new platform, word by word, and was capped by the appearance of Reagan in the hall after midnight to reveal that it would be Bush for vice president in November—just as the smart money had always suggested. The reality of the Ford-Reagan negotiations that is, the extent to which either side believed that the arrangement could be consummated, was in fact a matter of dispute for months thereafter. But for this segment of the convention audience, the event did not happen.

For those watching the same night of Republican politics on television, however, these negotiations were the centerpiece of the entire evening. They were the principal continuing story on all three networks and the item which drew the most network correspondents. They dwarfed the major substantive event from the podium, even as measured by total time. If the Republican party desired the American public to hear the details of its platform, it was clearly not getting its wish. If the party had something to gain from an exploration of the Ford possibility, it was seeing that possibility explored in the most difficult way possible. Indeed, if the television networks added life to the Reagan-Ford possibility early on, they also, in effect though surely not in intent, contributed just as powerfully to killing it off as the evening progressed. And all the while, those watching in the hall saw the detailed reading of the party platform; those watching from their living rooms saw a host of reporters working diligently on a story which never came to be—and possibly never was.[15]

Simple numbers were even better at distinguishing the new era from the old. Through 1976, at least two of the major networks had endorsed the notion of gavel-to-gavel coverage in principle, and both had actually provided more time for convention broadcasts than the national parties had provided for official sessions. After 1980, all three of the major networks abandoned that same abstract standard, and all provided significantly less time for convention broadcasts than the national parties provided for official sessions. The incident of the Ford vice presidency, then, merely suggested something further which raw statistics could not: the extent to which a qualitative change in the nature of convention coverage, and hence in convention products, and hence in convention *impact*, followed from the shift in total minutes of coverage.

More cuts, in any case, followed close upon this first round. These, in turn, were of a scale to render the Ford incident just another indication of the central thrust of the new era, not a measure of its outer reaches. The networks, building upon their experience with the first reductions of 1980 and in an environment where neither internal (organizational) nor external (political) criteria counseled otherwise proposed an even more severe reduction for convention coverage in 1984. This would inevitably increase the number of specific decisions by network news directors while it forged them into ever-sharper alternatives. This intensification would increase the impact of those decisions on the televised convention itself. These cuts, then, would directly bring into being the new, full-blown, bifurcated version of the convention.[16]

The Two Democratic Conventions of 1984

Party leaders, especially those in the Democratic party—the party out of power and thus the one which might hope (or need) to benefit most from its convention—were not at all happy with the new network consensus. But after a short period of public complaint, the relevant convention planners in both parties turned to adjusting the operation of their conventions to the new network schedule. As ever, this adjustment was made somewhat differently by each party. Yet once again, their adjustments, taken as a whole, both reflected and shaped the same basic structural development. For both parties, partly by intent but largely by effect, this meant the creation of two conventions—two realities—one local and one mediated, and the two perhaps as different as they had ever been.

The official sessions of the Democratic convention were to be considerably longer than their Republican counterparts. As a result, a greater share of that time would be eliminated from coverage by the constriction of network programming. The part of the convention which ultimately received almost no coverage—the major television networks could in principle have filmed parts and then replayed them during the evening, but in fact they did not—had two major elements. The first and most focused were the platform battles of the second afternoon. The second and more diffuse were the efforts to suggest the range of constituency groups which not only should be supporting the Democratic ticket but were in fact supporting Walter Mondale.

The Mondale camp had handled most platform conflicts in a way common to emerging nominees in the modern era. That is, they had been willing to split the difference in the Platform Committee or even capitulate rather than leave anything for a floor fight. This strategy had not worked on a plank put forward by the Hart campaign, calling for prohibition of the use of force in the Persian Gulf and Central America. It had also not succeeded on four planks from the Jackson campaign, which called for renunciation of the first use of nuclear weapons, sweeping reductions in defense spending, increased emphasis on affirmative action in public and private hiring, and abolition of the second (run-off) primary. In fact, conflicts engendered by Jackson during the nominating campaign had made the Mondale camp more willing than usual to fight these Jackson proposals directly, in order to reassure other constituency groups, especially Jews and southern whites, about the steadfastness of the nominee.[17]

By convention time, in any case, the Mondale camp had settled on a solution for two of the Jackson proposals, literally hammering out the compromise on affirmative action while this minority plank was before the full convention. On the two other Jackson proposals, on defense spending and on the run-off primary, the Mondale camp simply rallied its allies and defeated the minority reports. The Mondale leadership would have been happy to compromise further on the Hart proposal, but the Hart leadership was just as eager for an open contest. As a result, and facing possible defeat through defection of their own supporters, the Mondale leadership simply endorsed this minority report, urging their delegates to vote for it. The important point for viewers of the convention, however, was that none of this process— form or substance, compromise or conflict, victory or defeat—made any direct appearance on television.

The rest of the time left uncovered by the networks—the largest single use of time at the Democratic convention of 1984—was devoted to presenting speakers who could represent constituencies which the Mondale camp hoped to rally in November. Northerners and southerners, urbanites and ruralites, women and Hispanics, all were included. But the largest single subgroup—and hence the one most thoroughly *missed,* by television cameras and convention viewers— was black political leaders of all sorts. The percentage of black speakers at the podium for the Democrats in 1984 was probably the highest at any national convention, ever, in a deliberate attempt both to rally black voters and to counteract any potential unhappiness with—or stemming from—the Jackson camp. This fact, however, was just as thoroughly hidden from the general public by the pattern of television coverage.[18]

What television viewers did see, through the scheduling of convention planners and the cooperation of network officials, was a series of major speeches in the evening hours. On Monday, this meant the keynote, given by Governor Mario Cuomo of New York and widely believed to be one of the most effective keynote addresses in history. On Tuesday, the focal speech was from the third major candidate for the presidential nomination, the Reverend Jesse Jackson, and it too was considered an effective presentation. On Wednesday, the major speech was from the principal challenger to Walter Mondale, Senator Gary Hart of Colorado, and although it was not accorded as warm a critical reception as those before it, the speech did offer Hart one last chance to draw delegates to his cause for 1984, and otherwise to launch his presidential campaign for 1988. Nominations and balloting were held at the conclusion of the Hart speech and resulted without difficulty in the expected endorsement of Mondale. On Thursday evening, then, Geraldine Ferraro accepted the vice presidential nomination, Walter Mondale accepted the presidential nomination, and the convention adjourned—all with full television coverage.

The Two Republican Conventions of 1984

The differences in the convention available to observers on site and the one available to observers at home were thus substantial for the Democratic convention of 1984. They were destined to be substantial for its Republican counterpart too, thereby confirming the arrival of the new era of convention coverage—and of its leading product, the bifurcated convention. But these differences were themselves destined to diverge substantially from those on the Democratic side, thereby confirming the range of variation possible for bifurcated conventions in the new era. The Republicans also planned a small number of major speeches in the evening hours, for what they hoped would be the maximum audience among the viewing public. But they began with an additionally elaborated plan to use the times when they did *not* expect network coverage, for events supporting the party's senatorial and congressional candidates around the country. In this effort, they were ultimately to score some clear successes, to find themselves caught by surprise on other aspects of revised coverage, and to generate a small but continuing, open conflict with the networks over a tiny part of their agenda, the film introducing President Reagan for his acceptance speech.

The two morning sessions of the convention, the least likely to attract live network coverage, were tailored from the start to use the *local* convention for more focused political purposes. Monday morning was devoted to clearing the obligatory thank-yous and lesser commendations so that the evening sessions could be targeted to national concerns. Tuesday morning was more directly consequential in its own right, since it was aimed deliberately at home state campaigning. Short filmed introductions for a set of candidates—congressional candidates first, senatorial next—were followed by short appearances by the candidates themselves. These introductory films had been developed specifically to turn over to the candidates for use in their states, but the national committee then took the strategy a step further by filming *the convention as it responded to these films* and, especially, to the candidates, and delivering this film too for use in home state campaigning. Without a reduction in national television time, it would have been wasteful to invest sessions of the convention in one congressional race in Kansas, Mississippi, or Ohio. But after that cutback, it became actively advantageous to use the convention as a backdrop for these candidates at home, in the full—and accurate—expectation that the networks would skip these sessions anyhow.

The pattern of major speeches for the evening sessions was roughly similar to that on the Democratic side. Yet an unwillingness—or inability—to focus on one major speaker per evening did force the networks to make additional choices, or surrender the role of their news teams entirely. The result was a slightly less predictable pattern of coverage. The two main speakers of the first evening, Jeane Kirkpatrick, ambassador to the United Nations, and Katherine Ortega, treasurer of the United States and the designated keynoter, both secured extensive attention from the networks. But the range of major speakers on the second evening included at leave five "name" Republicans and forced the networks to pick and choose—which they did in large part by presenting snippets from each, supplemented by extended reports from various reporters and by commentary from the anchors. The nominating speeches for the president and vice president on Wednesday evening then restored both predictability and attention. And Thursday featured the acceptance speeches by the candidates themselves, again fully covered.

The one item in this schedule which became a head-to-head conflict between convention planners and network news directors was the film introducing the president, on which the networks by a two-to-one vote—CBS and NBC no, ABC yes—directly defeated convention officials by failing to show all but a few snatches of the film. Otherwise, the difference in the convention as a local event and as a mediated phenomenon, or at least the difference not expected by convention strategists, was a more subtle one. Many of the speakers presented to the full convention over the four-day period consciously emphasized the desire of the Republican party to reach out to all disenchanted Democrats and the welcome which such Democrats could expect to find. But the speakers who received the largest individual allocations of time from the party, and who were actually covered or at least sampled by the television networks, included only one of those underlining this outreach theme, while they managed to include most of the more partisan speakers, laying out a traditional Republican attack on the Democratic party.[19]

In the final, larger irony, the bifurcation of both conventions probably contributed to the practical goals of convention planners in both parties. For the Democrats in particular, the result of being forced to condense and plan within sharp limits was a clear and decided benefit. The party offered a small and consistent set of themes from major actors representing diverse groups of putative supporters, while both the more ritualistic and the more conflictual elements of the convention were successfully kept off camera. The convention thus became an apparently successful launching pad for the Mondale-Ferraro campaign, and polls seemed to confirm that it had accomplished its short-run goal. Immediately before the convention, Mondale trailed the president by 15 points; immediately afterward, that gap had substantially closed. For the Republicans, the result was a bit more mixed. The effort to help Republican candidates around the country was an evident technical success, just as the effort to secure network coverage of the Reagan film was a clear and measurable defeat. The focus on more partisan approaches, at the expense of appeals to Democrats, was an unintended product of the interaction of convention strategists and network news directors. But the convention was nevertheless apparently successful in launching the general election campaign, at least by the traditional measure of gain in the polls.

What had also happened, however, was a widening of the gap between the two conventions—the local and the mediated conventions, that is—to an unprecedented extent. What that might mean for the future of the convention as an institution could be only dimly perceived as the second of these gatherings recessed. Adaptations to the coming of the bifurcated convention would necessarily play a part in shaping that future. But so would a set of much larger changes, from the forces of social evolution and deliberate reform. The possible further impact of those forces is thus the tantalizing last question in any analysis of the convention. Extrapolation from evolutionary forces, and mental imposition of deliberate reforms, have to be the core of any answers. But their use requires a detour through the message of postwar conventions about the changing shape of the American politics outside.

Conclusion

Evolution and Reform:
The Convention and
a Changing American Politics

For its audience, the charm of a national party convention remains a mix of what it has always been. There is the element of momentous decision, of course. Even in an era when the convention merely ratifies rather than makes its central decision, that act still confirms one of two possible alternatives for the most important political office in the United States, and perhaps the world. There is the element of contention and conflict too. Few conventions occur without some evident struggle—over platform, over rules, perhaps over the presidential nomination itself—and that struggle acquires the intrinsic attraction of disputes which are larger than those of daily life. Finally, there is the element of sheer spectacle as well. If this is the aspect most satirized in conventions, it still possesses an almost automatic, visceral fascination—the proverbial cast of thousands, the rhetoric and symbols of a rich national history, the high drama and low comedy of democratic politics in action.

For the analyst, the charm of a national party convention is not unrelated to these surface manifestations. Because the current incarnation can be established and dispatched in just three to five days, the convention lends itself to a more nearly comprehensive understanding than do institutions, such as the presidency, with greater organizational and temporal extension. This makes it possible to look at the full array of changing convention operations, at major activities, critical participants, internal politics, and external impacts—even, in principle, at their interaction. Yet if the convention as a composite institution has been constantly changing, conventions have in fact been doing so for much of American history; a changing convention has inevitably looked out upon—has influenced and been influenced by a changing, larger, national politics. As a result, this same bounded character of the convention permits its use as a window, as a source both of concrete examples and of a larger perspective, on the (changing) national politics around it.

In this blend of continuity and change, in any case, lies the inherent attractiveness of the national party convention, as a theater for politicking, as an evolving institution in its own right, and as a window on a larger American politics. Chapters 1 through 8 have been intended to tell this story of continuity and change for the postwar convention in considerable detail. A much-foreshortened summary of that account forms the beginning of this chapter. But because the convention has sat in the midst of a larger and more consequential politics, which offered continuity and change, evolution and reform, on a parallel but necessarily far grander scale, this summary is simultaneously the beginning of an effort to use the convention as a window on that politics. Such an elaboration of its major external implications requires a return to the story of the postwar convention, to squeeze it for larger developments reflected in the convention and for concrete clues about their interaction, as observed through this smaller institutional world. A search for these implications, then, forms the bulk of this concluding chapter.

The Convention as Subject: A Changing Political Institution

For most of its institutional history, the national party convention was practically centered on the creation of a delegate majority behind a major-party candidate for president of the United States. The nomination of such a candidate was the original—and really sole—reason for creating the convention; the presence of that nomination was what produced the accretion of most other convention activities. In the early 1950s, however, in response to a set of larger, external, social forces, the nomination effectively departed the convention. Elements of the nationalization of presidential politics were the fundamental cause of this informal departure, but a change in the strategic calculations of key actors—party officials at that time—was the more immediate cause. These officials discovered that preservation of their influence required attention to explicitly national rather than purely local events in presidential politics. This realization implied that candidate affiliations had to be cemented earlier, to the point where candidate majorities were reliably effected in advance of the convention.

The behavior of these party officials, on the other hand, was at bottom a response to a changed political environment rather than a deliberate decision of their own, even collectively. Environmental changes made it easier for local opponents to challenge them from below, while making it easier for national contenders to challenge them from above. Thus the growth of national government provided everyone, not just these party officials, with an increased stake in the outcomes of presidential politics. The widening reach of national media of information made everyone more able to follow presidential politics nationally, while it encouraged everyone *else* to follow that politics independently. A more highly educated and middle-class society came to prefer a politics based on partisan independence and direct personal activity. And the decline of political parties as electoral organizations made party officials less able to resist these external changes. Individually, each of these elements adduced toward the nationalization of presidential calculations. Cumulatively, they removed presidential nominations from the national party convention.

Without formal decision by anyone, then, the nomination left the convention, and it has remained outside, in the process of delegate selection, ever since. The Democratic and Republican conventions of 1952, the first without a candidate initially nominated before the end of the Second World War, were also the last to feature a nomination realized within the convention hall. Approximately a generation later, after the disastrous Democratic convention of 1968, many of the same continuing forces from the nationalization of politics combined with a much more focused reform movement to extract sweeping alterations in the process of delegate selection—and to lock the nomination, procedurally, outside the convention. An old order dominated by a mix of internal party institutions gave way to a new order based on presidential primary elections. The key actors in this new order changed simultaneously, with party officials giving way to rank-and-file participants, or at least to those who turned out for the burgeoning primaries and participatory conventions.

The calculations of these new key actors, however, were essentially unchanged in their practical impact. These calculations still centered on national developments; they still produced delegate majorities in advance—often well in advance—of the national convention. In fact, when compared to party officials, these newly central rank-and-file participants were less initially informed and less ideologically rooted, and hence even more easily moved by early developments in nominating politics. The resulting tendency for the "bandwagon" (by which a nominating majority was created) to roll earlier and earlier was reinforced by a similar recurring movement among financial contributors and campaign activists. It was reinforced again, most powerfully, by the concentration of the national media on the earliest contests. In response, the convention, once the central forum for this nominating politics, became a fallback mechanism for a set of unlikely circumstances, effectively the nominator of last resort.

A marked shift in the political identity of those who became delegates to these evolving conventions followed hard upon the interaction of reform in the institutions of delegate selection and evolution in the environment for nominating politics. Yet here, it was principally self-conscious reform, albeit as augmented by environmental forces, which was both directly and indirectly influential in altering the identity of these delegates—their social backgrounds, their organizational attachments, their policy preferences, and their political styles. Directly, procedural reform devastated those institutional arrangements which created delegates through an official party structure, while it replaced them with arrangements which provided no certified place for the official party. Indirectly, procedural reform devalued the informal assets of party officials as well: a nominating politics which required multiple, independent, national campaigns made it very difficult to mobilize an extended party behind one candidate; candidates who needed early commitment and personal loyalty, above all, found party officials less useful even as individual participants.

The practical result was very close to the eclipse of the official party in the politics of presidential selection, and the diminution of party officials as national convention delegates. The major impact of this result on the convention, in turn, was to drive it further in the direction of the dominant ideology of its party—Democrats to the left, Republicans to the right. Party officials as a formal, organizational category were distinguished among political elites by their concern with presenting a broad party program, one capable of electing a wide array of party candidates, normally by moving both program and candidates toward the political center. When their influence at national conventions declined, and when even those party officials who did attend were less likely to offer this traditional orientation, the delegates as a collectivity were freed of that moderating restraint, and the convention as an institution moved off from the political center.

The withdrawal, constriction, or outright defeat of the official party, however, was only part of the change in delegate identities. Presidential aspirants could hardly hope to build the independent nominating campaigns required by a reformed politics out of individual pieces, so that the support of some existing framework remained an operational necessity. By the same token, organizational leaders outside the official party structure could hardly remain ignorant of this fact for long. The result was the rise of the organized interests, of interest groups and issue organizations, as the base for nominating campaigns. The result was also the coming of the interested partisans, of interest group representatives and independent issue activists, as the national convention delegates produced by these campaigns. In response, the convention changed additionally as an environment for internal politicking.

Not only did these interested partisans not face a broad range of constituencies to knit together for November, but they needed very specific—and noticeable—policy successes to satisfy their organizational membership at home. Not only did they not want to see the nominee move toward the political center in anticipation of the general election campaign, but they needed to use the convention to lock in their putative gains from the politics of nomination. The balance of ideologues over simple partisans thus continued to rise, to the point where those who were distressed by that balance began to look for ways to reintroduce the official party, through guaranteed formal representation if necessary. Their efforts, by then, were probably bootless, for they also confirmed the transformation of the political parties, from a collection of officeholders to an aggregation of activists in their organizational essence, and from partisans to ideologues as national convention delegates.

More Elements of Change in the Convention

The disappearance of the nomination almost automatically promoted a second major activity as the political centerpiece of these postreform conventions, just as change in the identity of convention delegates almost automatically contributed a different set of internal conflicts around this newly central activity. With the nomination gone but press attention continuing, many participants came to see the convention as a means to advance various external campaigns. For the nominee and top officials, this meant orchestrating the convention to set out the themes of—and effectively to launch—the general election campaign. For many others, however, it meant focusing the convention on some *other* concern, be that a future presidential bid, a current legislative effort, or supportive publicity for a nascent cause, group, or program.

Recurring lines of conflict followed this newly central activity. A division between the nominee and his remaining challengers provided one such line, and it was always the most serious when it surfaced. But a division between the convention leadership and the delegate rank and file, and thus often between the successful nominee and some minority of his own supporters, was a second recurring line of conflict, more reliably present and perhaps more diagnostic of the internal environment for postreform convention politicking. The nominee reliably aspired to move toward the political center and toward an identification with the general public. Many delegates preferred to affirm his ideological distinctness and to secure his group attachments from the nominating campaign.

Struggles over the focus of the convention were an obvious way to establish this balance. Moreover, indications were that these struggles still mattered. A sizable minority of the general public claimed to reach a voting decision during the convention, a claim which no candidate dared cavalierly dismiss. Beyond that, the convention was the last real opportunity for many participants to secure something concrete from the nominating campaign, while the internal course of that convention inevitably determined the extent to which the nominee could use it to set out his themes, even as it relentlessly painted a picture of the candidate and his party, whether their launching effort was successful or not.

The foci for these conflicts were those continuing activities which had always been at the organizational heart of the national convention—the mechanics for nominating a president, of course, but also the mechanics for nominating a vice president, affirming delegate credentials, adopting procedural rules, and proclaiming a party platform. Yet in an era when the launching of external campaigns had become the central activity of the convention, and when the reformed cast of participants was increasingly drawn to presidential politics by a concern for specific issues and interests rather than by simple partisanship and electoral calculation, the internal politics of each of these arenas was naturally, perhaps inevitably, different as well. The priority for these various theaters of conflict changed; the strategies of the participants within these theaters changed; eventually, the very organization of each arena—and hence the internal structure of the national party convention—began to change in response as well.

As between the two major nominations, the confirmation of a president dropped in priority, in an era when that nomination was effectively settled. At the same time, the selection of a vice president unequivocally rose—as a publicity device, a bargaining chip, or a symbolic reward. Among committees, Platform was up substantially, thanks to the promise of policy commitments, however ethereal these might be. Rules gained marginally, as the apparent source of regulations which might shape a nomination—perhaps still at this convention, definitely by the next. And Credentials dropped sharply, thanks to developments in both parties which made prior outcomes decisive. In strategic terms, dissident delegates sought policy demands which were sufficiently extreme to attract the attention of viewers at home. Nominees, from the other side, sought to compromise with these demands, even when they appeared to be politically indigestible, so as to get on with the business of orchestrating the convention. In the process, regardless of the outcome in any given convention, the resulting party programs became increasingly divergent. In the process, a new set of convention participants—perhaps the key intermediaries in American party politics—was initiated forcefully into these newly divergent views.

Implicit in this shift in the central activity of the convention (to the politics of launching one or another campaign) and in the effort by most participants to influence one or another of these launchings was the notion that *public impressions* were the principal measure of success. From there, it was but a small step to the perception that this reward came not through some official resolution but rather through a press portrait, to be gained indirectly from developments at the convention. As it happened, the departure of the nomination coincided precisely with the rise of television as the principal source of convention news—so that efforts to shape public impressions of the convention became conflicts over coverage by national television networks. The audience for television coverage soared instantaneously. Efforts to manipulate that coverage followed hard upon this trend.

In fact, the resulting conflict over press portraits of the convention quickly became a three-cornered affair. First were the historically dominant struggles, among candidates and delegates over the substance of the convention—but played out, in the television era, with continuing attention to their impact on a viewing audience. Second were some existing but newly augmented struggles, between partisan actors and network news officials, over priorities and perspectives for the televising of conventions. Third were the latest and least visible of these conflicts, within television news departments themselves, over what was initially a question of proper focus but ultimately became a question of the proper *amount* of coverage too. These struggles, like those around the traditional agenda, began to change the very structure of the convention, altering its physical appearance through the introduction of television equipment, its procedural pace through the generation of comprehensive scripts, and even its practical behavior through the banning of extended floor demonstrations.

The fact that television coverage via national network news was the central element in modern press portraits of the convention was almost immediately recognized by the active participants. Yet even they could be excused for concentrating on the details of that coverage during the period, from the early 1950s through the late 1970s, when its parameters remained essentially stable. Nevertheless, as the organizational and political environment for decisions about coverage changed, this gavel-to-gavel standard came under pressure. Organizationally, the networks saw their audience stagnate while operational and programming costs continued to rise. Politically, and more consequentially in the end, not only had the convention lost the nomination itself but additional events of obvious consequence—six months of presidential primaries on one side, the institutionalization of national debates on the other—began to chip away further at the importance of the convention.

In response, all three national networks reduced their coverage for 1980, cutbacks which they extended in 1984. The result was the unintended but effective creation of what might reasonably be called the bifurcated convention, with one convention on site and another (via television) at home, each powerfully different one from the other. There were in truth antecedents to this development, in coverage controversies from previous gatherings. There were concrete and immediate impacts as well, when the 1984 Democratic and Republican conventions featured noteworthy differences between local and mediated events—and thus emphasized the extent of press choices inherent in the new parameters. But what remained as the 1984 conventions adjourned was a realization that responses to the arrival of the bifurcated convention, by convention actors and network personnel alike, were the most obvious and immediate element of flux in the further evolution of the national party convention.

The Convention as Window on a Changing National Politics

That was the story of the convention as an evolving political institution. It was the story most relevant to the experience of participants. It was the story best seen by viewing audiences as well, though whether they would recognize its institutional sweep rather than just its anecdotal detail depended crucially on an instinct for the larger framework. In any case, it was the chronicle closest to the real allocation of benefits and costs to those on the outside. As such, it had to provide the most concrete understandings. Yet despite all that, the rewards of studying the convention in its own right—of focusing in on the national party convention—are not nearly all of its potential rewards. Indeed, it is possible to use the same developments but in effect to reverse the focus, to study the convention not for itself but for what it might reveal about other matters, and thus to seek a very different kind of political understanding.

This is true because the convention occasionally played a central role in major developments in American politics. But it is also true because the convention, even when its internal events were hardly major, still sat at the procedural center of that politics and thus tapped—sampled—its major developments. Some of this came through direct institutional linkage. The presidency and the political parties, for example, were formally and intrinsically connected to the convention, so that additional insights on those institutions could hardly be absent from a look at this one. Much of the convention's value as a window came more indirectly and informally, though. Thus most other major "actors" in American politics—individuals, of course, but also groups and factions, organizations and institutions, even issues and themes—can be seen in some fashion within the convention as well. The convention cannot offer a scientific sample of these agents, but it can provide the corresponding if lesser virtue that most of these agents did make an appearance, in a physically and temporally bounded context.

What the convention lost by being an institution in decline, then, it arguably compensated by being a concrete and comprehensible viewing point on the political system for which it was no longer, even arguably, the practical center. This was most immediately and consequentially apparent in the case of those two grand movements, the nationalization of politics and the imposition of procedural reform, which were reshaping not just the national party convention but the national political life around it. The convention gave both movements a set of specific and visible components; those movements gave American politics a very different set of operational contours. These could best be described abstractly as the coming of a fluid and unbrokered political environment, featuring electoral coalitions in campaigns for public office and policy coalitions inside the institutions of government which were increasingly truncated, segmented, and evanescent. But these contours can best be observed concretely through the changing character of intermediary organizations, of political parties and organized interests.

Within the convention *and* within the larger society, in fact, the decline of political parties as the central device for constructing political coalitions was matched by the rise of an increasingly diverse array of organized interests, as supplemented by a growing body of individual political activists, who were motivated principally by intense concern with narrow and focused issues. Of necessity in such an environment, campaigns for public office and then attempts to affect public policy became increasingly matters of individual entrepreneurship. Subsequently and perhaps of necessity as well, independent political entrepreneurs, who needed to build personalized electoral campaigns and issue-specific policy coalitions, turned to adapting political institutions to their personal needs for public attention—and thus adapted them to the larger political environment as well.

The specific adjustments following from this effort ranged from the reorganization of substantive committees, in the convention as in the U.S. Congress, to alterations in the procedures for action on the floor of those institutions. Yet what this meant in a different sense was a series of institutional manipulations aimed not so much at affecting the details of public policy directly as at using political institutions to communicate with—really to search for and then communicate with—organizable publics on the outside, forming them into subsequent policy coalitions if possible. That endeavor ultimately led all the relevant actors to a further concern with the structure of *press coverage* of those institutions and thus to an augmented concern with using the mass media to communicate with external publics—or with each other. And that effort, at the end of this chain of actions and reactions, produced not just another round of reforms in the internal structure of major governmental institutions but actual shifts in the comparative power of these institutions themselves.

What resulted was a new era characterized by altered social forces, reformed political institutions, shifting links between citizens and government, and even a new mechanics for politicking—the arrival of a comprehensive bifurcated politics. Abstractly, in the convention as in the society around it, the diagnostic aspect of this politics was the way institutional behavior and press portraits of it increasingly diverged, along with the growing primacy of external portraits rather than internal machinations. Said differently, politics as a process came increasingly to involve turning every element of political life toward communicating with organizable publics rather than trying to create continuing coalitions among major political actors. Nevertheless, however dangerously grand and abstract such a summary may seem, the convention still provides the practical window—the examples, the perspective, the analogues, and the referents—to make it measurable and concrete. Indeed, the elements of that politics can best be surveyed concretely by using the convention as a window to examine them.

The Nationalization of American Politics at Large

These analytic possibilities were evident in the very first part of the postwar convention story, in the nationalization of presidential politics and the departure of the presidential nomination. This was a crucial chapter in its own right: when nationalization removed the nomination from the convention, it set off a chain of events involving changed participants, substitute activities, shifting lines of conflict, altered foci for the resulting struggles, and a bifurcated character to the underlying institution. Yet seen from a different perspective—seen from the convention looking out, rather than from the outside looking in—the nationalization of presidential politics as registered in the convention was only a large but still concrete piece of an even larger and more diffuse nationalization in American politics as a whole. In fact not only did the elements of this larger nationalization have analogues in the convention but these fully developed external elements themselves invaded the convention hall. In other words, it was precisely these larger elements of a new American politics which broke over the convention and removed the nomination.[1]

The movement of governmental policy making from local and state to national levels, for example, which accompanied the growth of government generally, was a far larger element of American politics in the mid–twentieth century than its role even in the nationalization of presidential politics might suggest. No one questioned the fact of a growing governmental role in a society whose increasing complexity appeared to provide a permanent place—some would say "need"— for intervention, adjustment, or melioration by government. Few questioned the fact that policy initiatives, directives, and financing were increasingly national within this growth. Thus even state and local officeholders looked first to the national level for the funding to pursue their policy goals. Beyond that, more and more political activists and ordinary citizens looked to the national level for solutions to the ever-larger set of issues now subject to some governmental action, issues—such as school prayer, toxic waste, or even criminal justice—which increasingly could be addressed only at the national level.

The same picture of a composite nationalization of American politics in general can be seen by looking out through the convention via the other components of the nationalization of presidential politics, and the additional changes seen this way are every bit as striking. The appearance and multiplication of national media, for example, contributed by itself to this composite shift, in national politics as in the national convention, by providing both the means for following national developments and implicit encouragement to focus on them. From the other side, the decline of political parties as extended organizations again meant, as it did for the nomination and the convention, that the major countervailing institution to this trend was increasingly irrelevant to American politics. Together then, these two trends, the rise of national media of information and the decline of inherently local political parties constituted a striking change in the grand process of intermediation, the process by which individual citizens are linked to the institutions of government.

These two trends were joined, finally, in a development which completed and unified the picture, by changes in the social base of American politics, especially as represented by increasing educational levels and a shifting—ever more middle-class—occupational structure. By the mid-1970s, these changes provided the sustenance for a diverse array of independent activists, who in turn helped give American politics a particularly fluid and unpredictable character. Indeed, by the mid-1960s, this trend had provided the key attentive constituency for extended structural reform—itself a central element in a changing national politics. But by the mid-1950s, this changing social base had already contributed a growing stratum of incipient participants, who looked principally to national government for their preferred solutions and who evinced a preference for mass media rather than party officials as the source of their political impressions. The result was not just nationalization in each individual influence on politics, or even in their collective effect, but nationalization in a third and larger sense as well, within the convention and out in the country at large.

On the way to the convention in the postwar period, an old pattern, in which local interests were secured locally and then negotiated nationally with the convention as a forum, gave way to a new pattern, in which local interests had to be pursued instead by attempting to influence national campaigns, while these were taking shape. That was, in the small, why the nomination had departed the convention. This shift, however, was only an introduction to the pattern characterizing policy struggles for American politics as a whole. In the larger version of this older pattern, local issues had once been pressed upon local officials—and most issues had been truly local, to boot. In the larger version of its modern counterpart, even self-consciously local issues, such as road construction or welfare management, had to be addressed through struggles over national allocation formulas, or even through national court decisions—and there were far fewer of these explicitly local issues than there would have been only a generation or two before.[2]

The Place of a National Movement for Reform

With the coming of the next chapter in the postwar convention story, with the coming of reform to the process of delegate selection and the institutionalization of the presidential nomination outside the convention, the parallels between convention developments and their larger national politics were extended and refined. Indeed, "parallels" understates the case, for the reform movement which had such impact on the convention as an institution was only part of a movement sweeping governmental institutions as a group, just as the nationalization of the politics of presidential selection had been only part of the nationalization of politics more generally. Yet here, the sequencing was reversed. The forces which comprised the nationalization of politics had formed and then rolled through the national party convention. The reform drive which was so influential in shaping the character of convention politics preceded—actually led—the movement which rolled through many other governmental institutions.

This larger national reform drive was in part itself a product of the nationalization of politics. At a minimum, the social changes associated with political nationalization had contributed what would become both the constituency and the leadership for institutional reform. That constituency was found among those middle- and upper-middle-class, politically interested citizens whose incipient view of politics involved a preference for partisan independence and direct participation, rather than partisan regularity and negotiations among official representatives. An additionally important aspect of this same development was the presence within this constituency of a set of independent activists who would pursue—and thus operationalize—those procedural preferences, better known on the Democratic side but present in Republican ranks as well. The declining strength of political parties as organizations, stemming from decades of other preceding reforms, also magnified the importance both of this larger constituency and of its activist leadership.

Yet the broader reform drive was also dependent for its specific goals on an evolving reform doctrine, one awaiting its opportunity for application but one incipiently attractive to this new proto-constituency for reform. While it had almost as many variants as exponents, this doctrine reliably emphasized the facilitation of direct participation by individually motivated citizens and the counterpart restraint (or even elimination) of participation by organized intermediaries, especially political parties. Finally, this national reform drive, while it appeared to require a specific internal crisis in order to succeed in any given political institution, also appeared to need a larger national crisis to trigger the emerging reform activists and bring together these other influences. If there was one single crisis which filled this need—which explained why reform surfaced during the middle and late 1960s and why it surfaced in so many arenas at about that same time—it was probably the escalation of the Vietnam War, along with accompanying extended protests.[3]

Within the convention in any case, the reform process followed what would become its archetypal course, from a changing environment with certain predispositions for reform, through a catalytic crisis in the institution to be reformed, to a subsequent politics which could convert emerging reform doctrine into specific institutional changes. In the convention, there was already the nationalization of presidential politics, which had removed the presidential nomination and which provided the larger environment within which a sweeping reform movement appeared. There was a specific crisis in the Democratic convention of 1968, where both external violence and internal disruption convinced many that a reform movement might avert future disasters. And there was a reform politics inside the Democratic party thereafter, with spillovers for the Republicans, one drawing heavily on independent activists with an emerging reform doctrine and one generating the procedural reforms which reworked the process of delegate selection. Moreover, quite apart from many unexpected practical consequences, these changes did embody the key values of the reform approach, in their insistence on direct participation by individuals and in their hostility toward mediation by official political parties.

Yet if the elements of this reform process were well and concretely encapsulated within the national party convention, they could as easily have been isolated in any number of other subsequent places. The reform of presidential campaign finance, for example, became an alternative showpiece for the same elements.[4] In this area, the grand components of the nationalization of politics again formed the environment for incipient reform. A specific catalyst, the Watergate crisis stemming from the reelection of Richard Nixon, again brought that environment into substantive focus. An extensive reform package, embodying the new reform doctrine, was again the result. This included, from one side, limits on individual contributions and, from the other, limits on the way those contributions could be spent, along with the requirement of public record keeping and the provision of federal matching funds—to attenuate further the connection between candidates and donors. Finally, the same general doctrinal orientation could be seen in this reform, in an emphasis on advantaging small contributors, in an effort to constrain large, organized interests, and in elimination of a role for the political party.

The Contours of American Politics in a New Political Era

With the passage of these reforms, a new American politics, best perceived through the convention but characterizing American society at large, had come into existence. There was not just the overarching nationalization of politics but the presence of all those factors which constituted this nationalization, just as there was, by the late 1970s, not just an extended reform movement but numerous institutional

products of that movement—to combine formal, institutional transformation with informal, changing, environmental forces. There was
an evolving character to the politics outside these newly altered institutions, one featuring individuals who could best be described as
independent activists, independent at least of extended political parties
and segmented in both their participation and their policy focus. There
was an evolving character to the politics inside these institutions too,
especially with the coalitions which were central to shaping their policy
product; these could best be described as truncated both in scope and
in duration.

The simplest abstract summary might describe the coming of this
new composite system as the arrival of an increasingly unbrokered
politics. Many elements of an older American politics were still very
much in evidence, in those regions, institutions, organizations, and
actors which were less affected by the forces of nationalization and
reform. There were additional twists to this evolving alternative as
well, in its individual electoral and institutional contexts. There were
even some countervailing tendencies, in unplanned developments running contrary to the national trend and in deliberate efforts to resist
it. But the arrival of an increasingly unbrokered politics, one probably
more in keeping with the preferences of the American public for the
conduct of public affairs, was the largest development introduced by
the story of the postwar convention—larger even than the nationalization of politics, larger than any (or all) of the subsequent institutional reforms.[5]

The diagnostic element in all this—really the principal intermediate
cause rather than just the diagnostic indicator—was the organizational
decline of the official party, its eclipse as anything more than a partisan
label. Again, this is most evident in the confined and comprehensible
theater of the national party convention, less easily measured (if even
more important) in the diffuse theater of national politics. Yet here,
the convention is remarkable not as a window on this particular trend
but as a previous exception to it, that is, in the extent to which it
managed to resist this larger development for so long. Nominations
at other levels and even for other offices at the national level had been
forcibly moved outside the official party structure long before the same
thing happened with the presidency. Accordingly, the eclipse of the
party in the politics of presidential selection, and the diminution of
party officials at the national party convention, marked the true end
of an era in American politics.

The implications of the demise of party and of the decline of party officials were instant and far-reaching. Political parties were the major available agents for building coalitions—for serving as institutional brokers—across the wide and diverse geographic areas, across the multiple governmental levels, and across the separate governmental institutions of American society. Parties in the United States had never been preeminent, much less uncontested, in this activity. That was one of the distinctive features of American politics. Nevertheless, when they suffered a noteworthy further deterioration in their ability to undertake the building of coalitions in the postwar period—to provide the framework for campaigns for public office and to be the framework for the coordination of subsequent governments—that development was perhaps the central structural fact of its political era. Its further implications for the translation of demands upon government only emphasized that centrality.

Within the convention, the elements of this further deterioration in the role of political parties are easy to identify. The positional advantage which was previously guaranteed to the official party by party-based institutions of delegate selection was reduced sharply for the Republicans and eliminated for the Democrats by a move to institutions which were outside the official party structure. Those informal advantages which party officials retained by virtue of their practical experience were then rapidly devalued by a new politics of presidential selection, one requiring national, independent, and personal campaigns of all the contenders. The official party could not serve even in principle as the basis for more than one of these campaigns, but presidential contenders were in fact encouraged to seek support from organized entities other than the official party. Moreover, party officials needed to wait before going with a presidential contender, while presidential aspirants came to look on party officials as a mixed blessing even when they could be convinced to move.

Within national politics, parallel developments had actually preceded this decline. The guaranteed role of the official party in selecting candidates to local, state, and most other national offices had been under increasingly effective attack since the turn of the century, and only a few states, such as Connecticut and Virginia, retained much semblance of positional advantage. In turn, the informal powers of the official party had been under even more sustained assault: directly, through the efforts to eliminate the jobs, favors, and contracts on which extended party organizations had once been built, but indirectly too, through governmental programs which were far more important to their recipients than small, intermittent, concrete party benefits. There were still semblances of an extended official party in a few areas of the country. But in most, campaigns for public office had long been—as they finally became with the presidency—matters of individual entrepreneurship, to be built personally, independently, and with little attention to the official party structure.[6]

Intermediation in a New American Politics

In the absence of a preeminent role for parties, the coalitions in American electoral politics were almost inevitably less wide-ranging, less temporally extended, and thus more fluid and easily replaced. While this surely gave that politics an increased air of unpredictability—in the society at large as in the national party convention—it did not mean that coalitions, and hence the structure of politics overall, became truly atomized, truly decentralized to the individual citizen. This may have been the goal of some reformers; it was never a realistic possibility. For with the decay and constriction of the most extensive and best organized vehicle for the construction of coalitions in electoral politics, that role fell to the next most extensive and next best organized—though the drop was often a perilously long one. Put less abstractly, with the decay of political parties, their role was increasingly usurped by an array—itself growing and changing—of interest groups and issue organizations.[7]

The tasks associated with securing public office and then operating governmental institutions still required organizational units for their effective accomplishment. At a minimum, it was far simpler to construct a campaign (and then a government) by tapping previously existing organizations. Beyond that, the leaders of those organizations were not slow in seeing an opportunity to press forward and take advantage of the demise of the organized party. What resulted was an increased role for the organized interests, and hence for interested partisans, in the formation of political coalitions. Probably, this result alone would have implied more segmented coalitions in American politics, with a shorter life and a more limited policy focus. But actual changes in the constellation of available organized interests, the interest groups and issue organizations which could conceivably benefit as political parties declined, then went on to guarantee this result.

In effect, this evolving truncation of political coalitions was more segmental and fluid than it needed even in principle to be because the universe of available organized interests had also changed during the postwar period. The previously dominant interests in each party, organized business for the Republicans and organized labor for the Democrats, had been joined by a much wider array of organizations, especially ones built around a specific constituency or cause. While the agenda of American politics had never been well summarized by the notion of business versus labor, that agenda was further altered by a set of issues, ranging from foreign interventions through the well-being of endangered species to the place of religion in public life, which were further than ever from being effectively summarized in that—or any—simple dichotomy. Needless to say, that agenda was in part altered by these new issues precisely because economic interest groups were joined by organizations with new and different foci.[8]

It was still true that no single organization in this new constellation had the breadth and persistence of an AFL-CIO or a National Chamber of Commerce. Yet these organizations were just as clearly a smaller part of the organized environment than they had been a generation ago. Beyond that, the newer organizations gained additional countervailing advantages by being increasingly constructed of middle- and upper-middle-class activists, with a dominant concern for the issue or interest at their center, and thus from being particularly effective in the new, reformed, unbrokered politics. Indeed, as these activist-based organizations began to reach into additional sectors of American society, as religious evangelicals did, for example, with a lower-middle-class and working-class constituency, the tendency for the grand old interests of partisan politics to become a shrinking share of coalition formation seemed guaranteed.

Within the convention, again, the National Education Association or the Moral Majority, the Campaign for Safe Energy or the Congressional Club—to name but two pairs of partisan interests from only one convention year—could achieve remarkable prominence and remarkable impact. In the nation at large, within the U.S. Congress, for example, the major, continuing, economic interests might not be as easily supplanted. Yet if they were more consistently present in Congress, the agenda even of that body continued to expand beyond their central concerns, a situation encouraging these major interests to confine themselves politically to those concerns, or risk accumulating enemies who might invade *their* home territory. Beyond that, candidates *running* for Congress, when they turned to building their electoral coalitions and to staffing governmental offices thereafter, were

likely to find the self-styled independent activists of the newer organized interests more useful than the lobbyists of these older, allegedly
larger interests.

Institutional Responses to a New American Politics

A world of fluid and unbrokered politics, with segmented and temporary electoral coalitions, was not long in producing additional consistent changes in the political institutions into which these developments fed. Some of this was a nearly automatic response to the
external environment, as the main activities of these institutions shifted
to accommodate a changing national politics around them, quite apart
from the conscious wishes of their major actors. Some of it was deliberately strategic, an explicit response to the goals of new institutional
incumbents, as these individuals began to adapt the internal structure
of their recently conquered institutions in order to pursue their own
changing, more personal needs. Some of the resulting change even
began to have impacts in the other direction, as institutional alterations
produced further exaggerations in the drift of the political environment
outside. All this subsequent change, in any case, attested to the increasing congruence among a changing general environment for politics, a changing electoral politics within it, and a changing internal
institutional politics—to the point where it became quickly and increasingly difficult to separate changes in one of these elements from
changes in the others.[9]

The shift in the central activity of the national party convention is
perhaps the perfect example of the process by which a changing overall
environment could work an almost automatic change in a particular
political institution. For most of its history, the making of the nomination was the central activity of the convention, from which everything else followed. Yet when that activity departed, in response to
a changing external environment, it was quickly replaced by the effort—by struggles—to use the convention to launch and support one
or another external campaign. That shift would not have occurred,
of course, without the facilitative response of key political actors, and
a changing electoral politics in fact went on to contribute a noticeably
different cast of internal participants to translate the forces of a
changing overall environment. Yet this change in participants was not
in itself deliberate, and the resulting delegates still acted more as con-
duits than as shapers of external political forces.

This new central activity, this new publicizing use of the convention, had always, in truth, been incipiently present. Yet before the 1950s, it had as reliably been overshadowed by struggles to control the nomination itself. When that nomination departed but when press and public attention continued, it was in some sense natural for campaign launching to receive greater institutional emphasis. The focus on this activity, however, was specifically and pointedly facilitated by the arrival of a changing cast of participants, by the shift from party officials to interested partisans. These new key actors had hardly created the preconditions for their own appearance, and they were not consciously determined to change the main activity of the institution they inherited. Yet they *were* predisposed to use the convention to pursue the causes or interests which had motivated their participation in the first place, a predisposition which was reinforced by the absence of nominating possibilities. Accordingly, when almost everyone among them—nominees and challengers, convention officials and rank-and-file delegates—turned to the possibilities for using the convention to communicate with the outside world, that activity became the central one at postreform conventions.

What appeared to be a development peculiar to the convention, on the other hand, was only a focused and particular parallel to larger and general developments elsewhere. Outside the convention, in fact, the same tendency toward harnessing any available institution—any available piece of an institution, really—to the raising of issues and the publicizing of causes was an increasingly central feature of American national politics. This was true even in Congress, the putative hallmark institution for old-fashioned coalition building and for an old-fashioned politics of brokerage as usual. There, more and more activity was devoted to showing that individual representatives and senators were working on issues of concern to organized publics on the outside, or even to an undifferentiated general public.[10] Again, a changing overall structure of politics is the major explanation for this response. And again, the changing electoral politics which accompanied it contributed a new cast of participants, with newly discovered needs for guaranteeing their survival and influence. These individuals then became the specific means by which environmental forces produced changed patterns of behavior within political institutions.

The U.S. Senate was the first house of Congress to show this shift, to the institution as publicizer and communicator above all. Yet even the House of Representatives, the archetypal, internal, legislative "machine," moved toward this pattern within a decade of its emergence. Indeed, more and more of the internal activity of each institution was devoted to efforts by individual legislators not just to publicize issues and communicate with constituencies but to *locate* concerns which could serve this purpose—which could be both uniquely theirs and attractive to major publics. Once more, while the changing larger environment might well have been sufficient to dictate this institutional shift, there was also a major change in the character of electoral coalitions, which made a powerful further contribution. In this, representatives and senators, whose fortunes were increasingly individualized and entrepreneurial, and for whom the process of attaining public office had underlined that fact, were inherently inclined to search for personalized sources of public attention, once they had successfully reached that office.

Further Ramifications inside Political Institutions

Second-order effects perhaps inevitably followed. The overall environment might have nearly automatic impacts on the operation of political institutions, but individual actors within those institutions did not need to sit and merely watch these impacts roll on. At a minimum, they were free to look for ways to alter the internal structure of their institution, so as to bend both new forces and old institutions to their personal purposes. In passing, of course, this activity extended the impact of ongoing political change. Beyond that, the electoral environment supported such an effort additionally, by encouraging the search for ways to use the institutions of government to communicate with outside publics and to mobilize personal coalitions. Most officeholders, after all, had arrived not as party products but as individual entrepreneurs. The key actors within any or all of these institutions were, accordingly, predisposed to attend to modifying the structure of their institution in order to facilitate using it to launch and support their external campaigns—indeed, as many external campaigns as possible.

Informal modifications of recurring patterns of behavior were one way to address this changing political environment. Self-conscious reforms of the internal structure of political institutions were another, more easily observed, and often more dramatic response. By virtue of its physical and temporal limits, the convention makes both processes particularly self-evident. The recurring informal shift in strategies and counterstrategies for internal convention conflict, for example, a shift quickly characterizing both political parties, was an immediate, conscious response to the postreform environment. Thus from one side, interested partisans, convention after convention, sought policy promises and rules changes which were too extreme for the nominee to accept with impunity, precisely because these partisans valued the public attention of a battle. From the other side, nominees sought to compromise and accept these proposals, even when they would never dream of campaigning on them, so that these nominees could be free to orchestrate the convention for their own preferred impact on the viewing public.

More formal changes in convention structure show this same dynamic—by which a changing larger environment is converted into further reforms in internal organization through conscious adjustment by key participants—at a further, more explicit, and more concrete extension. For example, the move in the Democratic party to take the deliberations of convention committees outside the convention proper can best be understood as the product of reinforcing desires by both sides of a recurring convention conflict. From one side, individual delegates—dissidents, but many of those supporting the nominee as well—desired to use those committees to pursue as many of their programmatic causes as possible. Moving the committees provided additional time for that pursuit. From the other side, convention leaders desired to allow the nominee to launch his personal campaign with as little extraneous tension as possible. Moving the convention committees helped relegate any publicity efforts by dissident delegates to another locale, while it provided additional time to contain the potential damage from any surviving contrary initiatives.

Within other institutions of national government, very much the same development was occurring. Congress is, once again, not only a useful example but a veritable catalog of concrete reforms aimed at adapting the institution to a new American politics.[11] As more and more representatives and senators were independently elected, and as they came to realize that the key to their reelection—to their use of the institution of Congress—lay in communicating with various publics, these actors too began to search for additional ways to make their institution contribute to their personal goals. Given the nature of Congress, the first stop was its committees and subcommittees, the place where the detailed work of legislation occurred—but increasingly the place where legislators might seize an issue and gain public attention as well.[12] Thus representatives and senators moved to distribute the key positions, committee and subcommittee chairs, more broadly. They followed by distributing the resources of these bodies, both staff and hearing time, more broadly too. They completed the process by introducing electoral checks on committee leaders, to guarantee that these leaders did not interfere in increasingly independent subcommittees or attempt to recapture committee resources.

Beyond that, national legislators moved to liberalize provisions for pursuing their personal goals even after the committee stage, on the very floor of their institutions. A small part of this involved the modification of formal arrangements, especially in the House, which had previously reinforced the primacy of committee products, arrangements such as rules restricting floor amendments. A much larger part was simply a growing disinclination, except in the most extenuating circumstances, to follow the old norm that committee products should be respected.[13] The relaxation of those rules and the erosion of those norms did not make the formation of political coalitions, especially extended and continuing coalitions, any easier. Indeed, these changes took the fluidity and segmentation of electoral coalitions a step further inside Congress, exaggerating the flux of the new electoral politics. These altered arrangements did, however, increase the ability of individual legislators to pursue their personal goals—or at least to pursue public attention for those goals—and that was the deciding factor in their implementation. It was also, of course, the means by which changes in a larger environment were brought, effectively if not so consciously, into another political institution.

Countervailing Developments in a Changing Political System

The cumulative, largely consistent trend of all this change can still be overstated. Or at least, there were countervailing tendencies, and if these were not the dominant factors of their era, and if they gave no promise of imminent reversal of those factors which were dominant, they still contained the seeds of a cautionary note. Elements from the nationalization of politics, after all, had been present for as long as seventy-five years before their extension and interaction had removed the nomination from the convention. In the same way, the countervailing elements in an increasingly unbrokered national politics might ultimately prove that there was nothing ineluctable about the drift even of a grand political environment. Two more focused examples, the increasing reach of coherent ideologies and certain different efforts at institutional engineering, had at least some potential for building and then sustaining larger political coalitions, and are thus noteworthy for their countervailing implications.

The first of these, some halting but undeniable movements toward increased ideological coherence among partisan political activists, is again most easily observed within the convention. Although the major change in the character of convention delegates was the eclipse of the official party and the rise of the organized interests, the delegates produced by that change were also increasingly both more internally consistent in their ideological preferences and more ideologically divergent, Democrats versus Republicans. Through 1984, the principal product of this ideological elaboration had been greater internal tensions over efforts to use the convention to launch various external campaigns. But the increasing ideological divergence of party platforms was also a much more concrete product of this ideological coalescence. If this coalescence spreads further among those active in presidential nominating campaigns—and the consistency of platforms from year to year suggests that this spread is indeed occurring—such a development would have further practical consequences. At a minimum, it would contribute toward giving the convention itself a more fixed and continuing coalitional character. At the extreme, it would imply that only certain candidacies are viable in the politics of presidential selection— very liberal for the Democrats, very conservative for the Republicans.

Moreover, there is at least some reason to believe that the same ideological coalescence is proceeding apace in the world outside the convention.[14] Once more, it is not just that parties are declining as electoral organizations, while being rivaled by organized interests— although this is occurring, with the same apparent thrust toward ideological divergence. It is also that those party activists who remain to do the work of the party are themselves more likely either to be recruited from the interest groups and issue organizations or to be motivated specifically by ideological concerns. This suggests an increased uniformity among campaign activists, across geographic areas and at various federal levels, perhaps even with party platforms—this was certainly the intent of proponents—as the touchstone for that uniformity. Presumably in any case, if candidates need to mount campaigns by means of political activists who hold increasingly consistent and divergent ideologies, those candidates will either fail or bring their own views into line—and a generation of candidates with these newly desirable preferences would have the potential for making the political parties appear stronger rather than weaker in most institutions of national government. Indeed, again at the extreme, this recoalescence might cause the general public to move decisively toward one party or the other, creating reliable popular majorities around a clear-cut program.

More deliberate institutional engineering, with the effect of guaranteeing larger and more stable political coalitions, was a more incipient and halting feature of a politics moving very much, generally, in the opposite direction. Yet there were some initiatives along precisely these lines in the postwar period, and they were at least far more concrete and concretely interpretable than any evolving ideological trends. Within the convention, for example, the drive among the new generation of delegates to extend the influence of decisions reached within the convention hall, if successful, promises to provide some added institutional reach to the convention as a theater for internal politicking or even to spread the increasingly ideologized views of convention delegates out into national politics directly. Thus dissident delegates in the Democratic convention have concentrated on extending the hold of the party platform over any succeeding presidential administration, while their counterparts on the Republican side have worked at extending the reach of convention decisions into their national committee. On the other hand, the more important facts remain that these delegates have been only partially and formalistically successful and that there appear to be powerful institutional constraints on their ultimate practical triumph—in the independent base of an elected president, for example, and in the short-term nature of the convention itself.

Outside the convention, within the U.S. Congress, there has actually been somewhat more success, albeit with a more clearly circumscribed potential, at increasing the prospect for larger and more stable coalitions through institutional engineering. In Congress, this move has centered on strengthening political parties.[15] Indeed, the parties in each house, in part alarmed by the very difficulty of building broad and continuing coalitions, have begun to emphasize decisions reached within the party caucus—a gathering of the full party membership into a committee of the whole—as a guide to, a restraint upon, and ultimately a punishment for, membership behavior. These efforts have not attained the continuity across either time or policy which would make them serious challenges to the dominant drift of congressional (much less national) politics. They might well produce consensual and

moderate party coalitions, perhaps with rapidly shifting party positions, even then. But they exist, and they do run potentially counter
to most other national trends.

The Press, the Public, and a New Political Dynamic

A noticeably different American politics was nevertheless emerging,
forcefully and on many fronts. Moreover, the final element of this
politics not only was inherent in all the others but tied them together
in an additional sense—by being integral to the mechanics of politicking in a new order. In the most global sense, this final element
was the arrival of a recurring struggle over press portrayal of political
activity. If communication with and mobilization of sectors of the
general public was the essence of politicking in a new era, and if public
impressions were thus inevitably a critical resource in that politics,
press portraits were still the major intermediary product. If efforts to
shape those portraits could be the key to subsequent political success,
that fact raised further questions about the place of the mass media
of information, of the press, in the structure of American national
politics—about strategies for utilizing the press from one side and
about their own institutional operations from the other.

Seen more concretely, the central dynamic of a new American politics was the effort to use electoral campaigns and governmental institutions to communicate with elements of the general public, most
commonly by way of the mass media of information—by way of press
coverage of these campaigns and institutions. The place of the press
and of reportage, of "the news," was inherently open to exaggeration,
whereby this struggle for coverage, along with the internal decisions
affecting it, became the essence of politicking rather than its intrinsic
accompaniment. A growing role for mass media did not imply that
those media "made" rather than merely recorded the news, or even
that their standards for recording events would introduce deliberate
"bias" into public perceptions. Yet at bottom, most of the main elements of the new, unbrokered politics, whatever their roots and however they might be expressed, still revolved around efforts to communicate with outside publics—and thus most commonly around *press
coverage* of the actions of the major participants.[16]

This was self-evidently true when the ultimate goal was the shaping
of the impressions, and then the actual mobilization, of the general
public—and there were more attempts to achieve this directly in the

new politics. But it was also true when the target was some segment of that public, those with more specialized concerns for the topic at hand. The members of this incipiently attentive public could be attached to the various interest groups and issue organizations; they could merely be a more concerned sample of an unattached, general public. Getting their attention, in any case, could assure the survival of political leaders; it could also lead to concrete policy successes. The chain of political communication, however, hardly stopped at that point. An even more specialized audience within this attentive public were those political activists who increasingly energized the evanescent coalitions, the partial and limited alliances, which were the hallmarks of an evolving national politics. Indeed, it was not just that press coverage might communicate with these individuals but that they themselves were trying to use the media of information to pursue their various goals—and to communicate with each other.

In fact, it was possible to take this communication and intended mobilization even further, to the direct institutional operatives of American politics, and this was the most cost-effective strategy of all when circumstances permitted. As a first step, a more specialized but increasingly consequential audience were the staff members of various governmental institutions. These individuals were rarely decision makers in their own right. But they were a growing body within the attentive public; they could be extremely influential on policy matters which did not generate controversy; and they might be central to the forming of coalitions even around those issues which did. At the end of this chain of potential audiences were public officials themselves, the key actors in major governmental institutions as well as a recurring subject of press coverage of political events. Their electoral prospects were inevitably if indirectly shaped by press portraits, of course. But they might be influenced directly too by successful attempts to use press coverage to disseminate information and focus attention. Indeed, at the extreme, successful efforts to garner press attention, followed by anticipatory action by public officials, could obviate the need for an external coalition.[17]

There were still distinctions, not just within this potential audience but within the mass media too. There was in fact a multitude of "mass media" with an obvious potential for public communication, including not just network television but daily newspapers, radio stations, journals of political opinion, and even membership publications for the various organized interests. On the one hand, if the evening television news did not cover a hearing on the minimum wage or prayer in the schools but if the *AFL-CIO Federationist* or *Christian Voice* (respectively) did, even that was some gain for the issue and its proponents. On the other hand, television news, for the daily business of Congress as for the daily course of the convention, drew reliably the largest audience. That audience subsumed those individuals who could also be addressed, for reinforcement or countervailing argument, by the other, more limited, mass media. And those facts led most political actors to "keep score" via television. Indeed, television news surely came closest to success in suggesting that its content *was* the content of public concerns of the moment. In one sense, this impact was more ambiguous than it might appear, because network news directors often took implicit guidance on the crucial stories of the day from the major national newspapers or from more specialized publications. But that fact did not reduce the reach, or the direct institutional impact, of the national television networks.[18]

Institutional Adaptations to a Changing Political Dynamic

At the center of the mechanics of politicking in a new political order, then, was the attempt to use the institutions of government to communicate with a differentiated or general public, to build (inevitably temporary) coalitions by mobilizing sectors of that public, and at some point to convert those coalitions into governmental policy. It is not surprising that the principal means for accomplishing these goals began to elicit further changes in the operation of those institutions—indeed, that these key media of communication almost began to compel such changes. Within the convention, the discovery of not just the need but the means for doing all this had in fact been almost instantaneous. With the nomination gone but with press coverage remaining—indeed, and especially, with the serendipitous arrival of gavel-to-gavel coverage by the national television networks—major convention actors had not only seen the convention achieve a new central activity, in the launching of various external campaigns. They had also seen, dramatically represented on the floor of the hall, the means for both pursuing and intensifying that effort.

A three-cornered conflict over press coverage was the immediate result. Convention actors did continue to struggle over the concrete products of convention machinery, over (two) nominations and (three) committee reports. Moreover, these could still be of independent consequence, though they were increasingly pursued in a manner aimed at choreographing them for direct news coverage as well. Yet convention actors also and increasingly struggled to shape news coverage for its own sake, whether through careful advance consideration of what might and might not be reported or through an attempt to negotiate with—even to pressure—decision makers in the news media. Finally, news officials themselves were to acquire a part of this struggle, within their own organizations, when they faced the question of what to cover, of how to define convention "news."

When these officials ultimately responded to that question with a sharp cutback in coverage, they would alter—by main force—the character of the convention as a political institution. Yet well before that, the changing political dynamic of which all this conflict was a part would create direct changes in the operation of the convention, just as it would lead on to indirect adjustments when the occupants of the convention changed their institution further, to address a new political environment. Again, however, the forces which led to a shift in the central activities of the convention, and the calculations which led convention actors to begin to alter their institution, were hardly peculiar to the convention. These were, after all, largely external forces; they could reasonably produce corresponding alterations elsewhere.

Accordingly, it is hardly surprising that a composite political environment, which emphasized the integration of news strategies and news media within the convention, elicited similar strategies and a similar focus in other institutions outside.[19] Thus the attention of representatives and senators to the utilization of news media for publicizing their individual efforts was an obvious and immediate structural parallel. At a minimum, they too struggled to pursue concrete policies, with one eye on maximizing favorable press coverage. But in truth, they too were increasingly inclined to seek coverage for its own sake, as a means to publicize a given cause or issue while portraying their personal efforts in a favorable light—with specific legislative consequences to follow. In a new version of time-honored congressional parlance, they were inclined to meet the old institutional question "What would you rather have, a bill or an issue?" with a new institutional response, "The issue, thank you."

The coming of a new central activity, the launching of one or more external campaigns—its coming to the convention or to the Congress—had been additionally accompanied by conscious institutional adaptations. Convention committees had been subsequently reorganized; congressional committees and subcommittees had been even more substantially altered. Not surprisingly, there were again second-order adjustments to the internal structure of these institutions with the coming of a focus on the structure and operation of the mass media, especially television. Within the convention this adaptation meant that proceedings were streamlined, through systematic scripting; that decorum was emphasized, through sharp limitations on demonstrations; and that the hall itself was redesigned to facilitate television coverage, to the point where it was often dominated by television equipment.

Within the Congress, the most dramatic parallel development was the struggle over the presence of television cameras themselves. Live television coverage had come to the convention in 1952; it did not come to the House until 1979; it did not follow in the Senate until 1986. Once introduced, however, it was widely embraced and quickly integrated.[20] Indeed, explicit conflict over the role of television equipment again followed almost immediately upon its introduction, as when representatives argued over the use of their empty chamber in the making of after-hours partisan advertisements. The more consequential parallels, however, in the convention as well as in the houses of Congress, had come from the underlying change in central institutional activity, whereby delegates and legislators came to focus on using their institution to communicate with outside publics of all sorts. The introduction of television cameras, to that, despite their apparent physical insistence, was quite secondary to this earlier, larger change.

Political Dynamics and Changing Institutional Power

The focus on explicit efforts to communicate with various outside publics through political institutions by way of the mass media of information—even if it was central to the mechanics of politicking in a new political era—still missed one final, crucial aspect of that dynamic. This was the way in which a politics adapted critically to the structure of the news media made some inevitable further changes in the power of the institutions involved. Part of this impact was obvious, though no less consequential for being so. The integration of mass media and media strategies into the process of politics represented an inherent transfer of institutional power to those media themselves. A second and even more consequential part of this development was perhaps a good deal less obvious. For the existing institutions of government possessed an inherently differing potential to make use of this coverage, so that when a new political dynamic demanded its utilization as a key to political power, the comparative power of various governmental institutions itself began to shift.

The more straightforward aspect of this institutional shift was widely noted or at least frequently decried by various institutional actors. In a politics where the organization of the news media, strategies for shaping media coverage, and the press portraits which resulted were a central feature, there was an inevitable transfer of influence to the media of information themselves. This was not necessarily an intended outcome. Given the continuing stream of criticism which it produced when recognized, it was not necessarily enjoyed by its inheritors. Indeed, it did not even work in its essential outlines as its most vocal critics asserted—through personally biased decisions by news executives or personally biased commentary by news reporters, all of whom operated in a more technically, normatively, and professionally constrained world than frustrated partisans might have been willing to acknowledge. Yet if press coverage, especially through news programming, was a central element of the new American politics, then the decisions about coverage which news directors inevitably made, in a world of infinite events but fixed resources and limited time, were necessarily an important part of the total picture.[21]

A set of constraints stemming from the organization of national news media still operated both to reduce and to channel any such influence, quite apart from constraints on the impact of the news itself resulting from the level of attention and the pattern of values and self-interest within the public on the receiving end. Many events were still consensually "news" for most media, and the criteria underlying that consensus—major actors working toward public policies with obvious practical impact—limited deliberate influence from the start. Moreover, not just these events but many others in a sort of middle ground were primarily responsive to the activities of orthodox political actors—institutions, organizations, and individuals—rather than to any inherent selectivity, consensual or idiosyncratic, on the part of news media. In this sense, the frequent arguments about bias, pitting alleged conservative owners or advertisers against alleged liberal reporters or commentators, were far less consequential than attackers or defenders were inclined to admit. Nevertheless, the major, shaping role of national news media on the new American politics—and there remained substantial room for just such a role—was still organizationally inherent in certain ways of addressing the news about politics, ways which had nothing to do with deliberate ideological bias.

Within the convention, these facts stood dramatically revealed when the television networks, in response to organizational changes of their own but even more to changes in the larger environment for politics, cut the total amount of convention coverage. In doing so, they confirmed the decline of the convention, by pronouncing it to possess decreasing news value. In doing so, they simultaneously accelerated that decline, in an era when the launching of external campaigns (which required extensive press coverage for its success) was a central activity of the convention. But in cutting back, the networks also enhanced the importance of the choices among events for broadcast which they were now increasingly forced to make. In meeting that challenge, finally and unintentionally, they managed to create the bifurcated convention.

It would have been hard to find a more dramatic summary comment on the evolving state of convention politics, with its growing focus on press portraits and its associated partial transfer of power to the press, or on the uses of the convention as a window on American politics more generally. Within the other institutions of national government, this development was not as dramatically capsulized, because there was no similarly striking change in the amount of institutional coverage for the president, Congress, or even the Supreme Court. But in a second sense, what was missing with these other institutions was not the equally extended impact but only the attention-getting incident for focusing and underlining this development. For the greater continuity of coverage with these other institutions masked an even more dramatic difference in *levels* of institutional coverage—and thereby masked an even more extreme contribution.

Concomitant with the rise of the presidency in American national politics, for example, and of its increased predominance in the balance with Congress, was the rise both of the facility with which presidents could use national press portraits to impose their own issues as a national agenda and of the counterpart, only partially related tendency of the national press to concentrate on the presidency rather than on Congress. The increasing tendency of students of the presidency to focus on the advantages of that institution in communicating with the general public (as well as with specialized publics) as an important part of "presidential power" was in this sense a tribute to the importance of this underlying imbalance in coverage by national news

media.[22] Indeed, if patterns of press coverage could produce two institutions out of one, as they did in creating the bifurcated convention,
they could do something equally important by attending to one institution at the expense of another: they could feature one (the presidency) which existed both on site and at home and another (Congress)
which existed only on site. Again, they did not do so as a deliberate
exercise of power. But their role was still implicit in the arrival of a
new political structure, involving necessarily their own operations and
behavior.

The Coming of a True Bifurcated Politics

The convention manages to suggest, then, that there was in fact a
new American politics—or at least a new incarnation of trends in that
politics, brought to a newly extended and recognizably distinct culmination. This was an increasingly nationalized politics, of course; it
occurred within extensively reformed institutions; its essential coalitions, in electoral campaigns and in public office, were temporally
unstable and substantively narrow. Those coalitions in turn were constructed—built, unbuilt, and built again—from a shifting and unpredictable interplay among weak political parties, active but segmented
organized interests, and political activists owing no reliable allegiance
to either. Perhaps inevitably, the resulting politics focused on raising
issues, on communicating with publics, and on mobilizing potential
coalition members. At a minimum, this guaranteed an increasingly
central place for the mass media of information. Beyond that, it hinted
at a shift in the comparative power of governmental institutions
themselves, based on their differing potential to benefit from this new
dynamic.

All that a review of this new political era lacks, when summarized
in such a highly condensed form, is a summary concept—to put it
back together even more concisely. Its impact on the convention,
however, surely contains an implicit suggestion. For this evolving
American political era was in its essence nothing less than the coming
of a bifurcated politics, the abstract and general extension of developments best seen concretely within the national party convention.
Said differently, this was a politics occurring simultaneously within
political institutions and in the atmosphere around them—among their
amorphous and sometimes unknowable extended publics. It was a
politics aimed increasingly away from the direct negotiations of elected

or appointed representatives and toward the building of coalitions within that larger public, coalitions which might then elicit public policies, with or without extended negotiations, at some unspecified subsequent point. Its central metaphor, finally, was the bifurcated convention, with a version on site, a version at home, a growing disjunction between the two—and increasing primacy for the more abstract and diffuse, external version.

Moreover, the bifurcation at the core of this new politics really was different. It was not the familiar practical division between electoral and institutional politicking. Both realms were now dedicated to the same general activity, to raising issues and mobilizing supporters. Nor was it an older theoretical division, between representative and participatory approaches to democracy. Elected representatives were still crucial actors, but the intermittent and unpredictable character of participatory activists and their organizations conditioned the behavior of these representatives in noticeably different ways. At the core of this new politics, instead, was the transition from an older era of brokerage and bargaining to a newer era of publicity and communication. It was still possible for the organized interests to build and to broker policy coalitions directly, and thus on occasion to secure their policy wishes with impressive speed—and with a concomitant *lack* of outside involvement. Indeed, as American society came to feature a fluid and segmental, unbrokered politics, there could be numerous, short and sharp policy surprises of this sort, because they were unconstrained by any broad and lasting, contrary coalitions.

Nevertheless, the ideal strategy for those desiring a governmental policy was still to use the opportunities presented by reformed institutions of government and a more fluid structure of politics to try to capture the attention of as many and as much of the relevant publics as possible. Success at this effort was the surest way to victory in public policy; it was the surest way to defeat the more direct, internal strategies of competitors as well. The reasons for this fact were again inherent in the specific elements, the contours, of this new American politics—in nationalized social forces, reformed political institutions, truncated electoral and institutional coalitions, further structural changes aimed at communicating rather than negotiating, and indirect and reciprocal influences from the mass media of information. Yet if the core concept is right—if the essence of this bifurcated politics was those coalitions, limited both in scope and in duration—then the details of its elaboration cannot in principle be taken too much further. Political flux cannot be intellectual stasis; practical malleability cannot be analytic precision.

If there is a certain analytic disappointment in that, in its failure to permit intellectual closure, there is also a scholarly—and very practical—promise. Indeed, if the convention as a political institution has been constantly changing, that change is itself an inherent argument that politics seen through the convention will continue to change. Viewed one way, the convention has a new central activity, a recognizably different cast of participants, revised lines of internal conflict, further institutional adjustments, even a very different kind of external impact—and these changes promise additional, further consequences all their own. Yet seen another way, these are also a small sample of a larger national politics, a bifurcated politics shifting rapidly and additionally around them. In that role, these changes offer one further, final assurance. If the convention has changed this much, in the postwar period alone, then surely it is pointless to seek a fundamental and fixed portrait of the national politics shifting simultaneously and again inevitably around it.

Afterword

Evolution and Reform beyond 1988: The Future of the National Party Convention

When the story of the convention has been told in its own right, and when that story has been reanalyzed as a guide to national politics, the *future* of the institution remains unaddressed. In one sense, recent history says that this is as it should be. Most of the developments in the postwar convention, along with most of the shifts in the politics around it, were unforeseen by even the most thoughtful contemporary observers. Nevertheless, the sheer amount of change encompassed by these developments, even in just the postwar conventions, certainly argues that there will be more, just as the major specific dimensions of this change provide insights, or at least tantalizing hints, about the direction and shape of the institutional future. Accordingly, an attempt to address the future of the convention, inherently speculative and necessarily less rigorous, becomes the final step in an aspiringly comprehensive work.

Extrapolations from each of the major elements of evolutionary change are one obvious means for projecting this future. The nationalization of presidential politics outside the convention, for example, and the shifting social identities of the delegates within it, are factors which will almost necessarily continue to change, with an associated potential for further influence on the convention. Indeed, a special place among these evolutionary forces must be reserved for press behavior and emerging patterns of media coverage, because they led most directly to the bifurcated convention. Further deliberate alterations of some key aspects of institutional structure—the mental imposition of further self-conscious reforms—are another obvious means of projecting the future. There are already major reforms on the landscape for 1988, in the southern regional primary, for example, and there are reforms on the horizon which dwarf even these, including a national presidential primary. In principle, such developments might revolutionize the convention, or they might be formal alterations without much practical effect. Finally, numerous partially independent interactions among these elements will surely be the most common further influences on the convention. Whether—and how—the convention might still *make* a nomination, for example, along with the possible cumulative impact of numerous continuing adjustments by the individual states, are questions with the greatest potential influence on the future of the institution. A search for interactions among the elements of evolution and reform is thus the final available means toward projecting a future for the national party convention.

Evolution: The Character of Politics and the Nature of Participants

Many of the changes in the postwar convention were the product not of deliberate alterations by convention principals but of the impact of general, often gradual, social forces—or of ramifications from these. Accordingly, those forces which had already proved consequential can be examined again, to see where they might be going and whether—and where—the convention might go with them. Among these, the components of the nationalization of presidential politics are the most obvious and most obviously significant. But the category of changing social forces with a potential impact on the convention as an institution surely includes further shifts in the character of convention participants as well, as it includes—last but certainly not least—further change in the nature of press coverage of conventions.

The components of the nationalization of politics—rising governmental activity, declining party organizations, burgeoning media of information, and a shifting social base for politics—changed enough in just the postwar period, and came together with such impact in the early 1950s, that no analyst can dismiss their potential for further surprises. Moreover, lesser redirections of these forces are evident everywhere in the late 1980s. There is a temporary halt in the growing policy role of national government. There is a new infusion of activist, issue-oriented officials in both political parties. There is increasing competition for existing national media both from the appearance of new, aspiringly national contenders and from the increased ease of entry for regional challengers. There is continued movement in occupational structure and demographic patterns in the society at large.

Nevertheless, none of these trends, these hesitations, or these hesitant countertrends—or even all of them together—appears likely to reverse the general drift of the nationalization of politics. The balance among national, state, and local governments, for example, might well shift marginally from one presidential administration to another. Yet demands for governmental intervention in society, and the contest to expand or contain the national government within that contest, show no signs of abating. Political parties as organizations might acquire a new generation of officeholders; their formal prerogatives within party politics show no signs of becoming more extensive as a result. Competition and diffusion among mass media of information, the clearest exception to this lack of evolutionary impact, would have their effects, indirectly, in quite other areas. The underlying shift in the character of society, toward ever higher educational levels and an ever more white-collar economy, gives no indication of moving in a fundamentally different direction.

The fate of a changing cast of convention participants, then, is the other evolutionary element from the politics of presidential selection which had been critical to reshaping the postwar convention and which is potentially critical to influencing its further evolution. Like the nationalization of politics, changing participants produced substantial impacts in the comparatively short period after World War II—and really in the much more concentrated period after 1968. Like the nationalization of politics, changing convention participants produced these impacts without the explicit intention of individual actors, though the changing nature of participants was at least a partial product of deliberate actions elsewhere. Finally, like the nationalization of politics, this other major evolutionary factor is presumably capable of extension, retrenchment, or redirection, with related impacts on the convention. Despite all that, it is another similarity which is most telling for the probable impact of any further shifts in the character of convention delegates.

This is the extent to which the principal thrust of that shift, from the official party to the organized interests as the main vehicle for nominating campaigns and from party officials to interested partisans as convention delegates, seems not only set in its general direction but largely impervious to the other social forces, which are themselves gradual, informal, and incremental. There was, admittedly, an evident countertrend, in the move to reintroduce party officials as delegates to their national convention, by means of ex officio status if necessary. But there was a leading and evident element of extrapolation as well, in exaggerated conflicts between the nominee and the delegates and in the procedural responses to that conflict within the convention, which followed the shift from party officials to interested partisans. Yet once again there is also good reason to expect sharp limits on both these contrary tendencies.

The move to reintroduce party officials to the convention is most easily observed among the Democrats, where it was pursued explicitly through "add-on delegates" in 1980, through "superdelegates" in 1984, and through even more of the same for 1988. Yet the product of these initiatives, impressive enough in raw numbers, did not begin to reintroduce these officials to the actual campaigns for a presidential nomination. Accordingly, they did not so much shape that contest as adjust themselves to it, with the result that their major potential impact was in meliorating conflicts inside the convention rather than in reintroducing alleged partisan virtues—concern with broad-based constituencies, with a moderate program, and above all ultimate electability—into the politics of presidential selection. Indeed, these counterreforms appeared at the very point when distinctions between party officials and interested partisans were becoming increasingly blurred, as party office itself came increasingly to be filled by interest group representatives and independent issue activists.

The major counterweight to this development, the major shift among convention participants which would extend existing trends, is equally obvious. It is the tendency of the previous shift toward interested partisans to ramify through the convention as an institution, influencing both general convention strategies and specific structural arrangements. In fact, it is probably no longer necessary for the underlying shift to continue, much less to be extrapolated, in order for it to heighten the recurring conflicts between nominee and delegates, in order to encourage efforts by both sides to use the convention to publicize their most favored issues and causes, and in order for them to try additionally to modify the structure of convention committees and the rules for floor procedure. Simple consolidation of previous gains is probably enough to guarantee all this. The reintroduction of party officials, of course, might be sufficient to see that these developments go no further; it is hardly sufficient to do much more.

Internal convention conflict stemming from a shifting cast of par-

ticipants, then, seems likely to remain in a rough kind of stasis, changing only idiosyncratically with the events of a particular presidential
year. On the other hand, if the interested partisans should become
recurringly predominant, there are tools at their disposal to make the
convention contribute increasingly to their causes. Augmented use of
the party platform, in both publicizing their agenda and trying to give
it influence with subsequent presidencies, is one example; augmented
intrusion by the convention into the operation of the national party
committees is another. Likewise, if emerging nominees and top party
officials should become recurringly predominant instead, or recurringly
concerned with the attitudes and activities of the interested partisans,
there are tools at their disposal to retaliate. They could, for example,
shift committee business further from the convention proper, or they
could place additional limits on access to the floor.

Evolution: Patterns of Coverage and Possibilities for Adaptation

Ironically, both developments point toward the same eventual outcome. If the interested partisans are increasingly successful, the remaining strategy for nominees and top party officials is obvious—
reform. If nominees and party officials are increasingly successful, dissident delegates likewise have only one alternative short of recurrent
defeat—again reform. Moreover, deliberate alterations sufficient to
rework the convention context, and even to terminate many postwar
convention trends, are not just theoretically available. They have supporters; they have draft legislation; they are incipiently on the national
agenda. Before anyone is likely to implement them, however, there
are additional changes in the operation of the convention which, while
less potentially far-reaching, are more certain to follow from evolutionary trends already in evidence.

Changing patterns of convention coverage by the mass media, and
the inevitable adaptations by convention participants to them, are the
central element in these other evolutionary trends. The potential for
media coverage to shape the convention is inherent in an era when
campaign launchings—which is to say, external impacts—are the major convention product. Indeed, that potential began to reach a new
kind of realization in 1980, one driven much further in 1984, with
cuts in the coverage of conventions by the television networks, with
the coming of the bifurcated convention in response, and with the
simultaneous need by all participants to adjust their behavior to this

brave new media world. The bifurcated convention was the latest twist on the convention as an evolving political institution; it is the newest stimulus for the next incarnation of the convention as well.

Yet there was a more concrete though less metaphorically dramatic aspect to a new politics of convention media, one which ran along-side—and contributed powerfully to—an increasingly bifurcated convention. This involved the changing composition of the total array of news media which provided their own reporters to cover the convention. The conventions of 1980, and again of 1984, saw a tremendous growth in the number of state and local media, especially television stations, which sent their own correspondents to the national convention. In one sense, this represented a greater variety in coverage, multiplying the points of public information while it diversified and localized them. More media outlets were offering slices of the convention; far more reporters were looking for locally relevant stories.[1] Yet in an odd but more consequential sense, both these developments largely continued, then buttressed, and then extended existing trends.

For example, the growth of state and local reportage, and the hunt for state and local "angles" on convention stories, served principally to reinforce the shift in the main activity of the convention toward the launching of various external campaigns. At the extreme, this augmented the tensions from those campaigns, as when the Ohio press picked up shoving matches between Carter and Kennedy supporters in the Ohio delegation at the Democratic convention of 1980—and national media took these (state) stories and made them truly national instead. More often, however, this growing presence of state and local news media merely added to the utility of state delegations as launching pads for *state and local* political concerns. The New Jersey delegation to the Republican convention of 1980, for example, could devote its off-duty hours to unveiling potential Republican candidacies for governor. The Louisiana delegation to the Democratic convention of 1984 could concentrate on showcasing a much wider array of state party protocandidates. Many other states could do the same sort of thing, albeit in a less grand and consciously choreographed fashion.

Ironically, on the other hand, this increased utility of the state delegations, especially for state party and public officials, did not lead these individuals to a heightened involvement with the full convention and thus to extra efforts at restraining internal conflict. Probably, state and local officials were less likely to try to use even their part of the national convention, even to launch purely state and local activities, when the full convention promised to be too conflictual. But more to the point, if the addition of more and more state and local media gave these officials further incentive to use their delegations for their own political purposes, quite apart from the general level of combat, it also increased their incentive to stay out of that combat. Like the presidential nominees at the center of the convention, major state and local party and public officials could best orchestrate their piece of the gathering by avoiding extended conflict. Unlike those nominees, however, they could avoid much of that conflict simply by taking no position on it, letting it play itself out as it might.

Seen differently, efforts by state political figures to insulate state and local coverage of their part of the convention from conflicts swirling through the full gathering were only confirmation, and reinforcement, for the arrival of the bifurcated convention, for the coming of an environment featuring one convention on site and another on screen, at home. Yet the emerging composite pattern of media coverage actually went much further in reinforcing this growing disjunction. For while the big-three television networks were cutting total transmissions—that was, after all, the initial stimulus for the bifurcated convention—and while they were being joined by ever more state and local media, they were also being joined by new *national* media, which moved back toward the old gavel-to-gavel standard. One of these was Cable-Satellite Public Affairs Network (C-SPAN), the Washington-based governmental affairs broadcaster; another was Cable News Network (CNN), the Atlanta-based public affairs station.[2] Both offered substantially more coverage direct from the podium. But both offered additionally, at a second level of impact, reinforcement to the segmentation of the convention audience—and that was probably their most important impact.

Those who were most interested in the convention could now watch it, live and in full, on C-SPAN and CNN. Those who were less interested could catch the expurgated transmission on the major national networks. This tendency, then, further reinforced the move toward the bifurcated convention, by reducing the demand for additional network coverage while reducing the likelihood that anyone would feel deprived of essential elements of the convention by the arrival of this bifurcated coverage pattern. As a result, what is strategically necessary in this new coverage era is not an assault on media patterns of coverage—these are both more varied and less responsive to pressure than in the past. Rather, what is necessary and perhaps inevitable is adaptation by all participants—by orthodox political actors as well as by professional news people.

In this, it is clear that most network news officials have been bothered by the extent to which their coverage is now shaped by the formal convention schedule, and hence by informal maneuvering among top convention officials. It is clear as well that many—not all—orthodox political participants have been bothered by the fact that a network focus on major agenda items has in effect limited coverage of their particular issues and conflicts. The obvious strategy for both, and the place where their desires might intersect, is in deviation from the formal convention agenda. For news officials, this could mean as little as a decision to spend less time covering presentations at the podium or as much as a plan to do more editing and reviewing—to handle live convention coverage as if it were the evening news. For participants, this could mean as little as redoubling their efforts to alert reporters to emerging items of conflict or as much as an effort to utilize, reschedule, or disrupt major convention speeches. Yet because these adaptations are already at a second level of analysis, depending crucially on what the participants of 1980 and 1984 have deduced from their experiences, there is little point in trying to predict them further.

Interaction: The Return of a Nominating Convention

One further implication from these three evolutionary trends is perhaps the most obvious, the most inherent of all: the presidential nomination itself is exceedingly unlikely to return to the national convention on a regular basis. The nationalization of politics removed that nomination, informally, from convention confines. Reform of the process of delegate selection then institutionalized the construction of a nominating majority, effectively and almost formally, outside the convention. The continuing interaction of these elements, of evolution and reform, appears sufficient to guarantee that this construction will not return to the convention on even an intermittent basis.

Yet all this does not imply that construction of a nominating majority might not return in some deviant year in the late twentieth century, in response to those acts of nature—illness, injury, or dramatic revelation—for which the convention still sits as the nominator of last resort. Indeed, the question is not so much whether the convention will ever again make a nomination. The question is when it might be called upon to do so; how an institution which has not undertaken this crucial activity for forty years (or more) would perform when called on; and finally, whether the general public, as well as important segments of the activist community, would still accept the convention as a legitimate nominator—or whether the exercise of this residual power would so outrage an implicit sense of propriety that it would become in effect the last nominating activity by a national party convention, leading to the sort of self-conscious reform which would make the convention function in a radically different manner if it survived to function at all.

If it is pointless even in principle to set an estimated date for this scenario, the character of majority building in a postreform convention—the question of how a true nominating convention would work—is scarcely more receptive to precise speculation. The mechanics of delegate selection, the nature of nominating campaigns, the expected central activity at a normal convention, its recurring lines of conflict, even the place of the mass media—all these have changed since the convention last made a presidential nomination. Beyond that, the character of a true nominating convention is partially dependent on the details of the year in which subsequent nominating activity would become essential, that is, on the circumstances by which the front-runner was derailed, on the character of the field of remaining contenders, on the identity of the delegates for front-runner and opponents, and on the situation among available alternatives. Nevertheless, certain continuing elements in a changed convention politics are almost inevitably relevant to the construction of any delegate majority.

The first is a decline in the size of those delegate blocs which are automatically available for bargaining and brokerage. The handpicking of sizable blocs through centralized slate making is increasingly difficult. Formal arrangements to create them afterward, as with the "unit rule," have effectively disappeared. There are still three main devices for assembling collectivities at the convention—state delegations, candidate campaigns, and the organized interests—but these too are of changing relevance to the formation of an ultimate majority. State delegations still organize the daily life of delegates, and that role reserves their place in any bargaining structure. Moreover, Republican delegates often manifest a concern with state loyalty and state advantage, a concern often lacking among their Democratic counterparts. Yet the role of such delegations in both political parties is also markedly in decline, as the mechanics of delegate selection and the politics of presidential nomination combine to fragment these delegations both formally and informally.

In their place, candidate campaigns have gained notably in prominence. The basic organizational change in the selection of delegates, after all, was from party-based to candidate-based campaigns for a nomination. Accordingly, delegates in an actual nominating convention could be expected to be receptive to cues both from the staff of the campaign which had produced them and from their fellow candidate supporters. Staffs have the extra advantage of being organized and in place, yet they suffer a major inherent disadvantage. In any plausible scenario for majority building, the front-runner has presumably been derailed—otherwise there would be no nominating convention—but no candidate defeated by that front-runner is likely to be the choice of delegates entering the convention committed to someone else. Moreover, once a candidate or candidates have become irrelevant, the influence of their (former) campaigns could be expected to decline.

The obvious alternatives, with an ever-greater role in delegate selection and an ever-greater place in the convention politics to follow, are the interest groups and issue organizations which created—and constitute—the postreform delegate population. Again there are important differences between the parties, with manifestly more explicit and coordinated activity by such groups at Democratic conventions and more emphasis on simple ideology on the one hand and on a continuing tension between organized interests and the official party on the other at Republican conventions. Yet the shift toward interested partisans, with their focus on group identifications and ideological concerns and with their usual effort to use the convention to cap the nominating campaign, is a trend broadly applicable to both political parties. If state delegations are in decline, and when candidate bonds are loosened, the organized interests are the obvious alternative rallying point.

The larger question for the long-run impact of a modern nominating convention, however, is whether most participants (and their audience) would go on to treat the need for this activity as a surprising, theoretically undesirable, but practically successful venture, so intermittent an occurrence that one could pay it no further heed, or whether the behavior of such a convention, when combined with the identity of the nominee and his or her fate in November, would lead to demands for reform—for deliberate structural change so as to prevent a re-currence. The answer is again partially dependent on the details of the concrete instance, as witnessed this time by a national television audience. Yet there are also changes in the politics of presidential selection with an obvious bearing on the likely public response, and these bode ill for the reception of any true nominating convention.

Most concretely, changes in the character of the delegates have given them central concerns at variance with those of a more general public while making it less likely that they would perform well even by standards both groups shared. The delegates themselves have been moving toward the ideological extremes and toward specific, evident subgroup identifications. The general public not only is less ideolog-ically articulated and more moderate but has an apparent preference for an orientation toward a "public interest." Beyond that, these same concerns on the part of the delegates probably reduce their ability to form a quick and simple majority, by whatever standards they might use. Indeed, the very absence of large and brokerable blocs, a much more neutral triumph of structural democratization, risks making the convention *look* less appealing, less decorous and less effective, quite apart from its representative character or the identity of its ultimate nominee. If viewers were also bothered by the facelessness of the del-egates, that is, by the fact that they had largely been elected as un-knowns but were now selecting a possible future president, the dis-pleasure of the general public might be complete.

In a very different way—at a different level of abstraction—there is also an unswerving grand trajectory in the movement of presidential nominations across American history, one that is surely not irrelevant to the response of that general public, or indeed of particular elites within it. In this, party representatives in Congress originally seized the presidential nomination. They gave way quickly enough to a larger and more geographically representative set of party officials. Those party officials in turn gave way, gradually and grudgingly, to rank-and-file identifiers in state presidential primaries and participatory conventions. And a sense of legitimacy has moved, ineluctably, with them all. If the convention then reasserted its practical ability to serve as a nominator—and especially if it did so in a nonconsensual fash-ion—this act might just as practically violate that fundamental sense of legitimacy, producing a chorus of demands for further reform.[3] Public sentiment already supports reform in the abstract; this particular outcome would surely produce a reform leadership as well. The course of reform politics would then determine the fate of—and perhaps eliminate—this nominating possibility.

Interaction: Evolutionary Change through Incremental Alterations

Such a reform politics would also provide, of course, one very concrete instance of the other grand means by which the convention might change, and by which it might change the politics around it—reform, that is, deliberate alteration in the rules, procedures, and formal structures of the convention and of the process of presidential selection which precedes it. Reform institutionalized the nomination outside the convention proper; reform was central to a shift in the participants inside, a major alteration which had set off numerous subsequent changes. Presumably, subsequent reforms could achieve the same magnitude of impact. In any case, major actors continue to make the attempt. In the 1980s, there have been numerous self-conscious, individual efforts for change in the states. There have been emerging, coordinated efforts at much more sweeping alterations nationwide. There are proposals under discussion which would dwarf even these.

This is not to say that such efforts are destined to bear fruit. Much less is it to say that successful efforts would imply the realization of intended impacts. The whole experience of deliberate reform in the politics of presidential selection is as much a history of unintended consequences, certainly with regard to the convention, as it is of the achievement of planned political change. Accordingly, the mental imposition of various reforms is even more speculative than the extrapolation of current social trends. Nevertheless, that fact did not dampen the enthusiasm of past generations of reformers; it is unlikely to have much relevance to the fate of future reforms. An effort to speculate on the future of the convention, in turn, can hardly wait for the resolution of these analytic problems, any more than it can wait for the natural extrapolation of broad and general social forces.

What this history of the postwar convention affirms more positively, however, is the analytic near certainty that most further changes in the convention will feature the *interaction* of evolution and reform. Even the most grand and general, abstract social forces have worked through existing institutional arrangements, sometimes while conducing toward the promulgation of deliberate reforms. Even the most self-consciously theoretical and deliberate, abstract structural reforms have acquired their impact when imposed on existing social forces, an interaction which probably began in the minds of the human actors who proposed them. The institutionalization of the nomination outside the convention, for example, resulted principally from the impact of the nationalization of politics on the institution of the convention, before it was codified through changes in the mechanics of presidential selection, just as change in the cast of convention participants, a direct and immediate response to sweeping structural reform, was still dependent for its ultimate impact on changes in the larger society on which it was imposed.

Such interactions can hardly fail to govern subsequent reform initiatives. Indeed, the true boundary between evolution and reform, where the changes which result might almost be ascribed to either, is probably found in those self-conscious, rolling alterations in the mechanics of delegate selection in the individual states which became a regular feature of politics in the postreform era. The first great round of reform in delegate selection between 1968 and 1972 was different— in its underlying theory, its institutional scope, and its practical impact. Subsequent lesser rounds followed in every presidential interim.[4] Yet if the individual pieces of these were, by definition, calculated and deliberate, the whole quickly came to represent a response as much to a shifting environment as to any intellectual doctrine, as much a feature of continuing politics as of any assault on politics as usual. This was true for each election between 1972 and 1984; it is evidently true for 1988 as well; it is likely to be true for any succeeding election.

Moreover, these limited, individual, state-based adumbrations, even when summed for the nation as a whole, have contributed less and less over time toward change in the national party convention—and most portents suggest that this too will continue to be the case. The precise outlines of the institutional matrix for delegate selection, along with the precise details of the presidential politics within it, have varied inevitably for every presidential nomination after 1972. Yet the fundamental outlines of that matrix and that politics have remained roughly stable since reform became an accepted political fact. Between 1968 and 1972, these formal mechanics changed enormously, to a system based principally on candidate primaries, secondarily on participatory conventions. After that, the system has remained roughly stable. Between 1968 and 1972, the organizational and strategic demands of the nominating politics within this matrix made it necessary for every candidate to create an independent, national, personal campaign and to put it to work from the beginning of the contest. After that, in both parties, no candidate with serious prospects for nomination failed to follow the pattern.

As a result of this institutional continuity and operational stability, the nature of convention delegates also assumed a rough continuity in the postreform era. At first, there was drama (and consequence) in the eclipse of the official party by the organized interests and in the replacement of party officials by interested partisans. Yet while the share of each general category continued to vary from election to election, and while the precise identities of the advantaged individuals varied a great deal more, it was the overall change in the characteristics of these delegates which shaped the convention as a context for internal politicking. Indeed, as time passes, as a changing society interacts with these reforms, and as the distinction between party officials and interested partisans begins to blur, further incremental changes even in these basic arrangements seem increasingly unlikely to alter the convention as an environment for politicking.

The sum of individual changes from year to year, then, does not threaten to change either the nature of nominating politics or the character of the delegates selected. On the one hand, without consequential change in those elements, there is little reason to expect a change in the convention as a context for internal politicking or a change in the array of efforts to influence the external impact of that convention—or at least there is no reason to expect such piecemeal reforms to contribute to a change in these key operational realms. On the other hand, there have been larger reforms in the wind since 1984, and there are observers who believe that these do have the potential for a much greater impact on the mechanics of delegate selection. If they do, they might well ramify through the convention and promise more consequential change, through reform.

Reform: The Coming of One or More Regional Primaries

The leading example of this possibility of further reform is an incipient "southern regional primary." Simple in conception and practical in its capacity to be realized, this plan requires individual southern states merely to move their presidential primaries to the same coordinated day, early in the nominating contest, so that the American South will become the premier—and decisive—arena for presidential politics. The motivation behind this plan is equally clear. Democratic party and public officials throughout the South have felt for some time that other regions of the country, especially the Northeast, have been determining presidential nominations, giving the Democratic nominee a set of un-attractive group identifications and an extreme ideological cast. Many Democratic strategists outside the South have agreed with this diag-nosis and have encouraged a response, citing the ability of the putative majority party to lose four of the last five presidential elections.[5]

In any case, the essentials of a southern regional primary were in place by late 1987. Alabama, Arkansas, Florida, Georgia, Kentucky, Louisiana, Maryland, Mississippi, Missouri, North Carolina, Okla-homa, Tennessee, Texas, and Virginia had all—in a marvel of cal-culated and coordinated political engineering—moved their primaries to the same temporal spot. Mississippi, Missouri, Oklahoma, South Carolina, and Virginia had all moved their caucuses there as well. The delegations from these states represent 30 percent of the total convention, 60 percent of those needed for nomination. Their date, the second Tuesday in March, is early enough to be decisive, following only the Iowa caucuses and the New Hampshire primary. If this new procedural stratagem works as intended, then, it will change the course of presidential politics. That alone would have the greatest potential consequences for the national party convention. But at a second level, if this plan works as intended, it will also change the character of convention delegates, limiting the organized interests and boosting the official party while reining in the ideological extremes and strengthening the center.

The implicit assumptions behind this reform, however, run opposite not only to the normal course of politics in the postreform era—that in some sense was part of their intent—but to the evolutionary thrust of those forces which have become central determinants of that politics, forces which do not appear to be purely (or even largely) dependent on the institutional arrangements through which their influence op-erates. For example, the southern regional primary is premised on the assumption that the southern electorate is noticeably distinctive. Oth-erwise, southern delegate contests could still be decisive without changing the character of presidential politics. Likewise, the plan is premised on the assumption that this arrangement is sufficient to overcome the normal dynamics of nominating politics, under which the bandwagon rolls from the very first contest. Otherwise, the south-ern outcome would be shaped crucially by preceding encounters. Fi-nally, the plan assumes that the political character of the delegates would change in tandem with these arrangements. Otherwise, the subsequent convention would present the same recurring and familiar problems for any—even any southern-backed—emerging nominee.

Despite the nationalization of politics, there is some evidence that the South still differs as a region on a number of politically relevant attitudes, although these differences are just as clearly declining over time.[6] More to the point, their importance is called into question by a fundamental fact of reformed nominating politics. Those who turn out in presidential primaries and participatory conventions are better educated, more informed, and more intense in their preferences, and they are singularly likely to make a national—not a regional—choice. This tendency is reinforced by the usual nominating dynamic, under which the field begins to narrow sharply after the Iowa and New Hampshire contests, so that success or failure in those states would most probably determine the available choices for the southern primary electorate and could well sway candidate outcomes in the South. Under those conditions, the new regional primary would most probably work not as its creators intend but in one of two other ways. Either it would become the final filter before the decisive contests, which would occur subsequently (and elsewhere), or it would actually and successfully terminate the campaign—by selecting among a set of options created in Iowa and New Hampshire.

As if that were not enough, the campaigns which might hope to benefit from this reform, like all the serious nominating campaigns before them, would have to be independent, personal, and national in composition. Indeed, this particular implication of reformed nominating politics is powerfully reinforced by a southern regional primary, because every candidate has to be prepared to campaign—just three weeks after the opening contest—in all of at least fourteen states at once. Candidates, accordingly, would be forced more than ever to rely on that same population of political actors which such campaigns have necessarily tapped in recent years, that is, only tangentially on party officials and heavily on interest group representatives and independent issue activists. Thus this first major, deliberate, prospective reform—the creation of a southern regional primary—appears to have the same reduced potential for changing the convention as that first major social extrapolation, in the component elements of the nationalization of politics.

Yet this device has a second major implication, one that renders its impact in 1988 even less consequential for the longer run. For whether a southern regional primary accomplishes its stated goals or not, it is sure to be an unstable reform. That is, it is very likely to produce pressures for *further* reform, and these are likely to overwhelm any direct impact it might have. It would not even have to affect the character of presidential politics in order to increase the pressures for counterpart arrangements in the other regions. Indeed, these stirrings were already in evidence by early 1987, in the mountain states and in the states around the Great Lakes, and other states would surely come to understand that their influence was dependent on being part of a regional bloc. The trend might conceivably reach the point where the national committee or even Congress felt compelled to rationalize the resulting process, by mandating a nationwide system of regional primaries. But even if reform politics stopped well short of that outcome, the southern regional primary of 1988—however it works—is not likely to work the same way ever again, because it is likely to be joined by other regional primaries.

It could also be joined by an ironic prognosis: either this comprehensive system of regional primaries would once again not produce much political change or it would lead on to ever more serious reform. The first option still appears the more likely. A comprehensive arrangement of regional primaries would probably exaggerate the bandwagon effect. Even without a separate Iowa and New Hampshire—and certainly with them—the first grand contest would effectively limit the field to a handful of major internal contenders. The next grand contest would probably settle the outcome, although some form of proportionality in the allocation of delegates might encourage the losers to struggle on for one more round. Beyond that, serious campaigns would still have to be formed as they have been throughout the postreform era, so that the identity of national convention delegates should also change marginally and idiosyncratically from year to year. As a result, even earlier nominations than before, with roughly the same cast of ultimate delegates, seem the most likely product of a proliferation of regional primaries.

The alternative is a more destabilizing outcome. If these huge primaries did confirm differing candidate preferences—if one candidate could win in the first regional primary, a second in the second, and so on—then suddenly, by means of deliberate reform, the nomination is likely to be thrust back into the convention. This would be the undeniable and direct product of self-conscious alterations in the mechanics of delegate selection. As with any number of other deliberate interventions, it would work almost opposite to the intentions of its framers. Yet the construction of a nominating majority at the national party convention would be a necessity, and the dynamics of majority building in a reformed convention—a process which has never yet occurred and with which no analyst can claim experience—could take any number of foreseeable turns.

More foreseeable, in any case, is the external response. For if the move to regional primaries was justified to the general public both as rationalizing the process and as increasing their control over the nomination—and it would almost have to be justified that way in order to get support—and if the move to regional primaries was backed by party and public officials as the means to make their particular regions determinative, as it is already being backed for 1988, then the return of the nomination to the convention might be viewed as legitimate *by almost no one*. In this sense, it would be an extremely unstable reform, likely to realize this possibility only once—before being reformed yet again. The direction of reform here is also very clear: this is one of the major routes to the creation of a national primary and thus to the one final reform with the most radical implications for the character and operation of the national party convention.

Reform: A National Primary and the Convention

The national primary as an idea is hardly new. Once nominations to most public offices came to be handled directly through public primary elections, rather than indirectly through an official party structure, the presidency became an obvious target for such treatment. In most visions, there would be nationwide Democratic and Republican primaries, presumably at some date late in the spring. The two victors would then square off for the general election campaign.[7] The details of this arrangement—details of the highest consequence, as it turns out—remain open both to serious debate and to the play of practical politics. But the national presidential primary has almost a historical inevitability. That is, it is in some sense the logical culmination of two hundred years of American selection procedures: first the congressional party caucus, then the national party convention, then a mix of state primary elections and caucuses, and finally the national presidential primary, eliminating official parties and exalting the individual voter.

The national primary, in any case, is much more than a mere procedural possibility, buttressed by the alleged drift of American political history, for it is clear that a number of evident practical routes lead ineluctably to this reform. The misfiring of regional primaries, of course, whether they had been formally or only informally created, would lead at least to demands for further rationalization of the process and for a return of the ultimate decision to the general public. The national primary is a logical institutional response. The need for any national party convention actually to make a presidential nomination, regardless of the stimulus, is likely to lead to similar demands. Beyond that, the next crisis at a national convention seems likely, by itself, to bring on the national primary. It was the disastrous Democratic convention of 1968 which led to the last great round of reform; whenever the next disastrous convention occurs, it should inevitably lead to demands for more. Finally, lesser currents already present in conventions might produce such an outcome without the need for a crisis. The general struggle between nominees and dissident delegates, for example, or the more specific effort to extend or restrain the institutional influence of the convention, leaves each side with reform as a last line of defense.

Regardless, the major reform in waiting is also the major available reform with a guaranteed impact on the convention.[8] This is true on the usual evolutionary grounds. The national primary would be such a substantial change, involving not just a massive revision in the formal mechanics of presidential nomination but a huge associated transformation in the practical nature of campaigns, that it could potentially reach into every facet of the convention. But this time, a guaranteed impact is inherent on simple reform grounds too. Thus there are arrangements for a national primary which *abolish* the convention; there are arrangements which make a return of the nomination more likely; and there are numerous intermediate arrangements, the most plausible of all, which could hardly fail to shape not just the locus of the nomination but the character of the delegates, the nature of major activities, the recurring lines of conflict, the contours of media coverage, and the ultimate impact on the general public.

The central procedural issue, even among proponents, is the question of what would constitute a sufficient plurality for nomination, and of how that plurality would be reached. Most arguments in favor of a national primary, along with most analyses of how it would actually work, concede that an absolute majority of the primary electorate is unlikely for one candidate if numerous contenders are free to enter. Although some candidates might announce their intention to run and then pull out when they failed to mount a national campaign, several serious contenders would surely last until the actual ballot, along with others who remained more to rally constituencies or to raise issues than with the realistic hope of being nominated for president. Accordingly, either some threshold well below a majority would have to be accepted to confirm a nomination or a second primary—a so-called runoff—would have to be instituted to create an absolute majority between the top two contenders.

In principle, of course, there is an alternative. If no candidate reaches a sufficient plurality in a first primary election, delegates for all the candidates could be dispatched to a national convention, to construct a majority in the time-honored fashion. In practice, this is a highly unlikely recourse. The abstract justification for a move to the national primary almost has to involve rationalizing the overall process while putting its ultimate choice in the hands of individual citizens. Reinvesting the nomination in the convention is a move in precisely the opposite direction. Moreover, it runs counter to not just the arguments but all the foreseeable stimuli for creation of the national presidential primary. If a convention explosion were the impetus to reform, reinventing the convention (albeit indirectly) is hardly an acceptable procedural response. If anomalies in the regional primary were the impetus, whether those regional primaries also produced a decision by the convention or merely devalued voters in later regional groupings, reinvigorating the convention is again an inconsistent answer.

The fate of the national party convention, accordingly, is crucially dependent not just on the specific details of a national primary plan but on its precise and specific references to the convention. That fate is made no more secure by the fact that these details would almost inevitably be secondary, extremely secondary, to arrangements for creating a sufficient plurality—and would thus be available as bargaining counters for the reform politics which had to produce the overall plan. With that level of complexity and at that extended remove, the precise details relevant to the convention can hardly be foreseen. What can be enumerated is only an array of institutional possibilities, which still cover a remarkable range.

At the extreme are those plans, not extreme in their prospects, in which the national party convention simply disappears. A national primary does not require a subsequent convention, and there are arguments for eliminating it when the primary is adopted. The two major-party nominees could still make nationally televised acceptance speeches after the primary, and these could be used to set out the themes, issues, and constituency appeals for the election campaign.

Indeed, general public attention might actually be enhanced by this arrangement. A vice presidential address, or even a keynote speech, could also be added, to retain supportive convention activities—and to eliminate those elements for which nominees have never cared. The campaign leading up to the primary would otherwise be responsible for introducing the candidate. The campaign leading away from it, including televised presidential debates, would yield the necessary impressions of the nominee as a potential president. The convention, in this view, could be discarded as extraneous at best, potentially damaging at worst.

At some remove are those plans in which a national primary election still makes the effective nomination but in which the convention is retained to introduce the nominee, rally partisan forces, and offer a party platform. How this version works would be dependent in part on convention rules but largely on the mechanics of delegate selection, and thus on the character of convention delegates. In one alternative, the candidate would be allowed to pick the delegates directly—in effect, to distribute tickets—after the national primary. This should guarantee a most pacific convention, one minimizing internal tensions, concentrating on orchestration for the fall campaign, and featuring a much foreshortened agenda—filling two or three evenings of televised proceedings.

If the convention—and delegates—were to be retained, however, it is unlikely that losing candidates would be denied *any* representation, and even less likely that the nominee or these losers would be entitled to select delegates after the event. Accordingly, candidates might well have to field a full slate of delegates before the national primary and might thus be influenced in creating this slate by the need to create a full and national nominating campaign—much as they are now. Many of the current tensions between delegates and candidates would thus be transferred into even a temporally shortened convention, again providing variability in the extent to which the candidate could orchestrate the convention but also providing variability in the extent to which the television networks might find this conflict worthy of coverage.

If new procedural rules went so far as to allow delegates for the other contenders to attend the convention—it is either that or make the delegate contest effectively winner-take-all—then this transfer of existing conflicts would in fact be guaranteed. Indeed, there would be less reason than in the current era for these delegates to concentrate on anything other than using the convention to salvage something from the nominating campaign, presumably by using it to publicize their particular issue and interest concerns. Once again there would be a regularly institutionalized struggle with the nominee, rising and falling in intensity from year to year, over orchestration of the convention. The result would thus be a heightened version of current convention dynamics. But the result would also be, in a final, ironic, and entirely fitting twist, further incentive not just for combat at individual conventions—the source of their inherent fascination—but for efforts at changing the convention as an institution, so as to benefit one side or another in this continuing convention struggle.

Notes

1. The Nomination and the Convention

1. The three inaugural conventions in direct line with current incarnations are presented comprehensively in James S. Chase, *Emergence of the Presidential Nominating Convention, 1789–1832* (Urbana, Ill.: University of Illinois Press, 1973).

2. Presidential nominations during the preconvention years, along with the shift into national nominating conventions, are covered fully and systematically in Richard P. McCormick, *The Presidential Game: The Origins of American Presidential Politics* (New York: Oxford University Press, 1982).

3. These and subsequent examples are most centrally collected in Congressional Quarterly, *National Party Conventions, 1831–1980* (Washington, D.C.: Congressional Quarterly, 1983). A richer and more extended complement is Richard C. Bain and Judith H. Parris, *Convention Decisions and Voting Records,* 2nd ed. (Washington, D.C.: Brookings, 1973).

4. Besides the central sources in note 3, the full sweep of examples is enumerated and organized in Paul T. David and Ralph M. Goldman, "Presidential Nominating Patterns," *Western Political Quarterly* 8 (1955), pp. 465–480. A different effort at categorization is Gary C. Byrne and Paul Marx, *The Great American Convention: A Political History of Presidential Elections* (Palo Alto, Calif.: Pacific Books, 1976).

5. An exception was William G. Carleton, "The Revolution in the Presidential Nominating Convention," *Political Science Quarterly* 72 (1957), pp. 224–240, whose prescience is emphasized by a tendency of texts on the subject to continue to assert the opposite even as much as a decade later.

6. A very useful collection on the topic is Rhodri Jeffrey-Jones and Bruce Collins, eds., *The Growth of Federal Power in American History* (Edinburgh: Scottish Press, 1983). A more narrowly fiscal survey is Charles L. Schultze, "Federal Spending: Past, Present, and Future," in Henry Owen and Schultze, eds.,

Setting National Priorities: The Next Ten Years (Washington, D.C.: Brookings, 1976), pp. 323–369.

7. The classic overview is Luther Frank Mott, *American Journalism, A History: 1690–1960*, 3rd ed. (New York: Macmillan, 1962). A helpful complement is Peter M. Sandman, David M. Rubin, and David B. Sachsman, *Media: An Introduction* (Englewood Cliffs, N.J.: Prentice-Hall, 1982), especially "Broadcasting," pp. 299–344.

8. V. O. Key, Jr., addressed this development and its implications repeatedly, especially in "Party Machine as Interest Group," in Key, *Politics, Parties, and Pressure Groups*, 5th ed. (New York: Thomas Y. Crowell, 1964), pp. 347–369, and more or less continuously in Key, *American State Politics: An Introduction* (New York: Alfred A. Knopf, 1956). A pointed and provocative recent treatment is Alan Ware, *The Breakdown of Democratic Party Organization, 1940–1980* (Oxford: Clarendon Press, 1985), especially "The Missing Party Work Force," pp. 70–106, and "The Decline of Party Structures," pp. 107–142.

9. Much of this material is comprehensively presented, with an appropriate disregard for political implications, in Victor R. Fuchs, *How We Live: An Economic Perspective on Americans from Birth to Death* (Cambridge, Mass.: Harvard University Press, 1983). An approach to many of these same facts as an explicitly political problem is Richard L. Rubin, *Party Dynamics: The Democratic Coalition and the Politics of Change* (New York: Oxford University Press, 1976), especially "Democrats and the Metropolis," pp. 11–29, and "The Changing Democratic Electorate and Elite Factionalism," pp. 87–106.

10. The coming of this self-consciously independent brand of politics was best captured in James Q. Wilson, *The Amateur Democrat: Club Politics in Three Cities* (Chicago: University of Chicago Press, 1962). A later elaboration is Norman M. Adler and Blanche D. Blank, *Political Clubs in New York* (New York: Praeger, 1975). An earlier attempt by Wilson himself to systematize the factors which caused people to approach politics in this manner is Peter B. Clark and James Q. Wilson, "Incentive Systems: A Theory of Organization," *Administrative Science Quarterly* 6 (1962), pp. 129–166.

11. An interesting attempt to formalize these criteria, using conventions from the period before the departure of the nomination, is William A. Gamson, "Coalition Formation at Presidential Nominating Conventions," *American Journal of Sociology* 68 (1962), pp. 157–171.

12. The process of amassing a delegate majority in 1952 was probably the most thoroughly studied of any such effort in American history, thanks to a five-volume series: Paul T. David, Malcolm Moos, and Ralph M. Goldman, eds., *Presidential Nominating Politics in 1952* (Baltimore: Johns Hopkins University Press, 1954), vols. I–V.

13. A participant-observer account of this critical dispute is Jacob M. Arvey, as told to John Madigan, "The Reluctant Candidate—An Inside Story," *The Reporter*, November 24, 1953, pp. 19–26.

14. The story of 1956, for both political parties, is presented in Charles A. H. Thomson and Frances M. Shattuck, *The 1956 Presidential Campaign* (Washington, D.C.: Brookings, 1960).

15. The campaigns of 1960 represented not just a new phase in presidential politics but a new phase in writing about that politics as well, in the inauguration

of what would become quadrennial reports from Theodore H. White. The first and best is White, *The Making of the President 1960* (New York: Atheneum, 1961). An extremely useful companion, focused on both conventions, is Paul Tillett, ed., *Inside Politics: The National Conventions, 1960* (Dobbs Ferry, N.Y.: Oceana Publications, 1962).

16. Again, both campaigns are chronicled extensively in David, Moos, and Goldman, eds., *Presidential Nominating Politics in 1952*.

17. For the evolution of this maneuver, see "Contest Exploitation and Convention Control," in Paul T. David, Ralph M. Goldman, and Richard C. Bain, *The Politics of National Party Conventions* (Washington, D.C.: Brookings, 1960), pp. 260–262.

18. The major events of Republican politics in 1964 are threaded through Theodore H. White, *The Making of the President 1964* (New York: Atheneum, 1965). Its scholarly companion is Milton C. Cummings, Jr., ed., *The National Election of 1964* (Washington, D.C.: Brookings, 1966).

2. Institutionalizing the Disappearance

1. The details of that gathering are recounted most tellingly in Theodore H. White, "The Chicago Convention: The Furies in the Streets," as a climax to the story of nominating politics, in White, *The Making of the President 1968* (New York: Atheneum, 1969), pp. 257–313. A reinforcing view is Albert Eisele, "Catastrophe—Chicago 1968," in Eisele, *Almost to the Presidency: A Biography of Two American Politicians* (Blue Earth, Minn.: Piper, 1972), pp. 344–364.

2. The links in this chain are extensively described in Byron E. Shafer, *Quiet Revolution: The Struggle for the Democratic Party and the Shaping of Post-Reform Politics* (New York: Russell Sage, 1983).

3. The recommendations themselves are contained in "Official Guidelines of the Commission," in Commission on Party Structure and Delegate Selection, *Mandate for Reform* (Washington, D.C.: Democratic National Committee, 1970), pp. 38–48. An effort to tease out their institutional implications is Byron E. Shafer, "The Meaning of the Mandate: Formal Rules and Practical Effects," in Shafer, *Quiet Revolution*, pp. 194–213.

4. A concise summary of this sequence and its products through 1984 is "Table 5.2: A Comparison of the Democratic Party's Reform Commissions," in William Crotty, *Party Reform* (New York: Longman, 1983), pp. 40–43.

5. This general categorization is shared by such diverse sources as Thomas R. Marshall, "Three Presidential Nominations Systems," in Marshall, *Presidential Nominations in a Reform Age* (New York: Praeger, 1981), pp. 17–64, and James W. Ceaser, "The Evolution of the Nominating System, 1789–1968," in Ceaser, *Reforming the Reforms: A Critical Analysis of the Presidential Selection Process* (Cambridge, Mass.: Ballinger, 1982), pp. 11–29.

6. This first great break in the mechanics of delegate selection was recognized as a major change in nominating procedures in its own time, as in Louise Overacker, "A Brief History of the Presidential Primary Movement in the United States," in Overacker, *The Presidential Primary* (New York: Macmillan, 1926), pp. 10–22.

7. These theoretical distinctions are elaborated at the beginning of Chapter 3, and their practical impact is summarized in Tables 3.1 and 3.2.

8. These twists and turns in the story of 1972 are, once again, most easily revisited in Theodore H. White, *The Making of the President 1972* (New York: Atheneum, 1973).

9. Indeed, perhaps the ultimate implicit tribute to this increased influence was the rise of studies of the media as it reported nominating politics. The first, more informal version was Timothy Crouse, *The Boys on the Bus* (New York: Random House, 1972). Central to the more scholarly literature are Thomas E. Patterson, *The Mass Media Election: How Americans Choose Their President* (New York: Praeger, 1980), and Michael J. Robinson and Margaret A. Sheehan, *Over the Wire and on TV: CBS and UPI in Campaign '80* (New York: Russell Sage, 1983).

10. The literature on participation in general is well summarized in Lester W. Milbrath and M. L. Goel, *Political Participation* (New York: Rand McNally, 1977). A more pointed overview, with particular attention to the forums for participation, is Sidney Verba and Norman H. Nie, "The Participation Input," in Verba and Nie, *Participation in America: Political Democracy and Social Equality* (New York: Harper & Row, 1972), pp. 23–121.

11. The work which opened up the study of mass and elite information and ideology was Angus Campbell et al., *The American Voter* (New York: John Wiley, 1960), especially "Attitude Structures and the Problem of Ideology," pp. 188–215. A particular focus on these factors as goads to, and constraints on, candidate support is Scott Keeter and Cliff Zukin, "Popularity of the Candidates," in Keeter and Zukin, *Uninformed Choice: The Failure of the New York Presidential Nominating System* (New York: Praeger, 1983), pp. 139–176.

12. This "front-loading" of press attention was first dramatically highlighted by Michael J. Robinson and Karen McPherson in "Television News Coverage before the 1976 New Hampshire Primary: The Focus of Network Journalism," *Journal of Broadcasting* 21 (1977), pp. 177–186. A recent return, with the same concern and the same conclusion, is William C. Adams, "As New Hampshire Goes . . . ," in Gary R. Orren and Nelson W. Polsby, eds., *Media and Momentum: The New Hampshire Primary and Nomination Politics* (Chatham, N.J.: Chatham House, 1987), pp. 42–59.

13. The presidential contest of 1976 marked the passing of the baton for leadership in chronicling individual campaigns from Theodore H. White to a set of "contenders," among whom Jules Witcover and Jack W. Germond were probably most successful. The initial effort in what would become this partnership was actually by Witcover alone, *Marathon: The Pursuit of the Presidency, 1972–1976* (New York: Viking, 1977). Also useful for following the events of that year is Martin Schram, *Running for President: A Journal of the Carter Campaign* (New York: Pocket Books, 1977), along with the collection of reminiscences by some major participants, in Jonathan Moore and Janet Fraser, eds., *Campaign for President: The Managers Look at '76* (Cambridge, Mass: Ballinger, 1977).

14. Jules Witcover returned in 1980 with Jack W. Germond, in Germond and Witcover, *Blue Smoke and Mirrors: How Reagan Won and Why Carter Lost the Election of 1980* (New York: Viking, 1981). A very useful scholarly coun-

terpart is Austin Ranney, ed., *The American Elections of 1980* (Washington, D.C.: American Enterprise Institute, 1981), especially Charles O. Jones, "Nominating 'Carter's Favorite Opponent': The Republicans in 1980," pp. 61–98.

15. A good narrative introduction to this Republican nominating contest is Jules Witcover, "The Delegate Hunt: The Republicans," in Witcover, *Marathon,* pp. 395–500. A useful and highly condensed, scholarly summary is Gerald M. Pomper, "The Republicans," in Pomper et al., *The Election of 1976: Reports and Interpretations* (New York: Longman, 1977), pp. 18–27.

16. The leading general treatment is Jack W. Germond and Jules Witcover, *Wake Us When It's Over: Presidential Politics of 1984* (New York: Macmillan, 1985). An even more useful scholarly counterpart is Austin Ranney, ed., *The American Elections of 1984* (Washington, D.C.: American Enterprise Institute, 1985). And once more, in what has also become a continuing series, the opening essay by Gerald M. Pomper, "The Nominations," in Pomper et al., *The Election of 1984: Reports and Interpretations* (Chatham, N.J.: Chatham House, 1985), pp. 1–34, is a helpful supplement.

17. Both phases of press expectations, the "mentioning process" and the establishing of benchmarks, are considered in Donald R. Matthews, " 'Winnowing': The News Media and the 1976 Presidential Nominations," in James D. Barber, ed., *Race for the Presidency: The Media and the Nominating Process* (Englewood Cliffs, N.J.: Prentice-Hall, 1978), pp. 55–78. The second and more consequential phase of press expectations, which involves setting goals and interpreting results, is also summarized with examples in Richard Joslyn, "The Nomination Campaign," in Joslyn, *Mass Media and Elections* (Reading, Mass.: Addison-Wesley, 1984), pp. 120–134.

18. Finance regulations and their evolution are summarized in the appendix to Herbert E. Alexander, *Financing Politics: Money, Elections, and Political Reform,* 3rd ed. (Washington, D.C.: Congressional Quarterly Press, 1983), pp. 163–176. The pressures toward "front-loading" in the finance bandwagon come through clearly in William J. Lanouette, "Campaign Spending: The Gamble Pays Off," *National Journal,* May 17, 1980, pp. 819–821. A wonderful—and perverse—example of the bandwagon at work is Michael J. Robinson, "Paid Media: Throwing It Away," from Robinson, "Where's the Beef? Media and Media Elites in 1984," in Ranney, ed., *The American Elections of 1984,* pp. 172–177.

19. Indeed, this activist bandwagon had become such a reliable part of reformed nominating politics that it could be detected before the first real contest, as when the withdrawal of front-runner Gary Hart in mid-1987 was followed immediately by speculative pieces on where his key staff members would be transferring their allegiance. One example among many is Jack W. Germond and Jules Witcover, "No Rush to Judgment for Former Hart Backers," *National Journal,* May 23, 1987, p. 1372.

20. In fact, the concept itself has dropped out of recent texts on presidential politics and appears to survive only as an occasional early threat by one or another state political leader. A more general and statistical approach to this decline, in a work with numerous provocative findings, is Howard L. Reiter, "Fewer Favorite Sons," in Reiter, *Selecting the President: The Nominating Process in Transition* (Philadelphia: University of Pennsylvania Press, 1985), pp. 27–28.

21. An attempt to formalize this recurring practical process is John H. Aldrich, "A Dynamic Model of Presidential Nominating Campaigns," *American Political Science Review* 74 (1980), pp. 651–669. A more explicit and detailed treatment is Elaine C. Kamarck, "Structure as Strategy: Presidential Nominating Politics since Reform," Ph.D. dissertation, University of California at Berkeley, 1986, especially "The Delegate Count and Strategies for Sustaining Momentum," pp. 165–197. A provocative elaboration is Larry M. Bartels, "Candidate Choice and the Dynamics of the Presidential Nominating Process," *American Political Science Review* 31 (1987), pp. 1–30.

22. Donald S. Collat, Stanley Kelley, Jr., and Ronald Rogowski created this statistic in Collat, Kelley, and Rogowski, "The End Game in Presidential Nominations," *American Political Science Review* 75 (1981), pp. 426–435. Calculations in Table 2.6 for the years after 1976, when the original article stops, were developed from the rolling totals in *Congressional Quarterly Weekly Report* for 1980 and 1984.

3. Changing Contours of Delegate Selection

1. The scope of this Muskie boom—this bubble, really—comes through clearly in reportage of the time, as, for example, "The Making of a Front-Runner," *Newsweek*, January 10, 1972, pp. 13–16.

2. A concise classification of these and other institutional arrangements for delegate selection and presidential nomination is James I. Lengle and Byron E. Shafer, "Reform," in Lengle and Shafer, eds., *Presidential Politics: Readings on Nominations and Elections* (New York: St. Martin's Press, 1980), pp. 3–6.

3. The initial text for Democratic party reform was Commission on Party Structure and Delegate Selection, *Mandate for Reform* (Washington, D.C.: Democratic National Committee, 1970), especially "The Official Guidelines of the Commission," pp. 38–48. These rather abstract strictures were then translated into specific institutional requirements by the commission staff through a series of "Compliance Letters," which adapted the guidelines for the individual state parties. In that sense, the national requirements of guidelines must be reassembled by summing these state reports.

4. Historical comparisons of the mechanics of delegate selection are made difficult by the lack of external attention to delegate politics in the era when most selection was done inside the official party and by the tendency for actual practice to vary significantly within similar formal rules. One useful historical resource is the series on state and national rules compiled by the Library of Congress for various congressional bodies. A recent version is Thomas M. Durbin, comp., *Nomination and Election of the President of the United States, 1984* (Washington, D.C.: Government Printing Office, 1984).

After reform, along with conscious external attention to it, available sources are much better. Perhaps the best is the continuing series from the Congressional Research Service, which was inaugurated with Carol F. Casey, comp., *Procedures for Selection of Delegates to the Democratic and Republican 1976 Conventions: A Survey of Applicable State Laws and Party Rules* (Washington, D.C.: Library of Congress, 1976). Also tremendously useful, for more than just their target years, are Paul T. David, Malcolm Moos, and Ralph M. Goldman, eds., *Presidential Nominating Politics in 1952* (Baltimore: Johns Hopkins University Press, 1954), vols. I–V, and Commission on Party Structure and Delegate Selection, "State-by-State Analysis," undated but surely late spring of 1972, Presidential Libraries, National Archives, Washington, D.C.

5. For a sense of this abstract difference in concrete operation, compare the nominating campaigns of 1948 and 1952, for example, with those of 1972 and 1976. The former can be found in Irwin Ross, *The Loneliest Campaign: The Truman Victory of 1948* (New York: New American Library, 1968), and in David, Moos, and Goldman, *Presidential Nominating Politics in 1952*. The latter are fruitfully compared through Ernest R. May and Janet Fraser, eds., *Campaign '72: The Managers Speak* (Cambridge, Mass.: Harvard University Press, 1973), and Martin Schram, *Running for President: A Journal of the Carter Campaign* (New York: Pocket Books, 1977).

6. The painful irrelevance of the alleged incipient exceptions, such as Hubert Humphrey for the Democrats in 1976 or Gerald Ford for the Republicans in 1980, makes the same point.

7. The metaphor of mist clearing and its associated calculations are used to great effect by John H. Kessel in "Nomination Politics," in Kessel, *Presidential Campaign Politics: Coalition Strategies and Citizen Responses* (Homewood, Ill.: Dorsey Press, 1980), pp. 3–44.

8. Indeed, this factor came rapidly to be recognized as affecting the strategies not just of those who might ally with candidate campaigns but of the candidates themselves, as when these filing deadlines began, early, to limit the options of potential entrants in the Democratic contest of 1988. See James A. Barnes, "Reluctant Bridegrooms," *National Journal*, June 20, 1987, pp. 1579–83, an analysis which resurfaces in Kevin Phillips, "Democratic 1988 Presidential Selection Calendar Perils," in Phillips, *The American Political Report*, June 26, 1987, pp. 4–5.

9. Historical notes and evidence of continuity of these considerations into the present are offered by Leon D. Epstein in *Political Parties in the American Mold* (Madison, Wis.: University of Wisconsin Press, 1986), especially "State and Local Structure," pp. 123–154, and "National Organization," pp. 200–238.

10. Although it was written for quite other purposes, an extended piece of evidence that these risks are very real is David Lebedoff, *Ward Number Six* (New York: Scribner's, 1972).

11. This pattern of calculations was the basis for the dichotomy between "purists" and "professionals" offered by Nelson W. Polsby and Aaron B. Wildavsky in the second edition of their dominant text *Presidential Elections: Strategies of American Electoral Politics* (New York: Scribner's, 1968), pp. 173–180. With the coming of reform and the associated change in the character of delegates, that dichotomy became less powerfully central.

12. Carter as a nonparty president emerges clearly in Austin Ranney, "The Carter Administration," in Ranney, ed., *The American Elections of 1980* (Washington, D.C.: American Enterprise Institute, 1981), pp. 1–36.

13. The source of much of this wisdom, and the stimulus to much of the rest, was Herbert McClosky, Paul J. Hoffman, and Rosemary O'Hara, "Issue

Conflict and Consensus among Party Leaders and Followers," *American Political Science Review* 54 (1960), pp. 406–427.

14. Figure 3.1 was developed from the scale scores in McClosky, Hoffman, and O'Hara, "Issue Conflict and Consensus," for the issue categories "public ownership," "government regulation," "equalitarianism," "tax policy," and "foreign policy." In the strictest terms it is not possible to equate the resulting scores and distribution in Figure 3.1 with those of Figures 3.2–3.4, because Figures 3.2–3.4 are built from a different survey item. Yet by setting the composite score of the general public at 0 in Figure 3.1 and calibrating the individual group scores to a dispersion with roughly the same parameters as those of Figures 3.2–3.4, it was possible to generate the graphic representation of Figure 3.1. I do not believe that anyone familiar with the 1960 article by McClosky et al. will feel that this representation does violence to its seminal argument.

15. The underlying survey instrument was painstakingly created, and the resulting data assiduously collected, by Barbara G. Farah, M. Kent Jennings, and Warren E. Miller, with support from the Russell Sage Foundation. The data have been most comprehensively analyzed, in a work which shows their scope far better than Figures 3.2–3.4, in Warren E. Miller and M. Kent Jennings, *Parties in Transition: A Longitudinal Study of Party Elites and Party Supporters* (New York: Russell Sage, 1986).

16. The idea for Figures 3.2–3.4 was solely the province of Barbara G. Farah, now director of news surveys at the *New York Times:* without an original draft paper from her on aspects of the same topic, and without numerous subsequent conversations, these figures would never have been created. The actual manipulation of survey data was then undertaken by Debra L. Dodson at the Institute for Social Research, University of Michigan, from the delegate study which became Miller and Jennings, *Parties in Transition.* The resulting figures were transformed so that the mean ideological self-rating of the full American public was set equal to 0 in each case.

17. This possibility gets serious exploration in Jeane J. Kirkpatrick, *The New Presidential Elite: Men and Women in National Politics* (New York: Russell Sage, 1976).

18. The most frequently cited versions of this argument are probably those contained in the reminiscences of old-fashioned party operatives, such as William L. Riordan, rec., *Plunkitt of Tammany Hall* (New York: Norton, 1940).

19. These responsibilities and their pursuit are canvassed explicitly in his larger survey of the literature on parties by Leon D. Epstein, "Political Parties," in Fred I. Greenstein and Nelson W. Polsby, eds., *Handbook of Political Science* (Reading, Mass.: Addison-Wesley, 1975), vol. IV, pp. 229–277.

4. The Rise of the Organized Interests

1. One very elegant attempt to synthesize these perspectives is James W. Ceaser, *Presidential Selection: Theory and Development* (Princeton, N.J.: Princeton University Press, 1979), especially "Martin Van Buren and the Case for Electoral Restraint," pp. 123–169, and "Woodrow Wilson and the Origin of the Modern View of Presidential Selection," pp. 170–212.

2. These rumblings from practitioners can be heard intermittently in state-level reform politics in Byron E. Shafer, "The Politics of Implementation Writ Small: Pennsylvania Accepts Reform," pp. 320–340, and "Re-creation of Reform: The Party Structure Commission and Proportionality," pp. 492–522, in Shafer, *Quiet Revolution: The Struggle for the Democratic Party and the Shaping of Post-Reform Politics* (New York: Russell Sage, 1983). Professional political scientists were slow to reformulate these views into a more general perspective, but eventual responses include Nelson W. Polsby, *Consequences of Party Reform* (New York: Oxford University Press, 1983), and David E. Price, *Bringing Back the Parties* (Washington, D.C.: Congressional Quarterly Press, 1984).

3. This perspective thoroughly informs the first of the hortatory documents which helped inaugurate the reform movement in the Democratic party, the report of the private body known as the Hughes Commission: Commission on the Democratic Selection of Presidential Nominees, *The Democratic Choice* (New York: Commission on the Democratic Selection of Presidential Nominees, 1968). The same perspective was carried along, with some procedural modifications, in the first of the official reform reports: Commission on Party Structure and Delegate Selection, *Mandate for Reform* (Washington, D.C.: Democratic National Committee, 1970). This view received almost simultaneous scholarly exposition in John S. Saloma and Frederick H. Sontag, *Parties: The Real Opportunity for Effective Citizen Politics* (New York: Random House, 1973), to be underlined and expanded later in William J. Crotty, *Political Reform and the American Experiment* (New York: Crowell, 1977).

4. The classic treatments of these organized groups in American politics are Arthur F. Bentley, *The Process of Government* (Chicago: University of Chicago Press, 1908), and David B. Truman, *The Governmental Process: Political Interest and Public Opinion* (New York: Knopf, 1951).

5. They certainly struck that early and perspicacious observer Alexis de Tocqueville throughout *Democracy in America* (New York: Vintage Books, 1945), 2 vols., especially in "Political Associations in the United States," vol. I, pp. 198–205. More contemporary treatments include L. Harmon Ziegler and Wayne G. Peak, *Interest Groups in American Politics,* 2nd ed. (Englewood Cliffs, N.J.: Prentice-Hall, 1972), and Norman J. Ornstein and Shirley Elder, *Interest Groups, Lobbying, and Policymaking* (Washington, D.C.: Congressional Quarterly Press, 1978).

6. A major study of the archetypal predecessor is Peter H. Odegard, *Pressure Politics: The Story of the Anti-Saloon League* (New York: Columbia University Press, 1928). A survey of one slice of its modern counterparts is Andrew S. McFarland, *Public Interest Lobbies: Decision Making on Energy* (Washington, D.C.: American Enterprise Institute, 1976). A different ideological portion of the same organizational category is Jeff Dionne, "With Their Man in the White House, Conservative Legal Groups Are Hurting," *National Journal,* November 11, 1983, pp. 2316–18.

7. Perhaps the best known of these negotiations in recent nominating campaigns revolved around organized labor in 1984. The background to negotiation is presented in Dom Bonafede, "Labor's Early Endorsement Will Prove a Psychological Boost and Then Some," *National Journal,* September 24, 1984, pp.

1938–41, with the outcome in Rob Gurwitt, "Unions Hope Endorsement of Mondale . . . Will Advance Labor's Legislative Goals," *Congressional Quarterly Weekly Report,* October 8, 1983, pp. 2080–81.

8. Efforts by the NEA on behalf of Carter are covered in, among others, David S. Broder and Kathy Sawyer, "Teachers' Union Becomes Powerful Force in Party Politics," *Washington Post,* January 20, 1980, p. A7, and Steven V. Roberts, "Carter Camp Making Gains by Courting Teachers' Votes," *New York Times,* January 28, 1980, p. B4. The result is documented in David S. Broder, "Teachers' Union: Vital Bloc for Carter," *Washington Post,* July 2, 1980, p. A1; Denis A. Williams and others, "The Teachers' Pet," *Newsweek,* July 14, 1980, p. 28; and Harrison Donnelly, "National Education Association: Teacher Organization Unites behind Carter—for a Price," *Congressional Quarterly Weekly Report,* August 9, 1980, pp. 2277–79.

9. Summary figures and convention activities are drawn from "Memo to Political Editors and Writers; From Phil King, Manager, Public Information Office; Re NEA Teacher Delegates and Alternates to the Democratic National Convention," National Education Association, August 10–14, 1980, with ten supporting enclosures.

10. Intimations that things might be different in 1980 could have been found in George Vecsey, "Militant Television Preachers Try to Weld Fundamentalist Christians' Political Power," *New York Times,* January 21, 1980, p. A21. One of the first national hints that this effort was producing results was Wallace Turner, "Group of Evangelical Protestants Takes Over the G.O.P. in Alaska," *New York Times,* June 9, 1980, p. B12. A more thorough, retrospective investigation is Bill Keller, "The Evangelical Lobby: Evangelical Conservatives Move from Pews to Polls, but Can They Sway Congress?" *Congressional Quarterly Weekly Report,* September 6, 1980, pp. 2627–34.

11. The CBS News Election and Survey Unit was one of the few to catch this incipient development, and the following figures are based on affirmative answers to the questions about ever having made a "decision for Christ." Needless to say, this portion of the text (as well as Table 4.1) is dependent on this data, graciously provided by Warren J. Mitofsky, director of the unit.

12. These include James Davison Hunter, *American Evangelicalism: Conservative Religion and the Quandary of Modernity* (New Brunswick, N.J.: Rutgers University Press, 1983); Robert C. Liebman and Robert Wuthnow, eds., *The New Christian Right* (Hawthorne, N.Y.: Aldine, 1983); and A. James Reichley, *Religion in American Public Life* (Washington, D.C.: Brookings, 1985).

13. The exception which proves the rule may well have been the New Hampshire chapter of the American Chiropractic Association in the nominating contest of 1980; Timothy B. Clark, "Carter and the Chiropractors—The Tale of a Political Deal," *National Journal,* February 16, 1980, pp. 269–272.

14. This point is demonstrated, and its implications strongly argued, in James I. Lengle, *Representation and Presidential Primaries: The Democratic Party in the Post-reform Era* (Westport, Conn.: Greenwood Press, 1981).

15. Indeed, at the Democratic convention of 1984, surely the zenith of labor influence in the postreform era, it was the Communications Workers of America and the American Federation of State, County, and Municipal Employees which

provided the organizational infrastructure for the labor effort by supplying the publicity and the whip system.

16. For further bits of evidence and some extended speculation on this possibility, see the concluding chapter, especially "Intermediation in a New American Politics."

17. Two useful surveys are Edwin M. Epstein, *The Corporation in American Politics* (Englewood Cliffs, N.J.: Prentice-Hall, 1969), and Graham K. Wilson, *Unions in American National Politics* (New York: St. Martin's Press, 1979).

18. Suggestive but not conclusive numbers are found in Warren J. Mitofsky and Martin Plissner, "The Making of the Delegates, 1968–1980," *Public Opinion* 3 (October–November 1980), pp. 36–43.

19. The precise regulations are contained in "Rule 13: Automatic Delegates," in Commission on Presidential Nomination and Party Structure, *Openness, Participation, and Party Building: Reforms for a Stronger Democratic Party* (Washington, D.C.: Democratic National Committee, 1978), pp. 100–102.

20. A highly instructive further analysis is Thomas E. Mann, "Elected Officials and the Politics of Presidential Selection," in Austin Ranney, ed., *The American Elections of 1984* (Washington, D.C.: American Enterprise Institute, 1985), pp. 100–128.

21. The specific provision is "Rule 8: Selection of Party and Elected Official Delegates," in *Report of the Commission on Presidential Nomination* (Washington, D.C.: Democratic National Committee, 1982), pp. 17–18, as amplified at pp. 38–42.

22. This fact did not, however, imply a complete absence of officially sanctioned inquiries into the need for reform. The Republican record in these considerations is covered by John F. Bibby, "Procedural Reform within the GOP," from Bibby, "Party Renewal in the Republican Party," in Gerald W. Pomper, ed., *Party Renewal in America: Theory and Practice* (New York: Praeger, 1980), pp. 103–107.

23. The process of—and possibilities inherent in—slate making have received comparatively little scholarly attention. An exception which underlines the range of outcomes potentially associated with manipulation of these subrules, albeit from Democratic experience, is William Cavala, "Changing the Rules Changes the Game: Party Reform and the 1972 California Delegation to the Democratic National Convention," *American Political Science Review* 68 (1974), pp. 27–42.

24. John F. Bibby notes this remaining distinction between national Democratic and Republican practices in Bibby, "Procedural Reform within the GOP." The particular array of slating arrangements which it has produced among Republican state parties is presented, in careful detail, in *Delegate Selection Procedures: 1980 Republican National Convention* (Washington, D.C.: Republican National Committee, 1980) and *Delegate Selection Procedures: Republican National Convention 1984* (Washington, D.C.: Republican National Committee, 1984).

25. One aid to hindsight should have been the extrapolation to the *organizations* participating in politics by James Q. Wilson from his early work on incentives toward various styles of political participation, in Wilson, *Political*

Organizations (New York: Basic Books, 1973), especially "Part I: A Theoretical Perspective," pp. 19–91.

26. The Republican situation during the long years of largely fictional southern parties is summarized in Paul T. David, Ralph M. Goldman, and Richard C. Bain, "The Republicans' Century of Controversy," in David, Goldman, and Bain, *The Politics of National Party Conventions* (Washington, D.C.: Brookings, 1960), pp. 165–168. For the coming of more seriously organized Republican parties in the region, see Numan V. Bartley and Hugh D. Graham, "The Emergence of Two-Party Politics: Republicanism in the New South," in Bartley and Graham, *Southern Politics and the Second Reconstruction* (Baltimore: Johns Hopkins University Press, 1975), pp. 81–110, and Jack Bass and Walter DeVries, "Two Party Politics: The Republican Rise," in Bass and DeVries, *The Transformation of Southern Politics: Social Change and Political Consequence since 1945* (New York: Basic Books, 1976), pp. 23–40.

5. The Convention and the Election

1. Thumbnail sketches of both these conventions, which suggest the deliberate efforts of their nominees to use this break with tradition as a means of promising a larger break with existing political practice, can be found in "1932 Conventions: Democrats," pp. 80–81, and "1944 Conventions: Republicans," pp. 86–87, in Congressional Quarterly, *National Party Conventions, 1831–1980* (Washington, D.C.: Congressional Quarterly Press, 1983).

2. Key steps in the development of televised coverage, along with the appearance of a national audience for it, are presented in the beginning sections of Chapter 7.

3. Indeed, the character of press treatment of this convention—and hence of the inadvertent and deleterious launching of its ultimate nominee—is a consistent threat through the comprehensive account in Robert K. Murray, *The 103rd Ballot: Democrats and the Disaster in Madison Square Garden* (New York: Harper & Row, 1976). A comprehensive report on the Republican convention of 1940, which captures the meteoric rise of its nominee and the growing fascination of the general public with him, is contained in Donald B. Johnson, *The Republican Party and Wendell Willkie* (Urbana, Ill.: University of Illinois Press, 1960).

4. The central research instrument in these recurring samples of public opinion is the one which began at the Institute for Social Research at the University of Michigan and was eventually institutionalized on a national scale through the Inter-University Consortium for Political and Social Research in its "National Election Studies," from which forty years of social science tables—including Table 5.1—have been drawn.

5. One of the most consequential of these earlier nominating conventions, featuring clear organization around issues and causes but politicking centered on the nomination itself, was the Democratic convention of 1896, which is the subject of a critical part of Stanley L. Jones, *The Presidential Election of 1896* (Lexington, Ky.: University of Kentucky Press, 1965).

6. The analysis which follows, of the sources and patterns of internal convention conflict, attests at a second level to the difference in this internal politicking

from the days before the departure of the nomination and the coming of extended procedural reform. Two concise summaries of the outlines for politics in that era, one popular and one scholarly, are Staff of the Republican National Committee, "The Nomination Game," in *Republican Report* 3 (February 1964), pp. 2–4, and Nelson W. Polsby, "Decision-Making at the National Conventions," *Western Political Quarterly* 13 (1960), pp. 609–619.

7. Doris A. Graber affirms this tendency in her overview of research, "Newsmaking and Newsgathering," in Graber, *Mass Media and American Politics* (Washington, D.C.: Congressional Quarterly Press, 1980), pp. 57–88. The argument that the electronic media exaggerate this tendency is conveyed forcefully in Kurt Lang and Gladys E. Lang, *Politics and Television* (New York: Quadrangle Books, 1968), especially at p. 107.

8. This motivation is, in fact, hardly limited to losing contenders for the current nomination. It can also influence the convention behavior of those who may be considering a run in the future. Moreover, reporters often spend some time assessing the performance of potential future candidates at a current convention. One recent example was the favorable attention—and press reviews—gained by Congressman Jack Kemp at the Republican convention of 1980, as in Frank Lynn, "Kemp, Counting Gains of Detroit, Isn't Ruling Out New York Races," *New York Times*, July 18, 1980, p. 7. Kemp was reprised in 1984, in Christopher Madden, "Will Jack Kemp Be the Man to Beat in 1988?" *National Journal Convention Daily*, August 22, 1984, p. 2. Some Democratic counterparts for that year can be found in Dennis Farney and David Rogers, "Rising Democrats: Convention Showcases Party's Potential Stars as Well as Its Leaders," *Wall Street Journal*, July 18, 1984, p. 1.

9. One attempt to treat these temporal and structural incentives in more formal terms is Benjamin I. Page, *Choices and Echoes in Presidential Elections: Rational Man and Electoral Democracy* (Chicago: University of Chicago Press, 1978), especially "Constancy and Change in Policy Stands," pp. 108–151.

10. Extensively developed overviews of these two continuing divisions can be found in Joseph Rogers Hollingsworth, *The Whirligig of Politics: The Democracy of Cleveland and Bryan* (Chicago: University of Chicago Press, 1963), and George E. Mowry, *The Era of Theodore Roosevelt, 1900–1912* (New York: Harper & Row, 1958).

11. A quick overview of these causes for expansion is James W. Davis, "Growth in Size of Conventions," in Davis, *National Conventions in an Age of Party Reform* (Westport, Conn.: Greenwood Press, 1983), pp. 42–44.

12. The single most useful source on individual conventions, year in and year out, are the convention issues of *Congressional Quarterly Weekly Report*. For the Democratic version in 1972 this was "Democratic Convention," *Congressional Quarterly Weekly Report*, July 15, 1972, pp. 1715–49 and 1777–82. That year was distinctive, however, in acquiring a book-length scholarly treatment of this convention as well: Dennis G. Sullivan, Jeffrey L. Pressman, Benjamin I. Page, and John J. Lyons, *The Politics of Representation: The Democratic Convention 1972* (New York: St. Martin's Press, 1974).

13. These events and surrounding maneuvers are covered in detail in Theodore H. White, "Confrontation in Miami," in White, *The Making of The President*

1972 (New York: Atheneum, 1973), pp. 158–192. Also fascinating for a viewpoint from the center is Lawrence F. O'Brien, "Miami Beach," in O'Brien, *No Final Victories: A Life in Politics from John F. Kennedy to Watergate* (New York: Doubleday, 1974), pp. 301–316.

14. The essential background is "Republican Convention," *Congressional Quarterly Weekly Report,* August 26, 1972, pp. 2115–76.

15. Useful comparisons of the conventions of 1972, offering further detail on these internal Republican events, are James W. Davis, "1972 Democratic and Republican Conventions," in Davis, *National Conventions: Nominations under the Big Top* (Woodbury, N.Y.: Barron's Educational Series, 1973), pp. 97–123, and "The Conventions," in Ernest R. May and Janet Fraser, eds., *Campaign '72: The Managers Speak* (Cambridge, Mass.: Harvard University Press, 1973), pp. 141–188.

16. The main contemporary source on the Republican convention of 1976 is "Ford and Dole: Winners of a Bruising Republican Nomination Contest," *Congressional Quarterly Weekly Report,* August 21, 1976, pp. 2247–75 and 2292–2317. A helpful scholarly supplement is the coordinate set of five pieces from Dennis G. Sullivan, Robert T. Nakamura, Martha Wagner Weinberg, F. Christopher Arterton, and Jeffrey L. Poressman, "Exploring the 1976 Republican Convention: Five Perspectives," *Political Science Quarterly* 92 (1977–78), pp. 633–682.

17. This and other tactics in the complete strategic chain are covered in Jules Witcover, "The Republican Convention," in Witcover, *Marathon: The Pursuit of the Presidency, 1972–1976* (New York: Viking Press, 1977), pp. 473–510, and, especially from the viewpoint of key participants, in "Republican Convention," in Jonathan Moore and Janet Fraser, eds., *Campaign for President: The Managers Look at '76* (Cambridge, Mass.: Ballinger Publishing, 1977), pp. 53–72.

18. The key journalistic source is again "Carter and Mondale: A United Democratic Convention Picks Its Candidates," in *Congressional Quarterly Weekly Report,* July 17, 1976, pp. 1867–81 and 1913–39. The comparatively low level of conflict is implicitly reaffirmed by the collection of anecdotes about the gathering, and the persistently bored tone, in Richard Reeves, *Convention* (New York: Harcourt Brace Jovanovich, 1977).

19. These and other internal maneuvers are also reported in Martin Schram, "July/Convention," in Schram, *Running for President: A Journal of the Carter Campaign* (New York: Pocket Books, 1977), pp. 222–241, and in Jules Witcover, "The Democratic Convention," in Witcover, *Marathon,* pp. 355–370.

20. A stimulating overview of the operation of two competing campaigns is F. Christopher Arterton, "Strategies and Tactics of Candidate Organizations," *Political Science Quarterly* 92 (1977–78), pp. 663–671.

6. Recurring Struggles over Tangible Products

1. A helpful and condensed overview of the formal framework for vice presidential selection is Allan P. Sindler, "The Framers, the Constitution, and the Congress on the Vice Presidency and Succession," in Sindler, *Unchosen Presidents:*

The Vice President and Other Frustrations of Presidential Succession (Berkeley, Calif.: University of California Press, 1976), pp. 12–26.

2. A different classification of vice presidential selections, more nearly atheoretical in its taxonomy but more diverse and pointed in its categories, is Jay A. Hurwitz, "Vice Presidential Eligibility and Selection Patterns," *Polity* 12 (1980), pp. 509–521.

3. One useful summary of formal organization and normal procedure is James W. Davis, "Convention Committee Activity," in Davis, *National Conventions: Nominations under the Big Top* (Woodbury, N.Y.: Barron's Educational Series, 1973), pp. 35–51.

4. Another introduction to the traditional structure of the convention, one peppered with historical examples of the fights which could well up around this internal structure, is V. O. Key, Jr., "Organization of the Convention" and "Platforms," in Key, *Politics, Parties, and Pressure Groups*, 5th ed. (New York: Crowell, 1964), pp. 412–422.

5. One leading journalistic account of this contest is Jack W. Germond and Jules Witcover, "A Campaign Held Hostage," pp. 79–92, and "Damaging to Our Country," pp. 141–165, in Germond and Witcover, *Blue Smoke and Mirrors: How Reagan Won and Why Carter Lost the Election of 1980* (New York: Viking Press, 1981). A forceful scholarly counterpart is Nelson W. Polsby, "The Democratic Nomination," in Austin Ranney, ed., *The American Elections of 1980* (Washington, D.C.: American Enterprise Institute, 1981), pp. 37–60.

6. The substantive background to these contests is provided in "Democrats in the Big Apple," *Congressional Quarterly Weekly Report*, August 9, 1980, pp. 2262–76. A more impressionistic view is John F. Stacks, "Jimmy and Ted," in Stacks, *Watershed: The Campaign for the Presidency 1980* (New York: Times Books, 1981), pp. 196–211.

7. On the convention as it unfolded, the best source is "The Democratic Quest," *Congressional Quarterly Weekly Report*, August 16, 1980, pp. 2347–73 and 2390–2437. A more impressionistic review is Elizabeth Drew, "The Democratic Convention," in Drew, *Portrait of an Election: The 1980 Presidential Campaign* (New York: Simon & Schuster, 1981), pp. 221–260.

8. The relation between the prior nominating campaign and internal convention politics comes through clearly in Charles O. Jones, "Nominating 'Carter's Favorite Opponent': The Republicans in 1980," in Ranney, *The American Elections of 1980*, pp. 61–98. The background to this convention's politics is covered in "Republicans Go to Detroit," *Congressional Quarterly Weekly Report*, July 12, 1980, pp. 1923–40.

9. The story of the convention is most comprehensively presented in "The Republican Challenge," *Congressional Quarterly Weekly Report*, July 19, 1980, pp. 1979–2012 and 2030–69. A comparison of the two conventions of 1980 is Theodore H. White, "The Conventions: On Stage and Off," in White, *America in Search of Itself: The Making of the President, 1956–1980* (New York: Harper & Row, 1982), pp. 312–343.

10. A much understated review of the impact of the selection of Bush and of the extent of the subsequent response by the Reagan team is Martin Tolchin, "Conservatives First Recoil, Then Line Up Behind Bush," *New York Times*, July

18, 1980, p. 9. The central procedural gambit in this short-lived revolt is presented in Larry Light, "Sen. Jesse Helms: Coy Campaign for Vice President," *Congressional Quarterly Weekly Report,* July 19, 1980, p. 2001.

11. The nominating campaign as it fed into the convention is well and concisely summarized in Charles O. Jones, "Renominating Ronald Reagan: The Compleat Politician at Work," in Austin Ranney, ed., *The American Elections of 1984* (Washington, D.C.: American Enterprise Institute, 1985), pp. 66–69. The convention itself appears comprehensively in "Going After the Democrats," *Congressional Quarterly Weekly Report,* August 25, 1984, pp. 2067–2128.

12. The campaign and the convention are usefully summarized by Jack W. Germond and Jules Witcover in *Wake Us When It's Over: Presidential Politics of 1984* (New York: Macmillan, 1985). The convention itself is thoroughly covered in "The Democrats: Looking to November," *Congressional Quarterly Weekly Report,* July 21, 1984, pp. 1719–95 and 1799.

13. The best source for these detailed maneuvers is what was at the time a new day-by-day edition of *National Journal,* the Washington political weekly. These appeared as *National Journal Convention Daily* for July 15–19, 1984. A summary of the decision about a vice presidential candidate is "Special Report: Geraldine Ferraro, Mondale's Gamble," *Congressional Quarterly Weekly Report,* July 14, 1984, pp. 1675–86.

14. For the two additional and idiosyncratic nominations from 1980, for example, see *1980: Official Report of the Proceedings of the Democratic National Convention* (Washington, D.C.: Democratic National Committee, 1980), pp. 540–552.

15. A short summary of this most difficult and pressure laden of the vice presidential selections in the postreform era is Alan Ehrenhalt, "Ford's Task: Finding a Winning Formula," *Congressional Quarterly Weekly Report,* August 21, 1976, pp. 2247–48. A more extended and thematic rendering is Jules Witcover, "The Selection of Bob Dole," in Witcover, *Marathon: The Pursuit of the Presidency, 1972–1976* (New York: Viking Press, 1977), pp. 504–510.

16. For 1984 this was Rule 6, Section C, of "Affirmative Action": "State Delegate Selection plans shall provide for equal division between delegate men and delegate women and alternate men and alternate women in the convention delegation. Notwithstanding sub-paragraph A(2) above [forbidding the use of mandatory quotas to achieve such results], equal division at any level of delegate or committee positions between delegate men and delegate women or committee men and committee women shall not constitute a violation of any provision thereof." *Report of the Commission on Presidential Nomination* (Washington, D.C.: Democratic National Committee, 1982), p. 35.

17. Preparations for such an eventuality, along with explicit threats, are contained in Sandra Salmans, "Mondale Warned by Women's Group," *New York Times,* June 30, 1984, p. 6; Salmans, "Women May Fight for Ticket Spot, NOW Leader Says," *New York Times,* July 2, 1984, p. 1; and Howell Raines, "Mondale's Tough Choice," *New York Times,* July 3, 1984, p. 1. The resulting decision is chronicled in its larger context in Jack W. Germond and Jules Witcover, "What a Gas!" in Germond and Witcover, *Wake Us When It's Over,* pp. 368–379.

18. Reports from the interim politics of this commission at critical points include Christopher Lydon, "Democrats Name Panel on Delegates," *New York*

Times, September 22, 1973, p. 14; Lydon, "Democrats Vote to Abolish '72 Quotas for Delegates," *New York Times,* October 28, 1973, p. 42; and Lydon, "Using Rules to Make Ends Meet," *New York Times,* November 4, 1973, sec. IV, p. 3. The product of all this effort is summarized in William J. Crotty, "The Reform Controversy Continues: A Reappraisal of the McGovern-Fraser Commission's Actions," in Crotty, *Political Reform and the American Experiment* (New York: Crowell, 1977), pp. 245–247.

19. This arrangement is presented in "Rule 19: Monitoring and Compliance Review," in *Democrats All: A Report of the Commission on Delegate Selection and Party Structure* (Washington, D.C.: Democratic National Committee, 1973), pp. 22–24.

20. The proposal itself is Hart for President Campaign, "The Democracy Package," mimeo, 10 pp., as revised June 25, 1984. The highlights of its progress are presented concisely in Ronald Brownstein, "Democratic Rules Pact Could Change Nature of 1988 Primary Campaign," *National Journal,* June 30, 1984, pp. 1255 and 1279.

21. The product of this reform commission is described in Rhodes Cook, "Brushing Aside Complaints, DNC Approves Rules for 1988," *Congressional Quarterly Weekly Report,* March 15, 1986, p. 627. The politicking on the way to that product is reviewed in Cook, "Harmony Is In, Bickering Out as Democrats Consider Rules," *Congressional Quarterly Weekly Report,* March 1, 1986, pp. 509–510.

22. The crucial opening round in this struggle is covered in Robert G. Kaiser, "Democrats Adopt Plank Opposing Nuclear Power," *Washington Post,* June 24, 1980, p. A1. Yet given the outcome—a continuing retreat by the Carter leadership—the story can be followed as reasonably in the convention releases of the Campaign for Safe Energy, especially "Democrats Reject Carter on Issues of Nuclear Power and Solar Energy," August 11, 1980; "Coalition Claims Victory on Carter Solar 'Cave In,' " August 12, 1980; and "Vice-Presidential Nominating Petitions to Be Submitted for Major Speech on Nuclear Power and Solar Energy," August 13, 1980.

23. The final stages in this conflict are recorded in "Debates on Platform Minority Report No. 16," pp. 404–412, and "Remarks of Congressman Edward Markey of Massachusetts," pp. 494–497, in *1980: Official Report of the Democratic National Convention.*

24. The suspicion that this temporal shift might be necessary, even in the presence of a thoroughgoing triumph by eventual nominee Reagan, along with the decision to schedule platform hearings earlier, is covered in Steven R. Weisman, "G.O.P. Aides Note Signs of Dispute about Platform," *New York Times,* June 19, 1984, p. 1.

25. The substance of these recommendations and their fate are included in Richard C. Bain and Judith H. Parris, "1972: The Republican Contest," in Bain and Parris, eds., *Convention Decisions and Voting Records,* 2nd ed. (Washington, D.C.: Brookings, 1973), pp. 338–343.

26. These subsequent efforts are noted in Rhodes Cook, "GOP Convention Rules Adopted without Dispute," *Congressional Quarterly Weekly Report,* July 19, 1980, p. 2012, and Cook, "GOP to Keep Existing Rules for 1988 Presidential Race," *Congressional Quarterly Weekly Report,* August 25, 1984, p. 2092.

27. The career of these proposals is apparent in Alan Ehrenhalt and Rhodes Cook, "Platform Deliberations," *Congressional Quarterly Weekly Report*, August 14, 1976, pp. 2180–83; along with Richard L. Madden, "Reagan's Plank Criticizes Ford-Kissinger Policies," *New York Times*, August 17, 1976, p. 1; "Text of Platform Proposal," *New York Times*, August 17, 1976, p. 23; Christopher Lydon, "Submergence of the Issues Frustrates Left and Right," *New York Times*, August 19, 1976, p. 26; and Bernard Gwertzman, "An Ironic Kissinger Shrugs Off Rebuff on Platform," *New York Times*, August 19, 1976, p. 26.

28. This triumph was recorded officially in "Presentation of Rules Committee Report Part III, Sections 1, 2 and 3 by Donald Siegelman of Alabama," in *1980: Official Report of the Democratic National Convention*, pp. 460–461.

29. The official product of this enterprise is *Report of the Commission on Platform Accountability* (Washington, D.C.: Democratic National Committee, 1984).

30. The numerous surviving proposals from this list are included in "Report of the Committee on Rules and Order of Business," *Official Report of the Proceedings of the Thirty-Second Republican National Convention* (Washington, D.C.: Republican National Committee, 1980), pp. 194–213. The practical upshot is contained in Adam Clymer, "G.O.P. Retains Brock as Chief," *New York Times*, July 19, 1980, p. 1, and Charles Mohr, "A Party Chief and Survival," *New York Times*, July 19, 1980, p. 6.

31. These platforms are collected in their entirety, for all major political parties from 1840 through 1976, in Donald B. Johnson, comp., *National Party Platforms*, 2 vols. (Urbana, Ill.: University of Illinois Press, 1978).

32. The two platforms of 1976 are compared in Richard L. Madden, "Two Party Platforms Show Sharp Contrast on Issues," *New York Times*, August 15, 1976, p. 1. The most consistently attentive student of political party platforms in recent years is probably Michael J. Malbin; his more fully developed thoughts, focusing especially on the platforms of 1980, are contained in Malbin, "The Conventions, Platforms, and Issue Activists," in Ranney, ed., *The American Elections of 1980*, pp. 99–141. Finally, the platforms of 1984 can be compared directly from "Text of 1984 Democratic Party Platform," *Congressional Quarterly Weekly Report*, July 21, 1984, pp. 1747–80, and "Text of 1984 Republican Party Platform," *Congressional Quarterly Weekly Report*, August 25, 1984, pp. 2096–2117.

33. The traditional argument over the consequentiality of national party platforms is concisely summarized in James W. Davis, "Platform Committee Report," in Davis, *National Conventions in an Age of Party Reform*, (Westport, Conn.: Greenwood Press, 1983), pp. 99–120.

7. The Struggle over the Mediated Convention

1. Some of the most prescient—and still freshest—reflections on the arrival of televised coverage are from Kurt Lang and Gladys E. Lang, as collected in their *Politics and Television* (New York: Quadrangle Books, 1968).

2. Since the beginning of serious television broadcasting, the A. C. Nielsen Company has been the accepted arbiter of the size of the television audience. All

ratings figures used for the tables in this chapter are the official Nielsen ratings.

3. This context, and its varied internal developments, are considered explicitly in Chapter 8.

4. These efforts come through repeatedly, albeit often implicitly, in the comments of those charged with managing conventions for the successful nominee, as recorded in the series of symposia at the Kennedy School of Government after recent presidential contests: Ernest R. May and Janet Fraser, eds., *Campaign '72: The Managers Speak* (Cambridge, Mass.: Harvard University Press, 1973); Jonathan Moore and Janet Fraser, eds., *Campaign for President: The Managers Look at '76* (Cambridge, Mass.: Ballinger Publishing, 1977); Jonathan Moore, ed., *The Campaign for President: 1980 in Retrospect* (Cambridge, Mass.: Ballinger Publishing, 1981). For specific and pointed efforts along these lines in 1984, see the final two sections of Chapter 8.

5. These changes are covered with a broader focus in Luther Frank Mott, *American Journalism, A History: 1690–1960*, 3rd ed. (New York: Macmillan, 1962). Those who doubt the consequential nature of the arrival of *radio* as a mass medium might consider its impacts on the very organization of the convention, as noted in Pat Cranston, "Political Convention Broadcasts: Their History and Influence," *Journalism Quarterly* 37 (1960), pp. 187–189.

6. This larger organizational context in the case of television is powerfully conveyed in Edward Jay Epstein, *News from Nowhere: Television and the News* (New York: Random House, 1973). It is brought specifically into American politics, with a continuing focus on what is and is not "news," in Austin Ranney, *Channels of Power: The Impact of Television on American Politics* (New York: Basic Books, 1983).

7. The general strategic framework for the assault on Rule F(3)c is set out in Elizabeth Drew, "The Democratic Convention," in Drew, *Portrait of an Election: The 1980 Presidential Campaign* (New York: Simon & Schuster, 1981), pp. 221–260. Some reflections of major candidate operatives on confronting that framework are offered in "The Democratic Convention," in Moore, *The Campaign for President*, pp. 167–182.

8. Central elements from the negotiations over the televising of these conflicts come through clearly in Hedrick Smith, "Carter Aides Yield on TV Debate Time and Win Unity Vow," *New York Times*, August 6, 1980, p. 1, and Smith, "Kennedy Will Speak at the Convention on Economy Planks," *New York Times*, August 7, 1980, p. 1.

9. More precisely, the women's minority planks appeared on the convention rostrum at about 3:50 on the afternoon of Tuesday, August 12, 1980, well before national network coverage had begun; by contrast, Kennedy appeared at about 8:35 that evening—prime time by anyone's standards.

10. A useful condensation of the first battle over network coverage of convention films is in Pat Cranston, "Political Convention Broadcasts," pp. 191–192.

11. This controversy receives focused attention in Martin Schram, "Two Networks Refuse to Show Film," *Washington Post*, August 24, 1980, p. A9, and Tom Shales, "Battle Hymn of the Republicans," *Washington Post*, August 24, 1980, p. B1.

12. These and other tendencies in television reporting are threaded throughout Ranney, *Channels of Power*. A comparison with one major element of print journalism, the wire services, is Michael J. Robinson and Margaret A. Sheehan, *Over the Wire and on TV: CBS and UPI in Campaign '80* (New York: Russell Sage, 1983).

13. The movement over time among these various foci is covered in David Paletz and Martha Elson, "Television Coverage of Presidential Conventions: Now You See It, Now You Don't," *Political Science Quarterly* 91 (1976), pp. 109–131. A subsequent update is contained in Joe Foote and Tony Rimmer, "The Ritual of Convention Coverage in 1980," in William C. Adams, ed., *Television Coverage of the 1980 Presidential Campaign* (Norwood, N.J.: ABLEX Publishing, 1983), pp. 69–88.

14. This story gets extended attention, in a fashion emphasizing both the visceral impact of televised events and the visceral import of television news decisions, in Theodore H. White, *The Making of the President 1968*. It is perhaps best capsulized in this passage:

"Slowly, his anger grew as he watched the television sets and what was to be the penultimate climax on his way to the Presidency, a milestone in the career of the 'politics of joy.' Alioto rose on screen to nominate him; back and forth the cameras swung from Alioto to pudgy, cigar-smoking politicians, to Daley, with his undershot, angry jaw, painting visually without words the nomination of the Warrior of Joy as a puppet of the old machines. Carl Stokes, the black mayor of Cleveland, was next—to second Humphrey's nomination—and then, at 9:55, NBC's film of the bloodshed had finally been edited, and Stokes was wiped from the nation's vision to show the violence in living color.

"The Humphrey staff is furious—Stokes is their signature on the Humphrey civil-rights commitment—and Stokes' dark face is being wiped from the nation's view to show blood, Hubert Humphrey being nominated in a sea of blood." White, *The Making of the President 1968* (New York: Atheneum, 1964), pp. 301–302.

A more extended overview of television news organization and behavior at that convention is Thomas Whiteside, "Corridor of Mirrors: The Television Editorial Process, Chicago," *Columbia Journalism Review*, Winter 1968–69, pp. 35–54.

15. The earliest set of these negotiations, the one with the greatest—if still limited—impact, is covered in Charles A. H. Thomson, *Television and Presidential Politics: The Experience in 1952 and the Problems Ahead* (Washington, D.C.: Brookings, 1956), especially the section "Preparations" in "Television and the National Conventions of 1952," pp. 12–21.

16. This incident is noted in Thomson, *Television and Presidential Politics*, pp. 13–14.

17. For a review of these essentially cosmetic adaptations in recent times, see Ronald Brownstein, "Image Is Key at a Modern Convention," *National Journal Convention Daily*, August 20, 1984, p. 1.

18. A useful overview of these changes in convention operations, including network efforts *not* to be unduly influenced by them, is Charles H. Fant, "Televising Presidential Conventions, 1952–1980," *Journal of Communication* 30 (1980), pp. 130–139.

8. Coverage Levels and Institutional Character

1. A short overview of this very one-sided debate is contained in "Conclusions," in Pat Cranston, "Political Convention Broadcasts: Their History and Influence," *Journalism Quarterly* 37 (1960), pp. 192–194. Evidence supporting the dominant network view—that the conventions had been both widely watched and, perhaps especially, a benefit to television in competition with other news media—is in Charles A. H. Thomson, "The Immediate Response," in Thomson, *Television and Presidential Politics: The Experience in 1952 and the Problems Ahead* (Washington, D.C.: Brookings, 1956), pp. 42–54.

2. A useful device for putting this change in perspective in the development of television network news is "Appendix A: Chronology," in Eric Barnouw, *Tube of Plenty: The Evolution of American Television* (New York: Oxford University Press, 1975), pp. 469–478. A more thematic rendering is Edwin Emery, "Radio and Television: Revolution in Communication," in Emery, *The Press and America: An Integrative History of the Mass Media*, 3rd ed. (Englewood Cliffs, N.J.: Prentice-Hall, 1972), pp. 587–616. The specific structure of network competition at the conventions of 1964 is a continuing theme in Herbert Waltzer, "In the Magic Lantern: Television Coverage of the 1964 National Conventions," *Public Opinion Quarterly* 30 (1966), pp. 33–53.

3. The argument by network news people was always more explicit and public, whereas that of programming and marketing officials was at first more implicit and remained more private. Yet the outlines of both already show through in early analyses, as in Cranston, "Political Convention Broadcasts," Thomson, *Television and Presidential Politics,* or Kurt Lang and Gladys E. Lang, "The Televised Conventions, 1952," in Lang and Lang, *Politics and Television* (New York: Quadrangle Books, 1968), pp. 78–149.

4. The Library and Archives at CBS News retained all these detailed ratings figures across time and graciously made them available for Tables 8.2, 8.3, and 8.7.

5. Overviews of convention coverage for 1964, 1968, and 1972, and of its interaction with the character of convention events, include, respectively, Waltzer, "In the Magic Lantern"; Thomas Whiteside, "Corridor of Mirrors: The Television Editorial Process, Chicago," *Columbia Journalism Review,* Winter 1968–69, pp. 35–54; and Leonard Zeidenberg, "More Light, Less Heat, in Wake of Miami Beach," *Broadcasting,* July 17, 1972, pp. 16–22.

6. A concise introduction to the substance of this debate, showing both the scope of the organizational effort required to cover a convention and the rise of doubts about its value, is "The Press of the Press," *Congressional Quarterly Weekly Report,* August 21, 1976, p. 2261.

7. Defenses of convention coverage by various news people are contained in Robert W. Merry, "For a TV Producer, Covering Convention is a Series of Challenges," *Wall Street Journal,* July 17, 1980, p. 1. Curiously, while these arguments were losing ground within the three established networks, they received a much more favorable—indeed, a triumphant—hearing within the aspiring competition, as in Peter W. Kaplan, "Cable's CNN Takes Up the Conventions' Gauntlet," *New York Times,* August 19, 1984, sec. II, p. 1.

8. A glimpse of the earlier commercial balance can be found in "Philco Still

Counting the Chips from $3,000,000 Political Gamble," *Advertising Age,* November 17, 1952, pp. 44–45. Precise figures on the shifting balance of direct and indirect costs are difficult to secure, in part because the base for comparison is not consensually obvious, but highly suggestive numbers are offered by Edwin Diamond, head of the News Study Group at the Massachusetts Institute of Technology, in Diamond, "Presswatch," *National Journal Convention Daily,* July 15, 1984, p. 12.

9. Especially useful on media coverage of the nominating politics of 1976 are F. Christopher Arterton, "Campaign Organizations Confront the Media-Political Environment," pp. 3–24, Arterton, "The Media Politics of Presidential Campaigns: A Study of the Carter Nomination Drive," pp. 25–54, and William E. Bicker, "Network Television News and the 1976 Presidential Primaries: A Look from the Networks' Side of the Camera," pp. 79–110, all in James David Barber, ed., *Race for the Presidency: The Media and the Nominating Process* (Englewood Cliffs, N.J.: Prentice-Hall, 1978).

10. Comprehensive and provocative views on the presidential debates of 1976 are contained in Sidney Krause, ed., *The Great Debates: Carter vs. Ford 1976* (Bloomington, Ind.: Indiana University Press, 1979), and Austin Ranney, ed., *The Past and Future of Presidential Debates* (Washington, D.C.: American Enterprise Institute, 1979).

11. From the perspective of the networks, the major deliberate cut in convention coverage would come four years later, so that this first reduction was more an effort to tailor traditional reporting to the "real politics"—or lack thereof—at the 1980 conventions. Indeed, the scope of the network efforts which did remain and the extent of competition among them are evident in Tony Schwartz, "Networks Are Running Hard for the Viewer's Acclamation," *New York Times,* July 14, 1980, p. A11, and Bernard Weinraub, "Party Delegates Outnumbered by News Media's Delegates," *New York Times,* August 12, 1980, p. B14. Nevertheless, intimations that the old standard had been generally breached, and that further cuts were to come, could be found in Steven Rattner, "Extent of News Coverage Questioned at Convention," *New York Times,* July 17, 1980, p. B8, and Ed Hickey, "Overkill at Detroit May Mark Final Year of Full Coverage," *TV Guide,* July 26, 1980, pp. 1–2.

12. The process of gearing up to offer the campaign is thoroughly described in Dom Bonafede, "The Press in 1984," *National Journal,* December 3, 1983, pp. 2520–25. The first explicit announcement that these preparations would not, in all probability, culminate in gavel-to-gavel coverage of the conventions on network television was "Wyman's Rifle-Shot Approach to Broadcast Journalism," *Broadcasting,* October 12, 1981, pp. 78–82. And recognition that NBC would emulate CBS in this regard can be found in Frank J. Prial, "3 TV Networks May End Full Convention Coverage," *New York Times,* May 31, 1983, p. C15.

13. The story of this convention is well summarized in Theodore H. White, "Barry Goldwater's Convention: Coup at the Cow Palace," which underlines the efforts by the Goldwater staff to contain these potentially harmful demonstrations and focus the gathering on their intended message, in White, *The Making of the President 1964* (New York: Atheneum, 1965), pp. 190–220. In turn, the dismay of Goldwater supporters at the apparent press portrait of their convention comes

through clearly in Aaron Wildavsky, "The Goldwater Phenomenon: Purists, Politicians, and the Two-Party System," *Review of Politics* 27 (1965), pp. 386–413.

14. An extended account of the putative Ford candidacy is Jack W. Germond and Jules Witcover, "Cronkite's Co-Presidency," in Germond and Witcover, *Blue Smoke and Mirrors: How Reagan Won and Why Carter Lost the Election of 1980* (New York: Viking Press, 1981), pp. 166–190. Shorter but even more barbed accounts include "Beating around the Bush-Ford Story," *Broadcasting*, July 28, 1980, pp. 28–30, and Stephen Smith, "A Convention House of Mirrors," *Time*, July 28, 1980, pp. 54–55.

15. Accounts of this incident which focus expressly on the role of television news, especially as underpinned by the competitive urge of the major national networks, are Daniel Henninger, "The Night the TV News Dam Broke," *Wall Street Journal*, July 18, 1980, p. 12; Arlie Schardt, "TV's Rush to Judgment," *Newsweek*, July 28, 1980, pp. 72–75; and John J. O'Connor, "TV: Covering the Big Story That Never Became Reality," *New York Times*, July 18, 1980, p. A12. An account with the same substantive focus but featuring a multiple defense of the network role in this story is A. O. Sulzberger, Jr., "Officials of 3 Networks Defend Coverage of Night of Speculation," *New York Times*, July 18, 1980, p. A12.

16. While the concept of a bifurcated convention was not one with which professional convention observers could be familiar, the phenomenon itself was not lost on the perceptive. Thus after 1980, Jack Rosenthal, in "The Editorial Notebook" section, contributed a witty play on the Peter Sellers movie *Being There* by arguing that one could no longer reasonably watch a convention from the floor. Rosenthal, "Being There," *New York Times*, July 22, 1980, p. A18.

17. The overall strategy, however, of compromise bordering on surrender, still occasioned surprise among reporters with a different model of the convention in mind, as in Warren Weaver, Jr., "Mondale Forces Put Foes' Plans in the Platform," *New York Times*, June 20, 1984, p. 1.

18. Again, perceptive observers were well attuned to the phenomenon of the bifurcated convention. A particularly wry version was offered by Donald Hewitt of CBS News: "I loved it when the *New York Times* had a very strong piece by John Corey on how terrible it was that the networks weren't carrying gavel to gavel. And I knew why he didn't like that: because the reporters had nothing to watch. They'd go to San Francisco. And they went to Dallas. And they get very upset if we're not carrying gavel to gavel because they're back in their hotel rooms and they want to see what's going on. I had a picture taken, which I sent to the *New York Times*, at the moment they rapped the gavel at the Democratic convention in San Francisco last time. And I took a picture of the press section. There wasn't one guy in there. You know where they were? They were all back in the hotel rooms watching us." Donald Hewitt, Transcript of Remarks, Yale University, April 21, 1987.

19. In this case at least subsequent written commentary from print reporters in the hall came much closer to capturing the intention of Republican planners, as with Dick Kirschten, "GOP Courts Democratic Voters," *National Journal Convention Daily*, August 22, 1984, p. 1.

Conclusion. Evolution and Reform

1. Although it was written as much to comment on appropriate directions for the further analysis of American politics as to analyze actual redirections within that politics, one recent piece which considers many of the specific elements of political nationalization in tandem is Nelson W. Polsby, "Contemporary Transformations of American Politics: Thoughts on the Research Agendas of Political Scientists," *Political Science Quarterly* 96 (1981–82), pp. 551–570.

2. There is no recognized inventory of specific policies under this newer pattern, but recent examples would certainly include the process of developing a federal highway bill in 1987 or the maneuvering to contest the promotion of a new justice of the Supreme Court in that year. On the highway bill, see especially Paul Starobin, "Conferees Head for Collision on Highway Bill," *Congressional Quarterly Weekly Report,* February 21, 1987, pp. 327–339, and Starobin, "Highway Bill Veto Overriden after Close Call in the Senate," *Congressional Quarterly Weekly Report,* April 4, 1987, pp. 604–607. On the nomination of Robert Bork to the Supreme Court, see Nadine Cohodas, "Much at Stake as Senate Gets Ready for Bork," and Elder Witt, "Divided High Court Awaits New Direction," *Congressional Quarterly Weekly Report,* July 4, 1987, pp. 1429–31 and 1432–34, respectively, along with Tom Watson, "Polarized Senate Prepares for September Hearings on Bork," *Congressional Quarterly Weekly Report,* July 11, 1987, pp. 1495–99.

3. A different sort of framework for thinking about reform as a political impulse is Edward C. Banfield and James Q. Wilson, "Reform," in Banfield and Wilson, *City Politics* (New York: Vintage Books, 1963), pp. 138–150. A far-reaching but still not comprehensive roster of reform initiatives in national politics during the late 1960s and 1970s is William J. Crotty, *Political Reform and the American Experiment* (New York: Crowell, 1977).

4. A useful introduction to the drive for campaign finance reform and its impacts is Herbert E. Alexander, *Financing Politics: Money, Elections and Political Reform,* 2nd ed. (Washington, D.C.: Congressional Quarterly Press, 1980).

5. A very different kind of comprehensive investigation, which nevertheless offers clear parallels to these notions, is Morris Janowitz, *The Last Half-Century: Societal Change and Politics in America* (Chicago: University of Chicago Press, 1978). My own previous attempt to produce a synthesis is Byron E. Shafer, "The Changing Structure of American Politics," Inaugural Lecture Series (Oxford: Oxford University Press, 1986).

6. A helpful overview is Samuel J. Eldersveld, *Political Parties in American Society* (New York: Basic Books, 1982). A collection which emphasizes even more this individualization in party politics is Joel L. Fleishman, ed., *The Future of American Political Parties: The Challenge of Governance* (Englewood Cliffs, N.J.: Prentice-Hall, 1982).

7. This tension *between* political parties and organized interests is actually a recurring theme in the study of American politics, as in the writings of one of the earliest self-conscious "political scientists," Henry Jones Ford, at the turn of the twentieth century. See most especially Ford, "Politics and Administration," *Annals of the American Academy of Political and Social Science* 16 (1900), pp.

177–188, and Ford, *The Rise and Growth of American Politics* (New York: Macmillan, 1898).

8. The usual inventory of organized interests—huge but hardly exhaustive—is Denise Akey, ed., *Encyclopedia of Associations: National Organizations of the United States,* 2 vols., 19th ed. (Detroit: Gale Reference Service, 1985). A provocative attempt to knit these and other organizations into a thematic overview is Nelson W. Polsby, "Interest Groups and the Presidency: Trends in Political Intermediation in America," in Walter Dean Burnham and Martha Wagner Weinberg, eds., *American Politics and Public Policy* (Cambridge, Mass.: MIT Press, 1978), pp. 41–52.

9. This general way of thinking about political change has been more commonly used in work on the political development of underdeveloped countries. Some relevant studies include C. E. Black, *The Dynamics of Modernization: A Study in Comparative History* (New York: Harper & Row, 1966); Gabriel A. Almond and G. Bingham Powell, Jr., *Comparative Politics: A Developmental Approach* (Boston: Little, Brown, 1966); and Samuel P. Huntington, *Political Order in Changing Societies* (New Haven: Yale University Press, 1968).

10. Recent examples of such activity include Nadine Cohodas, "Press Coverage: It's What You Do That Counts," *Congressional Quarterly Weekly Report,* January 3, 1987, pp. 29–33, and Bob Benenson, "Hometown Celebrities: Savvy 'Stars' Making Local TV a Potent Tool," *Congressional Quarterly Weekly Report,* July 18, 1987, pp. 1551–55.

11. A useful enumeration and analysis is Leroy Rieselbach, *Congressional Reform* (Washington, D.C.: Congressional Quarterly Press, 1986). The interaction between the goals of individual members and the structure of the legislature, along with efforts to bring the two into line, is a central focus of Roger H. Davidson and Walter J. Oleszek, *Congress and Its Members* (Washington, D.C.: Congressional Quarterly Press, 1981).

12. Activity—and alteration—in congressional committees is the central focus of Steven S. Smith and Christopher J. Deering, *Committees in Congress* (Washington, D.C.: Congressional Quarterly Press, 1984), and Joseph K. Unekis and Leroy N. Rieselbach, *Congressional Committee Politics: Continuity and Change* (New York: Praeger, 1984).

13. Trends in this area are summarized in the marvelously titled working paper by Steven S. Smith, "Revolution in the House: Why Don't We Do It on the Floor?" Brookings Discussion Papers in Governmental Studies, No. 5, September 1986. The same tendencies show up in a wider context in Norman J. Ornstein, "The Open Congress Meets the President," in Anthony King, ed., *Both Ends of the Avenue: The Presidency, the Executive Branch, and Congress in the 1980s* (Washington, D.C.: American Enterprise Institute, 1983), pp. 185–211.

14. Hints at this larger development, along with substantial evidence for other contrary developments, can be found in Sidney Verba and Norman H. Nie, *Participation in America: Political Democracy and Social Equality* (New York: Harper & Row, 1972), especially "The Types of Participators: Their Orientations to Politics," pp. 82–94, and in David R. Mayhew, *Placing Parties in American Politics* (Princeton, N.J.: Princeton University Press, 1986).

15. The presence of these countervailing initiatives is noted explicitly in Rie-

selbach, *Congressional Reform,* and Roger H. Davidson and Walter J. Oleszek, *Congress against Itself* (Bloomington, Ind.: Indiana University Press, 1977). For the specific rise and role of the party caucus, see Randall B. Ripley, "Party Leadership," in Ripley, *Congress: Process and Policy,* 3rd ed. (New York: Norton, 1983), pp. 204–246.

16. Surely the best comprehensive analysis of the role of the major emergent medium is Austin Ranney, *Channels of Power: The Impact of Television on American Politics* (New York: Basic Books, 1983). Also tremendously helpful, both for a focus on the full array of national press and for analysis of its internal operation, is Stephen Hess, *The Washington Reporters* (Washington, D.C.: Brookings, 1981).

17. Several small but pointed examples of the direct impact of editorial comment by the news media can be found in Burt Solomon, "The Editorial 'We,' " *National Journal,* August 2, 1986, pp. 1881–83.

18. The public's own sense that television is the most effective communicator is affirmed directly in "And That's the Way It Is Today," *Public Opinion,* August–September 1979, pp. 30–31. Yet the larger institutional structure of the news media also shapes television news, and this effect is the subject of Stephen Hess in "News Organizations" and "Beats," in Hess, *The Washington Reporters,* pp. 24–66.

19. This development has been most widely recognized in the presidency, where it is richly documented in Michael Baruch Grossman and Martha Joynt Kumar, *Portraying the President: The White House and the News Media* (Baltimore, Md.: Johns Hopkins University Press, 1981). But it has certainly come to characterize Congress too, as discussed in Michael J. Robinson, "The Three Faces of Congressional Media," in Thomas E. Mann and Norman J. Ornstein, eds., *The New Congress* (Washington, D.C.: American Enterprise Institute, 1981). Even the Supreme Court is not immune, as attested by David M. O'Brien, "The Court and American Life," in O'Brien, *Storm Center: The Supreme Court in American Politics* (New York: Norton, 1986).

20. The hesitant introduction of television into the Senate is covered in Jacqueline Calmes, "Senate Agrees to Test of Radio, TV Coverage," *Congressional Quarterly Weekly Report,* March 1, 1986, pp. 520–521. Its subsequent affirmation is covered in Calmes, "Senate's Romance with TV Ends in Marriage," *Congressional Quarterly Weekly Report,* August 2, 1986, pp. 1744–45. The coming of perhaps the major internal battle over media use in the television era in the House is the subject of Diane Granat, "Televised Partisan Skirmishes Erupt in House," *Congressional Quarterly Weekly Report,* February 11, 1984, pp. 246–249. The counterattack is presented in Granat, "The House's TV War: The Gloves Come Off," *Congressional Quarterly Weekly Report,* May 19, 1984, pp. 1166–67.

21. This general view—emphasizing structural over explicitly ideological influences—is usefully summarized, and dissenting views are introduced, in Austin Ranney, "Bias in Television News," in Ranney, *Channels of Power,* pp. 31–63.

22. There is powerful but implicit testimonial to this development in the fact that most scholarly books which look at the interaction of press and national governmental institutions look at the presidency as the institution in question. There is, however, no need to stop at such unobtrusive measures; a strong, explicit

testimonial to this intrinsic advantage can be found in Samuel Kernell, *Going Public: New Strategies of Presidential Leadership* (Washington, D.C.: Congressional Quarterly Press, 1986).

Afterword. Evolution and Reform beyond 1988

1. This proliferation of convention journalists in the absence of any proliferating belief in the consequence of convention stories was one of the factors behind the cutback by national networks of convention coverage for 1980. It was also the source of numerous editorial comments, in 1980 and 1984, on the irony in having 10,000 reporters to cover 3,000 delegates—usually to the effect that each *delegate* should be assigned to interview three and a third reporters. A mild version of such analyses is Bernard Weinraub, "Party Delegates Outnumbered by News Media's Delegates," *New York Times,* August 12, 1980, p. B14. A version from one locality is Dennis McDougal, "After S.F. Media Blitz, Top 40 Radio May Sound Good," *Los Angeles Times,* July 17, 1984, pt. VI, p. 1.

2. The rise of CNN as a major source of convention news is the focus of Peter W. Kaplan, "Cable's CNN Takes Up The Conventions' Gauntlet," *New York Times,* August 19, 1984, sec. II, p. 1. A sense of the transition from the major networks to operations like CNN can be gained from Howard Rosenberg, "The Convention Story—Where's the Beef?" *Los Angeles Times,* July 17, 1984, pt. VI, p. 1. The surrender of the public television field to C-SPAN is confirmed in UPI, "PBS Abandons Convention Plan," *New York Times,* February 8, 1984, p. C21. And the move by C-SPAN to meet that challenge on a broad scale—with a small budget—is reported in UPI, "Novel Campaign Views on Cable," *New York Times,* February 15, 1984, p. A14.

3. Indeed, the Gallup Organization has been asking the American public about its support for a national presidential primary for about thirty-five years, and the response has never been less than two-to-one in favor of the arrangement. These polls are collected in *Gallup Opinion Index* No. 174 (1980), p. 19.

4. A highly condensed and useful way to follow these perturbations is "Appendix E: State Systems for Choosing National Convention Delegates, 1968–84," in Austin Ranney, ed., *The American Elections of 1984* (Washington, D.C.: American Enterprise Institute, 1985), pp. 330–332.

5. The development and implementation of a southern regional primary, largely at the impetus of state Democratic parties, is chronicled in Rhodes Cook, "Will 'Super Tuesday' Mean Southern Trouble?" *Congressional Quarterly Weekly Report,* May 9, 1987, pp. 875–880. The evolving Republican side of this institutional adventure is the subject of James A. Barnes, "The GOP's Super Tuesday," *National Journal,* May 9, 1987, pp. 1120–22.

6. An examination of these contrasts in the course of a somewhat different enterprise is John R. Petrocik, *Party Coalitions: Realignment and the Decline of the New Deal Party System* (Chicago: University of Chicago Press, 1981). A look specifically at turnout for a key segment of the southern electorate is Jeffrey E. Cohen, Patrick R. Cotter, and Philip B. Coulter, "The Changing Structure of Southern Political Participation: Matthews and Prothro 20 Years Later," *Social Science Quarterly* 64 (1983), pp. 536–549.

7. The earliest versions of these proposals are considered in Louise Overacker, "Proposals for a National Presidential Primary," in Overacker, *The Presidential Primary* (New York: Macmillan, 1926), pp. 187–196. These and more recent versions are cataloged in Joseph B. Gorman, comp., *Federal Presidential Primary Proposals* (Washington, D.C.: Library of Congress, 1976).

8. An incisive analysis of a broader range of national concerns which touch on some of the same topics is Austin Ranney, *The Federalization of Presidential Primaries* (Washington, D.C.: American Enterprise Institute, 1978).

Acknowledgments and Project History

In *Bifurcated Politics* I consistently argue that the political institution at the center of the book has changed in response to evolutionary forces, to deliberate reforms, and especially to their interaction—and has then contributed to changing the larger politics around it. Accordingly, that such a book had its own unintended, indirect, and very practical roots; that it had its own deliberate, planned, and consciously developmental beginnings; and that their interaction very much shaped its progress, are facts which will surprise few of its readers. That this continually surprised its author is, I hope, simple testament to the normal creative process—though one can think of less charitable interpretations. In any case, there were clear and self-conscious intellectual roots, along with evident but indirect practical influences, and their interaction did indeed produce *Bifurcated Politics*.

The practical and accidental may appear to have had pride of place. Said more concretely, this book began at one level in 1979, with a small research budget, courtesy of the Russell Sage Foundation; with the usual public announcement of plans for holding the national conventions of 1980, courtesy of the two major political parties; and with personal connections at both party headquarters, a happy accident repeated neither before nor since. In a sense, then, when these circumstances came together and were superimposed on a long-term and continuing fascination with real politicking, observed live and direct, the research project which became *Bifurcated Politics* could be said to have been born. On the other hand, the book was just as surely—perhaps even preeminently—the product of a set of theoretical concerns raised but not ultimately addressed in its predecessor, *Quiet Revolution*.

That study of reform politics within the national Democratic party, was an attempt to range beyond the intimate details of this politics, not just to an examination of the national committee, reform organizations, the political press, and the ideology, substance, and symbolism of reform, but to such overarching concepts as institutional change and the circulation of elites. Nevertheless, the politics at its core was still—all too obviously—occurring within an even larger social context which served as the framework for the book and which received occasional direct notice, but which could not be a focus in such an already-sizable undertaking. Such factors as the changing nature of intermediary organizations in American politics, or, indeed, the changing demographic shape of American society, moved vaguely and in the background of *Quiet Revolution*. I could not reasonably address them there, though I continued to look for the opportunity to do so. *Bifurcated Politics* became the partial means for accomplishing that.

In the beginning, however, the inexorable calendar for the mounting of conventions converted this intellectual background into painfully practical maneuvering. A team of researchers for each convention, official credentialing and access not just to the arena but to the convention floor, and housing with one or another state delegation were the obvious immediate needs for such a project. Given that the out-party in American politics traditionally holds its convention first, it was the Republicans, for 1980, who had to confirm that such arrangements were possible. Happily, a key but disparate set of Republican actors were quick to do so. Michael J. Baroody, then Director of Public Affairs at the Republican National Committee, provided crucial introductions. The central person in this was Josephine J. Good, longtime Director of Conventions for the Republican party; she and her assistant, Peggy Oppenheimer, took the entire research team under their wings. In this, far more than facilitative mechanics were at issue, since Jo Good was also willing to tap her own and her predecessor's memories, stretching back through many conventions, for some helpful historical perspective. I then tapped a boyhood spent in Pennsylvania as the touchstone for an argument that the research team for the Republican convention ought rightfully to be housed with the Pennsylvania delegation. Governor Richard Thornburgh and State Chairman

Martha Bell Schoeninger accepted that argument, though it really fell to John "Mike" Krauss, Executive Director, to handle the logistics.

The Democratic party, as it has perhaps through much of American history, proved more easily accessible but more difficult to organize for these purposes. The critical person on the inside, who provided the largest single injection of help in either party, was Elaine C. Kamarck, then Executive Director of the Compliance Review Commission. It was Elaine who introduced me to Robert E. Neumann, the Deputy National Chairman, and it was his two assistants, Diane Dewhirst and Maggie Williams, who ultimately managed logistics for this project on the Democratic side. It was also Elaine who made the initial introduction to Paul Tipps, State Chairman of Ohio and a man whose curiosity produced housing for the project with the Ohio delegation. His assistant, James "Pat" Leahy, brought us into the full range of delegation activities, from the distribution of souvenirs to the defusing of social tensions among the members.

The research team for the Republican convention consisted of John F. Bibby, Charles O. Jones, James I. Lengle, Nelson W. Polsby, and me. The team for the Democratic convention consisted of Richard F. Fenno, Jr., Thomas E. Mann, Geoffrey Smith, and again Lengle, Polsby, and me. We were fortunate to be joined at both conventions by Michael J. Malbin, who, while formally working for *National Journal,* lent us his considerable energy and expertise at many points. One *could* take the 1980 conventions and make this array look systematic: Bibby on Republican officialdom and Mann on its Democratic counterpart; Lengle on selected state delegations; Malbin on committee politics; Polsby on the news media; Jones and Fenno on the composite levels of the convention as seen through individual actors; Smith on Anglo-American comparisons. The truth, however, is far more complex.

While there was an initial, rough outline guiding the entire undertaking, it was also true that the purpose of deploying such a team throughout both conventions was to accumulate insights for further systematic attention. Accordingly, all participants were encouraged to pursue personal interests, and to write about and publish the products of that pursuit as they chose. What they owed to me as the project director was a set of notes on personal observations at the end of each convention day, along with a longer set of reflections after they returned home. The attempt to integrate these with my own personal observations after the fact, and especially the long and lonely task of isolating the structural factors which could give them pattern and explanatory power, was nevertheless the essence of the enterprise. A secondary virtue of extensive fieldwork was to reinforce the participants' confidence—most especially my own—that they did indeed have a grip on "the real convention."

In the aftermath of these two conventions, the impressions gained from direct experiences with them did alter the initial outline, and in substantial ways. The two conventions of 1980 were particularly useful in confirming that the distinction among party officials, interest group representatives, and independent issue activists was important to understanding the internal functioning of conventions. That distinction then led to the notion that divisions between the leadership and the rank and file—indeed, between the emerging nominee and his own delegates—were often crucial to convention politics. By the same token, direct perceptions of conflict over *portrayals* of the convention, in both parties in 1980, led ineluctably to an expanded focus on the integral role of the press and press coverage—and ultimately, I would like to think, to even larger discoveries, including the notion of the "bifurcated convention."

This fieldwork, some related library work, and much subsequent theorizing were continued in the interim between the 1980 and 1984 conventions at the Russell Sage Foundation, where I was a Resident Scholar. At first, I had some vague hope of finishing the book within this interim. But priority for the completion of *Quiet Revolution* made that unlikely, and the impending arrival of the next round of conventions effectively dismissed it. In the meantime, two people made major, further contributions to the evolving manuscript. The first of these was Miriam Feldblum, who began as my research assistant on *Quiet Revolution*. That experience obviously did not dissuade her from taking the same role on *Bifurcated Politics,* and her contribution is evident not just in a wide array of supporting labors but in a set of challenging questions as well. At two points along the way when Miriam could not provide these remarkable services, Steven Waldman filled in. I suspect that he came away pondering—and perhaps cursing?—the sheer amount of labor which can go into creating a few tables or a small set of arguments in such an enterprise.

By the time there was a reasonably comprehensive draft manuscript to all this, the 1984 conventions were already imminent. It seemed foolish not to add them to the fieldwork behind the book. For 1984, then, Peggy Venable, the new Director of Conventions at the Republican National Committee, took this project under her protection, and she and her assistant, Nellie McCormack, really managed all our logistics, additionally aided by Belinda Skaggs and Sheila Kolb of the Housing Office. A much larger number of actors at the Democratic National Convention eventually had some role in our appearance there, but Congressman Tony Coelho of the Democratic Congressional Campaign Committee became the formal leader of consequence among them, as John Orlando, the Counsel to that Committee, became the major operative on our behalf. Diana Walsh arranged housing, and we were set to attend another pair of conventions.

My abbreviated team of researchers for the Republican Convention this time included John F. Bibby, Charles O. Jones, and David C. Kozak, who was also instrumental in gaining the help of the Democratic Congressional Campaign Committee. The counterpart team for the Democratic Convention was Richard F. Fenno, Jr., Thomas E. Mann, and again Kozak and me. James A. Barnes, then at CBS News, was a companion, confidant, and unfailing source of questions for both ventures. I count it a tremendous benefit to have been able to rely as well upon the personal connections, generously applied, of John Bibby on the Republican side of the aisle and Tom Mann on the Democratic side. Indeed, "connection" radically undervalues what was a willingness not just to make introductions and to tap long-established personal acquaintances, but to advise continually on the inner workings of party councils and to think about changes in those inner workings as these two scholars had observed them over time.

I count my opportunity to observe the two other people who attended more than one round of conventions with me, Chuck Jones and Dick Fenno, as one of the major bonuses of the entire adventure. Chuck's ability to gain access to any party function and then actively to fit in—it would be easy (and fun) to summarize this by asserting that "there is a man with a sportcoat for every occasion," but it would desperately understate the character of that talent—is a skill which I can only wistfully admire. Anyone who has read the written work of Dick Fenno can imagine the pleasure of working with him in the field. Only those who have been able to enjoy the latter experience, however, can be fully and appropriately daunted by his ability to unwrap an individual political encounter, drawing from it layer after layer of meaning and implication. The apparent effortlessness of all this—and to succeed, it must at least appear to be effortless—belies a constant self-consciousness about useful observations and relevant questions, along with a powerful analytic capacity for interpreting both.

That was the fieldwork—and the team in the field. With the benefit of hindsight, it is possible to see further adjustments in an evolving manuscript as a result of attendance at the 1984 conventions, again over and beyond the incidents and examples which those conventions produced and which have been melded into the text. What stands out, in particular, is the coming of the "bifurcated convention"—as concept and as phenomenon—a lesson which I believed I had learned at the conventions themselves, but which was then powerfully reinforced by the anomalous questions of professional colleagues afterward. When I asked those colleagues about one or another development at the convention, to be met only with a blank look, or when they queried me persistently about some development which was either trivial or nonexistent in my (direct) experience, it was most often the reality of the bifurcated convention which underlay this mutual puzzlement. When this led on to the metaphor of a "bifurcated politics," the conventions of 1984 could take the most immediate credit.

When it came to converting observations into social explanations—using those observations to look for the factors which gave pattern to political behavior, and then working back from those patterns to more objectifiable indicators which could help those who did not share the observation to share the perception nevertheless—I had the assistance of a smaller but even more crucial cast. Two people, in particular, put more energy into this project than it (or its author) can ever repay, and probably more than wisdom or hindsight would ever have counseled them to contribute. David B. Truman read and commented on every chapter at least twice, and if I hesitate to note that fact, it is largely for fear of signaling others to swamp him with manuscripts, demanding the same treatment. From the difference between "occur" and "transpire" at one end of the continuum, to the perennial question at the other of whether the particular topic was really new or only a new incarnation of a historic American phenomenon, he provided more short-run attention than any author deserves—and more long-run impact than the critic himself can imagine.

I have tried once before to sum up the process of working with Robert K. Merton, in the limits which Acknowledgments inevitably permit. I failed then, and surely I shall fail again. An edited draft chapter, if I could bear to make it public, would automatically attest to some of this process, with its red-penned comments and rubber-stamped queries, affirming energy at all points and sheer perseverance at many. A tape of a long chat at Christmas of 1985, if only I possessed it, would be an even more diagnostic instrument, since that talk produced, for example, the title to this volume—without its having been spoken during the course of the conversation. The perils of working with two such men, for whom scholarly work—yours and theirs—is never good enough, are somehow (and miraculously) overcome by their willingness to come back repeatedly to your text as it is offered. I have no doubt that others will find sufficient flaws in this manuscript to guarantee that the contributions of these two remain obscured. The author, however, surely knows.

The manuscript to which they responded was in some sense the product not just of these direct human labors, but of the tolerance of a number of formal institutions, and of the indirect supporting skills of a number of other individuals. The manuscript was begun at the Russell Sage Foundation, so it is a particularly happy outcome that the Foundation should be associated with the ultimate product, some years later. The manuscript surely benefited from a year of research leave spent in the Department of Political Science at Florida State University, where I expected to spend a much longer time. During that year, James Lee Ray and William J. M. Claggett provided a constant good colleagueship which was critical to the progress of this manuscript in general and diffuse but essential ways. The fact that this interval was only a year is due to the creation of the Mellon Chair at Oxford, for which I departed in late 1985.

The Mellon Professorship then facilitated and constrained progress on the manuscript, probably in equal measure. The demands of a new post—in what was effectively a new world—surely took time that would have gone directly into the book. On the other hand, some of those demands were redirected to its benefit. Thus the opportunity to teach "The National Party Convention in American Politics" as a set of undergraduate lectures inevitably forced me to confront the problem of "translating" the major points of the book to one very interesting sample of the "intelligent lay audience." Likewise, the opportunity to teach the manuscript in a graduate course, along with the presentation of pieces in successive graduate workshops, gave it a test with a consciously professional audience. In this, Giles Alston, Bill Claggett (once again), Peter Gellman, Isabel Harrison, Nicol Rae, and Nancy Walker were a remarkable crew of critics and fellow authors, ranging in their contributions from a stream of tough questions to a charming roster of alternative titles.

Late in the process—meaning, in this case, the summer of 1987—I was able to apply two relevant, and remarkable, sets of survey data. The first of these was the continuing survey of national convention delegates undertaken by the Election and Survey Unit of CBS News for every convention since 1968. Warren J. Mitofsky has supervised the collection of this data—surely one of the unsung resources on politics in our time—and was the central figure in making it available. The second body of survey data was that on the 1972, 1976, and 1980 delegates, before, during, and after their convention experience, collected by Barbara G. Farah, M. Kent Jennings, and Warren E. Miller. Kent and Warren have dwarfed my own use of these data in their book *Parties in Transition: A Longitudinal Study of Party Elites and Party Supporters*. Barbara has shaped my use of these data more directly, and she and her colleague Debra L. Dodson not only advised on data analysis but provided the actual preliminary product from which key tables were developed. No reader can possibly see—though the author surely knows, with a mix of anxiety and awe—the extent to which both bodies of data served not so much as a stimulus but as a kind of late test of arguments which had long before been elaborated on the basis of observation alone.

Finally, any such project has a technical support system which manages to be simultaneously obvious, hidden, and essential. At the Russell Sage Foundation, Priscilla Lewis, the Director of Publications, took great good care of this manuscript in its early stages. Eric Wanner, the President, then took the critical initiatives with Harvard University Press, while remaining involved and supportive through the rest of the process. At Harvard, Michael A. Aronson, General Editor, labored mightily to guarantee that the book came out on schedule. Camille Smith, Senior Editor, then accepted—and implemented—that mandate.

Beyond all those is the one to whom this book is dedicated. It may be that there is no creativity without pain, no production without cost. Those who accept this possibility even come to find a rough justice in it. They can never find justice in the fact that these costs are shared. No dedication can be more than a side-payment on that balance.

Index

institutions, even the coming of a new and different sort of American politics.

Bifurcated Politics tells the story of most of the postwar conventions, along with the nominating campaigns that preceded them. But it also develops a picture of the changing American politics around those stories. It will become the definitive study of the national party convention.

Byron E. Shafer is Andrew W. Mellon Professor of American Government, Oxford University. He is the author of *Quiet Revolution: The Struggle for the Democratic Party and the Shaping of Post-Reform Politics.*